REVIT® ARCHITECTURE 2010

NO EXPERIENCE REQUIRED™

REVIT® ARCHITECTURE 2010
NO EXPERIENCE REQUIRED™

Eric Wing

WILEY

Wiley Publishing, Inc.

Senior Acquisitions Editor: Willem Knibbe
Development Editor: Tom Cirtin
Technical Editor: Lynda Jensen
Production Editor: Rachel McConlogue
Copy Editor: Liz Welch
Production Manager: Tim Tate
Vice President and Executive Group Publisher: Richard Swadley
Vice President and Publisher: Neil Edde
Book Designer: Franz Baumhackl
Compositor: James D. Kramer, Happenstance Type-O-Rama
Proofreaders: Nancy Hangar and Publication Services, Inc.
Indexer: Jack Lewis
Project Coordinator, Cover: Lynsey Stanford
Cover Designer: Ryan Sneed
Cover Image: Eric Wing. Cover images used by permission of the C&S Companies®. All rights reserved.

For general information on our other products and services or to obtain technical support, please contact our Customer Care Department within the U.S. at (877) 762-2974, outside the U.S. at (317) 572-3993 or fax (317) 572-4002.

Wiley also publishes its books in a variety of electronic formats. Some content that appears in print may not be available in electronic books.

Library of Congress Cataloging-in-Publication

Wing, Eric, 1970-
  Revit architecture 2010 : no experience required / Eric Wing. — 1st ed.
    p. cm.
  ISBN-13: 978-0-470-44722-2 (paper/website)
  ISBN-10: 0-470-44722-2
  1. Architectural drawing — Computer-aided design. 2. Architectural design — Data processing. I. Title.
  NA2728.W48 2009
  720.285--dc22
                              2009009727

Dear Reader,

Thank you for choosing *Revit Architecture 2010: No Experience Required*. This book is part of a family of premium-quality Sybex books, all of which are written by outstanding authors who combine practical experience with a gift for teaching.

Sybex was founded in 1976. More than thirty years later, we're still committed to producing consistently exceptional books. With each of our titles we're working hard to set a new standard for the industry. From the paper we print on, to the authors we work with, our goal is to bring you the best books available.

I hope you see all that reflected in these pages. I'd be very interested to hear your comments and get your feedback on how we're doing. Feel free to let me know what you think about this or any other Sybex book by sending me an email at nedde@wiley.com, or if you think you've found a technical error in this book, please visit http://sybex.custhelp.com. Customer feedback is critical to our efforts at Sybex.

Best regards,

NEIL EDDE
Vice President and Publisher
Sybex, an Imprint of Wiley

To my Dad.
You would have pretended to understand
what you were reading in this book
just to make me feel good.
I miss that.

ACKNOWLEDGMENTS

Before I even pondered writing a technical book such as this one, I was the guy who bought them and studied them from front to back. This specific page, however, I always thought was somewhat superfluous…bordering on self-indulgence. As I sit here now, after finishing 23 chapters, I can categorically say that the 750-word allotment only scratches the surface of the list of people close to me who have been tremendously inconvenienced by my unavailability and, conversely, by my temperament during the rare occasions when I was available. Of course, topping this list is the family: Jennifer, Cassidy, and Jacob. You guys really came through for me, and there is no way I could have written a single chapter without your support. How does a couple weeks at Disney sound? I won't even bring my laptop (unlike last time).

Also, I'd like to thank Grandma and Baci for constantly watching and being with the kids.

On the technical side, thanks to Willem Knibbe for acquiring the book and working with me on my manuscript, and for his constant patience as I lumbered through each chapter. Thanks, of course to Technical Editor Lynda Jensen for keeping my east, west, and all of my words straight. And to Tom Cirtin for keeping me on format and on schedule. (He is hounding me for these acknowledgments as well.) One more thanks goes to Cal Schilling for modeling and rendering our office building for the cover when I didn't have time.

ABOUT THE AUTHOR

Eric Wing lives in Syracuse, New York, with his family. He is the BIM manager for C&S Companies, which is a full-service engineering/architectural firm headquartered in Syracuse. Eric's degree is in architectural engineering, which he obtained from Delhi University. In addition to writing this book, Eric has written *Revit Structure Fundamentals*, and cowrote *Mastering Revit Structure* (Wiley, 2009). Also, Eric is the director of the Autodesk User Group training program (ATP), and is a columnist for *AUGIWorld* magazine. He also writes a monthly Revit column for AUGI's *HotNews*. In addition to writing, Eric is a nationally recognized speaker, consultant, and trainer. He is also a bass player in a Syracuse band called Jemba when time allows.

CONTENTS AT A GLANCE

CONTENTS

CHAPTER 9   Ceilings and Interiors   381

CHAPTER 10   Stairs, Ramps, and Railings   435

INTRODUCTION

A h! Why does one need a big, thick technical book? Well, it is true that the best way to learn is to just do it! But do you ever just *do* it and not fully *get* it? Books can serve either as the basis for learning or as a supplement for your learning. No one book will teach you everything you need to know about a specific application, but you may never learn everything you need to know about an application without a book. When written appropriately, the book you purchase is there to start you off using good practices. If you have already started, the book is there to serve as a desktop reference. And lastly, a book can merely serve as confirmation that you are approaching an application in the correct manner.

Revit Architecture is no exception. Although this application has proven to be easy to learn, and easy to get the feel of, it is still a deep, sometimes complicated application with many procedures that require step-by-step instruction to fully understand.

Also, this book has been written by an author who is "in the trenches" using Revit Architecture, Revit Structure, and Revit MEP simultaneously every day. So, yes, you could figure out all of this information on your own, but sometimes it is nice to let someone else figure it out for you and pass that knowledge along to you in the form of a book.

Instead of lengthy paragraphs of text that ultimately lead to no tangible information, this book addresses each subject in a step-by-step approach with literally over a thousand pictures and screenshots to make sure you are on track.

Also, this book also uses an actual project and will relate to real-world scenarios. As you are following the step-by-step procedures in the book, you will be encouraged to try many procedures on your own, and also to embellish the procedure to fit your own needs. If you would rather stick to the instructions, this book allows you to clearly do so as well. The book's project uses a five-story office building with a link (corridor) to a three-story multiuse building. The book's website provides the model (plus additional families) you will need for each chapter so that you can just open the book, jump to your chapter of interest, and actually learn something! Also, this book is flexible enough that you can substitute your own project if you do not want to follow the book's examples.

This book does not waste time and space with examples of other people's triumphs, but is designed for you to open it to any random page and learn something.

Who Should Read This Book

Revit Architecture 2010: No Experience Required. Does that mean if you have used Revit you won't find this book advanced enough? No. This book is designed for anyone who wishes to learn more about Revit Architecture. Also, this book is intended for architects, architectural designers, and anyone who is using a CAD-based platform to produce architectural-based drawings.

What You Need

BIM can be tough on hardware. This book recommends that you have 4GB of RAM with a 4GB processor. Also, you should be running at 512MB for your graphics. If you are under these specifications (within reason), in most cases you will be fine. Just realize, however, that you when your model gets loaded, you could start slowing down. All Revit applications are intended to run on a PC-based system. Windows XP or higher is recommended.

What Is Covered in This Book

Revit Architecture 2010: No Experience Required covers the full gamut of using the software and is organized as follows:

Chapter 1: The Revit World   This chapter introduces you to the Revit Architecture 2010 interface and jumps right into modeling your first building.

Chapter 2: Creating a Model   This chapter starts right off with placing walls, doors, and windows. Also, this chapter is designed to point you in the right directions in terms of using reference planes and all-around best practices.

Chapter 3: Creating Views   This chapter shows you how to navigate the Revit Project Browser and to create new views of the model. Also, you will learn how to create specific views such as elevations, sections, callouts, plans, and of course our favorite: 3D perspectives.

Chapter 4: Working with the Revit Tools   In this chapter, you will learn how to use the everyday drafting tools needed in any modeling application. You will become familiar with such actions as trim, array, move, and copy. Although it seems remedial, this is one of the most important chapters of the book. It gets you on your way to the "Revit Feel."

Chapter 5: Dimensioning and Annotating   In this chapter you will learn how to annotate your model. This includes adding and setting up dimensions, adding and setting up text, and using dimensions to physically adjust objects in your model.

Chapter 6: Floors   Yes! Just floors. In this chapter, you will learn how to place a floor. You will also learn how to add materials to a floor and how to pitch a floor to a drain.

Chapter 7: Roofs   In this chapter we discuss the ins and outs of placing roofs. You will learn how to model flat roofs, sloping roofs, pitched roofs, and roof dormers. In addition, you will learn how to pitch roof insulation to roof drains.

Chapter 8: Structural Items   In this chapter you delve into the structural module of Revit Architecture. The topics we cover include placing structural framing, placing structural foundations, and creating structural views.

Chapter 9: Ceilings and Interiors   This chapter focuses predominately on interior design. Placing and modifying ceilings will be covered as well as adding specific materials to portions of walls and floors. You will also learn how to create soffits.

Chapter 10: Stairs, Ramps, and Railings   This chapter focuses on the creation of circulation items. You will learn how to create a simple U-shaped multistory staircase to start; then we move on to creating a custom winding staircase. From there you will learn how to create a custom wood railing. You will be adding ramps to the model in this chapter as well.

Chapter 11: Schedules and Tags   In this chapter you will start bringing the BIM into your model. This chapter focuses on adding schedules and adding annotation tags to specific objects and materials in your model. Most importantly, in this chapter you will learn how your model is parameter driven and how these parameters influence the annotations.

Chapter 12: Detailing   In this chapter you will learn how to simply draft in Revit. The procedures allow you to draft over the top of a Revit-generated section, or create your own drafting view independent of the model. You will also learn how to import CAD to use as a detail.

Chapter 13: Creating Specific Views and Match Lines   In this chapter you will learn how to take advantage of the multitude of views you can create, and how to control the visibility graphics of those views to create plans such as furniture and dimensional plans.

Chapter 14: Creating Sheets and Printing   This chapter explores how to produce construction documents using Revit. The procedures include creating a new drawing sheet, adding views to a sheet, creating a title block and a cover sheet, and plotting these documents.

Chapter 15: Creating Rooms and Area Plans   The focus of this chapter is to create rooms and areas. The procedures lead you through the placement of rooms, and you will learn how to set the properties of those rooms. We also discuss how to create room separators and how to create gross area plans. This chapter also guides you through the creation of a color fill floor plan.

Chapter 16: Advanced Wall Topics   In this chapter you will focus specifically on the creation of compound walls. By using the Edit Assembly dialog, you will learn how to add materials, split walls, and add sweeps and reveals such as parapet caps, brick ledges, and brick reveals. Creating stacked walls is also addressed.

Chapter 17: Creating Families   This chapter focuses on the topic of creating families. The procedures start with a simple wall sweep family, then move on to creating a door family with an arched header. You will also learn how to create an in-place family.

Chapter 18: Site and Topography   In this chapter you will learn how to place a topographical surface into your model. We also discuss how to control point-by-point elevations in your site. Splitting and then creating subregions to create swales and berms will be covered. You will also learn how to utilize an imported CAD site plan and place a toposurface over the top of the CAD lines. We also explore rotating your project to true north.

Chapter 19: Rendering and Presentation   In this chapter you will learn how to use the Revit rendering tools using the mental ray rendering engine built into the Revit GUI. This chapter also shows you how to create walkthroughs as well as solar studies.

Chapter 20: Importing and Coordinating Revit Models   This chapter focuses on the ins and outs (pun intended) of importing and exporting CAD formats as well as linking Revit Structure models. The procedures include configuring CAD layering settings as well as linking and importing AutoCAD for plans and sections. You will also learn how to link Revit Structure and perform a copy/monitor operation as well as use the Revit collision detection.

Chapter 21: Phasing and Design Options   This chapter explains how to create an existing floor plan, then moves through demolition into new construction. You will also learn how to create alternates using design options.

Chapter 22: Project Collaboration   In this chapter you will learn how to use Revit in a multiuser environment. The procedures in the book will lead you through activating worksharing, and then creating a central model. You will then move to creating local user files as well as saving to central and placing "requests to relinquish."

Chapter 23: BIM Management   Our final chapter shows you how to create a Revit template you can use at the start of each Revit project. You will also learn how to configure settings such as line weights, dimensions, text, and custom tags, such as levels structural grids and view titles.

Included with the book are Revit Architecture project files that follow along with the instruction. Each chapter will have one or more actual Revit models that have been completed up to the point of the instruction of that specific chapter, or even that specific section of the chapter to allow the reader to jump in at any moment. Also included with the book are custom families that accompany the lessons as well as additional families and projects that can be downloaded as a bonus. You can download the accompanying files at `www.sybex.com/go/revit2010ner`.

Contacting the Author

As you are reading along, please feel free to contact me at `ewing@cscos.com`, and I will be glad to answer any question you have. In addition, if you would like me to come speak or train at your firm, feel free to give me a shout. You can also visit my company's website at `www.cscos.com` and click the BIM link. You can also go directly to `www.bimnation.com`

Sybex strives to keep you supplied with the latest tools and information you need for your work. Please check the website at `www.sybex.com`, where we'll post additional content and updates that supplement this book if the need arises. Enter revit architecture in the Search box (or type the book's ISBN — 9780470447222), and click Go to get to the book's update page.

CHAPTER 1

The Revit World

▶ Getting comfortable with the Revit Architecture interface

▶ Learning to use the Design ribbon

▶ Navigating through the Project Browser

▶ Learning about file types and families

Before we get started, I think we should set the record straight. I'm sure you have seen plenty of presentations on how wonderful and versatile this 3D Revit revolution thing is. And I'm sure you may be thinking, "This all seems way too complicated for what I do. Why do I need 3D anyway?"

The answer to that question is: you don't. If you think about it, what do you do to get a job out — that is, after the presentation has run its course and you are awarded the project? Your first step is to redraw the plans. Next comes the detail round-up game we all have come to love: we pull the specs together, and then we plot. This is quite a simple process, and guess what? It works. Well, it has worked up until this 3D thing showed up. Now it seems to have turned into this convoluted process in which we have no real clue as to where things are coming from, drawings are not looking very good, and it is taking three times as long to get a drawing out the door. Well, if you just bought this book, welcome to the Revit world. In Revit, you will find that the vast majority of the processes you will encounter are in a flat 2D platform. Instead of drafting, you are placing components into the model. Yes, these components do have a so-called third dimension to them, but there is a logical methodology that drives the process. If you need to see the model in 3D, it is simply a click away. That being said, remember this: there is a big difference between 3D drafting and modeling.

 N O T E   The paragraph you just read will be the longest one of the book. This book is designed to cut to the chase and show you how to use Revit Architecture in a step-by-step fashion without having to read through paragraph after paragraph just to find the answer you are looking for. Datasets are provided at the book's accompanying website (www.sybex.com/go/revit2010ner), but if you choose to, you can use your own model as you go through the book. If you do not wish to read this book cover to cover, don't! Although I recommend going from front to back, you can use the book as a desk reference by jumping to a desired topic. The datasets will be added in phases to accommodate this type of usage. Either way, get ready to learn Revit Architecture!

With that preamble behind us, let's get on with it.

The Revit Architecture Interface

Toto, we are not in AutoCAD anymore!

No, we are not. First of all, there is no command prompt and no crosshairs. Stop! Don't go away just yet. You will get used to it; I promise. Unlike most CAD applications, Revit Architecture is heavily "pared down," so to speak. It's this way for a reason. It was designed for architects and architectural designers. You do not need every command that a mechanical engineer would need. An electrical engineer would not need the functionality that an architect would require.

What you will find as you start getting comfortable with Revit is that there are many, many choices and options behind each command.

Let's start at the beginning:

1. To open Revit Architecture, click the icon on your desktop (see Figure 1.1), or choose Start ➤ All Programs ➤ Revit Architecture 2010 (see Figure 1.2).

FIGURE 1.1: You can launch Revit Architecture from the desktop icon.

2. After you start Revit, you see the Recent Files window shown in Figure 1.3. The top row lists any projects you have been working on; the bottom row lists any families you have been working on.

3. If you are firing up Revit for the first time, both of these columns will be blank. At the bottom of each column, you are given a choice of creating a new model or of browsing for an existing one (see Figure 1.4).

4. Click the New… button.

5. The New Project dialog shown in Figure 1.5 opens. You can choose to use the default template or no template, or you can even create a

brand-new template by clicking the Project Template radio button. (We will cover template creation later in the book.) For now, just click OK to create a new project using the default template. You do not need to alter anything in this dialog.

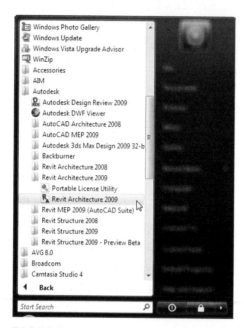

FIGURE 1.2: You can also launch Revit Architecture using the Windows Start menu (this shows the Windows Vista operating system).

FIGURE 1.3: The Recent Files window lists any recent projects or families you have worked on.

FIGURE 1.4: You can create a new model or browse for an existing one.

FIGURE 1.5: The New Project dialog allows you to start a new project using a preexisting template file, or you can create a new template file.

Now that the task of physically opening the application is out of the way, we can delve into the application. At first, you are going to notice many differences between Revit and CAD. Some of these differences may be off-putting, while others will make you say "I wish AutoCAD did that." Either way, you will need to adjust to a new workflow.

The Revit Workflow

In Revit, there is certain feel you AutoCAD converts will need to get a grasp of. Some of you will find this new workflow easy to adapt to while others will find it excruciatingly foreign. (To be honest, I found the latter to be the case at first.) Either way, it is a simple concept. You will just need to slow down a bit from your AutoCAD habits.

Executing a command in Revit is a three-step process:

1. At the top of the Revit window is what is called the Ribbon. Built into the ribbon is a series of tabs. Each tab contains what is called a panel. This will be your Revit launch pad! Speaking of launch pad, click the Wall button on the Home tab, as shown in Figure 1.6.

2. Once you click the Wall button, notice that Revit adds an additional tab to the Ribbon with options specific to the command you are running, as shown in Figure 1.7. This allows you to make different choices based on the placement of a wall. You may also notice that Revit places an additional Options bar below the ribbon for more choices.

The Home tab

FIGURE 1.6: The Design bar is the backbone of Revit Structure.

FIGURE 1.7: The Options bar replaces the command prompt from AutoCAD. MicroStation users will be more familiar with this method.

3. Once you have made your choices from the Ribbon and the Options bar, you can place the object into the view window. This is the large "drawing area" that takes up two thirds of the Revit interface. To place the wall, simply pick a point in the window and move your pointer. The wall starts to form. You can press the Esc key to exit the command.

Using Revit is not generally as easy as this, but keep in mind this basic three-step process:

1. Start a command.

2. Choose an option from the appropriate tab.

3. Place the item in the view.

Revit appears to offer a fraction of the choices and functionality that AutoCAD or any drafting program offers. This is true in a way. Revit does offer much fewer choices to start a command, but how many choices does an architect or an architectural designer need? Revit keeps its functionality focused on architecture and construction. It is the dynamic capabilities of the application during the placement of the items, as well as the functionality of the objects after they have been placed in the model that gives Revit its robust capabilities. Never judge a book by its cover — unless, of course, it is the book you are reading right now.

Let's keep going with the main focus of the Revit interface. This is the Ribbon. You will be using the Ribbon exclusively within Revit.

The Ribbon

You will be using the Ribbon for all of the commands you execute in Revit. As you can see, you don't have much of a choice to do otherwise. However, this is good, because it narrows your attention to what is right in front of you. When you pick an icon on the Ribbon, Revit will react to that with a new tab giving you the specific additional commands and Options you need. In addition, Revit also keeps the existing tabs that can help you while you are in the current command, as shown in Figure 1.8. Again, the focus here is to keep your eyes in one place.

In this book, there will be a few terms thrown at you that you will become familiar with. Of course we just discussed the Ribbon, but mostly you will be directed to choose a tab, and to find a panel on that tab.

To keep the example familiar, when you selected the wall button, your instructions will read: "On the Build panel of the Home tab, click the Wall button."

FIGURE 1.8 The Ribbon breakdown.

WHAT'S THAT TOOLBAR ABOVE THE RIBBON?

This toolbar is called the Quick Access toolbar. It is filled with some popular commands. One special function of this toolbar is the cursor icon. You are to use this button when you wish to terminate a command. To the left of this toolbar is what we are calling the Revit Home button. By clicking this button, you have access to more Revit functions that will be covered later in the book.

Now that you are starting to see how the ribbons and the tabs flow together, let's take a look at another feature within the Ribbon panels that allows you to reach beyond the immediate Revit interface.

The Change Element Type Menu

When you pick the wall button, an entirely new set of commands appears. What you will immediately notice is that there is a picture of the item you are placing in the model (in this case it's a wall). Below that picture is a menu that says "Change Element Type." Once you click this menu, you will see that there is an entire list of additional walls to choose from, as shown in Figure 1.9.

FIGURE 1.9 The Change Element Type Menu

The objective of the next exercise is to start placing walls into the model:

1. Open Revit Architecture using the default template.

2. On the Home tab, click the Wall button.

3. In the Change Element Type menu, select Exterior - Brick and CMU on MTL. Stud.

4. On the far left side of the Element panel is the Element Properties button, shown in Figure 1.10. Click this button.

FIGURE 1.10: The Element Properties button gives you access to many variables associated with the item you are adding to the model.

Clicking the Element Properties button provides you with a new world of choices and options. You will soon see that the power of Revit is hiding just below the surface.

Element Properties

Hidden within the Options bar is a single button that will gain you access to a multitude of choices and parameters. Although this dialog will contain different information for each item, the format will stay the same. One of the many wonders of Revit Architecture is the fact that most procedures, dialogs, and processes are virtually the same as the next. Master how to build a wall, and you have mastered how to build a roof and a floor.

Within the element properties you will see two categories, as shown in Figure 1.11. In this figure, the first category, Type Parameters, is grayed out, and you cannot select anything. In the other category, Instance Parameters, you can edit settings directly. There is a huge difference between the two.

Instance Parameters

The items that can be immediately edited are called *instance parameters*. This means that these parameters will change only the object being added to the model at this time. Also, if you select an item that has already been placed in the model and click the Element Properties button, the instance parameters will change only that item you have selected. This makes sense — not all items are built equally in the real world. Figure 1.12 illustrates the instance parameters of a typical wall.

Type Parameters

The type parameters (see Figure 1.13), when edited, will alter every item of that type in the entire model. To access the type parameters, click the Edit Type button while still in the Element Properties dialog, as Figure 11.14 shows.

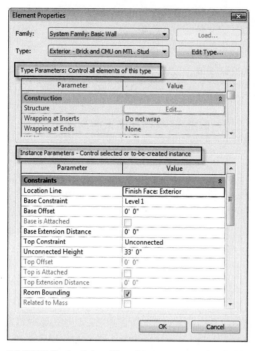

FIGURE 1.11:   The element properties hold a wealth of parameters and control over families in Revit.

FIGURE 1.12:   The instance parameters will change only the currently placed item or the currently selected item.

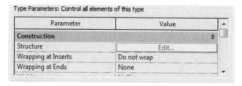

FIGURE 1.13:   The type parameters, when modified, will alter every occurrence of this specific wall in the entire model.

FIGURE 1.14: The Edit Type button allows you to access the type parameters.

At this point, you have one of two choices. You can either make a new wall type (leaving this specific wall unmodified) by clicking the Duplicate button, or you can start editing the wall's type properties, as shown in Figure 11.15.

 WARNING I cannot stress enough that if you start modifying type properties without duplicating the type, you need to do so in a very deliberate manner. You can easily affect the model in an unintended manner. We will discuss the specifics of all of the wall's type parameters in Chapter 16, "Advanced Wall Topics."

FIGURE 1.15: The type parameters are used to modify the wall system's global settings.

Now that you have gained experience with the Element Properties dialog, it is time to go back and study the rest of the Options bar as it pertains to placing a wall:

1. Since we are only exploring the element properties, click the Cancel button twice to return to the model.

2. Back in the Options bar, find the Location Line: menu. This will allow you to set the wall justification. Select Finish Face: Exterior (see Figure 1.16).

3. On the Options bar, be sure the Chain checkbox is selected, as Figure 1.16 shows. This will allow you to draw the walls continuously.

FIGURE 1.16: By selecting Finish Face: Exterior, you know the wall will be dimensioned from the outside finish.

4. In the Draw panel, there is a series of "sketch" options. Since this specific wall is straight, make sure the Line button is selected, as shown in Figure 1.17.

FIGURE 1.17: You can draw basically any shape you need.

Get used to studying the Ribbon and the Options bars — it is going to be your crutch as you start using Revit Architecture! Of course, at some point you need to physically start placing items in the model. This is where the view window comes into play.

The View Window

To put it simply, the big white area where the objects go is the view window. As a result of your actions, this area will become populated with your model. Notice the background is white — this is because the sheets you plot on are white. In Revit, what you see is what you get … literally. In Revit, you aren't counting on color #5, which is blue, for example, to be a specific line width when you plot. You will be able to see immediately what the thickness of all of your "lines" are going to be *before* you plot. What a novel idea. See Figure 1.18.

FIGURE 1.18: The view window collects the results of your actions.

To continue placing some walls in the model, keep going with the exercise. If you have not been following along, you can start by clicking the Wall button on the Home tab. In the Change Element Type menu, select Exterior - Brick and CMU on MTL. Stud. Make sure that the wall is justified to the finish face exterior. You may now proceed:

1. With the Wall command still running and the correct wall type selected, position your cursor in a similar location to the illustration in Figure 1.19. Now, pick a point in the view window.

2. With the first point picked, move your cursor to the left. You will notice that a few things are happening. One is that the wall seems to be snapping in a horizontal plane, and there is a blue dashed line that apparently locks the horizontal position. In Revit, there is no "Ortho." Revit will align the typical compass increments 0, 90, 180, 270, and 45 degrees.

72' - 0"

FIGURE 1.19: The procedure for "drawing" a wall in Revit Architecture

3. Another thing you will notice is a blue dimension extending from the first point to the last point. Although dimensions cannot be typed over, this type of dimension is a temporary dimension, and is there for just that. Type **100**, and press the Enter key. (Notice you did not need to type the foot mark ('). Revit thinks in terms of feet.) The wall is now 100' long. See Figure 1.19.

4. With the Wall command still running, move your cursor straight up from the endpoint of the 100'-long wall you just drew. Look at Figure 1.20.

80' - 0"

90.000°

FIGURE 1.20: How Revit Architecture works is evident in this procedure.

5. Type **80** and hit Enter. You now have two walls.

6. Move your cursor to the right until you "run into" another blue alignment line. Notice that your temporary dimension says 100'–0".

Revit understands symmetry. Once you see this alignment line, and the temporary dimension says 100'–0", pick this point.

7. Move your cursor straight down and type **16**.

8. Move your cursor to the right and type **16**.

9. Hit the Esc key.

Do your walls look like Figure 1.21? If not, try it again. You need to be able to do this and to be comfortable with this procedure (as much as possible).

FIGURE 1.21: Working with Revit starts with the ability to work with the view window, and learning the quirks and the feel of the interface.

To get used to the Revit flow, always remember these three steps:

1. Start a command.

2. Focus on your options.

3. Move to the view window, and add the elements to the model.

If you start a command, then focus immediately on the view, you will be sitting there wondering what to do next. Do not forget to check your options and the appropriate ribbon tab.

Let's keep going and close this building by using a few familiar commands. If you have never drafted on a computer before, don't worry. These commands are simple. Starting with the easiest but most important is the topic of being able to simply select an object.

Object Selection

Revit has a few similarities to AutoCAD and MicroStation. One of those similarities is the ability to perform simple object selection, and to be able to execute common modify commands. For this example, we are going to mirror the two 16'–0" L-shaped walls to the bottom of the building:

1. Type **ZA** (zoom all).

2. Click the Modify button on the Design bar.

3. Near the two 16'–0" L-shaped walls, pick (left-click) and hold down the pick button at a point to the right of the walls but below the long, 100'–0" horizontal wall.

4. You will see a window start to form. Run that window past the two walls. Once they are highlighted, as illustrated in Figure 1.22, let go of the pick button, and the walls are selected.

FIGURE 1.22: Picking a "crossing" window to select two walls

There are two ways to select an object: by using a crossing window or by using a box. Each plays an important role in how you select items in a model.

Crossing Windows

In Revit, you can select items in one of two ways. A *crossing window* describes an object selection method in which the window being placed only needs to cross through the objects in order for them to become selected. A crossing window will always start from the right and end to the left. The crossing window, when being placed, is represented by a dashed-line composition (see Figure 1.22).

Boxes

A box is an object selection method that will only select the items that are 100 percent inside the window being placed. This method is useful when you want to select only specific items while passing through larger objects that you may not want in the selection set. A box always starts from the left and works to the right. The line type is a continuous line (see Figure 1.23).

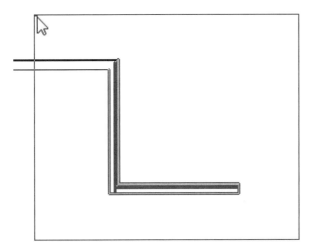

FIGURE 1.23: To select only objects that are surrounded by the window, select a box. This will leave out any item that may only be partially within the box.

Now that you have experience selecting items, you can execute some basic modify commands. Let's begin with mirroring, one of the most popular modify commands.

Modifying and Mirroring

You will find that Revit Architecture requires that you select items first, and then execute a command. This is true for most action items, and is certainly true for every command on the Modify toolbar.

1. Make sure only the two 16'–0" walls are selected.

2. Once the walls are selected, you will see the Modify Walls tab appear. On the Modify panel, click Mirror ➤ Draw Mirror Axis, as shown in Figure 1.24.

3. Your cursor will change to a cross hair with the mirror icon illustrating that you are ready to draw a mirror plane, as shown in Figure 1.25.

FIGURE 1.24: The Ribbon adds the appropriate commands.

FIGURE 1.25: There are options you will have to choose for every command in Revit.

4. Make sure the Copy checkbox is selected (see Figure 1.25).

5. Hover your cursor over the inside face of the 80'–0"-long vertical wall until you get to the midpoint. Revit will display a triangular icon, indicating that you have found the midpoint of the wall. See Figure 1.26.

FIGURE 1.26: Revit has snaps similar to most CAD applications. In Revit, you will only get snaps if you choose the draw icon from the Options bar during a command.

6. Once the triangular midpoint snap appears, pick this point. Once you pick the point where the triangle appears, you can move your cursor directly to the right of the wall. You will see an alignment

line appear, as illustrated in Figure 1.27. Once the alignment line appears, you can pick another point along the path. Once you pick the second point, the walls are mirrored and joined with the south wall. Again, refer to Figure 1.27.

FIGURE 1.27: Mirroring these walls will involve first, picking the midpoint of the vertical wall, then second, picking a horizontal point along the plane.

Now that you have some experience mirroring items, it is time to start adding components to your model by utilizing the items that have been placed previously. If you are not getting it, retry these first few procedures. Rome was not built in a day. (Well, perhaps if they had Revit, it would have sped things up!) You want your first few walls to look like Figure 1.28.

FIGURE 1.28: Your building should look like this illustration.

Building on Existing Geometry

Now that you have some geometry to work with and you have some objects placed in your model, Revit starts to come alive. The benefits of using building information modeling (BIM) will become apparent quickly, as explained later in this chapter. For example, because of the fact that Revit knows that walls are walls, you can add identical geometry to the model by simply selecting an item and telling Revit to create a similar item.

Suppose you wanted a radial wall of the same exact type of the other walls in the model. Perform the following steps:

1. Type **ZA** to zoom the entire screen.

2. Press the Esc key.

3. Select one of the walls in the model — it does not matter which one.

4. Right-click on the wall.

5. Select Create Similar, as shown in Figure 1.29.

FIGURE 1.29: You can select any item in Revit and create a similar object by right-clicking and selecting Create Similar.

6. On the Place Wall tab, click the Start-End-Midpoint Arc button, as shown in Figure 1.30.

FIGURE 1.30: Just because you started the command from the view window does not mean you do not have to look at your options.

7. Again with the Options? Yes. Make sure your Location Line: is set to Finish Face Exterior.

8. With your wheel button on your mouse, zoom into the upper corner of the building and select the top endpoint of the wall, as shown in Figure 1.31. The point you are picking is the corner of the heavy lines. The topmost, thinner line actually represents a concrete belt course below.

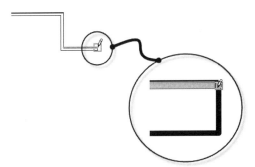

FIGURE 1.31: Select the top corner of the wall to start your new radial wall.

9. Select the opposite, outside corner of the bottom wall.

10. Move your cursor to the right until you see the curved wall pause. You will also see an alignment line and a tangent snap icon appear as well. Revit understands that perhaps you want an arc tangent upon the two lines you have already placed in your model.

11. Once you see this, pick the third point. Your walls should look like Figure 1.32.

FIGURE 1.32: The completed exterior walls should look like this illustration.

Just because you have placed a wall in the model, that does not necessarily mean it looks the way you would like. In Revit Architecture, there is a lot you can do with view control and how objects are displayed.

View Control and Object Display

Although this is a nice way to add walls to a drawing, it does not reflect the detail you are going to need to produce construction documents. Well, the great thing about Revit is that you have already done everything you need to do. You can now tell Revit to display the graphics the way you want to see them.

The View Control Bar

At the bottom of the view window, you will see a skinny toolbar (as illustrated in Figure 1.33). This is the View Control bar. It contains the following functions:

FIGURE 1.33: The View Control bar controls the graphical view of your model.

Scale   The first item on the View Control bar is the scale function. It gets small mention here, but it is a huge deal. In Revit, you change the scale of a view by selecting this menu. Change the scale here, and Revit will scale annotations and symbols accordingly. See Figure 1.34.

Detail Level   The detail level allows you to view your model at different qualities. You have three to choose from: Coarse, Medium, and Fine. See Figure 1.35.

FIGURE 1.34: The scale menu allows you to change the scale of your view.

FIGURE 1.35: The detail level control allows you to set different view levels for the current view.

If you want this view to appear with more graphical information you would select the Fine choice. To see how the view is adjusted using this control, follow these steps:

1. Select the detail level icon and choose Fine.

2. Zoom in on a wall corner. Notice the wall components are now showing in the view.

T I P When you change the view control in a view, it is not a temporary display. You are telling Revit how you want to plot this view. If you see it on the screen, you will see it when it comes out of the plotter.

There are other items on the View Control bar, but we'll discuss them when they become applicable to the exercises.

The View Tab

Since Revit is one big happy model, you will quickly find that simply viewing the model will become quite important. Within Revit, there is some functionality that you can take advantage of in the form of the Navigation bar. To activate the Navigation bar, first go to the view tab, then click the User Interface button. Make sure the Navigation bar is activated, as shown in Figure 1.36.

One item we need to look at on the Navigation bar is the steering wheel.

FIGURE 1.36: The View tab produces the Navigation bar.

The Steering Wheel

The steering wheel, allows you to zoom, rewind, and pan. When you pick the steering wheel icon, a larger control "panel" will appear in the view window. To choose one of the options, you simply pick (left-click) one of the options, and hold the pick button as you execute the maneuver.

To use the steering wheel, follow along:

1. Pick the steering wheel icon from the Navigation bar, as shown in Figure 1.37.

2. Once the steering wheel is in the view window (as illustrated in Figure 1.37), click (left-click) and hold the Zoom choice. You can now zoom in and out.

FIGURE 1.37: You can use the steering wheel to navigate through a view.

3. Now click and hold the Rewind choice in the steering wheel. You can now find an older view, as shown in Figure 1.38.

FIGURE 1.38: Because of the fact that Revit does not include zoom commands in the Undo function, you can rewind to find previous views.

4. Do the same for the Pan choice. The Pan function is found on the outer ring of the steering wheel. Once you press and hold Pan, you can navigate to other parts of the model.

Although you can do all of this with your wheel button, some users still prefer the icon method of panning and zooming. For those of you who prefer the icons for the previous items, you will also want to use the icons for the traditional zooms as well.

Traditional Zooms

The next items on the Navigation bar are the good old zoom controls that you are used to. The ability to zoom in, zoom out, and pan are all included in this function, as shown in Figure 1.39.

FIGURE 1.39: The standard zoom commands

Of course, if you have a mouse with a wheel, you can zoom and pan by either holding down the wheel to pan or by wheeling the button to scroll in and out.

Thin Lines

Back on the View tab, you will see an icon called thin lines, as shown in Figure 1.40. Let's talk about what this icon does.

In Revit Architecture, there is no such thing as layers. Line weights are controlled by the actual objects they are representing. In the view window, you see these line weights. As mentioned before, what you see is what you get. Sometimes, however, these line weights may be too thick for smaller-scale views. By clicking the thin lines icon as shown in Figure 1.40, you can force the view to display only the thinnest lines possible to still see the objects.

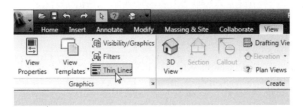

FIGURE 1.40: Using the thin lines icon will allow you to "operate" on the finer items in a model.

To practice using the thin lines function, follow along:

1. Pick the thin lines icon.

2. Zoom in on the upper-right corner of the building.

3. Pick the thin lines icon again. This toggles the "mode" back and forth.

4. Notice the lines are very heavy.

The line weight should concern you. As mentioned earlier, there is no such thing as layers in Revit Architecture. This topic is addressed in Chapter 13.

The next icon on the View toolbar is the show mass icon. This will be addressed in Chapter 16.

Default 3D

This icon actually brings us to a new discussion. Complete the following steps that will move us into the discussion on how a Revit model actually comes together!

1. Click the default 3D icon, as illustrated in Figure 1.41.

FIGURE 1.41: The default 3D icon will be heavily used.

2. On the View Control bar, click the Model Graphics Style button and choose Shaded with Edges, as illustrated in Figure 1.42.

FIGURE 1.42: The Model Graphics Style button enables you to view your model in color. This is typical for a 3D view.

A word of caution: if you do turn your shadows on, do so with care. This could be the single worst item in Revit in terms of performance degradation. Your model *will* slow down with shadows on.

3. Again on the View Control bar, select Shadows Off and turn the shadows on, as illustrated in Figure 1.43, and again in 1.45.

FIGURE 1.43: Shadows create a nice effect, but at the expense of RAM.

Within the 3D view is the ViewCube. It is the cube in the upper-right corner of the view window. You can switch to different perspectives of the model by picking on the quadrants of the cube (see Figure 1.44).

FIGURE 1.44: The ViewCube lets you freely look at different sides of the building.

 TIP   The best way to navigate a 3D view is to press and hold the Ctrl key on the keyboard. As you are holding down the Ctrl key, press and hold the zoom wheel on your mouse. Now move the mouse around. You will be able to dynamically view the model.

FIGURE 1.45: The 3D model with shading and shadows.

Go back to the floor plan. Wait! How? This brings us to quite an important topic in Revit: the Project Browser.

The Project Browser

Revit is the frontrunner of BIM. BIM is sweeping our industry for a reason. One of the biggest reasons is the fact that you have a fully integrated model right in front of you. What this means is that when you need to open a different floor plan, elevation, detail, drawing sheet, or 3D view, you can find it all right here in the model.

Also, this means our workflow is going to change. In most cases, it is going to change drastically. When you think about all the external references and convoluted folder structures that comprise a typical job, you can start to relate it to the way Revit uses the Project Browser. Within Revit, you are using the Project Browser instead of the folder structure previously used in CAD.

This changes the playing field. With CAD, the process of closing the file you are in and opening the files you need to work on is restructured in Revit to enable you to stay in the model. You never have to leave one file to open another. You also never need to rely on external referencing to complete a set of drawings. Revit and the Project Browser will put it all right in front of you.

To start using the Project Browser, follow along:

1. To the far left of the Revit dialog is the Project Browser (see Figure 1.46).

FIGURE 1.46: The Project Browser is your new Windows Explorer.

2. The Project Browser is broken down into categories. One category is Floor Plans. In the Floor Plans category, double-click on Level 1.

3. Double-click on Level 2. Notice that your display level is set to Coarse. This is because any change you make on the View Control

bar is for that view only. When you went to Level 2 for the first time, that change has not been made yet.

4. In the view window, you will see little icons that look like houses (see Figure 1.47). These are elevation markers. The elevation marker to the right might be in your building. If this is the case, you need to move it out of the way.

5. Pick a box around the elevation marker. Once both the small triangle and the small box are selected, move your mouse over the selected objects.

6. Your cursor will turn into a move icon. Pick a point on the screen and move the elevation marker out of the way.

FIGURE 1.47: Elevation markers are shown in plan as these symbols. If you are to move them, it must be done by picking a window. There are two actual items in an elevation marker.

WARNING   Hey! What happened to my elevation? You are in Revit now. Items such as elevation markers, section markers, and callouts are no longer just "dumb" blocks. They are linked to the actual view they are calling out. If you delete one of these markers, you will delete the view associated with it. If it is a view that you and your design team has been working on, you lost that view. Also, if you move an item it needs to be done deliberately and with caution. This elevation marker you moved has two parts. The little triangle is actually the elevation. The little box is the part of the marker that records the sheet number the elevation will wind up on. If you do not move both items by placing a window around them, it will leave the elevation's origin where it was. Once this happens, your elevation will look like a section, and it will be hard to determine what happened.

7. In the Project Browser, find the Elevations (Building Elevations) category. Double-click on South.

8. Also in the Project Browser, notice there is a 3D category. Expand the 3D category, and double-click on the {3D} choice. This will bring you back to the 3D view you were looking at previous to this exercise.

Now that you can navigate through the Project Browser, adding other components to the model will be much easier. To start with, we can begin to add some windows.

Windows

By clicking on all of these views, you are simply opening a view of the building, not another file that is stored somewhere. For some users this can be confusing. (It was for me.)

When you click around and open all of these views, they stay open. You can quickly open many views. There is a way to manage these views before it gets out of hand.

In the upper-right corner of the Revit dialog, you will see the traditional close and minimize/maximize buttons for the application. Just below them are the traditional buttons for the files that are open, as shown in Figure 1.48. Click the X for the file.

FIGURE 1.48: You can close a view by clicking the X for the view. This does not close Revit, or an actual file for that matter — it simply closes that view.

In this case, you have multiple views open. This situation (which is quite common) is best managed on the View tab. To utilize the Window menu, perform the following steps:

1. On the Windows panel of the View tab, click the Switch Windows button, as shown in Figure 1.49.

2. Once the menu is expanded, look at the open views.

FIGURE 1.49: The Window menu lists all the current views that are open.

3. Go to the {3D} view by selecting it from the Window menu, by clicking the 3D icon at the top of the screen, or by going to the {3D} view in the Project Browser.

4. On the Windows panel, click Close Hidden Windows.

5. Close this window by pressing Esc on the keyboard.

6. In the Project Browser, open Level 1.

7. Go to the Window Panel and select Tile.

BUT I USED TO TYPE MY COMMANDS!

Well, you still can. In the Revit menus, you may have noticed that many items have a two- or three-letter abbreviation to the right. This is the keyboard shortcut associated with the command. If you want, you can make your own, or you can modify existing keyboard shortcuts. In Windows Explorer, go to C:\Program Files\Revit Architecture 2010\ Program\ KeyboardShortcuts.txt. Within this .txt file, you can find the shortcut you wish to add. By removing the semicolon, you can put your shortcut between the quotation marks. For example, change the string that looks like this:

```
menu:"Window-Arrange Icons"
```

to this:

```
"WA"menu:"Window-Arrange Icons"
```

Save the text file. The setting will not take effect until you close Revit Architecture and open it back up again.

---

8. With the windows tiled, you can see the Level 1 floor plan along with the 3D view to the side. Select one of the walls in the Level 1 floor plan.

Notice it is now selected in the 3D view to the side. These views you have open are mere representations of the model from that perspective. Each view of the model can have its own independent view settings.

You are at a good point now to save the file. And this brings the book to a good point to discuss the different file types, and their association to the BIM model.

File Types and Families

Revit Architecture has a somewhat unique way in which it saves files and utilizes different file types to build a BIM model. To learn how and why Revit has chosen these methods, follow along with these steps.

1. Click the save icon (see Figure 1.50).

FIGURE 1.50: The traditional save icon will bring up the Save As dialog if the file has never been saved.

2. In the Save As dialog, click the Options button in the lower-right corner (see Figure 1.51).

FIGURE 1.51: The Options button in the Save As dialog will allow you to make some choices in how the file is saved.

3. In the File Save Options dialog, you will see at the top a place where you can specify the number of backups, as shown in Figure 1.52. Set this value to 1.

    The reason Revit does this is because, when you click the save icon, Revit actually duplicates the file. It will simply add a suffix of "001" to the end of the filename. Each time you click the save icon, Revit will record this save and add another file called "002," leaving the "001" intact. The default is to do this three times before it starts replacing the 001, 002, and 003 with the three most current files.

4. Under the Preview section, you can specify which view this file will be previewed in. I like to keep it as the current view. That way, I can get an idea if the file is up-to-date based on the state of the view. Click OK.

FIGURE 1.52: The Options in the Save As function allow you to specify number of backups as well as the view it will use for the preview.

5. Create a folder somewhere, and save this file into the folder. The name of the file used as an example in the book is called NER.rvt. (NER stands for "No Experience Required.") Of course, you can name the file anything you wish, or you can even just do your own project using the steps and examples from the book as a guideline.

Now that you have experience adding components to the model, it is time to investigate exactly what it is we are adding here. Each component is a member of what Revit calls a *family*.

UNDERSTANDING THE REVIT ARCHITECTURE FILE (.rvt)

The extension for a Revit Architecture file is .rvt. There are three separate Revit applications: Revit Architecture, Revit Structure, and Revit MEP. All three Revits share the same .rvt file extension. You can open a Revit file produced in any of these three applications directly. You do not need object enablers to read items that do not pertain to that discipline.

System and Hosted Families (.rfa)

As mentioned earlier, a Revit model is based on a compilation of items called families. There are two types of families: system families and hosted families. A system family can only be found within a Revit model and cannot be stored in a separate location. A hosted family is inserted similar to a block (or cell) and is stored in an external directory. The file extension for a hosted family is .rfa.

System Families

System families are inherent to the current model and are not inserted in the traditional sense. You can only modify a system family through its element properties within the model. The walls you've put in up to this point are system families, for example. You did not have to insert a separate file in order to find the wall type. The system families in a Revit Architecture model are as follows:

Walls

Floors

Roofs

Ceilings

Stairs

Ramps

Shafts

Rooms

Schedules/quantity takeoffs

Annotation items

Views

System families define your model. As you can see, the list pretty much covers most building elements. There are, however, plenty more components not included within this list. These items, which can be loaded into your model, are called hosted families.

Hosted Families

All other families in Revit Architecture hosted in some way by either a system family or a level. For example, a wall sconce is a hosted family in that, when you

insert it, it will be appended to a wall. Hosted families carry a file extension of
.rfa. To insert a hosted family into a model, follow these steps:

1. Open the NER.rvt file or your own file.

2. Go to Level 1.

3. On the Home tab, select the Door button.

4. On the Place Door tab, click the Load family button, as shown in
   Figure 1.53.

FIGURE 1.53: You can load an RFA file during the placement of a
hosted family.

5. Browse to the Doors directory.
   (Note that if you are on a network, your directories may not be the
   same as in this book. Contact your CAD/BIM manager (or whoever
   loaded Revit on your computer) to find exactly where they may have
   mapped Revit.

6. Notice there is a list of doors. Select Single-Raised Panel with
   Sidelights.rfa, and click Open.

7. On the Place Door tab, click the Change Element Type menu, as shown
   in Figure 1.54. Notice that not only did you bring in the raised panel
   door family, but you also have seven different types of the same door.
   These types are simply variations of the same door. You no longer
   have to explode a "block" and modify it to fit in your wall.

FIGURE 1.54: Each family .rfa file will contain multiple types associated with that family.

8. Zoom in on the upper-left corner of the building as illustrated in Figure 1.55.

9. To insert the door into the model, you must place it in the wall. (Notice that before you hover your cursor over the actual wall, Revit will not allow you to add it to the model, as shown in Figure 1.55.) Once your pointer is directly on top of the wall, you will see the outline of the door. Once you see this, pick a point in the wall. The door is inserted. (We will cover this in-depth in the next chapter.)

FIGURE 1.55: Inserting a hosted family (.rfa)

You will be using this method quite a bit in this book and on a daily basis when you use Revit. One thing to note is the fact that when a family is loaded into Revit Architecture, there is no live path back to the file that was loaded. Once it is added to the Revit model, it becomes part of that model. To view a list of the families that are within the Revit model, go to the Project Browser and look for the Families category. Within the Families category, you will see a list of the families and their types, as Figure 1.56 shows.

FIGURE 1.56: All of the families as listed in the Project Browser

The two main Revit files have been addressed. Two others are still crucial to the development of a Revit model.

Using Revit Template File (.rte)

The .rte extension pertains to a Revit template file. Your company surely has developed a template for your own standards or will soon. An RTE file is simply the default template that has all of your companies standards built into it. When you start a project, you will use this file. To see how an RTE file is used, follow these steps:

1. Click the Revit Home button and select New ➤ Project.

2. In the resulting dialog, as shown in Figure 1.57, click the Browse button.

3. This will throw you into a category with several other templates. You can now choose to use a different one.

4. Click Cancel twice.

FIGURE 1.57: A new Revit model is based on an RTE template file.

Whenever you start a project, this is the type of template you are going to use. When you are starting a new family, however, you will want to use an RFA.

Using Revit Family Files (.rft)

The .rft extension is another type of template, only this one pertains to a family template. It would be nice if Revit had every family fully developed to suit your needs. Alas, it does not. You will have to develop your own families. You will start with a family template. To see how to access a family template, perform these steps:

1. Click the Revit Home button, and select New ➣ Family to open the browse dialog shown in Figure 1.58.

FIGURE 1.58: The creation of a family starts with these templates.

2. Browse through these templates. You will most certainly use many of them.

3. Click the Cancel button.

Tempting? I know! We will thoroughly cover creating in Chapter 17, "Families." As mentioned earlier, you are only going to get to a certain point before you run out of Revit provided content. If you are feeling brave, go ahead and play around in one of the templates. You have nothing to lose (except time).

Are You Experienced?

Now You Can...

- ☑ navigate the Revit Architecture interface and actually start a model

- ☑ find commands on the Design bar and understand how this controls your options

- ☑ find where to change a keyboard shortcut to be similar to what you had in CAD

- ☑ navigate through the Project Browser

- ☑ understand how the Revit interface is broken down into views

- ☑ tell the difference between the two different types of families, and understand how to build a model using them

CHAPTER 2

Creating a Model

▶ Placing exterior and interior walls

▶ Adding reference planes

▶ Joining walls

▶ Using the Split command

▶ Editing a cut profile

▶ Adding doors

▶ Adding openings

▶ Adding windows

Now that you have a solid working knowledge of the Revit Architecture interface and you understand how it differs from most other drafting applications, it's time to move on to creating the Revit model.

The first chapter had you add some exterior walls to the model, and this chapter will expand on that same concept. You will also be placing some of the components that were introduced in Chapter 1, such as doors and windows. Revit is only as good as the families that support the model.

To kick off the chapter, we will focus on the accurate placement of interior and exterior walls. We also have a lot to learn about the properties of walls and how to tackle tricky areas where the walls just won't join together for us.

Placing Walls

In Chapter 1 we placed some walls and then added some exterior walls to the model. In this section you will be adding more walls to the model. While adding walls to the model is not difficult, we need to explore how to control these walls when adjacent items start moving around and corners get "fussy." Also, we will examine proven methods to ensure accuracy before you start traveling down the wrong path.

Adding Exterior Walls

To continue with the perimeter of the building, let's add some more exterior walls. The first few walls we added to our model were pretty basic in terms of layout. It would be nice to have only square geometry! The reality is you are going to encounter walls at different angles and dimensions to which you cannot just line up other walls. To get around this, let's add what are called *reference planes* to help us lay out our building. At the end of this section, our building's perimeter will look like Figure 2.1.

The objective of the next set of procedures is to establish some strong working points, then add walls along those guidelines. We will also use these rules to make the necessary adjustments later in the section.

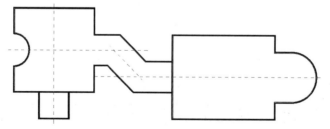

FIGURE 2.1: The footprint of our completed building

Reference Planes

Reference planes are construction lines that you can place in your model to establish center lines and to use as an aid in terms of symmetrical geometry. If you add a reference plane in one view, it will show up in another. If you add one in a plan view, you can see that same plane in an elevation. This is a great way to build using a common reference. Also, reference planes, by default, will not plot.

The only drawback to reference planes is that they suffer from overuse. Try to only use them as what they are: a reference. To practice using reference planes, follow these steps:

1. Open the file you created in Chapter 1. If you did not complete that chapter, open the file called NER-01.rvt, which you can download from the book's website at **www.sybex.com/go/revit2010ner**. (You can also use your own building. You will, of course, have to realize that the dimensions specified here will not be consistent with your model).

2. On the Work Plane panel of the Home tab, click the Ref Plane ➤ Draw Reference Plane button, as shown in Figure 2.2.

FIGURE 2.2: The Ref Plane command is on the Basics tab of the Design bar.

As you move through the exercises in this book, you will discover that the Ref Plane command is found elsewhere in the program.

3. Draw the reference plane through the center of the building, extending each end past the exterior walls. (Remember, this is a construction line. You can go long if you need to). See Figure 2.3 for an idea of where the line should go.

4. If the line is not the length you would like it, you can stretch it. First select the line; at each end, you will see blue grips. Simply pick (left-click) the grip and stretch the reference plane to the desired length, as in Figure 2.3.

5. Start the Ref Plane command again.

6. Press Esc, then click the Ref Plane ➤ Pick Existing Line/Edge, as shown in Figure 2.4.

7. Set the Offset to 15'–0" (remember, you can just type 15). See Figure 2.4.

FIGURE 2.3: You can grip-edit reference planes to the required length.

FIGURE 2.4: Ref Plane: Pick Existing Line/Edge.

8. Hover your pointer above the mid-reference plane. Notice a blue alignment line will appear either above or below.

9. Move your pointer up and down. See the alignment line flip? When it flips to the top, pick the middle line. It will add the line to the top.

10. With the Ref Plane command still running, hover over the middle line again. This time, offset the alignment line down. Your plan should now look like Figure 2.5.

FIGURE 2.5: Reference planes are used here to aid in the placement of walls.

T I P   Notice you did not actually use the "offset" command. Revit Architecture has the offset function built into most of the commands you will be running. All you have to do is to remember to look at your Options bar and you will be OK!

Adding More Walls

Let's add some walls! To do so, follow along with the next set of steps. (Before we start, here's a tip. In this procedure we're going to add walls in a counterclockwise direction, so follow along in that manner. But know that Revit assumes you will add walls in a clockwise manner. In the future, try adding the walls clockwise; it "forces" the exterior of the wall to the outside.) OK, now back to adding walls!

1. Press the Esc key.

2. Select one of the exterior walls in the model and right-click.

3. Select Create Similar. (You can still start the wall command from the Home tab. If you do, make sure you select Basic Wall: Exterior - Brick and CMU on MTL. Stud.)

4. On the Options bar, make sure the Location Line is set to Finish Face Exterior.

5. Start drawing your new wall from the intersection of the west wall (the one on the left) and the upper reference plane, as shown in Figure 2.6. Make sure you are using the face of the wall and not the ledge below. The blowup in Figure 2.6 can help you.

 N O T E   Make sure the new wall is from the brick face and not the ledge below. If the wall does not automatically join after placement, try again.

FIGURE 2.6: Drawing a single wall from a defined starting point

---

6. If the wall is starting on the wrong side of the reference plane, tap your spacebar. This will flip the wall to the correct side.

7. Type 25 and press Enter.

8. Press Esc.

9. Do the same for the other side. Your plan should now look like Figure 2.7.

FIGURE 2.7: The two walls drawn here are 30'–0" from finish face to finish face.

10. Start the Wall command again.

11. From the top 25'–0" wall, pick (left-click) the corner of the finish face (again, the brick face and not the ledge below). The wall may be in the wrong orientation, so tap the spacebar to flip it if it is.

12. Move your cursor up and to the left at a 135° angle (Revit will snap at 45° intervals).

13. Once you move your cursor far enough in this direction, Revit will pick up the north finish face of the building drawn in the previous procedure. Once these two alignment lines appear, pick the point on the screen, as shown in Figure 2.8.

14. Once this point is picked, draw a horizontal wall to the left 25'.

15. From the left point of that wall, draw a wall up 25'.

16. From the top of that wall, draw another wall to the left 80'.

17. Draw a wall down 25'.

18. On the Place Wall panel, click the Start-End-Midpoint Arc button, as shown in Figure 2.9.

FIGURE 2.8: Allow Revit to guide you in the placement of walls.

FIGURE 2.9: Draw a radial wall using the arc through three points method.

19. Since the Wall command is still running, the next point to pick is the endpoint of the arc. Pick a point straight down at a distance of 30'–0".

20. Once the second point is picked, move your pointer to the right until Revit snaps it to the tangent radius. (You may not get a tangent snap, but Revit will hesitate once you have reached the tangency.)

21. On the Options bar, check the line button to the right of the arc passing through three points icon. This will allow you to draw a straight wall again.

22. Draw a wall straight down from the end of the arc 25'.

23. Draw a wall to the right 80'.

24. Draw a wall straight up 25'–0".

25. Press Esc. Your building should look like Figure 2.10.

FIGURE 2.10: The building up to this point

The next few walls will be a little tougher. You are going to have to place them using the imbedded offset function within the Wall command. Remember, you need to keep watching the Options bar for this one.

1. Start the Wall command.

2. On the Draw panel, click the Pick Lines button, as shown in Figure 2.11.

FIGURE 2.11: Using the pick lines icon from the Options bar will allow you to add a wall by using an offset from another object.

3. On the Options bar, you will see an Offset input. Type 30 and press Enter.

4. Move your cursor over the outside face of the wall, as Figure 2.12 shows. Once you see the alignment line appear below the wall, pick the outside face, as in Figure 2.12.

5. Repeat the procedure for the angled wall. Make sure you offset the wall to the left. See Figure 2.13.

FIGURE 2.12: Adding a wall using the built-in offset function may take a couple tries to get the method down.

FIGURE 2.13: Creating the bottom of the corridor

Wall Adjustments

You've probably noticed that the walls are joining themselves together. This behavior is inherent to Revit. For the previous procedure, however, you will be left with a gap between the bottom two walls. It was too far for Revit to realize these walls need to be joined. You can fix this by following these steps:

1. Pick (left-click) the bottom diagonal wall. You will see a number of blue icons and dimensions appear, as shown in Figure 2.14. Each of these icons plays a role in the adjustment of the wall.

FIGURE 2.14: By selecting a wall, you will get a chance to make adjustments such as stretching the ends by picking the blue grips.

2. On each end, you will see a solid blue grip. Pick the right solid blue grip and drag the wall down to meet the reference plane, as shown in Figure 2.15.

FIGURE 2.15: Stretching the wall using the blue grip

3. Select the horizontal wall to the right.

4. Pick the left blue grip, and drag this wall's end to the left until you hit the bottom corner of the diagonal wall. The two walls will join together (see Figure 2.16).

FIGURE 2.16: The walls are automatically joined when you "pull" the end of one into another.

5. We need to add another part of the building. Right-click on one of the exterior walls and select Create Similar.

6. On the View toolbar, set the detail level to Coarse, as shown in Figure 2.17.

FIGURE 2.17: Sometimes setting the graphic display to Coarse can make the placement of other walls easier.

7. On the Options bar, change the offset to 15'–0".

8. Pick the midpoint of the wall, as shown in Figure 2.18.

9. Draw the wall 25'–0" down from the wall by typing **25** and pressing Enter.

10. Once you pick the 25'–0" distance, move your cursor up, back toward the wall, as shown in Figure 2.19.

11. Draw a wall across the front of the two walls, as shown in Figure 2.20. Make sure it is flipped in the right direction.

12. Set the detail level back to Fine. Your walls should look like Figure 2.20.

FIGURE 2.18: Adding the new walls requires picking the midpoint of this wall. Make sure your offset is set to 15'–0" on the Options bar.

FIGURE 2.19: By using the Offset command as you are drawing walls, you can use one common centerline.

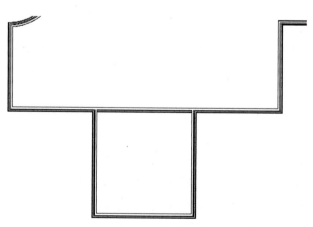

FIGURE 2.20: The completed walls for the south side of the building

DOES IT MEASURE UP?

In Revit, you have access to the Tape Measure, which is the same as the distance command in AutoCAD. To verify whether your walls are at the distances you want them to be, pick the Tape Measure button as shown here. Once the distance is measured, the Options bar will show you the result.

Adding Interior Walls

Interior walls are basically the same as exterior walls in terms of how they are placed in the model. This is a good thing. Luckily you can be slightly more relaxed with the justification. Now that there is a footprint to the building, it is much easier to see whether the walls need to be adjusted.

We'll start with laying out an elevator shaft and a stairwell, using an 8" CMU wall system. To follow along, either keep going with the model you are developing or open the file NER-02.rvt.

1. Zoom into the northwest corner of the building, as shown in Figure 2.21.

2. On the Home tab, select the Wall button.

3. In the Change Element Type menu, select the Basic Wall: Generic - 8" Masonry.

4. For the starting point, pick the corner as shown in Figure 2.21. The wall will probably be in the wrong orientation, so if necessary, tap the spacebar to flip the wall's orientation.

5. Draw move your cursor downward and type 12. The wall will be 12'–0" long.

6. Move your cursor to the right and type 10.

7. Move your cursor back up the view and pick the exterior wall.

8. Hit the Esc key. You should have three walls that look like Figure 2.22.

FIGURE 2.21: Start drawing the 8" CMU elevator shaft in the corner indicated here.

FIGURE 2.22: The elevator shaft begins to take shape.

At this point, you have some walls in the model. It is time to look at ensuring that these walls are accurately placed, so you need to check the dimensions.

Using Temporary Dimensions to Gain Control of Your Model

Once items are placed in a model, you are usually going to need to make some adjustments. Revit does a good job with this; however, there are some rules that need to be adhered to. The goal here is to have a clear 10'–0" dimension on the inside faces of the shaft. At this point, you should assume that you do not. This is where temporary dimensions come into play:

1. Select the right, vertical CMU wall. You will see a blue temporary dimension appear along the bottom wall. This dimension is indicating the centerline increments, as shown in Figure 2.23.

2. On the temporary dimension, you will see some blue grips. If you hover your cursor over one of them, a tooltip will appear indicating that this grip represents the "witness line."

FIGURE 2.23: Temporary dimensions, like the one shown here, can be adjusted to measure from different wall faces by picking the witness line grip.

3. Pick the grip to the right side of the dimension. Notice it moves to the outside face of the wall. Pick it again, and notice it moves to the inside face. This is exactly where we want it.

4. Pick the grip to the left of the dimension twice to get it to read from the inside face of the CMU wall.

5. Notice the actual increment in the dimension is blue. Select the blue dimension, type 10, and press Enter. The wall that was selected will move to accommodate the new increment, as shown in Figure 2.24.

FIGURE 2.24: The wall that is selected is the wall that will move once you type the new dimension.

Temporary Dimension Settings

Revit takes the default for the temporary dimensions from the center of the walls — which is typically the last place you want the dimension to be taken from. You can change some settings to fix this:

1. On the Manage tab, click Settings ➤ Temporary Dimensions, as shown in Figure 2.25.

FIGURE 2.25: This command lets you control where the temporary dimensions are taken from.

2. In the Temporary Dimensions Properties box, select Faces under Walls.

3. Under Doors and Windows, select Openings, as shown in Figure 2.26.

FIGURE 2.26: This is the most popular configuration.

4. Click OK.

5. Select the wall to the left. You may not see any dimensions at all. Always remember to look up at the Ribbon area. Click the Activate Dimensions button, and you will now see a 10'–0" dimension.

6. Underneath the dimension, you will see a small blue icon that also looks like a dimension. If you hover your mouse over it, a tooltip will appear indicating that you can make the temporary dimension permanent, as shown in Figure 2.27. Once you see this tooltip, click the icon.

FIGURE 2.27: You can make temporary dimensions permanent.

7. Press Esc.

8. Select the right wall. Notice the permanent dimension turns blue. We know that anything that turns blue in Revit can be edited. You can change this increment anytime you wish.

9. Press Esc again without changing the dimension.

We need one more shaft wall to create a separation between the exterior walls and the shaft, as shown in Figure 2.28. Perform these steps:

1. Right-click on any CMU wall and select Create Similar.

2. On the Draw panel, select the Pick Lines button.

3. On the Options bar, type **10** in the Offset field.

4. On the Options bar, be sure the Location Line is set to Finish Face Interior.

5. Offset the south CMU shaft wall. This will separate the shaft from the exterior and create a little chase.

6. Press Esc twice. Figure 2.28 shows the elevator with the shaft wall. Make sure you check your dimensions before proceeding.

FIGURE 2.28: The elevator with the shaft wall

The next task is to mirror these walls to the other side:

1. Pick a window around all of the masonry walls.

2. On the Modify Walls tab, click the Mirror ➤ Pick Mirror Axis button, as shown in Figure 2.29.

FIGURE 2.29: The Mirror command is activated only when you have objects selected.

3. Pick the horizontal reference plane in the center of the building. Your walls are now mirrored, as shown in Figure 2.30.

4. Save the model.

We are starting to get the hang of adding different wall types — but we aren't done yet. We still need to add quite a few interior partitions.

DID YOU SELECT TOO MUCH?

If you picked a window around all of the walls and now have more items selected than you wish, you can simply press the Shift key on your keyboard. This will remove the item form the selection set. If the opposite happened, and you wanted to add an item, you press the Ctrl key and pick the item(s) you want added. Your cursor will always show a plus or a minus sign, as shown here.

FIGURE 2.30: The elevator shaft is now mirrored.

Placing Interior Partitions

The majority of your tasks in Revit involve placing interior partitions. Given the dimensional nature of placing these types of walls in Revit, you don't need to bother with reference planes as often as when you are placing the exterior walls.

Given that, creating interior partitions is somewhat easier than the exterior variety, as you will see in a moment. With the exterior, careful placement and constant double-checking is crucial. With interior partitions, the typical method is to get the wall where you "think" you need it. You can then go back and make adjustments without disturbing too many adjacent items.

To start adding interior partitions, we will begin with the necessary lavatory and egress first, and then fill the spaces with some offices. When completed, this stage will look like Figure 2.31.

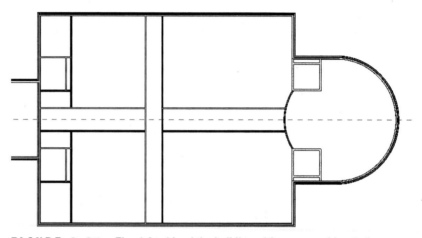

FIGURE 2.31: The right side of the building with egress and lavatories

The objective of the next procedure is to start adding our interior partitions:

1. To get started, open the building you have been working on. If you did not complete the last procedure, open the file called NER-03.rvt found on the book's website. Or, of course, you can keep going on your own project.

2. Make sure you are on Level 1.

3. On the Home tab, click the Wall button.

4. In the Change Element Type menu, select Basic Wall : Interior - 6⅛" Partition (2-hr).

5. On the Draw panel, click the Pick Lines button.

6. For the Height, instead of Unconnected choose Level 2 from the menu.

7. For the Location Line, choose Finish Face Exterior.

8. On the Draw panel, click the STart-End-Midpoint Arc button.
   (See Figure 2.32.)

FIGURE 2.32: Choosing options should be old hat by now!

9. Pick the left corner of the upper CMU walls

10. Pick the left corner of the bottom CMU walls.

11. Move your cursor to the left, and specify a radius of 20'–0", as shown
    in Figure 2.33.

12. Press Esc twice.

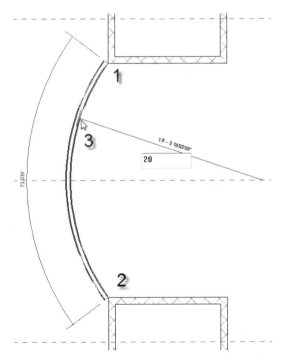

FIGURE 2.33: Drawing an arched wall requires a three-point method. It is
similar to the Start-End-Direction command in AutoCAD.

We now need to add some corridor walls. You can do this using the center reference plane you established earlier:

1. Right-click on the radial wall and select Create Similar.

2. On the Draw panel, click the Line button.

3. For the Location Line, choose Finish Face Interior.

4. For the Offset (on the Options bar), add a 4'–0" offset.

5. To start placing the wall, pick the intersection of the center reference plane and the radial wall, as shown in Figure 2.34.

6. Move your cursor to the left. Notice the wall is being drawn but at an offset of 4'–0" from the "line" you are drawing up the middle of the building.

FIGURE 2.34: Drawing corridor walls using an offset can be a great timesaver.

7. For the second point of the wall, pick the intersection of the left-most wall.

8. Now move your cursor back to the right. Notice the other side of the wall is being drawn at a 4'–0" offset. This time, it is on the opposite side of the reference line.

9. Pick the intersection of the reference plane and the radial wall as the second point, as shown in Figure 2.35.

FIGURE 2.35: Completing the main corridor. You will still have to drag the walls together to join up.

Let's now clean up the gaps between the radial wall and the two corridor walls:

1. Make sure you are not still in the Wall command by pressing Esc or by selecting the Modify button on the Quick Access bar.

2. Select the top corridor wall. On the right end of the wall is a blue grip. Pick it and drag the top corridor wall into the radial wall.

3. Repeat the step for the bottom wall. (See Figure 2.36.)

FIGURE 2.36: Getting a grip on the grips!

 W A R N I N G   Picking a grip on the end of a wall also means you are going to get a temporary dimension. Look at it! If it does not say 8'–0" to the inside face of the corridor, you have a problem. Discovering these discrepancies early in the design stage is much better than finding out you have a dimensional issue when the drawings are going out the door. If the increment is not 8'–0", first verify that the temporary dimension is going to the inside face. If not, pick the blue grip and move the witness line to the inside face of the walls. If the dimension is still off, move the witness line to the center reference plane. Now just type 4 and press Enter. Repeat the process for the other wall. Always check dimensions like this. The time you save could be your own!

The next step is to get the lavatories in. These will show up at the east end (left side) of the building. Refer to Figure 2.37 for the dimensions and follow along:

1. Right-click on one of the corridor walls and select Create Similar from the menu.

2. Look at your options, and create the lavatories shown in Figure 2.37. All of the dimensions are taken from finish inside face.

FIGURE 2.37: The lavatory at the east side of the building

3. Once the lavatory walls are drawn in, mirror the walls to the other side of the building, as shown in Figure 2.38.

FIGURE 2.38: Both the Men's and Women's lavatories. The actual rooms will be added in Chapter 15.

We now need another corridor running north and south as shown in Figure 2.39. The best way to approach this is to add another reference plane, and then add the walls in a similar fashion to the method applied to the east/west corridor. To open up the central area, some 45° walls will be added at 4'–0". To accomplish this, start by following these steps:

FIGURE 2.39: This is the finished corridor layout.

1. On the Work Plane panel of the Home tab, click Ref Plane ≻ Draw Reference Plane..

2. Draw a reference plane from the midpoint of the top exterior wall to the midpoint of the bottom exterior wall.

3. Click the Tape Measure button. Make 100% sure this is the center of the building. You are going to rely heavily on this line.

4. Start the Wall command.

5. On the Options bar, be sure Location Line is set to Finish Face Interior and that the offset is 4'–0".

6. Pick the top intersection of the reference plane and the exterior wall.

7. Draw the wall down to the bottom of the building.

8. Keeping the Wall command running, draw the other side of the corridor by picking the same two points along the reference plane.

TIP   Are the reference lines really necessary? No, they are not. But it is a good, sound approach to laying out your building. These lines will be used heavily throughout the life of your project.

You now have an area in the middle of the building where four walls intersect each other. You can now add some 45° walls there to open the corridor at this area, as shown in Figure 2.40:

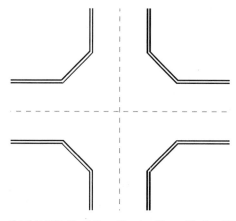

FIGURE 2.40: The corridor with the 45° walls added

1. Zoom into the intersections of the corridors.

2. On the Work Plane panel of the Home tab, click Ref Plane ➤ Draw Reference Plane.

3. On the Draw panel, select the Pick Lines button and change the offset to 4'–0".

4. From the finish inside face of the top, horizontal corridor wall, offset the reference plane up. See Figure 2.41.

TIP   This can be tricky to get the reference plane going in the correct direction. If it is being stubborn, and is still trying to offset the line down, just move your cursor up a little. The reference plane will change direction.

Walls : Basic Wall : Interior - 6 1/8" Partition (2-hr) :
Reference

FIGURE 2.41: Adding yet another reference plane to the model. You will delete this one.

Once the reference plane is established, you can add the new wall. It can be as simple as just drawing the wall in, but there are still a few little procedures you should be aware of:

1. Start the Wall command by right-clicking on one of the corridor walls and selecting Create Similar.

2. On the Options bar, be sure the wall's Location Line is justified from Finish Face: Interior.

3. Pick the intersection of the reference plane and the inside finished face of the left, vertical corridor wall (see Figure 2.42).

FIGURE 2.42: Adding the 45° wall

4. Once you pick the start point, move your cursor to the left and down at a 45° angle (you can approximate the angle, Revit will "snap" you to the correct angle).

5. At a 45° angle, pick the endpoint at a location within the horizontal, top corridor wall (see Figure 2.42).

EYEBALLING WITH ACCURACY

You may notice when you are using temporary dimensions that the increment always seems to "snap" to even increments. This is no accident. If you choose Settings ➤ Snaps on the Manage tab, you will see values for Length Dimension Snap Increments and Angular Dimension Snap Increments. These values change based on the zoom percentage. The closer you zoom in, the smaller the increments get. You can also change these values by typing in a semicolon and adding a new increment to the end of the list, as shown here.

WARNING   If you proceed with just assuming that these walls are 4'-0" from the inside face, you may be making a big mistake. Take distances after you add walls — especially if the walls are not 90°.

The next task is to mirror the walls. This part is going to be easy since you put those reference planes in there!

1. Select the 45° wall.

2. Pick Mirror ➢ Pick Mirror Axis from the Modify Walls tab.

3. Pick the vertical reference plane. And voilà! The wall is mirrored (see Figure 2.43).

FIGURE 2.43: Using the Mirror command in conjunction with a reference plane is a good example of thinking ahead.

4. Select the two 45° walls, and mirror them about the horizontal reference plane. You should now have four 45° walls, as shown in Figure 2.44.

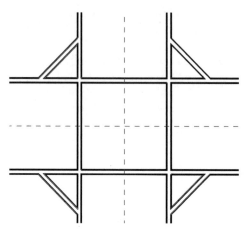

FIGURE 2.44: Stuck inside these four walls

5. You can now delete the reference plane by simply selecting it and clicking the Delete button.

Now it's time for some further cleanup. Although all of the modify commands will be featured in Chapter 4, "Working with the Revit Tools," we can still use some here. Already, the Mirror command has been "borrowed" from that chapter. We might as well "borrow" the Split command as well!

1. On the Edit panel of the Modify tab, select the Split button, as shown in Figure 2.45.

FIGURE 2.45: Using the Split command

2. Always look at the Options bar! Check the Delete Inner Segment button.

3. Pick a point along the top, horizontal corridor wall near the intersecting 45° wall.

4. Pick the second point along the same wall, only on the opposite side (see Figure 2.46).

FIGURE 2.46: Split the wall at two points. If Delete Inner Segment is selected, the result will eliminate the wall between the two points.

5. Repeat the process for the other three walls. You should now have an open central area for your corridor, as shown in Figure 2.47.

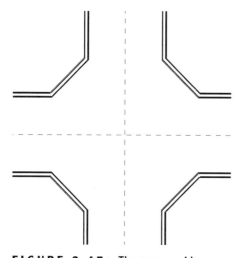

FIGURE 2.47: The open corridor

N O T E   If the Split command is giving you a splitting headache rather than splitting the walls, keep trying. We will also cover this in Chapter 4. Commands such as Split do require a different "touch" than in AutoCAD.

Looking back, we have accomplished quite a bit. Laying out walls, then modifying them to conform to your needs is a huge part of being successful in Revit, but we are not done yet. The next few processes will involve dealing with different types of walls that merge together. Historically, this has been an issue. Although Revit tends to clean these areas up a little better than other modeling applications, there still are going to be some "sticky" areas. Let's create a situation where this will occur!

Editing Wall Joins

There is a separate function in Revit that deals with editing wall joins specifically: the Edit Wall Joins command. It can come in quite handy. To get started,
let's add some more walls to an already busy corner of the building:

1. Zoom into the northwest corner of the building, as shown in Figure 2.48.

FIGURE 2.48: The northwest corner

2. Start the Wall command. Make sure it is the same 6⅛" two-hour partition you have been using.

3. To start the wall, pick the intersection where the CMU wall abuts the
   finish inside face of the exterior wall. See Figure 2.49.

FIGURE 2.49: Adding to the mess in the corner

4. The wall may be flipped in the wrong direction. If it is, remember to
   hit the spacebar. This will flip it up to the proper orientation.

5. Pick the second point of the wall at the corridor in the middle of the building. Press Esc twice. The intersection should look like Figure 2.50.

FIGURE 2.50: The wall and the resulting intersection

6. Zoom back in on the intersection. If the view does not resemble Figure 2.50 in terms of line weight, click the thin lines icon, as shown in Figure 2.51.

FIGURE 2.51: Click the thin lines icon to see how the walls are actually joining together.

7. On the Edit Geometry panel of the Modify tab, click the Wall Joins button, as shown in Figure 2.52.

FIGURE 2.52: You'll find the Edit Wall Joins button on the Edit toolbar.

8. Hover your pointer over the intersection. Revit will display a big box, as shown in Figure 2.53.

9. Once you see the big box, pick anywhere within the area. This will establish that this is the intersection you wish to edit.

FIGURE 2.53: Choosing the intersection you wish to edit

Once you pick the intersection, you will see some additional lines show up. This exposes how Revit is actually looking at the corner.

10. On the Options bar, you will now see some choices for configuring this intersection. Select the Miter option, as shown in Figure 2.54. This option is the most popular.

Although a wall of this type would never actually have a 45° miter in real life, mitering the corner in Revit allows for a more uniform join between adjacent walls.

Displaying Wall Joins

Usually, in a plan view such as this, there will be no wall joins shown at all. Typically only the outside lines join and an enlarged detail would show the specific construction methods. But in some cases, you would want Revit to reveal this information. In Revit, you have three choices for the display:

Clean Join   This will join the same materials in each wall together.

Don't Clean Join   This will take one wall and indiscriminately run it straight through to the end.

Use View Settings   In the view properties, you can specify the default for how the wall intersections are to be displayed (see Figure 2.55).

FIGURE 2.54: Adding a mitered join

FIGURE 2.55: Choosing a display option

The objective of the next procedure is to investigate where the wall join settings are located:

1. Choose Use Display Settings.

2. Press Escape a few times and click on the drawing.

3. Type VP to open the View Properties dialog.

4. In the View Properties dialog, you will see a category for Wall Joins. It is set to clean all joins; it is also unavailable for editing. If your view's detail level is set to Fine, the default is to clean all joins. If it is set to Coarse, as shown in Figure 2.56, you have a choice between joining the same wall types or cleaning all joins.

5. Do not change anything here, and just click Cancel. Press Esc.

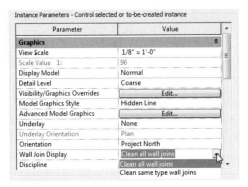

FIGURE 2.56: Choosing a display level in the view's properties

Disallow Wall Join

There is another item to deal with when walls join together. In some cases, you may not want walls to automatically join even if they are the same exact wall type. To learn how to prevent this behavior, follow along:

1. Select the long, horizontal 6⅛" wall that comes into the corner, as shown in Figure 2.57. You will see a blue grip to the right of the intersection. This represents where the wall's extents are.

2. Hover directly over the blue grip.

3. Once the blue grip highlights, right-click.

4. Select Disallow Join (see Figure 2.57).

FIGURE 2.57: By right-clicking on the wall's end grip, you can tell Revit to disallow that wall's join function.

5. Once the wall is un-joined, you can pick the same blue grip and slide the wall back to where you would want it to terminate. Of course, you will have to do this manually (see Figure 2.58).

6. Once the wall slides into place, select it.

7. Notice there is an additional blue T-shaped icon. Hover your cursor over this icon; you will see that you can pick this icon to allow the walls to join back up again, as shown in Figure 2.58.

8. Pick this button to allow the join.

FIGURE 2.58: Allowing the walls to join back again

As mentioned earlier, your ability to edit wall joins can determine how quickly you start either liking, or disliking, Revit. This book took a few extra steps in the effort of joining walls, but the experience will carry through, project after project.

There is one more area we need to investigate before we leave this corner: the area within the chase. Suppose you do not want to run the gypsum into this area. This is a common situation that can cause people to have fits with Revit. Let's try to avoid those fits right now!

Editing the Cut Profile

A plan view is simply a section taken 4'–0" up the wall from the finish floor. In Revit, you can manually edit the profile of any wall cut in plan. This is extremely useful if you need to take sections of drywall out of specific areas without creating or adding an entirely new wall. To do this, perform the following steps:

1. Zoom in on the right side of the elevator shaft at the intersection of the exterior wall, as shown in Figure 2.59.

2. Select the west CMU wall, and drag it out of the exterior wall by picking and dragging the blue grip at the end of the wall (see Figure 2.59).

FIGURE 2.59: Pick the blue grip and drag the CMU wall out of the exterior wall.

3. Right-click on the blue grip on the endpoint of the wall.

4. Select Disallow Join.

5. Pick the blue grip and drag the wall end back to the face of the wall behind the gypsum (see Figure 2.60).

FIGURE 2.60: The method is to pull the CMU out of the wall, disallow the join, and then drag it back into the face of stud.

6. On the Edit Linework panel of the Modify tab, click the Cut Profile button, as shown in Figure 2.61.

7. Pick the finish face of the exterior wall. You are selecting the gypsum layer to be cut out of the shaft (see Figure 2.61).

FIGURE 2.61: Click the Edit Cut Profile button and select the gypsum.

8. You now need to draw a very short line from the inside face of the wallboard to the outside face, as shown in Figure 2.62. Press Esc.

9. Once the short line is drawn in, you will see a blue arrow. This arrow indicates the side of the material you wish to keep. If you pick (left-click) the arrow, it will flip direction. Make sure it is flipped to the right.

FIGURE 2.62: This line indicates where the wallboard will be cut. The blue arrow indicates the side of the material that will remain.

10. Notice you now have an additional tab called Create Cut Profile Sketch. Additionally, this tab contains a Cut Profile panel, which allows you to finish the Cut Profile. What you see here is called the Sketch Mode. Since you are done "sketching" the cut profile, click Finish Cut Profile, as you can see in Figure 2.63. Figure 2.64 shows the final result.

FIGURE 2.63: Clicking Finish Sketch will finalize the session and complete the command.

N O T E   If you receive an error that says "Ends of the sketched loop do not lie on the boundary of the face being modified" when you are trying to finish the sketch, it is because you have not drawn the line exactly from point to point. This line cannot cross over, or be shy of, the material you are trying to split. If you are getting this error, select the magenta line. You will see two familiar blue grips. Pick the grip that does not touch the face of the material and drag it back.

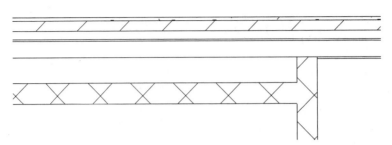

FIGURE 2.64: The finished wall with the finish deducted from the core of the chase

Go through and do the same thing to the south side of the building, starting at the edit Wall Joins section.

There are plenty more walls left to add, but we need to save something for Chapter 4. At this point, it sure would be nice to start adding some doors and windows to the model!

Placing Doors and Windows into Your Walls

Adding doors and windows is one of the easiest things you will do in Revit Architecture. Finding the correct door or window becomes a bit harder. Creating a custom door or window takes time and patience. This portion of this chapter will focus on adding these items to the model. Chapter 17, "Families," will drill down into the specifics on the creation of these custom families.

Adding Doors

Placing a door in Revit Architecture can seem annoying and somewhat unnecessarily tedious at first. But like anything else in Revit, once you get the method down, you will find your groove.

1. Either continue working in the model that you are following along with, or go to **www.sybex.com/go/revit2010ner** and navigate to the file called NER-04.rvt. The model is completed up to this point. Of course, you can translate these lessons to your own project as well.

2. On the Home tab, click the Door button.

3. In the Change Element Type menu, choose Single-Flush: 36"×84" (see Figure 2.65).

FIGURE 2.65: Adding a door.

4. Move your cursor over to the south wall near the elevator shaft, as shown in Figure 2.66. Notice that if your cursor is not within a wall, you get the "NO" sign. Revit will not allow you to just place a door into space. A door is considered a hosted family.

5. Once you get your cursor positioned approximately where Figure 2.66 shows, move your pointer up and down. Notice the door's direction will change. This is typical behavior for a door.

6. Press the spacebar. Notice the door will flip direction.

7. Make it so the door is facing outward and to the left, as shown in Figure 2.66. Once it is, pick (left-click) a point on the wall. If you accidentally put it in wrong, don't worry — we can fix it. Press Esc.

FIGURE 2.66: Placing a door will always require a host. Remember, you can press the spacebar to change the orientation, and move your cursor up and down to flip the direction.

YIKES, LOOK AT MY WALLS!

When you place a door or any opening into a compound wall, you need to tell Revit specifically how to wrap the materials. By default, Revit will stop the brick and any other finish right at the opening. Obviously this is usually not the case. The following steps will guide you through wrapping materials at an insert:

1. Select the exterior wall.

2. On the Modify Walls tab, click the Element Properties button, as shown here.

3. In the Element Properties dialog, click Edit Type, as shown here.

    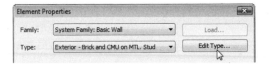

4. Where it specifies wrapping at inserts, select Both.

5. Click OK twice.

Notice that when the door is placed, a tag shows up and has an automatic number within it. In Revit, once you place a door you should go right back and select it. This will highlight the door and "turn on" a few different options. Follow these steps:

1. Click the Modify button on the Quick Access toolbar. This will disengage you from the Door command.

2. Pick the door you just added to the model. Notice there are blue temporary dimensions. Let's make sure these dimensions are going where we want them.

   A. On the Project Settings panel of the Manage tab, click Settings ➤ Temporary Dimensions, as shown in Figure 2.67.

FIGURE 2.67: Select Settings ➤ Temporary Dimensions.

   B. Make sure that walls are going to faces and that doors are going to openings.

   C. Click OK.

Now that the temporary dimensions are configured the way we need them, we can start using them to manipulate the placement of our doors:

1. Select the door again.

2. Move the left witness line to the outside face of the CMU wall, as shown in Figure 2.68.

3. As you know, in Revit Architecture anything that turns blue can be edited. Click on the blue dimension that extends from the CMU wall, drag it to the right of the elevator shaft, and change it to 1'–0" (see Figure 2.69).

FIGURE 2.68: Moving the witness line to a more appropriate location

FIGURE 2.69: Change the temporary dimension.

Placing Wall Tags

Notice the tag that shows up? This is an automatic feature of Revit. Another thing that is automatic is the tag's number. Under normal circumstances, Revit will number it incorrectly. Luckily you can renumber it:

1. Select the door.

2. Pick (left-click) the number in the door tag.

3. Change the number to 101.

4. With the door still selected, notice you have flip arrows as well. If the door is not in the orientation you see in the previous figures, click these arrows to flip the door.

5. Mirror this door and its tag about the buildings centerline.

Loading Families

It would be nice if the seven doors available in the Revit model were all you needed. They, of course, are not. Revit, like most other CAD and applications that use *building information modeling*, does not load every single component into the drawing or model. File size is just as much of a concern in Revit as it is in AutoCAD. If you need a different door, you have to go get it:

▶

Most items that are added to the Revit model can be selected and flipped in the same method. Also, if you select the items to be flipped and press the spacebar, it will have the same effect.

1. On the Home tab, click the Door button.

2. On the Place Door tab, click the Load Family button, as shown in Figure 2.70.

FIGURE 2.70: Click Load on the Options bar.

3. Find the Doors directory; navigate to Double-Flush.rfa and click Open.

4. Select Double-Flush : 72"×84" from the Type Selector in the Options bar.

5. Place the double doors in the wall, as shown in Figure 2.71.

FIGURE 2.71: Placing the double doors

6. Mirror the door using the center reference plane.

7. Add bathroom doors, as shown in Figure 2.72. Use Single-Flush: 36"×84"?

8. Label them accordingly.

9. In the exterior wall that divides the east building form the corridor, add a Single Raised Panel with Side Lights : 36"×84" door centered upon the opening.

10. Change the tag to read 100B, as shown in Figure 2.73.

Normally the doors will automatically "find" the center of the wall. But to make sure, you can type SM. This will tell Revit that you want to snap to the middle.

FIGURE 2.72: Adding lavatory doors. You will have to renumber the tags.

FIGURE 2.73: Add a new corridor door. If this door is not loaded into your model, you have to click the Load button on the Options bar.

We need to add more doors and interior partitions, but they will be best suited for Chapter 4 where we can be more accurate. In the meantime, however, let's add some simple openings.

Placing Openings in Your Walls

Openings are categorized with doors but need to be added to the model using the Component command. No, really. It's true. Follow along:

1. On the Home tab, click Component, as shown in Figure 2.74.

FIGURE 2.74: Clicking Component on the Home tab.

2. On the Place Component tab, click the Load Family button.

3. Browse to the Doors directory.

4. Find the file called Opening-Cased.rfa and click Open.

5. On the Place Component tab, click the Element Properties button.

6. Click Edit Type...

7. Click Duplicate.

8. Call the opening 84"×84".

9. Under Dimensions, change the Width to 7'–0".

10. Click OK twice. Then Esc to clear the Command.

11. Zoom into the area shown in Figure 2.75, and place an interior - 6⅛"
Partition (2-hr) wall as shown. This is the wall you will place the
opening into.

12. Click Component, and place the Opening into the wall as shown in
Figure 2.75.

FIGURE 2.75: The new opening

Add two more doors, and we are finished with this section:

1. On the Home tab, click Door.

2. From the Change Element Type menu, pick Double-Flush : 72"×84".

3. Add the double doors to the ends of the vertical corridor, as shown in Figure 2.76.

4. Label them as 100C and 100D.

FIGURE 2.76: Two new corridor doors

Again, there are plenty more doors and partitions that we can add to the model, but they will be added in Chapter 4. Let's move on to adding some windows!

Adding Windows

Doors, windows, openings … it's all the same really. Once you have experience adding one, the other is just as easy!

The objective of the next procedure is to add some windows to the model.

1. On the Home tab, click the Window button, as shown in Figure 2.77.

FIGURE 2.77: Adding a window is the same as adding a door.

2. Select the Fixed : 36"×72" window from the Change Element Type menu.

3. Add the window to the corner of the building, as shown in Figure 2.78. Be careful with the placement. If your cursor is toward the exterior of the wall, the window will be orientated correctly.

FIGURE 2.78: Depending on the side of the wall your cursor is on, you can add a window to the correct orientation.

4. Add two more windows to the east wall adjacent to the wall you just put the first window in. Use your temporary dimensions to ensure you are placing the windows 1'–0" from the opening to the wall.

5. Mirror the windows. See Figure 2.79.

FIGURE 2.79: Placing the windows to the corner of the building and mirroring them

6. Select one of the windows that have been placed. Notice the temporary dimensions and the flip arrows.

7. Change the tag to read A. (All of the windows are type A.)

8. You will get a warning stating that you are changing a type parameter. Click OK.

Now that the windows are in place, it is time to investigate how they are built by taking a look at their properties.

Window Properties

Again, just as with doors and openings, you can check the element properties to tweak the unit even further:

1. Select one of the windows.

2. On the Modify Windows tab, click the Element Properties button, as shown in Figure 2.80.

FIGURE 2.80: The Element Properties button. You must select a window to get this button to display on the Options bar.

3. The dialog that appears first contains the instance parameters. Anything you change here applies to only the one window you have selected. Click the Edit Type button.

 TIP   If you know that you want to change an instance parameter (such as sill height) for every window in the model, you can. Knowing that an instance parameter only applies to one item, instead of picking just one window, you can pick a window, right-click, and choose Select All Instances. From there you can click the Element Properties button. This will subsequently change every window because you had every window selected.

4. Scroll down until you see Type Mark. Notice this value is set to A. This is the property you changed by typing the value into the tag in the model. Revit works both ways. If you change a symbol in the model, it will change the parameter value within the family. See Figure 2.81.

Windows are among the most difficult items in Revit to use out of the box without any real customization. In Chapter 17, we will dive into creating some custom Revit windows. For now, however, remember the lessons learned in this chapter. They will go a long way.

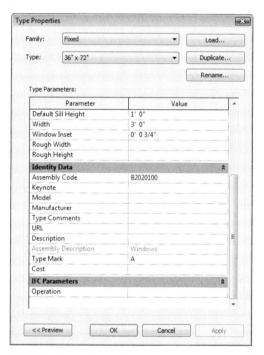

FIGURE 2.81: Changing a type parameter changes every window of that type.

Are You Experienced?

Now You Can...

- ☑ place exterior walls

- ☑ place interior walls

- ☑ add reference planes

- ☑ join walls

- ☑ use the Split command

- ☑ edit a cut profile

- ☑ add doors

- ☑ add openings

- ☑ add windows

CHAPTER 3

Creating Views

▶ Creating and managing levels

▶ Adding sectional and elevational views

▶ Controlling your views for aesthetic values

One of Revit Architecture's strongest points is the fact that it is one single model. This single model, however, has to be broken down into a tangible format that allows the user to navigate through a project. Chapters 1 and 2 featured the Project Browser (and it will be featured in this chapter as well), but what is the Project Browser actually managing? Well, it's simply managing views of the model. Here's an example: in the Project Browser, under Floor Plans you usually see Level 1. This is a view of the model that just so happens to be a floor plan. Under Elevations (Building Elevations), you see East Elevation, North Elevation, South Elevation, and West Elevation. These are exactly the same as the floor plans in the sense that they are simply views of the model.

This chapter focuses on the creation of views and their relationship to the model. We will start with possibly the most important function in Revit: creating levels. The power of Revit comes with the single-model concept. By being able to add levels to a model, you are also adding floor plans. This two-way interaction is what makes Revit the BIM choice for many users.

Creating Levels

As you wander through the floor plans in the Project Browser, you will see Level 1 and Level 2. Not every job you will work on will have only a Level 1 and a Level 2. Our task in this section is to create new levels that are appended to floor plans.

To follow along, open your model you have been working on, or go to **www.sybex.com/go/revit2010ner**, and browse to the Chapter 3 folder. Open the file called NER-05.rvt. If you wish, you can use an actual project you are working on. You will just have to replace any names and specific dimensions with ones that are applicable to your project. Perform these steps:

1. In the Project Browser, double-click on the South Elevation. It is located under Elevations (Building Elevations), as shown in Figure 3.1.

   Notice at the right side of the building there are two symbols with a datum at the end. These are elevation markers. Unfortunately, right now they are somewhat obscured by the exterior wall. Zoom in to this area, as shown in Figure 3.2.

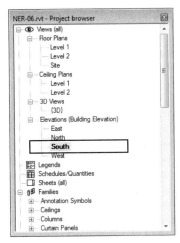

FIGURE 3.1: Finding an elevation in the Project Browser

 T I P   If, as you progress through the next few steps, you don't see what is shown in the next two figures, try zooming in more and repeating the instructions.

FIGURE 3.2: When dealing with levels, it is a good idea to zoom in close so you can manipulate them.

2. Select (left-click) Level 1. Notice you will get several blue icons, dimensions, and a lock.

Where the actual level line intersects the datum bubble, there is a hollow blue circle (grip), as shown in Figure 3.3, except that your view will be slightly obscured by the wall. Move the bubble so that you can see the grip clearly.

3. Left-click (pick) and hold the pick button. You can now drag the bubble to the left.

FIGURE 3.3: Picking the grip to drag the level out of the way

4. Once you get to a point where the level is outside the building, pick a spot to place the bubble and the annotation.

5. Press Esc, or select the Modify button on the Quick Access toolbar.

Now that the levels are physically in a position where they can be worked on, you can now start building on them.

Adding Levels

Adding an entirely new level in Revit Architecture is actually quite simple. But there are procedures that need to be adhered to in order to ensure you are adding the levels correctly.

When you are using the level feature in Revit, two procedural aspects stand out. One is to look at your Options bar after you start the command. The second is to click the Modify button when you have finished. It is very easy to get confused as to how Revit wants you to proceed with adding a level, and it is also easy to inadvertently create multiple levels. Remember, in Revit you are always in a command.

If you hover over any item in Revit Architecture and pause for a second, you will see what is called a tooltip.

To add a level, follow along:

1. On the Datum panel of the Home tab, click the Level button, as shown in Figure 3.4.

FIGURE 3.4: Adding a level from the Datum panel on the Home tab

2. On the Draw panel on the Place Level tab, you will see that you can either draw a line or pick a line, as shown in Figure 3.5. Make sure Pick Lines is checked.

3. Also on the Options bar, you will see the Make Plan View option. Make sure it's checked.

4. At the end of the Options bar, you will see a field for an offset. Type **10** and press Enter. Basically the approach here is to pick Level 2 and create a new level that is offset 10'–0" above (see Figure 3.5).

FIGURE 3.5: Choosing the options for the Level command

5. With the options set, hover your cursor over Level 2.

   Notice that, when you come into contact with Level 2 a blue dotted line appears. If you move your cursor slightly above the Level 2 line, the blue alignment line appears above Level 2. If you inch your cursor slightly below Level 2, the blue alignment line appears below Level 2.

6. When you see the blue line appear above Level 2, pick the Level 2 line, as shown in Figure 3.6.

FIGURE 3.6: Waiting for the alignment to appear

TIP   You may be starting to notice that speeding through the commands as you may have done in AutoCAD is not helping you any in Revit. In Revit you will find that you need to slow down a bit, and let Revit "do its thing." Once you start getting the hang of this behavior, you can speed up again.

7. You should now have a Level 3 at 20'–0" (see Figure 3.7).

WARNING   Just because you have created a new level, this does not tell Revit to shut down the command. Notice the Options bar is still active and the Level button still has the focus. If you start "clicking around" in the view area, you will start creating levels. Every time you pick a point on the screen, a new level will show up. Also, Revit does not care if you have a level on top of another level. This situation can get ugly fast.

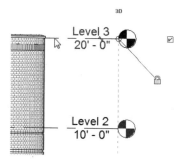

FIGURE 3.7: The completed Level 3. Remember, you are still in the Level command until you tell Revit to stop.

8. With the Level command still running, create Levels 4, 5, 6, and 7. Your elevation should now look like Figure 3.8. Also, look at your Project Browser. It should not have any additional levels.

FIGURE 3.8: Levels 1 through 7 are now complete.

9. On the Basics tab of the Design bar, pick the Modify button. You have now safely terminated the Level command. (You can also press the Esc key on your keyboard.)

Now that you have some experience adding levels, it is time to investigate the actual physical level to see how it can be manipulated and modified.

The Composition of a Level

Levels have controls that allow the user to adjust their appearance. As it has been stated throughout the book, when you select a family you will see that multiple items turn blue. The blue color indicates that these items can be modified. When you select a level, a few additional items will appear.

To investigate further, follow along:

1. Zoom in on Level 7.

2. Select Level 1 by picking (left-clicking) on either the text or the actual level line itself. This will put the focus on the level line. Notice the text that turns blue. We know that any blue item can be modified (see Figure 3.9).

FIGURE 3.9: The selected level

3. Click on the blue Level 7 text. This will allow you to edit the name of the level.

4. Type **Parapet**, as shown in Figure 3.10, and press Enter.

FIGURE 3.10: Renaming the level

5. Revit will ask you if you want to rename any corresponding views. Choose Yes (see Figure 3.11). Level 7 is now the Parapet level, as shown in Figure 3.12.

By renaming corresponding views, you are telling Revit to keep the level and its corresponding view named accordingly.

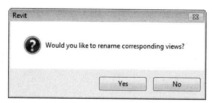

FIGURE 3.11: Click Yes to rename corresponding views.

FIGURE 3.12: The renamed level

6. With the Parapet level still selected, click on the 60'–0" field.

7. Type 52 and press Enter. This will physically drop the level to the true elevation.

You will now have two slightly overlapping levels. This can be fixed by manipulating some of the controls that show up when you select the level.

Press the Esc key a couple of times to clear any command that may be active and follow along:

1. Select the Parapet level.

2. The blue items will "light up." One of them is the choice to add an elbow, as shown in Figure 3.13. Click it, and Revit will bend the level.

FIGURE 3.13: You can add an elbow to the elevation marker.

3. Now that the elbow has been added, it will need to be moved. Notice that there is a blue grip at each bend point. Pick the blue grip, as shown in Figure 3.14, and drag the Parapet level out of the level below.

Can't you just type over the dimension? In Revit, you cannot have an inaccurate increment. If you type a new value to any increment, the model will change to reflect this new dimension.

FIGURE 3.14: Dragging the level to a new position using the grips provided

4. The line of the level will still be in the way. Notice the two blue grips are still available. Pick and drag the horizontal line out of the way of the Parapet text, as shown in Figure 3.15.

FIGURE 3.15: Making the final adjustments to the level

Now that the Parapet level has been established, it is time to make modifications to Level 6. Luckily the procedures will be the same as when you made the modifications to the Parapet level:

1. Press Esc to clear any commands.

2. Select Level 6.

3. Pick the blue text that says Level 6.

4. Rename it to **Roof**.

5. Press Enter.

6. Click Yes to rename the corresponding views.

7. Press Esc. Your levels should look like Figure 3.16.

Parapet
52' - 0"

Roof
50' - 0"

FIGURE 3.16: The Roof and the Parapet levels

Other Level Adjustments

There are three more adjustments we still need to review before we can move on. If you notice, the level lines are projected all the way to the other end of the building. Only level heads and level data are displayed on the right side of the level line. You can control the other end of the level as well.

To follow along, pan over to the left side of the building where the level lines seem to just stop, as shown in Figure 3.17, and perform these steps:

1. Select the Parapet level.

2. Notice the small blue box to the left of the level? Pick it. It will turn the level information on at that end of the building (see Figure 3.17).

FIGURE 3.17: You can check the box that appears to turn the level information on at the other end of the building.

3. Turn the Roof level on as well. Use the blue adjustment icons (elbow icons) to move it out of the way (see Figure 3.18).

Parapet
52' - 0"

Roof
50' - 0"

FIGURE 3.18: Controlling the visibility of the level at the other end

With the two upper levels established, we can now constrain some walls up to these levels. Sometimes the best way to do this is to look at the model from a 3D view:

1. Click the default 3D view icon on the Quick Access toolbar at the top of your screen, as shown in Figure 3.19.

FIGURE 3.19: Clicking the default 3D view icon

2. The next step is to select all of the walls you want to be extended to the Parapet level. In this case only the east building will go all the way up to this level. Select the walls as shown in Figure 3.20. (Be sure to select all of the elevator shaft walls as well.) You must hold the Ctrl key to add to the selection.

FIGURE 3.20: Selecting the walls that extend to the Parapet level

3. On the Modify Walls tab, select the Element Properties button, as shown in Figure 3.21.

FIGURE 3.21: Selecting the Element Properties button

4. In the Element Properties dialog, under the Instance Parameters change the top constraint to Up to Level : Parapet, as shown in Figure 3.22. Click OK. Your walls should now extend to the Parapet level, as shown in Figure 3.23.

FIGURE 3.22: Setting the top constraint Up to Level: Parapet

5. On the Views menu bar, choose (double-click) the South Elevation.

6. Start the Level command again.

FIGURE 3.23: The east side of the building is now constrained to the Parapet level.

7. Offset Level 4 up 4'–0". Remember, you are in the Level command. You must choose to pick lines on the Options bar. Also, you must specify an offset of 4'–0" on the Options bar.

8. Offset another level up from Level 4 2'–0".

9. Rename the 4'–0" offset level to **East Parapet**.

10. Rename the 2'–0" offset to **East Roof** (see Figure 3.24). You will have to add elbows to the levels to see the names and elevations.

FIGURE 3.24: Adding two new levels for the east side of the building

11. Deselect the Display Bubble checkbox to the *right* of the level line by clicking the Hide Bubble checkbox.

12. Display the bubbles to the *left* side of the level line by checking the Display bubble box, as shown in Figure 3.25.

East Parapet
34' - 0"

East Roof
32' - 0"

FIGURE 3.25: Using the display bubble toggles to switch the display to the appropriate side of the building

13. Zoom back in to the right side of the building. There should now be two blank level lines above Level 4.

14. Select the East Parapet level. Notice you still get some blue icons that appear. One of those icons says 3D.

15. Pick (left-click) the 3D icon. It now says 2D. The larger hollow blue grip now turns to a smaller, solid grip. This will allow you to drag the level end without dragging the rest along with it. It also ensures this modification does not affect other views (see Figure 3.26).

Level 5
40' - 0"

2D

Level 4
30' - 0"

FIGURE 3.26: Turn off the 3D extents so you can drag the level end freely and without disturbing any other view.

16. Repeat the procedure for the EastRoof level. Now both of the blank ends are set for 2D extents.

17. Select one of the levels activating the grips.

18. Pick the blue grip and drag the end to the left side of the building approximately to the location shown in Figure 3.27. Notice that the two 2D lines are locked to one another.

19. Add another level 2'–0" above Level 3 and call it **Corridor Parapet**.

20. Turn on the level information on the left side.

FIGURE 3.27: You can drag the 2D level ends wherever you want them.

 W A R N I N G   Having to adjust a level's display in different views is something that you will have to do on almost every project. It is good to keep in mind that, if the 3D button is left on, moving the level in the current view will also move it in other views — sometimes for the better, and sometimes for the worse. Switching to 2D can eliminate some aggravation.

21. Turn off the level information on the right side.

22. On the right side, turn on the 2D extents.

23. Drag the right side of the line to an area approximately as shown in Figure 3.28.

FIGURE 3.28: All of the levels are in place for now.

Now it's time to move these walls to their proper levels. Again, in this case it may be a little easier to go to a 3D view so we can get a good perspective on the results of constraining the tops of the walls. Perform the following steps:

1. Click the default 3D icon.

2. In the 3D view, select the east side of the building, excluding the corridor and the three walls to the south, as shown in Figure 3.29. (You will need to press and hold the Ctrl key for multiple selections.)

FIGURE 3.29: Selecting the west part of the building

3. On the Modify Walls tab, select the Element Properties button.

4. In the Element Properties dialog, set the Top Constraint to Up to Level : East Parapet.

5. Click OK. In the 3D view, your walls should grow to meet the new constraints.

6. Press Esc.

7. Select the corridor walls as well as the three south walls whose tops remain unconstrained.

8. On the Modify Walls tab, select the Element Properties button.

9. Set the Top Constraint to Up to Level: Corridor Parapet (see Figure 3.30). Click OK.

10. Go back to the South Elevation. Adjust your levels to appear as shown in Figure 3.31.

11. Save the model.

FIGURE 3.30: The final walls are constrained to the corridor parapet level.

FIGURE 3.31: The final look of the building

Creating Building Sections

As your model starts to develop, you will begin to see areas that need further attention. (Certainly the area where the corridor hits the west building needs to be fixed.) This brings us to a good point. Sections in Revit Architecture, when placed into the model, not only help us build a set of construction documents, but also help us to physically work on the model. For example, we need to fix the east wall of the east wing. We don't have any good views established that focus directly on this area. This is the perfect place to add a section!

To begin, open your model you have been working on, or go to
www.sybex.com/go/revit2010ner and browse to Chapter 3. Open the file called
NER-06.rvt. If you wish, you can use a project you are working on. You will just
need to replace any names and specific dimensions with ones that are applicable to
your project. To add a section and some cool wall modify commands, follow along:

1. Zoom in on the area where the corridor meets the east wing of the
   building.

2. On the Create panel of the View tab, select Section, as shown in
   Figure 3.32.

FIGURE 3.32: The Section command is found on the Create panel of the
View tab.

3. A section takes two picks to place into the model. You must first pick
   the point for the head; then you must pick a point for the tail. To place
   the section as shown in Figure 3.33, first pick a point above the corridor and to the right of the vertical wall.

4. Once the first point is picked, move your cursor straight down the
   view. Once you are positioned directly below the bottom corridor wall,
   pick the second point. (See Figure 3.33.) If the section is looking the
   wrong way, that's fine. We will fix that in a moment.

5. Now that the section is placed, it looks like we are going to have to
   flip it to look at the wall we intended to modify. Pick the section. You
   will see a few blue icons appear. The one we are interested in is the
   icon that looks like a double arrow. This is a flip grip. It is the same
   thing we saw in the doors and windows. (See Figure 3.34.)

FIGURE 3.33: Placing the section into the model

FIGURE 3.34: Once you select the section, you will see the flip grip.

6. Once you see the "flip grip," pick it. It will flip the section into the correct direction.

WARNING   We may be jumping ahead here, but here's a word of caution: if you cut a section in Revit Architecture, then place detail components and draft over the top of that section, you are stuck. Do not flip or move the section once you have drafted over the top of a section. The results will be bad. The walls will move, not your linework, leaving you with a mess.

With the section flipped in the correct direction, you will see a dashed line that forms a box around part of the model, as shown in Figure 3.35. This forms the view extents of the section. Anything outside of this box will not be shown.

7. The vertical dashed line (to the left) will have a move arrow. Pick the move arrow and drag the crop region into an area as shown in Figure 3.35.

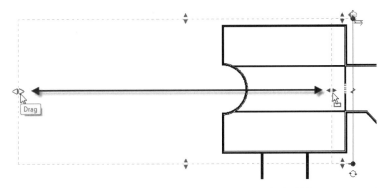

FIGURE 3.35: You can control how deep into the building you want the section to look.

 NOTE   If you don't have the section selected, you need to select it. You must pick the line of the section, not the bubble. Once you pick the line, the section is selected.

8. With the section still selected, notice you have a small, blue break icon in the middle of the section (see Figure 3.36). Pick the break line (it is called the "Gaps in Segments" icon). The section is now broken, and you will have grips controlling the ends of the break lines (see Figure 3.36).

FIGURE 3.36: Adding a gap in the section

9. At each end of the section you will see a blue icon that resembles a recycle figure. This controls what the section head will display. By selecting this "cycle" icon, you can choose to have a section head, a tail, or nothing. At the tail of the section, cycle through until you get a section head (see Figure 3.37).

FIGURE 3.37: Cycling through the display choices

With the section cut, it is time to open the view we have created. In the Project Browser, you will now see a new category called Sections (Building Sections). In this Sections category, you will have a view called Section 1. When you cut the section, you added a view to the project. This view will carry its own properties and can be drafted over (see Figure 3.38).

FIGURE 3.38: The Project Browser with the new section

 T I P   Be organized. Just because you are using BIM, that does not negate the need for basic organization. The first thing you should do when creating a section (or any new view for that matter) is to give it a name. If you don't, and leave it Section 1, Section 2, Section 3..., you find yourself wasting a lot of time looking for the right view.

At this point, it is time to name the section and open the view. We can also fix the gap in the wall while we are at it. Just perform the following steps:

1. In the Project Browser, right-click on Section 1.

2. Choose Rename from the context menu (see Figure 3.39).

3. Change the name of Section 1 to **East Corridor Section**.

FIGURE 3.39: You can rename the view by right-clicking in the Project Browser.

4. Click OK.

5. Double-click on the East Corridor Section in the Project Browser. This will open the section. You can see the two corridor walls, and the east wing beyond.

6. One thing you will notice immediately is the fact that the level information is running into the walls. To fix this, simply select the Parapet level. (Remember: select the actual line, not the datum head.)

7. Slide the elevation markers to the right, out of the way of the walls (see Figure 3.40).

8. Repeat the process for Level 1 and Level 2. Notice that when you slide these levels to the right, they will snap into place and align themselves to the rest of the levels.

9. Pick the left end of the level lines, and move them to the right as well. This will get all of the lines out of the way so that you can work on the section (see Figure 3.41).

FIGURE 3.40: You can adjust the levels by picking and dragging the blue grip at the intersection of the level line and the datum bubble.

N O T E   Notice that when you are adjusting the levels in the section the 2D icon appears. This means that any adjustments made here will not affect any other views. In a sectional view, Revit will automatically make the levels 2D. In an elevational view, however, Revit will make the levels 3D. If you want to make adjustments in an elevation, it is a good idea to turn these to 2D extents.

10. Also, add some elbows to the elevation markers. There are so many that the text elements collide with one another.

11. On the View Control bar, select Fine for the detail level, as shown in Figure 3.41. (Making adjustments like this to a view will become second nature to you very soon.)

FIGURE 3.41: On the View Control bar, set Fine as the detail level.

In Revit Architecture, you can also double-click on the actual annotation that refers to the view you wish to open. For example, if you want to open the West Corridor Section, and you are in a plan, all you have to do is double-click on the section bubble, and it will open the view. If you are in the section and you want to go back to a floor plan, you can double-click on a datum bubble, and Revit will open that view.

▶

Cutting a section is immensely helpful in terms of being able to view the model from basically any perspective you want. To go even further, when you cut a section you can also work on your model by modifying any item the section.

Making Building Modifications in a Section

Now that you have a good look at this side of the west wing, it is obvious that this wall needs to be repaired. In Revit Architecture, you can make a modification to a building in any view. This is good — and it can also be bad. Just remember that everything you do has a downstream effect on the entire model.

To follow along, open your model you have been working on, or go to www.sybex.com/go/revit2010ner and browse to Chapter 3. Open the file called NER-06.rvt. If you wish, you can use a project you are working on. You will just need to replace any names and specific dimensions with ones that are applicable to your project. The following procedure will guide you through making a modification to a wall's profile while in a section view:

1. In the Project Browser, find the East Corridor Section and open it by double-clicking on the name East Corridor Section.

2. In this section, select the West wall of the East wing, as shown in Figure 3.42.

3. Once you select the wall, look to your Modify Walls tab. There you will see a button that says Edit Profile, as shown in Figure 3.42. Click that button.

FIGURE 3.42: Clicking Edit Profile on the Modify Walls tab

You will now be presented with a magenta outline of the wall. This magenta outline can be modified to alter the wall's profile. If you look at your Ribbon, you will notice that Edit Profile has been added to the Modify Walls tab. This allows you to focus on the modification at hand (see Figure 3.43).

> When you select a wall, you will get options to modify that wall. Edit Profile is one of those options.

4. On the Draw panel of the Modify Walls ➤ Edit Profile tab, select the Lines button, as shown in Figure 3.43.

FIGURE 3.43: Adding additional lines to alter the wall's profile

5. With the Lines command running, move your pointer to the right, vertical magenta line.

6. Move your pointer up or down until you are aligned with Level 3, as shown in Figure 3.44.

FIGURE 3.44: Revit will align your cursor to levels, allowing you to accurately sketch a new profile.

7. Once you see that you are snapped and aligned with the magenta line and Level 3, pick this point. Your line will start.

8. Draw the line to the right until you intersect with the side of the wall to the right, as shown in Figure 3.45.

9. Once you see the intersection snap show up, pick (left-click) this point (see Figure 3.45).

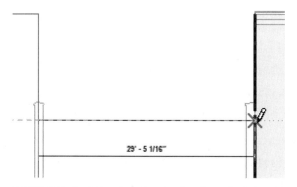

FIGURE 3.45: Drawing the line from the left wall to the right

10. Now, draw the line straight up the wall to the top. Make sure you do not snap to the top of the parapet. The point you want is to the top of

the brick, as shown in Figure 3.46. (All you are doing here is sketching the profile of the wall.)

FIGURE 3.46: Drawing another line from Level 3 to the bottom of the parapet

11. Continue drawing the line from the right to the left across the top of the wall. Snap to the endpoint of the wall to the left, as shown in Figure 3.47.

FIGURE 3.47: Drawing the line across the top

12. Press the Esc key, or pick the Modify button from the Quick Access toolbar on the Design bar.

13. Pick the vertical line to the left that goes from the bottom of the wall to the top.

14. Pick the top blue grip, and stretch the line down to Level 3.

15. You now have a closed loop, as shown in Figure 3.48.

FIGURE 3.48: Closing the wall by stretching the line using grips

 W A R N I N G   If you do not have a perfectly closed, continuous loop with your magenta lines, Revit will not allow you to proceed with finishing altering the profile of this wall. Make sure you have no gaps, overlaps, or extra line segments aside from the six lines you need to form the wall's outline.

16. On the Wall panel of the Modify Walls ➢ Edit Profile tab, click Finish Wall, as shown in Figure 3.49. Your finished wall profile should look like Figure 3.50 in the next set of steps.

FIGURE 3.49: Clicking Finish Sketch

There is one thing left to do before we leave this section: select the 2 hr fire rated partition wall that is only constrained to Level 2. Now that we have opened up this area, the wall can now go up to Level 3. To constrain the top of this wall to Level 3, follow along:

1. Select the wall, as shown in Figure 3.50.

FIGURE 3.50: Selecting the wall that needs to be altered

2. On the Modify Walls tab, select the Element Properties button, as shown in Figure 3.51.

3. In the Element Properties dialog, change Top Constraint to Up to Level : Level 3, as shown in Figure 3.51.

FIGURE 3.51: Choosing the element properties to change a wall's constraints is becoming old hat!

4. Click OK. The wall is now meeting the brick exterior.

5. In the Project Browser, double-click on Level 3.

6. Change the detail level to Fine (remember this is in the View Control bar at the bottom of the screen).

7. On the View tab, select the Section button.

8. Place a section as shown in Figure 3.52. Make sure the view range is set as shown, and that the extents are similar to the figure.

FIGURE 3.52: Adding another section to modify another wall

9. In the Project Browser, right-click on the new section and rename it to East Wing South Wall Section. We will use this section in Chapter 4.

Adding entire building sections is a great way to quickly break down the model into large segments so you can work. Another type of section, a wall section, however, allows you to view smaller portions of the item being detailed.

Adding Wall Sections

A wall section is basically the same as a building section. The only difference is that, when you place a wall section, Revit will hold the extents to a much smaller area. When you add a building section, Revit will want to extend to the farthest geometry. That being said, a wall section is usually placed to show only the item being cut, disallowing the geometry beyond to be seen.

Start by opening your model you have been working on, or go to www.sybex.com/go/revit2010ner and browse to Chapter 3. Open the file called NER-07.rvt. If you wish, you can use a project you are working on. You will just need to replace any names and specific dimensions with ones that are applicable to your project. To place a wall section, follow this procedure:

1. Go to Level 3 in the Project Browser.

W A R N I N G   If you are directed to go to a specific floor plan and your view looks nothing like the one shown in the book, you need to make sure you are not in a ceiling plan. Notice in the Project Browser that you have floor plans and ceiling plans. The two are quite different. Make sure you are in a floor plan.

2. On the View tab, pick the Section button (the same one you picked for the building section).

3. In the Change Element Type menu, select Wall Section, as shown in Figure 3.53.

4. Also on the Options bar, change the scale to ½"=1'–0".

5. Add the section through the corridor wall that was modified in the previous section of this chapter, as shown in Figure 3.53.

FIGURE 3.53: Changing the type of section from Building Section to Wall Section and adding it to the model

6. Right-click on the new section in the Project Browser. It will be in a category called Sections (Wall Section).

7. Select Rename.

8. Call the new section **Corridor Entry Section**. Click OK.

9. Open the Corridor Entry Section.

10. Change the detail level to Fine. Your section should look like Figure 3.54.

FIGURE 3.54: The wall section at ½" = 1'–0"

11. Save the model.

Now that we are narrowing down the types of sections we can use, it's time to venture into a specific type of section that can allow you to do a plan section detail.

Creating Detail Sections

There is a third type of section we need to discuss: the detail section. Revit refers to this type of section as a detail view, so that's how we will start addressing it.

To create a detail view, open your model you have been working on, or go to **www.sybex.com/go/revit2010ner** and browse to Chapter 3. Open the file called NER-08.rvt. If you wish, you can use a project you are working on. You will just need to replace any names and specific dimensions with ones that are applicable to your project. Perform the following steps:

1. Open the view called Corridor Entry Section (if you do not have it opened already).

2. On the View tab, select Section (yes, the same section we have been using all along).

3. In the Change Element Type menu on the Element panel, select Detail View : Detail.

4. On the Options bar, change the scale to 1½" = 1'–0".

5. Place a section horizontally, as shown in Figure 3.55. Make sure the section is flipped so it is looking downward.

FIGURE 3.55: Creating a plan section detail

6. In the Project Browser, you will see a new category called Detail Views (Detail). Expand the tree, and you will see your new detail. It is usually called Detail 0, depending on how many details have been added to the model previously.

7. Right-click Detail 0 and select Rename.

8. Rename the detail to **Plan Detail at Corridor Opening**.

9. Open the Plan Detail at Corridor Opening view.

With the detail open, you may only be able to see two dashed lines. This is because the crop region needs to be expanded, as explained in the nest section.

Crop Regions

The border that surrounds the detail is called a *crop region*. It dictates the extents of the specific view you are in. We can adjust this crop region and use it to our advantage. To learn how to make adjustments to the crop region, follow these steps:

1. Select the window surrounding the detail, as shown in Figure 3.56.

2. You will now see four blue stretch arrows at the midpoint of each line. Pick the top stretch arrows, and stretch the top region up until you can see the opening jamb, as shown in Figure 3.56.

FIGURE 3.56: Stretching the crop region to view the detail

3. Repeat the process for the bottom so you can see the entire opening.

4. With the crop region still selected, notice there are little break icons similar to the make elbow icons in the level markers. Pick the break icon, as shown in Figure 3.57. You can now slice part of the section away, resulting in two separate cropped regions.

5. Within the cropped regions, you will see blue move icons. If you do not see blue icons as shown in Figure 3.58, you need to select the crop region again.

6. Slide the sections closer together by picking the top icon and moving the section down.

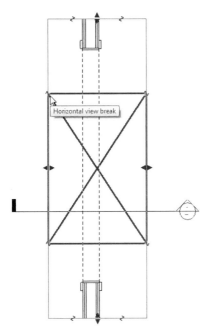

FIGURE 3.57: Splitting the section

FIGURE 3.58: Sliding the view regions tighter together

7. Save the model.

Now that we have some nice control over how the details are being shown, we can go back and learn how to make the actual section marker more aesthetically pleasing.

Splitting a Section Segment

One more section item, then we are done! Sometimes, it is necessary to split (or jog) a section. This is done when certain items need to be shown that are not necessarily in line with one another. You can accomplish this in Revit Architecture as follows:

1. Open the Level 1 floor plan.

2. On the View tab, select the Section button.

3. In the Change Element Type menu on the Element tab, select Building Section.

4. This time, pick a point above the corridor that connects to the west wing of the building for the section head, and then pick a point well below the bottom of the corridor, as shown in Figure 3.59.

FIGURE 3.59: Adding another section to the model

5. In the Project Browser, find the section you just made and rename it to West Corridor Section.

6. Select the new section marker.

7. On the Modify Views tab, pick the button called Split Segment.

8. Pick a point along the section line just below the corridor, as shown in Figure 3.60.

9. Move your cursor to the right. Notice a jog appears in the section. Place the jog into the building. The section is now jogged into the building.

Finally! We are done with sections. Just remember that by adding a section to the model, not only are you preparing to build your construction documents, but you are also enabling access to specific elements, thus allowing you to make modifications you otherwise could not have.

FIGURE 3.60: Jogging a section calls for splitting the segment.

Creating Callouts

Creating an enlarged area of your model is always going to be an item on every project you do. Luckily in Revit Architecture, callouts are not only easy to add to your model but are directly linked to the view they are referring to as well. This is crucial for project coordination. Another nice thing about callouts is the fact that you can make modifications to the callout view independently from the host view you are pulling the information from. The biggest change you will make is the scale. Yes, your callout can be at a different scale.

To follow along, open your model you have been working on, or go to **www.sybex.com/go/revit2010ner** and browse to Chapter 3. Open the file called NER-09.rvt. If you wish, you can use a project you are working on. You will just need to replace any names and specific dimensions with ones that are applicable to your project. Here's the procedure for adding callouts:

1. In the Project Browser, under Sections (Wall Sections), open the Corridor Entry Section.

2. Find the View tab on the Ribbon.

3. On the View tab, click the Callout button, as shown in Figure 3.61.

FIGURE 3.61: The Callout button is located on the View tab.

4. On the Options bar, set the scale for 1½" = 1'–0".

5. Pick a window around the area where the corridor fire wall meets the exterior wall with the brick façade, as shown in Figure 3.62.

6. In the Project Browser, notice there is a new section (Building Section). Its name is Callout of Corridor Entry Section — which is fine just the way it is. Press Esc.

7. Select the callout you just added by picking any point along the line. Notice a bunch of blue grips appear. These grips enable you to stretch the shape of the callout.

FIGURE 3.62: The callout area is directly related to the view it is calling out.

8. Pick the grip that connects the callout bubble to the leader coming from the callout window.

9. Drag the bubble to the location shown in Figure 3.63.

10. Pick the blue midpoint grip on the leader and create an elbow, as shown in Figure 3.63.

FIGURE 3.63: Adjusting the callout will be a common task.

11. In the Project Browser, find Callout of Corridor Entry Section under the Sections (Building Sections) category and open the view. (You can also double-click on the callout bubble to open the view.)

12. With the section open, select the crop region as shown in Figure 3.64.

FIGURE 3.64: Selecting the crop region

Once the crop region is selected, you will see an additional region that consists of a dotted line. This is called an annotation region. This gives you a "gutter" to place text outside the area that is physically being cropped.

13. Type WT. This will tile the windows you have open.
    Notice that the callout window is selected along with the crop region in your callout. That is because the two objects are one and the same (see Figure 3.65).

14. Stretch the crop region closer to the actual wall, as shown in Figure 3.65.

15. Save the model. We will use this detail for future chapters to get it ready for construction documents.

FIGURE 3.65: Modify the crop region by selecting it and stretching the grip.

The crop region and the callout outline are the same. If you modify one, the other changes accordingly.

Now that we have a callout created for a detail, it is time to go to the plan and create some callouts there. It would be nice to have some typical lavatory callouts as well as a typical elevator callout:

1. In the Project Browser, go to Level 1. (Make sure it is a floor plan, not a ceiling plan.)

2. Zoom in on the area shown in Figure 3.66.

3. On the View tab, select Callout.

4. Pick a window around the lavatory, as shown in Figure 3.66.

5. In the Project Browser under the Floor Plans category, you will see Callout of Level 1. Right-click on Callout of Level 1 and select Rename.

FIGURE 3.66: Creating a plan callout

6. Rename it to **Typical Men's Lavatory**.

7. Open the Typical Men's Lavatory view.

8. Notice the detail level is set to Coarse. Change it to Fine.

 T I P   You may have noticed that we have been opening up quite a few views. It is a good idea to close the views you don't need to have open. It could slow you down a tad. To do this, choose Window ➤ Close Hidden Windows.

9. Save the model.

10. Open the Level 1 floor plan.

11. Create a callout for the Women's room below the corridor (directly below the Men's room).

12. Call the new callout **Typical Women's Lavatory**.

13. Create one more callout around the elevator shaft in the east wing, as shown in Figure 3.67.

14. Call the new callout **Typical Elevator Shaft**.

Now that the "boring" views are out of the way, it is time create some perspective views of the model. Creating these views is just as easy but requires a specific procedure in which you'll take advantage of the Camera function.

FIGURE 3.67: The plan showing the three typical callouts

Creating a Camera View

This is by far the view you will have the most fun with. Revit Architecture seems to lend itself naturally to this type of view.

Taking a camera view is essentially telling Revit to look at a certain area from a perspective vantage point. Like a section or a callout, this view may never see the "light of day" in terms of actually going on a drawing sheet, but camera views are perfect to see how a model is coming along from a realistic point of view.

To follow along, open your model you have been working on, or go to www.sybex.com/go/revit2010ner and browse to Chapter 3. Open the file called NER-10.rvt. If you wish, you can use a project you are working on. You will just need to replace any names and specific dimensions with ones that are applicable to your project. To create a camera view, follow along:

1. Go to the Level 1 floor plan.

2. On the View tab, click the drop down arrow in the 3D button and select Camera, as shown in Figure 3.68.

3. Pick a point in the main corridor of the west wing, and move your cursor to the left down the hallway. We want to take a perspective view as if we were standing in the intersection of the two main corridors, as shown in Figure 3.69.

FIGURE 3.68: Adding a camera view

4. The second point you pick will be how far the camera is going to "reach" into the building. Pick a point past the corridor doors, as shown in Figure 3.69.

FIGURE 3.69: Placing the camera view in the main corridor

5. Unlike when you're placing a section or a callout, Revit will automatically open the new perspective view. This does not mean that it automatically has a name. In the Project Browser, you will see a new view within the 3D Views category. It is called 3D view 1. Right-click on 3D view 1 and name it **West Wing Corridor Perspective.**

6. On the View Control bar located at the bottom of the view, change the Model Graphics Style to Shading with Edges.

7. The next button to the right is the Shadows button. For a perspective view, turning the shadows on is okay if it is a relatively small view. In this example, go ahead and turn it on (see Figure 3.70).

FIGURE 3.70: The Perspective view down the east wing corridor

Once the camera is in place, it is difficult to determine how to modify it. You can do quite a bit to the view, but the following section will focus on modifying the actual camera in the plan.

Modifying the Camera

Once you place the camera into the model, Revit does not leave behind any evidence that the camera is there. If you need to make adjustments, or just see where the view is being taken from, perform the following steps:

1. Open the Level 1 floor plan.

2. In the Project Browser, find the West Wing Corridor Perspective view in the 3D Views category. Right-click on it and select Show Camera, as shown in Figure 3.71.

FIGURE 3.71: By finding the view in the Project Browser, you can tell Revit to show its origin in the plan.

The camera will now show up in the plan temporarily so you can see it.

In the view, you will see the camera icon itself, a triangle, and a straight line. The camera can be physically moved, and the grip on the midpoint of the triangle can also be adjusted to swivel and to look farther into the model. Figure 3.72 shows the exposed view.

FIGURE 3.72: The exposed view

Creating an Elevation

I saved the best view for last ... or at least the most popular. Elevations are essential for any project — so essential, in fact, that Revit provides four of them before you place a single wall into the model. The four shapes that represent houses that were in the model at the beginning of the book are elevation markers, as shown in Figure 3.73. These markers are typically handy but are most certainly in the way now. The first thing we need to do is to move one of them out of the way. The second thing we need to do is to create a few new ones!

To start manipulating elevations, follow along:

1. Go to the Level 1 floor plan. In the western part of the corridor, there is an elevation. Yours may be in a slightly different location than the book's example, but it needs to be moved nonetheless (see Figure 3.73).

FIGURE 3.73: The elevation marker is right in the way!

The action we are about to perform is to move the elevation marker. To move an elevation marker, however, we need to break down what an elevation marker is composed of. It is actually two separate items. The square box is the elevation. The triangle is the part of the marker that activates the view, as shown in Figure 3.74. To move this elevation marker, you must pick a window around both items and move them together. If you do not, the actual view will stay in its original location, leaving you wondering what is wrong with your elevation.

FIGURE 3.74: The elevation marker is broken down into two pieces. Both need to be moved together by picking a window around the entire symbol.

2. Pick a window around the elevation marker. Make sure you are not picking any other items along with it.

3. Move your mouse over the selection. Your cursor will turn into a move icon with four move arrows, as shown in Figure 3.75.

4. Drag the elevation marker to the east side of the building, as shown in Figure 3.75.

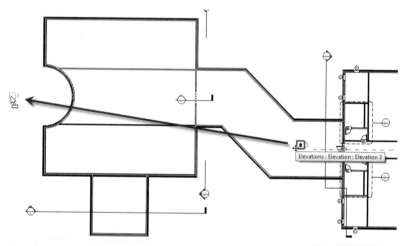

FIGURE 3.75: You can drag the elevation marker once the entire item is selected.

Now that the elevation marker is out of the corridor, it is time to make a new one. To do so, make sure you are in the Level 1 floor plan and follow along:

1. On the View tab, select the Elevation button, as shown in Figure 3.76.

2. One you pick the Elevation button, move your cursor around the perimeter of the building. Notice that the elevation marker will follow the profile of the exterior walls. This is a great thing!

 WARNING   When you are choosing to create an elevation of a radial wall, or nonlinear item, be sure you know exactly at which angle you are placing the elevation marker. When you are in the elevation view, you may get a false sense of dimensions based on the view's perspective. Draw a reference plane if you need to, and then place the elevation on that plane.

FIGURE 3.76: The Elevation button on the View tab

3. Pick a place for the elevation, as shown in Figure 3.77.

4. Once the elevation is placed, select the triangle. You will see the same extents window as you saw in the section (see Figure 3.77). This controls how deep into the model you are viewing, and it also shows you the length of the section. Because you placed this elevation up against a wall, Revit will stop the elevation at that wall.

5. Pick the top grip and stretch the elevation past the wall, as shown in Figure 3.77.

FIGURE 3.77: The elevation is placed. You can select the view arrow and move the extents of the elevation into the building.

6. In the Project Browser under Elevations (Building Elevations), you will see a new elevation. Right-click on it and rename it to **East Wing Southeast Elevation**.

7. Open the elevation.

8. On the View Control bar, change the scale to $1/4" = 1'–0"$.

9. On the View Control bar, set the detail level to Fine.

10. Save the model.

You have added a new exterior elevation. You can add an interior elevation as well. It is just as easy and much more fun!

Interior Elevations

The difference between an exterior elevation and an interior elevation is the same as the difference between a building section and a wall section. Both interior and exterior elevations are executed the same way: by selecting the View tab on the Design bar. The only difference is that you can make a choice between the two in the Type Selector in the Options bar. To add an interior elevation, perform these steps:

1. Go to the Level 1 floor plan.

2. On the View tab, select the Elevation button.

3. In the Change Element Type menu, choose Elevation : Interior elevation, as shown in Figure 3.78.

4. Hover your cursor in the corridor near a point shown in Figure 3.78. Notice that when you move your cursor up, the arrow flips up. When you move your pointer down, the arrow flips down.

5. Make sure the arrow in the elevation target is pointing up and pick a point along the horizontal corridor, as shown in Figure 3.78, to place the elevation.

6. Once you place the elevation, you will notice that the extents will be outside the building (in most cases this occurs, if it does not, you are good to go). On the right side, pick the blue grip and drag the right extent to the point shown in Figure 3.78.

7. In the Project Browser, you will see that you have a new elevation under the Elevations (Interior) category. Right-click the new elevation (Revit will call it Elevation 1 - a, or something similar) and call it **West Wing Corridor Elevation**.

FIGURE 3.78: Adding an interior elevation and making the adjustments

8. Open the new view called West Wing, Corridor Elevation.

9. Notice the crop region extends all the way up to the parapet. Select the crop region and drag the top down to Level 2, as shown in Figure 3.79.

FIGURE 3.79: Stretching the grip down to crop the view

In the elevation's view, you can drag the crop region down to show only that floor. If you would rather see all of the floors, perhaps you should use a section rather than an elevation.

N O T E   If you had floors already placed in the model, Revit would create the interior elevation to only extend to this geometry. Since we do not have floors, Revit does not know where to stop. If you happen to place an elevation without floors, then put them in later, Revit will not make the adjustment. You still have to do it manually.

Let's create some more elevations, shall we?

1. Go to Floor Level One Zoom into the west wing entry area, as shown in Figure 3.80.

2. On the View tab, select the Elevation button.

3. Place an elevation marker in an area similar to the one shown in Figure 3.80, and then move it to the center of the lobby.

 T I P   Notice that when you are trying to place the elevation in the entry area, it seems to be wandering all over the place. This is because the elevation is trying to locate the radial geometry. The safest bet in this situation is to find a straight wall and "aim" the elevation at that wall. In this case, you should aim the elevation at the bottom of the elevator shaft. Once the elevation marker is in place, you can then move it to where you need it to be.

FIGURE 3.80: Add the elevation marker as shown here, and then move it to a new location.

4. With the elevation marker centered in the lobby, select the round
bubble. Notice that four blue boxes appear, as shown in Figure 3.81.
This allows you to turn on multiple views. Check on all four views, as
shown in Figure 3.81.

FIGURE 3.81: Turn on all four views in the lobby.

With the four elevations turned on, you have some naming to do! Up to this
point, you have been going to the Project Browser to rename the elevations. Let's
explore another way to rename an elevation and to view its properties as well.

Elevation Properties

With each view comes a new set of properties. For example, when you made the
perspective view of the corridor you set Model Graphics Style to Shaded with
Edges, and you turned the shadows on. Normally in an interior elevation you do
not want to do this. Revit allows you to have separate view properties on a view-
by-view basis.

To access the View Properties dialog, follow these steps:

1. On the interior elevation with the four arrows, select only the arrow
facing up (north), as shown in Figure 3.82.

2. Right-click on the arrow and select Element Properties, as shown in
Figure 3.82.

FIGURE 3.82: Right-click the marker and select Element Properties.

3. In the Element Properties dialog, notice you have a wealth of information about that view. You also have a multitude of options as well. The option we are going to change is View Name, as shown in Figure 3.83. Find View Name under the Identity Data heading, and change it to **West Wing Entry North Elevation**, as shown in Figure 3.83.

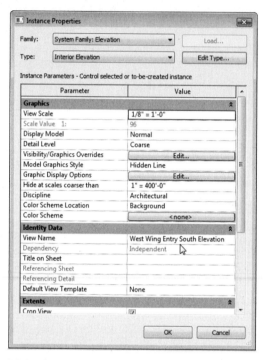

FIGURE 3.83: Changing the View Name to West Wing Entry North Elevation

By changing the value in the Element Properties dialog, you are, in effect, changing the name in the Project Browser. Again, change something in one place, and it will change in another.

4. Click OK.

5. Select the West Wing Entry North Elevation again. Notice the view's extents are stretching past the entry atrium. Pick the blue grips at the end of the elevations and bring them into the atrium area, as shown in Figure 3.84. Also, drag the view limit up to show the radial exterior wall (see Figure 3.84).

FIGURE 3.84: Making the adjustments to bring the view back into a reasonable range

6. Right-click on the elevation arrow facing left (east) and select Element Properties.

7. Change View Name to **West Wing Entry East Elevation.**

8. Click OK.

9. Right-click on the arrow facing down (south) and select Element Properties.

10. Change View Name to **West Wing Entry South Elevation.**

11. Click OK.

12. Right-click on the arrow facing right (west) and select Element Properties.

13. Change View Name to **West Wing Entry West Elevation.**

14. Click OK.

15. Select each elevation, and adjust the view's extents the same way you did for the north elevation.

16. Save the model.

One thing you will notice is the fact that the actual view names are showing up in the plan. This is nice, but unfortunately it leaves no room for anything else other than the actual view. Plus, most construction documents (at least none that I have ever seen) do not have these names right in the plan. We can turn this off.

Now that we can place and modify annotations, let's delve into the physical properties of these annotations.

Annotation Properties

Annotations all have properties we can modify. To change the elevation symbol properties, follow along:

1. On the Manage tab, click Settings ➤ Elevation Tags.

2. At the top of the Element Propertied dialog, you will see Family: System Family : Elevation Tag. Below that you will see Type. Change the Type from ½" square to ½" circle (see Figure 3.85).

3. In the Type Parameters, under Graphics, change the Text Position to Inside.

4. Uncheck Show View Name (see Figure 3.85).

FIGURE 3.85: Modifying the properties for the elevation markers

5. Click OK.

6. Zoom back in on the elevation markers. They should look like Figure 3.86.

F I G U R E   3 . 8 6 : The revised, less obtrusive elevation marker

   N O T E   It's Revit time! No longer will you see "dumb" placeholder information in a tag. When it comes time to create our construction documents and these views are put on sheets, Revit will then automatically fill out these tags with the correct information. To take it one step further, you can tell Revit not to print these annotations if the views they are representing are not on a sheet.

The ability to add elevations is a must. As you can see, physically adding an elevation is simple. It does, however, take practice to manipulate elevations to look the way you want.

Are You Experienced?

Now You Can...

- ☑ create levels, and constrain walls to stretch or shrink if the levels elevational information changes in any way

- ☑ cut wall sections and building sections through the model

- ☑ create detail views, allowing you to add plan sections through a wall or a building section

- ☑ create a callout view and control the crop region

- ☑ add a camera to the model, giving the user a nice perspective of a certain area

- ☑ create interior and exterior elevations within the model

CHAPTER 4

Working with the Revit Tools

▶ Using edit commands to modify a model

▶ Mastering tools to align and constrain geometry

▶ Employing tools to merge different wall types together

Y ou can get only so far with allowing a computer application to place architectural components into a model. At some point, the application needs to be flexible enough to enable users to employ their own set of drafting and modifying tools, thus allowing the architect or designer the freedom to create their own architecture and construction procedures. Revit Architecture does provide the basic modify and edit commands — which are quite common if you have experience with other drafting applications such as AutoCAD — but with a little more flair and some differences in procedure from that of a 2D drafting application.

In this chapter you will learn how to utilize the geometry you have already placed in the model to build an actual working plan. As you manipulate the plan, all of the other views you made in the previous chapter will reflect those changes. We'll start with the edit commands.

 N O T E   This chapter, like Chapters 1, 2, and 3, is an important chapter to be comfortable with. If you are not comfortable with the first few chapters, I recommend skimming back through them. Sometimes you can pick up something you missed and have a "light bulb" moment.

The Revit Architecture Edit Commands

You aren't going to get very far in Revit without knowing the edit commands. Up to this point, we have been avoiding most of the modify commands but simply could not avoid at least some of them. There will be some overlap in these chapters as many aspects of Revit span multiple topics.

The commands that we'll cover are Move, Copy, Rotate, Array, Mirror, Rotate, Align, Trim, and Split. Each command is as important as the next at this stage of the game. Some are obvious, while others can take some practice to master.

The first command, Move, is one you'll recognize from previous chapters. Move is probably the most heavily used command in Revit.

The Move Command

The Move command is generally used to create a copy of an item while deleting the original item.

Begin by finding the model you have been working on that you are using to follow along. If you have not completed the previous chapter procedures, open the file caller NER-11.rvt found at the book's website, **www.sybex.com/go/revit2010ner**. Go to the Chapter 4 folder to find the file.

To use the Move command, perform the following steps:

1. With the file open, go to Level 1 under the Floor Plans category in the Project Browser.

2. Zoom in on the east wing.

3. Select the south wall of the bump-out at the south side of the east wing, as shown in Figure 4.1.

4. On the Modify Walls tab, you will see the Move button, as shown in Figure 4.1.

FIGURE 4.1 Select the wall to be moved. The Move button now appears on the Ribbon.

5. Now that the Move command is running, you see some choices at the Options bar:

   Constrain If you check Constrain, you can only move at 0, 90, 180, or 270 degrees.

   Disjoin If you check Disjoin, when you move the wall, any walls that are joined to it will not be affected by the move. The wall will lose its join.

   Copy This option turns the Move command into the Copy command. Conversely, the Copy command allows you to uncheck this option and turn the Copy command into the Move command.

6. To start moving the item, you must first pick a base point for the command. Pick a point somewhere toward the middle of the wall, as shown in Figure 4.2.

7. Once you pick this point, move your cursor straight up. You will see a blue dimension. At this point you have two choices: you can either "eyeball" the increment, or you can type the increment you want (see Figure 4.2).

FIGURE 4.2 On the Options bar, you can see the choices available. The first point has been picked and the wall is being moved up.

8. Type in the value 2'–6" and press Enter. The wall has moved 2'–6". Notice the adjacent walls move with it. In Revit, there is no stretch command. See Figure 4.3.

 TIP Revit Architecture will accept a few different values for feet and fractional inches. For example, instead of typing 2'–6" (Which Revit will accept), you can type **2 6**. Just make sure you have a space between the 2 and the 6. Revit will accept that value. If there are fractional increments, you can type **2 6 1/2"**, and Revit will accept the value. Or you can type **2'-6 1/2"**.

> You may be thinking, "But I used to type my commands!" Well, you still can in Revit. If you type **MO**, Revit Architecture will launch the Move command. Remember, though, you need to have the item selected first!

Now that Move is officially in the history books, it's time to move on to Move's close cousin: the Copy command.

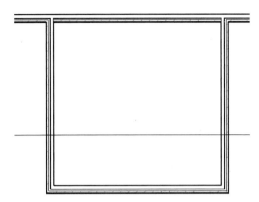

FIGURE 4.3 Moving the wall 2'–6" also means that any adjoining walls will be moved along with it.

The Copy Command

When you need to make duplicates of an item, Copy is your go-to player. The Copy command works like the Move command, except it leaves the initial item intact. You also will get the option of creating multiple copies if you need.

To start using the Copy command, follow along:

1. Make sure you are still in the Level 1 floor plan.

2. Zoom in so you are focused on the west wing in its entirety, as shown in Figure 4.4.

3. Pick the corridor wall, as shown in Figure 4.4.

4. Click the Copy command on the Modify Walls tab.

5. Zoom in on the wall close to the midpoint of the selected wall and the intersection of the horizontal wall that divides this portion of the building (see Figure 4.4).

6. If you hover your cursor in the center of the wall (not near the actual finish faces, but the core of the wall), you will see a blue dotted centerline indicating that you have found the center of the wall. Also, if you move your cursor to the right a little, you can position your cursor so that it picks up the horizontal wall's centerline. Once you pick up the horizontal wall's centerline, the centerline for the vertical wall will disappear. This is fine. You will now see that you are snapped to the endpoint of the horizontal wall. Once you see this, pick the point (see Figure 4.4).

7. Move to the right until you pick up the midpoint of the horizontal wall. Once you do, pick that point.

8. Repeat the procedure for the south side of the corridor, as shown in Figure 4.5. You will see that the ends of the walls do not meet. This is fine — we will modify theses walls with the trim command in a moment.

9. Save the model.

FIGURE 4.4 Creating a copy of the corridor wall

FIGURE 4.5 The two walls copied, segmenting the spaces north and south of the corridor.

The next step is to rotate an item. Although the Rotate command is a simple concept, Revit does have unique processes involved in this command.

The Rotate Command

The Rotate command allows you to change the polar orientation of an item or a set of items. This command may take a little practice to understand how it works. The good thing, however, is that once you have experience with the Rotate command, you will be better at other commands that share a similar process.

To use the Rotate command, follow along:

1. Open the Level 1 floor plan.

2. Zoom in on the east radial portion of the east wing, as shown in Figure 4.6.

FIGURE 4.6 The east radial portion of the east wing.

3. We are going to add a new reference plane and rotate it by 45 degrees. To do this, go to the Home tab, click the Ref Plane, and click the Draw Ref Plane button on the Reference panel (see Figure 4.7).

4. For the first point, pick the center point of the radial wall, as shown in Figure 4.7.

5. For the second point, pick a point outside the radial wall (again, see Figure 4.7).

Notice that the Copy command is one click away from being the Move command. Remember to always look at the Options bar for choices.

TIP   In Revit, sometimes finding the correct snap can be difficult. To over-come this, you can type the letter **S**, then the first letter of the snap you wish to use. For example, if you wanted to snap to the center of the arc, you would first start the Ref Plane command (any command works here, but we are using a reference plane as an example) and then type **SC**. This will snap to the center.

FIGURE 4.7   Establishing a reference plane.

 WARNING   Be careful when you are rotating items in this fashion. Figure 4.7 shows the second point extended past the radial wall, and that is where you generally want it; however, watch out for your snaps. When you pick the second point, be sure to zoom in on the area, ensuring you are not inadvertently snapping to the wrong point.

6. Press Esc.

Now that the reference plane has been added, you can rotate it into place. (Yes, you could have just drawn it at a 45° angle, but we are practicing the Rotate command here).

1. Select the reference plane you just drew.

2. On the Modify Reference Planes tab, select the Rotate button, as shown in Figure 4.8.

FIGURE 4.8   The Rotate command is active for the specific item you have selected.

3. Once you start the Rotate command, look back at the reference plane. Notice there is an icon that resembles a recycle arrow in the middle of your line. Revit will always calculate the center of an object (or group of objects) for the rotate point (see Figure 4.9).

4. Zoom in on the rotate icon.

5. We must move this icon to the left endpoint of the reference plane. To do so, pick (left-click) and drag the rotate icon to the endpoint of the reference plane, as shown in Figure 4.9.

FIGURE 4.9 Pick and drag the rotate icon to the endpoint of the reference plane.

6. With the rotate origin in the correct location, it is rotate time! Notice that if you swivel your cursor around the reference plane, a line forms from the rotate origin to your cursor. This indicates that the origin is established. You need to now pick two points. The first point you pick must be in line with the object you are rotating. In this case, pick a point at the right endpoint of the reference plane, as shown in Figure 4.10.

7. Now, when you move your cursor up, you will see an angular dimension. Once that angular dimension gets to 45°, pick the second point (see Figure 4.10).

FIGURE 4.10 To rotate an item, you must specify two points.

8. Press Esc.

If you type **RO**, you will be able to start the Rotate command. Just be sure you have something selected first.

As you are well aware, you'll use the Rotate command quite frequently. Now that you have some experience with the Rotate command and know how Revit wants you to move the pivot point, the next command, the Array command, will be easy for you to grasp.

ROTATE OPTIONS

While you are in the Rotate command, don't forget that you have options. The most popular option is to create a copy of the item you are rotating, as shown in this graphic.

Another popular option is to simply specify an angle. This can be difficult, however, because of the fact that the angle you think is correct could be the opposite of what you thought, resulting in you having to undo the command, then redo the rotation specifying a negative (−) value.

The Array Command

When you need to create multiple duplicates of an item, or a group of items, the Array command will be the logical choice. The Array command in Revit functions in a similar fashion to the Rotate command. The similarities of the Array command also extend to the Array command in AutoCAD. You have two basic choices:

▶ Radial, which allows you to array an item around a circle or an arc

▶ Linear, which allows you to array an item in a straight line, or at an angle

Let's look at the Radial array first.

Radial Array

The Radial array is based on a radius. If you need items to be arrayed in a circular manner, then the Radial array is your choice. Again, once you start the Array command, do not ignore the Options bar. It will guide you through most of the command.

To start using the Radial Array, follow these steps:

1. Select the 45° reference plane, as shown in Figure 4.11.

2. On the Reference Planes tab, select the Array button, as shown in Figure 4.11.

FIGURE 4.11 Select the item to be arrayed first, and then click the Array button on the Reference Planes tab.

3. With the Array command active, you will see some choices available on the Options bar, as shown in Figure 4.12. For this procedure, click the Radial Array button.

4. Check Group and Associate.

5. Set Number to 4.

6. Check the Move to: Last button (see Figure 4.12).

FIGURE 4.12 Setting the options for the Radial array

7. With the options set, focus your attention on the object being arrayed. Notice the familiar rotate icon. Pick and drag the blue icon from the midpoint of the line to the endpoint. This will pivot the array about this axis (see Figure 4.13).

FIGURE 4.13 Drag the pivot icon to the endpoint of the item being arrayed.

8. With the pivot point in place, specify two points for the array. The first point will be a point along the angle of the item being arrayed. The second point will be a point along the angle you wish to end with.

9. Pick the endpoint of the reference plane you are arraying.

10. Move your cursor down until you see 90°. Once you do, pick the second point (see Figure 4.14).

11. Click (left-click) off into another part of the view. This will establish the array. You should have four reference planes at this point, similar to Figure 4.15.

FIGURE 4.14   Specifying the two angles for the Radial array

12. Select (left-click) one of the reference planes. You will see a large dashed box surrounding the reference plane. You will also see a temporary arc dimension with a blue number 4 at the quadrant. It may be obscured by the arc, but it is there nonetheless (see Figure 4.15).

13. Click the number 4.

14. Change the count to 5.

15. You now have five reference planes, as shown in Figure 4.16.

   Getting the hang of the radial array may take a few projects to gain the experience you would like to feel comfortable. It will come if it is not there already. The next array type, the Linear array, follows the same concept as the Radial array, but it is more straightforward. Yes, pun intended.

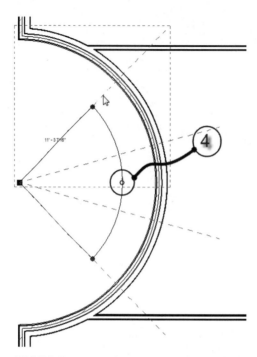

FIGURE 4.15 After the array is successful, select one of the arrayed members. Notice you can change the count.

FIGURE 4.16 The fact that you can control the number of items in an array group after the fact is quite advantageous.

Linear Array

Of course, you may wish to create an array along a line. This can be accomplished in Revit as well. Once the Linear array is completed, you still enjoy the same flexibility that you have with the Radial array in terms of being able to specify the number of items in the array.

The objective of this procedure is to create an array of windows along the north and south wall on the east side of the building. To do this, we will first need to establish two strong reference planes.

To learn how to use the Linear array command, follow along:

1. Zoom in on the east section of the east wing, as shown in Figure 4.17.

2. The next step is to add two reference planes. We will use these reference planes to establish the ends of our window array. To do this, go to the Ref Plane command on the Basics tab of the Design bar.

3. On the Options bar, keep the draw icon active, and add an offset of 1'–6" (remember you can just type **1 6**).

4. Pick the corner of the radial wall where it intersects the straight wall for the first point of the reference plane, as shown in Figure 4.17.

5. Pick a second point similar to Figure 4.17 to finish the reference plane.

FIGURE 4.17 Starting the Ref Plane command

If you are drawing the reference plane, and it keeps going below the wall as opposed to above the wall, you can tap the space bar as you are drawing the reference plane. This will flip the side of the wall it is being drawn on.

6. With the Ref Plane command still running, repeat the procedure for the top of the wall. You want to pick the top, outside face of brick, avoiding the concrete ledge below, as shown in Figure 4.18.

7. As you are drawing the reference plane, you will have to hit the spacebar to flip it in the correct direction.

FIGURE 4.18 The two reference planes are established.

Now we need to add a window based on the bottom reference plane. This window will then be arrayed up the wall to meet the northern reference plane.

1. On the Home tab, select the Window button.

2. Change the Element Type to: Fixed : 24" × 72".

3. Place the window approximately where it is shown in Figure 4.19. You will have to move the window in alignment with the reference plane.

FIGURE 4.19 Adding the window to be arrayed

4. After you place the window, press the Esc key on your keyboard.

5. Select the window.

6. On the Modify Windows tab, select the Move button.

7. Move the window from the bottom, outside corner down to the reference plane, as shown in Figure 4.20.

FIGURE 4.20 Moving the window into position

8. Press Esc.

9. Zoom out until you can see the entire wall.

10. Select the window you just inserted into the wall.

11. On the Modify Windows tab, select the Array button.

12. On the Options bar, select Linear Array, as shown in Figure 4.21.

13. Click Group and Associate (if it is not already selected).

14. For Number, enter 4.

15. Select Move to Last.

FIGURE 4.21 Choosing the Linear array options

I DON'T WANT TO MOVE ANYTHING!

The Move to Last and Move to Second choices are somewhat misleading. You are not actually "moving" anything. If you choose Move to Last, for example, Revit will place an additional item in the last place you pick, keeping the first item intact. Revit will then divide the space between the two items evenly based on the number of items you specific in the options. If you specify four items, Revit still has two items left to divide.

If you choose Move to Second, Revit will place an additional item at the second point picked (like Move to Last), but this time Revit will add additional items beyond the second item. The distance is calculated by the distance between the first two items.

16. Pick the top endpoint of the bottom window.

17. Move your cursor up the wall, and pick a point perpendicular to the top reference plane, as shown in Figure 4.22.

18. Once you pick the second point, you will have to wait a moment; then Revit will evenly fill the void with the two additional windows. Also, Revit will give you the option of adding additional windows. Enter a value of **5** and press Enter (see Figure 4.23).

FIGURE 4.22 "Moving" the window to the top reference plane

FIGURE 4.23 Changing the number of items in the array. You can always come back to the arrayed group and change this value at any time.

 N O T E Once your items are grouped and arrayed, you can still move the end item. It is good to note that not only can you move it in the direction of the array, but you can move it laterally to the array, causing a "step" in the array.

With the array completed, it is time to duplicate our efforts on the other side of the radial portion of this wall. As in CAD, at this point you have a few different choices. You can repeat the Array command, copy the items, or mirror the items.

The Mirror Command

The Mirror command does exactly as it sounds: it makes a copy of an object or a group of objects in the opposite orientation of the first item(s). The crucial point to remember is that you will need to specify a mirror "plane."

Although we simply could not avoid using this command in previous chapters, it's time to officially address and explore the mirror command. One aspect of the Mirror command that is most useful is the fact that, if you have reference planes existing in the model, you can simply pick these planes to accomplish the mirror, as opposed to sketching a plane in which to mirror about.

The objective of the following example is to mirror the windows to the south side of the east wall:

1. Zoom in on the windows you just arrayed.

2. Pick a window around the windows starting from the upper-left corner to the lower-right corner, as shown in Figure 4.24.

FIGURE 4.24 Selecting the items to be mirrored. Make sure you do not select the wall that the windows reside in.

 T I P Oops! I selected the wall. That's OK. You do not need to Esc out of the selection. Simply hold down the Shift key on your keyboard and pick (left-click) the wall. It will become deselected.

3. On the Modify Windows tab, select the Mirror ➤ Pick Mirror Axis button, as shown in Figure 4.25.

FIGURE 4.25 The Mirror button appears when you select an item.

4. Position your cursor over the center reference plane that is part of the radial array. When you pause, you will get a tooltip indicating that you are about to select the reference plane. Once you see this tooltip, select the reference plane, as shown in Figure 4.26.

FIGURE 4.26 Select the Pick Lines button from the Options bar. The line you are going to pick is the reference plane shown here.

5. Zoom out to check out the placement of the windows. Do not assume that everything went as planned. Your Level 1 floor plan should resemble Figure 4.27.

 N O T E   If the mirror went wrong, or you are not comfortable with the results, use the Undo button and try again. Now is the time to practice!

Now that the two straight walls have windows, it is time to array some windows within the radial portion. The problem is, however, when you insert a window along a radius you cannot snap it to the intersection of the reference plane and the wall. This is where the Align tool becomes critical.

Once you pick the reference plane, Revit will mirror the entire group of windows.

FIGURE 4.27 The finished east wall

The Align Tool

You are going to find yourself in a situation where two items need be in alignment with one another. The Align command is a great tool for accomplishing this. Actually, it's one of the most useful tools within Revit, and you will use it extensively. Overuse of this command is not possible! Since the Align function is a tool, you do not have to select an item first for this function to become available. You can select it at any time.

To practice using the Align tool, follow along:

1. Zoom in on the radial portion of the east wall, as shown in Figure 4.28.

2. On the Home tab, select the Window button.

3. In the Change Element Type menu, choose Fixed : 16" × 72".

4. Place it in the radial wall in a similar location as shown in Figure 4.28. Do not attempt to "eyeball" the center of the window with the reference plane. As a matter of fact, purposely misalign the window, as shown in Figure 4.28.

FIGURE 4.28 Place the window approximately in the area shown here.

5. On the Modify tab, select the Align button, as shown in Figure 4.29.

FIGURE 4.29 Select the Align button on the Home tab.

6. The Align tool needs you to select two items to work. First select the item you want to align *to*; pick the reference plane as shown in Figure 4.30.

7. Now that the reference plane is picked, you need to pick a point on the window: the centerline of the window. By looking at the window now, you will not see this line. If you hover your cursor over the middle of the window, you will then see a center line become highlighted. Once you see this center line, pick the window.

FIGURE 4.30 Choosing the items to be in alignment. Remember, you must choose the item you want to align *to* first.

The window will move into alignment with the reference plane, as shown in Figure 4.31.

FIGURE 4.31 The window is now in alignment with the reference plane.

8. Select the window.

9. Pick the Array button on the Modify Windows tab.

10. Do a radial array of the windows. You remember how, right?

N O T E   Adding reference planes, and working in a controlled environment, is very typical of Revit Architecture. You establish a reference plane, add a component, and then execute some command such as Array, Copy, or Move. Although it may seem like quite a few steps, you are now accurately, and deliberately, placing items in your model. The accuracy you apply here will propagate itself through the project in terms of elevations, sections, and drawing sheets.

Let's practice more with the Align tool. It is one of the most important modify tools in the Revit arsenal, and we don't want to understate its usefulness:

1. Zoom into the west wing of the building, as shown in Figure 4.32.

2. On the Home tab, select the Door button.

3. Place a Double Flush : 72" × 84" door in the radial corridor wall, as shown in Figure 4.32. As when you placed the window along the reference plane in the last procedure, don't try to eyeball and alignment.

4. Renumber the door to 100A.

FIGURE 4.32 Adding a double door to the west wing corridor

5. On the Tools toolbar, click the Align button.

6. Pick the horizontal reference plane.

7. Pick the center line of the door. Once the reference plane is aligned, pause for a moment without hitting Esc. You will see a little blue padlock. We can use this to lock the alignment.

Another nice feature associated with the Align command is the fact that, after your alignment is complete, you can physically lock the items together, allowing the two aligned items to move as one.

Locking an Alignment

Once you have aligned the items, you may notice a small, blue padlock icon. Within Revit Architecture, you have the ability to lock items together by using the Align tool. This is a great thing — and it can be a bad thing. It is great in the sense that, if the center reference plane moves for whatever reason, the door will also move. It is bad in the sense that, if the door moves, the center reference plane will also move.

When you align an item and you lock it, be sure this is what you want to do. It's simple: pick the padlock icon, as shown in Figure 4.33. You are now aligned and locked to the center reference plane.

FIGURE 4.33 The door is now aligned and locked.

There are also going to be times where you have two items that are already aligned but you just want to lock the items together. To do this, you are still going to use the Align command to access the lock option:

1. Zoom into the east side of the west wing at the corridor intersection.

2. Start the Align command.

3. Pick the double doors in the corridor.

4. Pick the center reference plane.

5. Pick the blue padlock to lock the doors to the center reference plane (see Figure 4.34).

Now that the Align command is out of the way, we can move on to the next item on the Modify tab: the Split command.

FIGURE 4.34 You can create a locked constraint by using the Align command even if the items were in alignment to begin with.

Split

The Split command takes the place of the conventional trim command because you cannot actually delete an entire area between two points in Revit. Using the Split command is the equivalent of the Break command in AutoCAD. The Split command can be used on walls and when you are editing an element in Sketch mode.

To use the Split command, find the model you have been working on that you are using to follow along. If you have not completed the previous procedures, open the file called NER-12.rvt found at the book's website, **www.sybex.com/go/revit2010ner**. Go to Chapter 4 to find the file. The objective of this procedure is to cut a notch out of a wall by using the Edit Profile function:

> **1.** In the Project Browser, open the Section (Building Section) called East Wing South Wall Section, as shown in figure 4.35.

FIGURE 4.35 Open the section called West Wing South Wall Section. It will put you in section, as shown here.

2. Select the wall beyond, as shown in Figure 4.36.

3. On the Modify Walls tab, click the Edit Profile button, as shown in Figure 4.36.

FIGURE 4.36 Select the wall beyond, and click the Edit Profile button on the Modify Walls tab

Once the Edit Profile option has been selected, you will be put into Sketch mode. You know you are in Sketch mode because your Ribbon will end with a Finish and a Cancel that you have to select to get back to the full model. Also, the wall you have selected will now consist of four magenta "sketch" lines, and the rest of the model is shaded into the background.

4. On the Edit Profile tab, click the Split button, as shown in Figure 4.37.

FIGURE 4.37 Select the Split button on the Edit Profile tab.

5. Once you select the Split button, look at your Options bar. Notice you can specify to delete the inner segment. Click the Delete Inner Segment button, as shown in Figure 4.38.

6. Pick the intersection of the bottom magenta sketch line and the inside face of the left wall for the first split point, as shown in Figure 4.38.

7. Pick the intersection of the bottom magenta sketch line and the inside face of the right wall, as shown in Figure 4.38.

FIGURE 4.38 To remove a segment of a line, you must use the Break command and select Delete Inner Segment from the Options bar.

Once these points are picked, the magenta sketch line will be segmented. Now you need to add more lines to the sketch. To do this, you must leave the Split command and follow along using the sketch tools on the Draw panel:

1. On the Draw panel of the Edit Profile tab, click the Lines button, as shown in Figure 4.39.

2. Click the Pick Lines button, as shown in Figure 4.39.

3. Pick the inside face of the left wall (#1 in Figure 4.39).

4. Pick the Level 3 Level (#2 in Figure 4.39).

5. Pick the inside face of the right wall (#3 in Figure 4.39).

6. Hit Esc.

FIGURE 4.39 Tracing the walls to form a notch. This is done by selecting the Pick Lines button, and picking the walls.

The next step is to get the magenta lines in a state where they form a continuous loop. This means that there can be no overlapping lines. Each line starts exactly where the last line ends. There can be no gaps or overlaps:

1. Hit Esc.

2. Pick (left-click) the horizontal magenta line that is traced over Level 3.

3. On each end, you will see a round, blue grip. Pick each grip and stretch the line to the intersection of the vertical magenta lines, as shown in Figure 4.40.

4. Select the left, vertical magenta line and stretch the top grip down to the intersection of the horizontal magenta line, as shown in Figure 4.40.

5. Select the right, vertical magenta line and stretch the top down to the horizontal magenta sketch line. You should now have a continuous loop (see Figure 4.40).

6. On the Wall panel of the Edit Profile tab, select the Finish Wall button, as shown in Figure 4.41.

7. Go to a 3D view at this point to check out your model (as shown in Figure 4.42). You can either click the 3D button on the Quick Access toolbar, or you can pick the {3D} view from the Project Browser.

The next set of procedures will focus on basic cleanup using the Trim command. Although a lot can be accomplished with this one, single command, there is a Revit method you will need to get used to.

FIGURE 4.40 Modifying the sketch lines by stretching the grips to form a continuous loop

FIGURE 4.41 Click Finish wall to get back to the model.

REVIT WANTS IT CLEAN!

As mentioned earlier, if you click Finish Sketch and Revit gives you a warning, as shown in the following graphic, you *must* be sure that you have no overlapping lines or gaps in your sketch. Revit is quite unforgiving and will not allow you to proceed.

FIGURE 4.42 The building in 3D up to this point. For this image, the shadows are turned on.

Trim

Any time you need to "cut" an item, or extend an item, you'll use the Trim command. In any design-based application, you won't get very far without the Trim command. Similar to the Split command, the Trim command can be used on walls and within Sketch mode. As mentioned earlier, however, there are specific procedures you need to conform to before you become comfortable using this command.

To use the Trim command, open the model you have been working on. If you have not completed the previous chapter procedures, open the file caller NER-13.rvt found at the book's website **www.sybex.com/go/revit2010ner**. Go to Chapter 4 to find the file.

To use the Trim command, follow this procedure:

1. With the file open, go to Level 1 under the Floor Plans category in the Project Browser.

2. Zoom in on the west wing. You will see two walls that do not quite reach their destination. These walls need to be trimmed.

3. On the Modify tab, select the Extend ➢ Trim / Extend Single Element button, as shown in Figure 4.43.

FIGURE 4.43 Click the Trim/Extend Single Element button on the Modify tab.

4. Zoom in on the area, shown in Figure 4.44.

FIGURE 4.44 Zoom in to this area to start trimming the walls.

5. To trim the vertical wall back to the horizontal wall, you must first pick the wall you want to trim *to*. In this case, select the north face of the horizontal wall, as shown in Figure 4.45.

6. Now you must pick a point along the vertical wall. The trick here is that you must pick a point on the side of the wall that you want to *keep*. Pick a point along the vertical wall above (north of) the horizontal wall, as shown in Figure 4.45. Once you do, the wall will be trimmed back.

FIGURE 4.45 Follow this procedure to trim the wall back.

7. Hit Esc. to terminate the command.

You may not always want to trim an item. There will be just as many times where you need to elongate an item to reach a destination point. This is better known in the drafting world as extend. To use the extend feature of this command, the process is similar. This time, however, you must first select the wall in which you want to extend an object, and then select the object to be extended:

1. Zoom in on the south part of the west wing.

2. On the Modify tab, click the extend ➤ Trim/Extend Single Element button.

3. Pick the south corridor wall. This is the wall you want to extend to.

4. Pick the vertical wall that does not quite intersect. Your walls should now look like Figure 4.46.

5. Save the model.

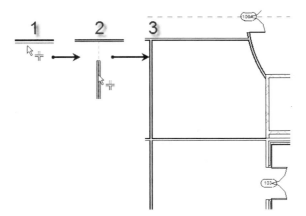

FIGURE 4.46 Stepping through this procedure to extend the wall

There is one more command to examine that is used in the basic day-to-day modification of a Revit model. You may have noticed that most of the commands we have used to place items in the model have had the offset command "built into" the options of that specific procedure. The next section will focus on offsetting items using the stand-alone Revit Offset command.

Offset

The Offset command allows you to create a copy of an item at a specified distance. As mentioned earlier, the need to offset an item crops up much less often in Revit Architecture than in a conventional drafting application. This is because, in Revit, the functionality is provided as an option in most commands. There are times, however, where you will need the good old Offset command.

To get used to using the Offset command, follow these steps:

1. Zoom in on the east part of the west wing. This is the area where the men's and women's restrooms are (see Figure 4.47). The objective is to offset the vertical wall to the right of the restrooms to the middle of the open space, as shown in Figure 4.48.

2. On the Modify tab, click the Offset button, as shown in Figure 4.47.

3. On the Options bar, click the Numerical button.

4. Enter 16' 2" in the Offset field.

5. Make sure Copy is checked.

6. Hover your cursor over the wall to the right of the lavatory, as show in Figure 4.47. You will see an alignment line appear to the right of the wall.

FIGURE 4.47 Choosing your options and picking the wall to be offset

7. Once you see the dashed alignment line appear, pick the wall. The new wall should be in the middle of the large room.

8. Repeat the process for the walls south of the corridor, as shown in Figure 4.48.

 WARNING   Be sure your math is correct. Once you offset an item, use the Measure command. I've mentioned this before, and I will mention it repeatedly throughout this book! You will be glad you did this now rather than later.

This concludes our discussion of Offset. Since this floor plan consists of some items we may like to repeat on other floors, we can now explore how to do this using the Copy/Paste command right from Windows.

FIGURE 4.48 Completing the floor plan by using the Offset command will be a common procedure.

Copy/Paste

Yes, this is the actual Microsoft Windows Copy/Paste. In Revit Architecture, you will be using this feature quite a bit. There is no better way to complete a space or a layout on one level and to use that layout on another level by copying the geometry.

To practice using the Copy/Paste function, we will select the two lavatories on Level 1, copy them to the Windows clipboard, and paste them to the remaining floors:

1. Zoom into the area where the men's and women's (these will be caps in the actual room tags later on in the book) lavatories are located.

2. Select the walls and doors that define both bathrooms, as shown in Figure 4.49. Also, select the corridor walls as well as the radial corridor wall at the westend of the building. Be sure to select the doors as well (see Figure 4.49).

FIGURE 4.49 Selecting the items to be copied to the clipboard

Remember, when you are selecting multiple items, you need to press and hold the Ctrl key to add to the selection set. If you see you have inadvertently selected too much, press the Shift key to deselect the items.

3. Choose Edit ➢ Copy to Clipboard. (Or you can press Ctrl+V.)

4. Go to a 3D view.

5. On the Modify Walls tab, Click Paste Aligned ➢ Select Levels, as shown in Figure 4.50.

6. In the next dialog, select Levels 2 through 5, as shown in Figure 4.50.

7. Click OK.

Your model should look like Figure 4.51. If it doesn't, go back and try it again.

N O T E   Just because you copied and pasted identical items does not mean they are linked in any way. If you move, edit, or even delete any of these walls, the walls you pasted will not be affected by this.

The last section in this chapter will focus on actual practice. We now have five floors in the west wing alone must have a layout added to them. We also need to add a layout to the east wing.

FIGURE 4.50 The Select Levels dialog allows you to choose which levels you are pasting the information to.

YOU MUST HEED THE WARNING!

If you see a warning dialog while pasting elements that says you have just created a duplicate and that double counting is going to occur, stop and undo the paste. Determine why Revit issued that waning. Did you already paste these elements to this level? Sometimes the top of the walls are above the level above. You can check this as well.

FIGURE 4.51 The west wing is starting to come together.

Creating the Plans

Now that you have added walls, doors, and windows, you can start to combine this experience with your knowledge of the basic Revit editing commands. In this previous section, you started to lay out the programs for your floor plans.

You can follow along with the book's examples up to floor 3. You can create your own plans for floors 4 and 5.

To get started, open the model you have been working on. If you have not completed the previous tasks, open the file called NER-14.rvt at the book's website, **www.sybex.com/go/revit2010ner**. Go to Chapter 4 to find the file.

To start building a floor plan to be copied to other levels, follow these steps:

    1. In the Project Browser, go to Level 1 under Floor Plans.

2. Start adding walls, doors, openings, and windows to resemble Figure 4.52. These doors and windows can be any type you like. If your model varies slightly from the example in the book, don't be concerned.

FIGURE 4.52 The first floor layout for the west wing

3. In the Project Browser, go to Level 2

4. Type VP to open the View Properties dialog.

5. In the View Properties dialog, set Underlay to None, as shown in Figure 4.53.

6. Create a floor plan layout similar to Figure 4.54. Make all of the dimensions as even and as round as possible. Use all of the commands and functions you have learned up to this point.

7. For the windows, go to a 3D view, and using Copy/Paste, align them up all the way to Level 5. This way, you know your windows are aligned, and you can follow this procedure in your room layout for each floor. See Figure 4.55.

 WARNING   When you use Copy/Paste, you may get the same Duplicate value warning we mentioned earlier. If you do, stop and undo. Make sure you are not pasting windows over the top of windows.

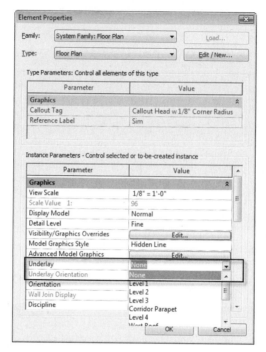

FIGURE 4.53 Switch Underlay from Level 1 to None.

FIGURE 4.54 The Layout for Level 2. Try to make the dimensions as even as possible, consistent with what is shown here.

FIGURE 4.55 Using Copy/Paste, align the windows to the higher floors. This will influence your floor layout for each level.

8. Go to Level 3, and create a floor plan similar to Figure 4.56. We did this by using Copy and Paste Aligned from Level 1. We added one wall to the northwest suite.

FIGURE 4.56 Level 3: This was mostly copied from Level 1 with the exception of the 18'–0" room that was added.

9. Go to Level 4 and create your own floor plan. The book will give no example. You are on your own!

10. Create one more floor plan for Level 5. Again, design your own layout. Be as creative as you wish.

11. Save the model.

If you got through that last procedure, and you are happy with the results, you are on your way to being efficient in Revit. This is because you just created a floor plan basically on your own. These last few steps were created to prove that Revit can be quite intuitive when approached with just a little experience.

If you are not comfortable with your results in this section, that's OK. I had an uncomfortable feeling the first time through too. Take a deep breath, and go back through where you think you got lost. Feel free to send me an email message if you have questions or concerns.

Are You Experienced?

Now You Can...

- ☑ use common editing commands to alter the appearance of your model

- ☑ use reference planes to establish good, accurate methods of layout

- ☑ array items, and change the count, length, and radius if needed

- ☑ align items and keep them constrained

- ☑ use locks to constrain an alignment to one another

- ☑ split items to remove a segment or to turn one item into two

- ☑ use the Copy and Paste Aligned commands to create multiple floors that are similar in layout

CHAPTER 5

Dimensioning and Annotating

▶ Adding dimensions to a model

▶ Modifying dimensions

▶ Using dimensions as a layout tool

▶ Constraining dimensions

▶ Placing text and annotations

T he principle topic of this chapter is the ability to dimension and annotate a model. Once the novelty of having a really "cool" model in 3D wears off, it is time to buckle down and produce some bid documents. This is where Revit needs to prove itself in terms of functionality. You should ask yourself, "Is Revit capable of producing drawings consistent with what is acceptable to national standards, and more importantly, my company's standards? And if so, how do I get to this point?" These are the questions the owners and managers are going to be asking you. (If you are, in fact, an owner or a manager, I suppose you can still just ask yourself these questions.)

The answers to these questions begin right here with dimensioning and annotations. This is where you can start to make Revit your own. Also, when it comes to dimensioning, you will find in this chapter that dimensions take on an entirely new role in the design process as well.

Dimensioning

I think you are going to like dimensioning in Revit. It is almost fun. Almost. Before we get started, there is one thing we should get out of the way: you cannot alter a dimension to display an increment that is not true. Hooray! As you get through this chapter, you will quickly learn that when you place a dimension, it becomes not only an annotation but a layout tool as well.

The dimension command has five separate types: Aligned, Linear, Angular, Radial, and Arc Length. Each has its importance in adding dimensions to a model and will be covered separately.

Let's get started shall we? To begin, open the file you have been following along with. If you did not complete the previous chapter, go to the book's website at **www.sybex.com/go/revit2010ner**. From there you can browse to Chapter 5 and find the file called NER-16.rvt.

Aligned Dimensions

The most popular of all the Revit Architecture dimensions is the Linear dimension. This type of dimension will be the dimension used 75 percent of the time.

An aligned dimension in Revit allows you to place a dimension along an object at any angle. The resulting dimension will be in alignment with the object being dimensioned. A Linear dimension, however, will only add a dimension at 0, 90, 180, or 270 degrees regardless of the item's angle.

There are certain procedures that go along with using an aligned dimension. To add one, perform these steps:

1. Go to the Level 1 floor plan.

2. Zoom in on the west wing of the building.

3. On the Annotate tab, click the Aligned button, as shown in Figure 5.1.

FIGURE 5.1 Starting the Dimension command from the Annotate tab

4. On the Options bar, you will see a row of choices as shown in Figure 5.2. Make sure that you have Prefer : Wall Faces selected.

5. The next menu allows you to choose if you want to pick individual references or entire walls. Select Entire Walls from the menu, as shown in Figure 5.2.

FIGURE 5.2 The Options button for the Dimension command. Notice the Options button at the far right.

6. On the far right of the Options bar is an Options button. This pertains to the options you can choose from when selecting the entire wall. Click the Options button.

7. In the Auto Dimensions Options, select Intersecting Walls. Do not select any other item (see Figure 5.3).

8. Zoom in on the north wall, as shown in Figure 5.4.

9. Pick (left-click) the north exterior wall. Notice that the dimensions are completely filled out.

FIGURE 5.3 The Auto Dimensions Options

10. Pick a point (to place the dimension) approximately 8' above the north wall (see Figure 5.4).

FIGURE 5.4 By choosing the Pick Entire Walls option, you can add an entire string of dimensions in one click.

11. In true Revit form, you are still in the command unless you tell Revit you do not want to be. In this case, click the Options button on the Options bar (the same one you clicked before).

12. Uncheck Intersecting Walls in the Auto Dimension Options dialog.

13. Pick (left-click) the same wall. You now have a dimension traveling the entire length of the building.

14. Move your cursor above the first dimension string you added. Notice the dimension will "click" once it gets directly above the first string.

15. Once you see the dimension snap, pick that point (see Figure 5.5).

In many cases, you will need the ability to pick two points to create the dimension. What a world it would be if everything was as easy as the dimension string we just added. Unfortunately, it is not.

FIGURE 5.5 Adding a major dimension by turning off the Intersecting Walls choice in the Dimension options

Aligned Dimensions by Picking Points

Nine times out of ten, you will be picking two points to create the dimension. Usually in Revit this is quite simple — until you get into a situation where the walls are at an angle that is not 90°. In a moment we will explore that issue, but for now, let's add some straight dimensions:

WARNING   Before you get started, it is good to note that this procedure is not easy. If it does come easy to you, great! If it does not, don't get discouraged. Keep trying.

1. Zoom in on the northwest portion of the west wing, as shown in Figure 5.6.

2. On the Basics tab of the Design bar, click the Dimension button.

3. On the Options bar, choose Individual References from the Pick menu, as shown in Figure 5.6, and do the following:

   A. Pick the north wall.

   B. Pick the horizontal wall that ties into the radial wall, illustrated as "2" in Figure 5.6.

   C. Place the dimension about 8' to the right of the vertical wall, as shown in Figure 5.6.

FIGURE 5.6 Placing the dimension by picking two points

4. With the Dimension command still running, pick the north wall again and do the following:

   A. Pick the center line of the door, as shown in Figure 5.7.

   B. Pick the horizontal wall that ties into the radial wall, illustrated as "3" in Figure 5.7.

   C. Pick a point inside (to the left of) the first dimension, as shown in Figure 5.7.

FIGURE 5.7 Adding a dimension string manually

W A R N I N G   When you are adding a string of dimensions, you must not stop and then resume the dimension string in the middle of the command. As you will see in a moment, when you add dimensions in a continuous line there is a lot you can do in terms of making adjustments to the objects you are dimensioning.

You will now see that the actual dimension values are blue. Also, you will see a blue EQ icon with a dash through it. (Refer back to Figure 5.7.)

5. Click the Blue EQ button, as shown in Figure 5.8. If the door was not exactly centered, this will force the door to move to an equal distance between the two walls.

FIGURE 5.8   You can use the dimension string to move the door by clicking the EQ button.

6. Hit Esc.

There may be times where you would like to display the dimensions rather than the EQ that Revit shows as a default. To do so, follow along:

1. Select the dimension.

2. Right-click.

3. Choose EQ Display, as shown in Figure 5.9.

The dimensions should now show an increment. But that increment is going to half the distance of the wall.

Pretty cool. There is one last item involving aligned dimensions that we should address: how you dimension along an angle.

Another way to tell Revit how you want the dimensions displayed is to select the dimension, then click the Element Properties button on the Modify Dimensions tab. Here, you will be given additional choices as to how you would like the dimensions displayed.

FIGURE 5.9 Toggle off the EQ display.

Dimensioning an Angle

No, not an "angel," an *angle*. Adding this type of aligned dimension is not the easiest thing to do in Revit. As a matter of fact, it can be quite difficult. This is why we need to address the process as a separate item in this book.

1. Zoom in on the corridor area.

2. On the Annotate tab, click the Dimension button.

3. On the Options bar, be sure Pick is set to Individual References.

4. Zoom in close to the intersection of the two walls, illustrated as "1" in Figure 5.10.

5. Hover your pointer over the core intersection, as shown in Figure 5.10.

6. Tap the Tab key until you see the square grip appear.

> **N O T E**   By tapping the Tab key, what you are telling Revit is that you wish to filter through different points. Once you arrive at the square grip, this tells Revit that you wish to dimension the angled wall.

7. Once the square grip appears, pick it (left-click). See Figure 5.10.

8. Move to the other intersection of the angled wall.

9. Hover your cursor over this core intersection, as shown in Figure 5.11.

10. Tap the Tab key until you see the same square grip.

11. Pick the square grip.

12. Now the dimension is following your pointer. Pick a third point about 8' away from the angled wall, as shown in Figure 5.11.

13. On the Design bar, select the Modify button. This will end the command.

FIGURE 5.10 Press the Tab key to select the point shown.

FIGURE 5.11 Picking the second point along the wall

Unfortunately, we had to dimension to the core of the wall. This is the last place we would ever need to take a dimension from. At this point, the dimension needs to be "stretched" to the outside finished face of the brick, as you'll see next.

Editing the Witness Line

Every dimension in Revit Architecture has its own grip points when selected. This is similar to most CAD applications. Two of these grips control what is called the *witness line*. The witness line is the line that is "attached" to the item being dimensioned. Because we had to take this dimension from the core of the wall, the witness lines need to be dragged to the outside face of the brick.

1. Select the angled dimension. Notice the blue grips appear.

2. On the left side of the dimension, pick and hold the grip in the middle of the dimension line, as shown in Figure 5.12.

3. Drag the blue grip to the outside face of the brick. You will know you are in the right spot because you will see a small dot appear, as shown in Figure 5.12.

FIGURE 5.12 Dragging the witness lines grip

4. Repeat the procedure for the other side.

Trust me — this is worth practicing now, before you get into a live situation. If you have already run into this, you know exactly what I mean.

There is just one more thing we need to look at in terms of "tweaking" and making adjustments to an aligned dimension: overriding a dimension's precision.

Overriding the Precision

Another unfortunate issue created by dimensioning a wall at an angle such as this is the fact that the dimension usually comes out at an uneven increment. In most cases, you do not want to override every dimension's precision just for this one, lone dimension to read properly. In this situation, you want to turn to the dimension's element properties:

1. Select the angled dimension.

2. On the Modify Dimensions tab, click the Element Properties button.

3. In the Element Properties dialog, click the Edit Type... button, as shown in Figure 5.13.

FIGURE 5.13 Clicking the Edit Type... button to create a new dimension style

4. Click the Duplicate button, as shown in Figure 5.14.

5. Call the new dimension style **Linear - 3/32" Arial - 1/4" precision.** Click OK.

6. Scroll down to the Text category. There, near the bottom, you will see a row for Units Format. Next to the Units Format row is a button that displays a sample increment. Pick it (see Figure 5.14).

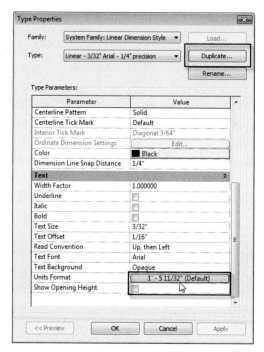

FIGURE 5.14 Select the button in the Text category to access the dimension's precision.

7. Uncheck Use Project Settings.

8. Choose To the Nearest ¼" from the Rounding drop-down (see Figure 5.15).

9. Click OK twice.

10. Click OK one more time to get back to the model. Notice the dimension is now rounded to the nearest ¼". In this case, it is rounded to a whole number.

Although aligned dimensions will bear the brunt of your dimensioning, there are still plenty of other dimension types waiting for you to use.

FIGURE 5.15 Changing the dimension's units. Notice some of the other choices you have available.

Linear Dimensions

Linear dimensions are used less frequently than most of the other dimensions. Unlike AutoCAD, where linear dimensions are the go-to dimension, they are put on the bench for most of the game in Revit. The best use for a linear dimension is in the situation where you would like to put a straight dimension across non-linear (angled) geometry, as follows:

1. Zoom back in on the corridor area.

2. On the Annotate tab, select the Linear Dimension button. Notice that you do not have the choice of selecting the entire wall. That option has been taken away. Instead, Revit requires you to pick a point.

3. Move your cursor over the inside corner at the bottom of the corridor, as shown in Figure 5.16. Make sure you are exactly over the exterior intersection of the brick. You will know you are there by the white dot that shows up, as shown in Figure 5.16.

4. Once you see the dot, pick the corner.

5. Pick the same spot on the other side of the wall, as shown in Figure 5.17. Once you pick the second corner, the dimension will follow your cursor in a straight direction.

FIGURE 5.16 Selecting the finished exterior corner of the brick. You will see a small white dot appear, indicating you can pick the start of the dimension.

6. Move your cursor to the left approximately 8', and pick the third point to place the dimension (see Figure 5.17).

FIGURE 5.17 When you add a linear dimension to an angled wall, you will get a straight dimension.

7. Hit Esc.

8. Select the new dimension.

9. On the Modify dimensions tab, select the **Linear - 3/32" Arial - ¹/₄"** style, as shown in Figure 5.18.

FIGURE 5.18 Changing the dimension to reflect the new rounded dimension.

10. The dimension is now rounded to the nearest ¹/₄".

Aligned and linear dimensions are the two dimension styles that pertain to straight dimensioning. The next three dimension procedures are used to add dimensions to angled and radial geometry.

Angular Dimensions

This type of dimensioning comes close to needing no introduction at all. But I will introduce it anyway.

Angular dimensions are used to calculate and record the angle between two items. These two items are usually walls. Of course, we will add an angular dimension to our lovely corridor walls:

1. Zoom back in on the corridor.

2. On the Annotate tab, select the Angular Dimension button as shown in Figure 5.19

3. For the first wall, pick the finished inside face of the upper-left corridor wall, as shown in Figure 5.19.

4. Pick the finished inside face of the angled corridor wall, as shown in Figure 5.19.

5. Move your cursor to the left about 8', and place the dimension as shown in Figure 5.19.

FIGURE 5.19 Placing an angular dimension means picking two walls, then a point to place the dimension.

6. Hit Esc.

7. Repeat the steps for the bottom of the corridor.

8. Add the rest of the dimensions, as shown in Figure 5.20. This will complete the dimensioning of the corridor area.

FIGURE 5.20 Finish placing the corridor dimensions.

If you would like to place the dimensions in different locations, feel free to do so.

The next set of dimensions will pertain to radial geometry. We can finally get out of this corridor!

Radial Dimensions

Radial dimensions are used to, well, measure the radius of an item. Luckily in Revit, we are using an application that knows you are adding a radial dimension to a building component. This means the many different choices provided by a CAD application are taken away, leaving just the basics.

The following procedure will lead you through adding a radial dimension:

1. Zoom in on the west radial entry in the west wing.

2. On the Annotate tab, select the Radial Dimension button.

3. Pick the outside face of the radial wall, as shown in Figure 5.21.

4. Place the radial dimension somewhere that makes sense. If your model looks like Figure 5.21, you may proceed. If it does not, go back and try it again.

5. Pan all the way to the east radial end of the east wing, as shown in Figure 5.22.

Keep in mind that you can add an angular dimension to physically change the angle of the items being dimensioned. Use caution, however, and be sure the correct items are being moved when you alter the angle.

FIGURE 5.21 Adding a radial dimension is as about as straightforward as it gets.

6. On the Annotate tab, select the Radial Dimension button.

7. Dimension to the finished outside face of the brick, and place your dimension to a similar location as shown in Figure 5.22.

FIGURE 5.22 Adding the second radial dimension

 WARNING   All too often, you can easily dimension from the wrong reference point. The reason this book is using a wall with a concrete ledge below the brick is to expose you to the fact that you need to be very deliberate in how and where you choose your references for dimensions. Don't be afraid to zoom in and out as you are adding your dimensions.

If you are careful in how you add a radial dimension, you are going to find this process quite simple. The next type of dimension, however, can be a little tricky.

Arc Length Dimensions

Measuring the length of an arc is a handy capability that was added back in the 2009 release. I have found the Arc Length dimension extremely useful in locating items such as windows along an arc. That is, in fact, what we need to do in the west wing of the building.

The following procedure will lead you through adding an arc length dimension:

1. Zoom in on the west radial entry of the west wing, as shown in Figure 5.23.

2. On the Annotate tab, select the Arc Length button as shown in Figure 5.23.

3. Pick the finish face exterior face of the brick.

4. Pick the center line of the window.

5. Pick a point along the exterior face of brick that runs along the vertical intersecting wall, illustrated as "3" in Figure 5.23.

6. Pick a point in which to place the dimension.

F I G U R E   5 . 2 3 Placing an Arc Length dimension involves four separate picks.

Let's try it again. This time the dimension will be taken from the first window (the one we just dimensioned) to the second window. The process will be exactly the same.

1. On the Annotate tab, select the Arc Length button.

2. Pick the exterior face of brick along the radial wall.

3. Pick the first window's center line.

4. Pick the second windows center line.

5. Pick a point to place the dimension. See Figure 5.24.

Now that you have experience adding dimensions to record placement of items, it is time to see how you can use dimensions to not only record the increments but also to physically use dimensions as an actual layout tool.

FIGURE 5.24: Adding a second Arc Length dimension

Using Dimensions as a Layout Tool

Using dimensions as a layout tool is my favorite topic when it comes to dimensions. "Okay, fine," you may say to yourself. "I can do that in CAD." Well, not quite. You see, in Revit you cannot alter a dimension to read an increment that it is not. You can, however, select the item you are dimensioning, and then type a new number in the dimension. At that point, the item you are dimensioning will move. The result of this is an accurate dimension.

The first item we need to explore is equally constraining a string of dimensions. You were exposed to this in the previous section of this chapter, but now, let's really dig in and gain some tangible experience using this tool.

To begin, open the file you have been following along with. If you did not complete the previous chapter, go to the book's web page at **www.sybex.com/go/revit2010ner**. From there you can browse to Chapter 5 and find the file called NER-17.rvt.

For this procedure, we will add some more walls to the east wing, and then constrain them using the EQ dimension function:

1. In the Project Browser, go the Level 1 floor plan (not a ceiling plan!).

2. Zoom into the west wing of the building.

3. Select one of the interior corridor walls, right-click, and select Create Similar from the context menu.

4. Draw five walls, as shown in Figure 5.25. They do not have to be an equal distance from one another.

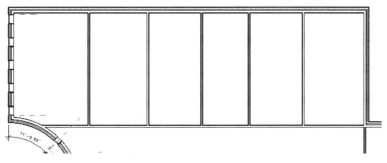

FIGURE 5.25 Adding the walls "willy-nilly"

5. On the Annotate tab, click the Aligned button.

6. Also on the Options bar, be sure the Prefer option is set to Center Core (see Figure 5.26).

FIGURE 5.26 Changing the options for the dimension

7. Zoom in on the left exterior wall, as shown in Figure 5.27.

8. Hover your pointer over the wall. Notice Revit is trying to locate the center of the wall? In this instance this is not what we want (even though we just told Revit to do that).

9. We want Revit to start this dimension string using the interior face of the finished wall. To do this, hover your pointer over the inside face of the wall, as shown in Figure 5.27.

10. Once you are over the inside face of the wall, tap the Tab key on your keyboard three times until Revit highlights the inside face of the wall.

FIGURE 5.27 Press the Tab key to filter to the desired reference of the wall.

11. Pick the inside face of the wall.

12. Move your cursor to the right until you pass over the first interior wall. Notice the core center line of the interior wall highlights. Once you see this, pick the wall, as shown in Figure 5.28.

 WARNING   Just like when we equally constrained the door in the previous procedure, you need to keep the dimension command running. If you hit Esc, undo the last dimension and start over.

13. Once you pick the first interior partition, move to the right and pick the center of the next wall.

14. Repeat the procedure until you get to the last wall (see Figure 5.28).

FIGURE 5.28 Adding a string of dimensions to the interior walls

Once you get to the exterior wall to the right, you will encounter the same issue. You want this string of dimensions to go to the inside face, not the core of the exterior wall:

1. Hover your cursor over the inside face of the wall and tap the Tab key on your keyboard until the inside face of the wall becomes highlighted. Once it does, pick the highlighted face of wall, as shown in Figure 5.29.

FIGURE 5.29 Press Tab to locate the inside face of the wall.

2. Once the inside face is located, pick it.

3. Move your cursor up the view. Notice the entire dimension string is following.

4. Placing a dimension in Revit is a little awkward, but you will get the hang of it. What you need to do is pick a point away from the last dimension in the string, as shown in Figure 5.30. It is almost as if you are trying to pick another item that is not there. Once you do this, the dimension will be in place.

FIGURE 5.30 Picking a point away from the last dimension to place the string

> If you placed the dimension string, then escaped out of the command, that's fine. You can simply select the string of dimensions again, and you will be back in business.

Now that the dimension string is in place, it is time to move these walls to be equal distances apart from one another. Notice that, once you placed the dimension string the familiar blue icons appeared. We can use them:

1. Find the EQ icon in the middle of the dimension string and pick it. The slash through it is now gone and the walls have moved, as shown in Figure 5.31.

FIGURE 5.31 Before and after the EQ icon is selected

2. Press Esc twice to let go of the selection.

Since these walls are not constrained to always be equal, this means that if one of the exterior walls is moved, these five interior partitions will always maintain an equal relationship to one another — that is, as long as this dimension string is still associated with the walls.

In Revit Architecture, you can choose to keep the walls constrained or to only use the dimension as a tool to move the walls around.

Constraining the Model

Constraining a model is an important topic, because such choices you make early in the design process can either be of great benefit or be a detriment to the project's flow. As you gain more experience using Revit Architecture, you are going to start hearing the term *overconstrained*. This is a term given to a model that has been constrained in so many places that any movement of the model forces multiple warnings and, in many cases, errors that cannot be ignored.

Given that, how you choose to constrain your model is up to you. You will learn how to constrain (and of course *un*constrain) your model in this chapter, but deciding when and where to constrain your model will certainly vary from project to project.

The string of equal dimensions we now have in place, in effect, has, by default, created a constraint with these walls. To unconstrain them, follow along:

1. Select the dimension string.

2. Press the Delete key on your keyboard.

Out Of Sight, Out Of Mind.

In CAD, you used to type **E**, then pressed Enter. This is no longer a good idea. If you do this to an item in Revit Architecture, it will only remove that element from the current view — not from the entire model. You are better off either selecting the item and pressing the Delete key on the keyboard, or selecting the item and clicking the delete icon, as shown here:

3. Revit will now give you a warning, as shown in Figure 5.32. The warning says:

A Dimension with Lock and/or EQ Constraints is being deleted, but the elements will still be constrained. Push "Unconstrain" to remove the Constraints or "OK" to leave elements constrained.

FIGURE 5.32 A Revit warning pertaining to the constraint of the walls

If you select Unconstrain, the EQ dimension will disappear as well as any constraint on the walls. If you move the exterior wall, the newly spaced walls will not reposition themselves.

4. Click OK. You will learn how to unconstrain these walls in a different method.

5. Select one of the interior walls that were part of the EQ dimension string.

6. On the Options bar, select the Activate Dimensions button, as shown in Figure 5.33.

 N O T E Sometimes, when you select an item that is being constrained, the dimensions will already be activated, and the Options bar won't provide this button. If you do not see the Activate button on the Options bar for this example, your dimensions have been activated already.

7. With the dimensions showing, you will now see the EQ icon. Click this icon, and it will release the constraint set for the walls. You are now free to move around the building.

FIGURE 5.33 Activating the dimensions

T I P   Notice in Figure 5.33 the anchor icon to the left of the dimensions. This determines which wall will remain stationary. This icon can be moved to any of the items involved in the constraint. For example, if you click and drag the anchor to the middle partition, then move one of the exterior walls, the middle partition will stay in place while the other walls move an equal distance to the right and left of the anchored wall.

Now that you have experience with dimension equality constraints, it is time to start learning about a different type of constraint that involves locking items together at a distance.

Locking a Dimension

There will be cases where you may want to always hold a dimension, no matter what else is going on around it. This can be done by physically adding a dimension to an item, then locking that dimension in place. For example, if you want to lock the middle space to a specific dimension, you simply add a dimension and lock it down. Sound easy? It is!

1. On the Annotate tab, click the Aligned Dimension button.

2. On the Options bar, change the Prefer option to Wall Faces, as shown in Figure 5.34.

3. Pick the inside faces of the two middle partitions, as shown in Figure 5.34.

4. Once you place the dimension, a blue padlock icon will appear. When it does, pick it.

5. Select the left wall that has been dimensioned.

6. Move the wall to the right 2'–0". Notice the right wall moves as well.

7. Click the Undo button, as shown in Figure 5.35.

8. Delete the dimension.

9. When you get the warning, click the Unconstrain button.

10. Save the model.

11. Add doors and windows to the plan, as shown in Figure 5.36. They can be any type of door or window you choose — just try to keep it close to the ones in Figure 5.36. Also, placement does not matter. We will adjust this in the next procedure.

FIGURE 5.34 You can add a dimension and lock the distance between two items.

FIGURE 5.35 Click the Undo button.

FIGURE 5.36 Adding doors and windows to the floor plan

In the next section, we will start using dimensions as a tool to physically start moving elements around. Although this one might seem like an exercise in futility, the practice is quite relevant to what you are going to be dealing with when you are on a project.

Using Dimensions to Move Objects

As I have mentioned before, you cannot type over a dimension and cause the value in that dimension to be inaccurate. Revit does provide tools to get around this. When you add a dimension and select the object being dimensioned, your dimension will turn blue. This is a temporary dimension, which can be edited. Consequently, the object being dimensioned will move.

The objective of this procedure is to select an item and modify the temporary dimension, in effect moving the object:

1. Zoom in on the left side of the east wing, as shown in Figure 5.37.

2. Select the door, as shown in Figure 5.37. Notice there is a blue dimension on both sides of the door. These are temporary dimensions.

3. Pick the blue text in the temporary dimension, as shown in Figure 5.37. (It might be obscured by the wall, but if you hover over it, it will become selected and you can select it at that point.)

4. Type 1. (This is the equivalent of 1'–0"). The door will move.

FIGURE 5.37 When you type a different value, the temporary dimension will move the object.

5. Press the Esc key to release the door.

This procedure used a temporary dimension that, when you select the item, appeared. Once you finished editing the dimension, it went away. In the next procedure, we will add a "real" dimension and do the same thing.

1. On the Annotate tab, select the Aligned Dimension button.

2. Place a dimension between the door and the wall, as shown in Figure 5.38.

FIGURE 5.38 Placing a dimension

3. Press the Esc key.

4. Select the door. Notice the dimension turns small and blue. It is now ready to be modified, as shown in Figure 5.39.

FIGURE 5.39 Making adjustments with the actual dimension

5. Once you see the dimension turn blue, select the text and type 1 (1'–0"). The door will adjust to the 1'–0" increment.

6. Press the Esc key.

7. Select the dimension.

8. Notice there is a blue grip just underneath the text. Pick the grip and move the text out from between the extension lines, as shown in Figure 5.40. Notice Revit will place a leader (an arrow pointing from the model to your text) in the text.

FIGURE 5.40 By grip-editing the text, you can slide it to a "cleaner" location. Revit will automatically leader the text to the dimension line.

This is a process that will take some time getting used to. That's okay, because it's a process worth getting used to. The next procedure will delve into making further modifications to dimensions, and a nice failsafe procedure embedded within the dimension properties.

Dimension Text Overrides

Although I just told you that you can't override a dimension, the following steps get around that. There will be many cases where you would just like to have text or, more commonly, a prefix or a suffix within a dimension. All three can be accomplished in Revit Architecture.

1. Select the 1'–0" dimension.

2. Notice the text turns blue. As you know, blue means that this item is editable in Revit. Pick the text. You should see the dialog in Figure 5.41.

The fact that temporary dimensions are displayed in Revit lends itself to another common process: the double check. All you need to do in Revit Architecture is to select any item, and the temporary dimensions will appear. (If not, remember to click Activate Dimensions on the Options bar.) You can simply look at the dimension. If it reads the value you expected, great! If not, change it. It's that simple.

FIGURE 5.41 The Dimension Text edit dialog

3. Under Dimension Value, click Override Text, as shown in Figure 5.42.

FIGURE 5.42 Any numeric value will trigger a warning in Revit. You simply cannot type a value over a dimension.

4. Type 1'–1" and press Enter.

5. You will get an error. Revit will not allow you to do such a foolish thing. Click OK.

6. Click Use Actual Value, as shown in Figure 5.43.

FIGURE 5.43 Under Dimension Value choose Use Actual Value, and type **TYP.** as the prefix.

7. Under Prefix, type TYP., as shown in Figure 5.43.

8. Click OK.

As a closing practice for dimensioning, move the rest of the doors along this wall to a 1'–0" increment from the finished inside face of the wall to the door opening. Also, dimension the floor plan as shown in Figures 5.44 and 5.45.

FIGURE 5.44 The dimensional layout for the north part of the east wing

FIGURE 5.45 The dimensional layout for the south part of the east wing

Adding Text

Text in Revit Architecture is going to be a love/hate relationship for every Revit user. You will love it, because it will automatically scale with the view's scale. You will hate it because the text editor is something of a throwback from an earlier CAD application. Either way, the procedure for adding text does not change with your feelings toward it.

To begin, open the file you have been following along with. If you did not complete the previous chapter, go to the book's web page at www.sybex.com/go/revit2010ner. From there you can browse to Chapter 5 and find the file called NER-18.rvt.

The objective of this procedure is to simply add text to the model, format it, and add and format a leader:

1. In the Project Browser, go to the Level 1 floor plan.

2. Zoom in on the west wing's radial entry area where the elevator shafts are, as shown in Figure 5.46.

3. On the Basics tab on the Design bar, click the Text button, as shown in Figure 5.47.

4. On the Options bar, in the Type Selector select Text : 3/32" Arial.

FIGURE 5.46 The radial entry

FIGURE 5.47 Click the Text button on the Basics tab of the Design bar.

5. Also on the Options bar is an option called Leader. Select the None button. It is the button with the A on it, as shown in Figure 5.48.

6. To place the text, you need to pick a window. Pick the point labeled "1" in Figure 5.48.

7. Pick the point labeled "2" in Figure 5.48.

8. Type **CMU SHAFT WALL**.

9. Click a point in the view outside of the text box. You now have a note in the model.

10. Press the Esc key.

11. Select the text.

12. On the Options bar, review the choices you have to leader the text.

FIGURE 5.48 To place leader-less text, you must pick a window.

13. Click the Add Left Leader button, as shown in Figure 5.49. It adds a leader to the left end of the text.

14. By clicking the grips and moving the text around, configure the text and the leader to resemble Figure 5.49.

FIGURE 5.49 Adding and stretching a leader

Adding Leader Text

You can add text to a model by placing a leader first and then adding the text within the same command. Although in Revit leaders can be added to all text, you have the option of adding text to a model with or without a leader.

The objective of the following steps is to place text with a leader:

1. On the Basics tab of the Design bar, select the Text button.

2. On the Options bar, click the Two Segments button, as shown in Figure 5.50.

3. Pick a point near the radial wall, as shown in Figure 5.50.

4. Pick a second point similar to 2 in Figure 5.50.

5. Pick a third point just to the right of the second point.

6. Type FULL HEIGHT RADIAL WALL.

7. Click an area outside of the text.

FIGURE 5.50 Adding a piece of leader text

Now that you can add text to a model, it is time to investigate how to modify the text once it has been added to the model. We can start with that arrowhead on the end of the leader.

Changing the Leader Type

It almost seems as though Revit uses the ugliest leader as a default, forcing you to change it immediately. The large arrowhead you see in Figure 5.50 is not the only arrowhead Revit provides — had that been the case, Revit would never have even gotten off the ground!

To change the arrowhead that Revit uses with a text item, follow this procedure:

1. Select the text you just added to the model.

2. On the Options bar, click the Element Properties button.

3. In the Element Properties dialog, click Edit / New.

4. Change the Leader Arrowhead parameter to Arrow Filled 15 Degree, as shown in Figure 5.51.

5. Click OK twice.

FIGURE 5.51 Changing the leader arrowhead

 T I P   You will not always have to do this procedure. These leaders should be set up in your template before you begin. Refer to Chapter 23, "BIM Management," for management issues regarding templates.

Now that's a handsome-looking arrowhead. The next item to address is how to modify the placement of text once it has been added to the model.

Modifying the Text Placement

With any text item in Revit, you can select the text in your model, and you will see grips for adjusting text: two grips on the text box, two on the leader, and a rotate icon.

The objective of the following short procedure is to modify the text placement and to make the necessary adjustments.

1. Select the text you just added to the model.

2. Pick the right blue grip.

3. Stretch the text window to the left until it forces the text to wrap, as shown in Figure 5.52.

FIGURE 5.52 Wrapping the text using the right grip

Observe the rotate icon. You don't need to rotate the text here, but notice it is there for future reference.

Modifying the placement of text is a straightforward process. Changing the actual font and size of the text in a model is another story, and involves further investigation

Text Properties

Of course, you can change the font for text. You can also change the height and the width. One thing to keep in mind, however, is that the text height you specify is the actual text height you want to see on the sheet. You no longer have to multiply the desired text height to a "line type scale." Revit understands that text is scaled based on the view's scale. This process is eliminated for you.

To modify the text appearance, run through the following procedure:

1. Select the last text item you added to the model.

2. On the Options bar, click the Element Properties button.

3. Click Edit / New.

4. Click Duplicate.

5. Call the new text $3/16$" Tahoma.

6. Change the Text Font setting to Tahoma.

7. Change the Text Size setting to $3/16$" (see Figure 5.53).

8. Change the Width Factor setting to .8.

FIGURE 5.53 Changing the text values in the Element Properties dialog

9. Click OK twice.

You have now successfully changed the text. Of course, this large, non-uniform text is not proper in this context. You can change that easily:

1. Select the text you just changed to Tahoma.

2. In the Type Selector menu on the Options bar, select 3/32" Arial. This will change the text back to the Arial text, keeping the new text type available for another time.

Are You Experienced?

Now You Can...

Revit does not use an SHX font. As a matter of fact, SHX cannot be used at all in Revit. Keep this in mind when you are setting up your company's templates. If you are using an SHX font, you will need to find an alternate font.

☑ add a multitude of different types of dimensions to your model by simply altering the options associated with the dimension command

☑ equally constrain items in a model by adding a string of dimensions and clicking the EQ button

☑ use your dimensions as a layout tool, keeping the items constrained even after the dimension is deleted

☑ add text to a model by starting either with a leader or just a paragraph of text

☑ change the text type and arrowhead type for leader text

CHAPTER 6

Floors

- ▶ Placing a floor in your model
- ▶ Pitching a floor to floor drains
- ▶ Building a floor layer by layer
- ▶ Creating shaft openings

t is going to be hard to convince you that floors are easy when an entire chapter is dedicated to this lone aspect of Revit Architecture. Well, floors *are* easy. The reason I'm dedicating an entire chapter to the subject is the fact that we need to address a lot of aspects to floors.

Adding a floor to a model is quite simple indeed, but in Revit Architecture, we are truly modeling this floor. That means that the structure and the finish can all be included when you create your floor. When a section is cut through this floor, you get an almost perfect representation of your floor system and how it relates to adjacent geometry, such as walls.

Floors, of course, are more than large slabs of concrete; therefore, you'll also be introduced to creating materials, and you'll learn how to pitch these materials to floor drains. Further, you will examine how to create sloped slabs as well.

The first area we are going to explore is how to place a slab into your model. It is as simple as it sounds, but you must follow certain steps, which I'll outline next.

Placing a Floor Slab

As you've learned up to this point, in Revit Architecture you do need to add items the way Revit wants you to add them, or else you will probably generate errors or, worse, inaccuracies in your model.

To begin, open the file you have been following along with.
If you did not complete the previous chapter, go to the book's web page at **www.sybex.com/go/revit2010ner**. From there you can browse to Chapter 6 and find the file called NER-19.rvt.

The objective of the following procedure is to create a floor slab to be placed into the model:

1. In your Project Browser, go to the Level 1 floor plan.

2. In the Level 1 floor plan, zoom in to the east wing.

3. On the Home tab, select the Floor button, as shown in Figure 6.1.
   Notice that the Home tab turns into the Create floor boundary tab as shown in Figure 6.2.

4. In the Create Floor Boundary tab, select the Floor Properties button, as shown in Figure 6.2.

5. In the Element Properties dialog, at the top you will see the Family, then the Type, as shown in Figure 6.3. The Family is System Family: Floor. The Type is 12" Generic - 12".

FIGURE 6.1 The Floor button on the Home tab

FIGURE 6.2 Selecting the Floor Properties button in the Sketch tab

6. To the right of the Type menu, you will see an Edit Type button. Click it (see Figure 6.3).

You are now accessing the Type Properties. This means that any change made here will have an effect on every slab of this type in the entire model.

 T I P   At this point, you always want to either create a new floor system or rename the current one. This will avert much confusion down the line when you have a floor called Generic - 12" and it is actually a 6" concrete slab on grade.

7. Click the Rename button, as shown in Figure 6.4.

8. Call it 6" Slab on Grade.

9. Click OK.

10. In the Structure row, there is a long Edit button, as shown in Figure 6.5. Click it.

FIGURE 6.3 Click the Edit / New button to start creating a new floor slab.

FIGURE 6.4 Rename the current floor. Since you will never have a Generic 12" floor in your model, it is a good idea not to keep this floor around.

You are now in the Edit Assembly dialog. This is where you can specify a thickness for your slab. You can also add layers of materials here as well.

Type Parameters:

Parameter	Value
Construction	☆
Structure	Edit...
Default Thickness	1' 0"
Graphics	☆
Coarse Scale Fill Pattern	
Coarse Scale Fill Color	■ Black
Identity Data	☆
Keynote	
Model	
Manufacturer	
Type Comments	
URL	
Description	
Assembly Description	Floor Construction
Assembly Code	B1010
Type Mark	
Cost	

FIGURE 6.5 Clicking the Edit button to access the structure of the floor

In the middle of the Edit Assembly dialog is a large spreadsheet-type field that is divided into rows and columns. The rows are defined by a structural component, and include a boundary above and below the structure. It is the Structure row that we are interested in here:

1. In the Structure row, you will see that it is divided into columns. Click into the first cell in the Material column within the Structure row, as shown in Figure 6.6.

2. You will see a small [...] button appear when you click into the Material cell. This is an indication that you will be given a menu if selected. Click the [...] button.

The term *layer* may throw you off a bit. Revit uses *layer* here to describe a component of the floor. This is not to be mistaken with the AutoCAD "layer."

Layers

	Function	Material	Thickness	Wraps	Variable	▲
1	Core Boundary	Layers Above	0' 0"			
2	Structure [1]	<By Category>	1' 0"	☐	☐	
3	Core Boundary	Layers Below	0' 0"			

Insert	Delete	Up	Down

FIGURE 6.6 By clicking in the Material cell within the Structure row, you can access the Materials dialog.

3. You can now choose a material from the menu. Scroll down until you arrive at Concrete - Cast-in-Place Concrete, and select it. Notice that to the right you can see that this material will display two different hatches. There is a sand hatch that will be visible for floor plans, and a concrete hatch that is visible for sections (see Figure 6.7).

FIGURE 6.7 The Materials menu

4. Make sure Concrete - Cast-in-place concrete is selected, and click OK.

5. Directly to the right of the Material column is a Thickness column. Currently there is a value of 1'–0". Click into the cell that says 1'–0", and change it to 6".

T I P   If you just type 6 and press Enter, you are going to wind up with a 6'–0"- thick slab. Be sure to add the inch (") mark after the 6. The value needs to read 6".

6. Click OK twice.

7. Click OK again to get back to the model.

Now that the slab has been created, we can place it into the model. You will notice that your Design bar has changed into what is called Sketch mode. You will now proceed to sketch the slab in place.

Sketching the Slab

The Create Floor Boundary tab is one of those items that you will need to get used to in terms of how Revit wants you to proceed; you are basically limited to the choices provided in this menu. Not to fear, you should have plenty of choices, but there is still that "feel" thing we keep talking about.

Here's what needs to happen: the perimeter of the slab must be drawn into the model. Since this is basically a slab on grade, we are going to pour the concrete to the inside finished face of the wall. We won't worry about a control joint between the wall and the slab at this point.

Picking Walls

The best way to add a slab is to use the Pick Walls button as much as possible (see Figure 6.8). In doing so, you are telling Revit that this edge of slab needs to move if this wall moves.

Let's start sketching the slab:

1. In the Create Floor Boundary tab, select the Pick Walls button, as shown in Figure 6.8.

FIGURE 6.8 Pick Walls ensures that that edge of your slab will move if the wall moves.

2. With the Pick Walls tool running, hover your mouse over the inside face of the wall, as shown in Figure 6.9.

WATCH WHAT YOU ARE PICKING!

As you are picking the walls to place your edge of slab, be careful. If you do not pick the inside face, there is a chance Revit will try to extend the slab to the core of the wall. If you zoom into the area that you are picking, you will see an alignment line appear. Make sure this line is where you want it, as shown here:

3. Once you see the wall become highlighted and you are sure you are on the inside of the wall, pick it (see Figure 6.9).

4. With the inside face of the wall picked, you need to move on to the next wall. Pick the inside face of the north wall.

   Notice that as you are picking the walls, a magenta "sketch line" appears on the inside face of the walls. This is another indicator telling you whether you are on the correct side of the wall.

5. Keep picking the walls, as shown in Figure 6.10. You need to have a continuous loop — no gaps and no overlaps.

6. Apply some basic modify commands as well. Figure 6.10 contains the commands you will need to accomplish, forming a continuous loop.

7. Once you have accomplished picking the perimeter of the east wing, click Finish Floor on the Create Floor Boundary tab, as shown in Figure 6.11.

FIGURE 6.9 Picking the inside face of the first wall

FIGURE 6.10 Selecting the walls

USING FLIP ARROWS

If you accidentally picked the wrong place in the wall, that's OK. If you press Esc, then select the magenta line, a flip arrow will show up. If you pick the flip arrow, the magenta line will flip back to the correct face of the wall, as shown here. Also, if there are other sketch lines that are on the wrong face, this one flip will take care of any connected sketch lines.

FIGURE 6.11 Click Finish Floor to finalize the floor sketch.

Once the floor is finished, you are going to have plenty of opportunity to practice adding floors in this model! We need to add a floor to the corridor as well as the west wing:

1. Zoom into the corridor, as shown in Figure 6.12.

2. On the Home tab, start the Floor command.

CLEAN UP THOSE CORNERS!

Revit Architecture won't let you finish if you have a gap or an overlapping line. If you get the error shown here, you need to go back into your sketch and see which corner is giving you trouble. If you do get the error dialog, you can click the Show button to have Revit show you where the issue is.

3. In the Create Floor Boundary tab, click the Pick Walls button.

4. Pick the three north walls of the corridor. Remember to keep the magenta line to the inside face (see Figure 6.12).

FIGURE 6.12 Picking the north walls of the corridor

5. To add the west edge of the slab, Revit will not really let you pick the wall. If you do, the magenta line will go either to the core center line or to the opposite face of the wall. At this point, click the Lines button on the Create Floor Boundary tab, as shown in Figure 6.13.

FIGURE 6.13 Sometimes you will need to click the Lines button to draw the edge of the slab freehand.

6. With the Lines button selected, select the Pick Lines button on the Draw panel, as shown in Figure 6.14.

7. Pick the face of the east wall as shown in Figure 6.14.

FIGURE 6.14 Pick the face of the west wall. The line will run past the corridor. That's OK. You will trim that in a moment.

8. On the Draw panel, click the Pick Walls button.

9. Pick the south corridor walls. (Remember to keep the magenta line to the inside of the corridor.)

10. Pick the east wall of the corridor. This time you want to be sure that the magenta line is to the left of the wall. This will ensure that the two slabs meet (see Figure 6.15).

FIGURE 6.15 Add the slab edge to the left side of the east corridor wall.

Now that you have the process of adding sketch lines to the model, you can start to look into how to clean up the sketch so we can finish.

Using Trim to Clean Up the Sketch

Now that the lines are placed, it is time to make sure you don't have any gaps or overlaps. And you do. It is time to fix this situation. To do this, you are going to use the basic modify commands we used in the previous chapter.

The issue here is the fact that the east wall has a giant gap at the bottom and an overlap at the top. The command you need to use here is the Trim command:

1. Pick the trim button from the Tools toolbar as shown in Figure 6.16.

2. With the corners successfully trimmed, click Finish Floor.

When picking the east wall of the corridor, you may find that Revit just will not let you pick the opposite face of the wall. This is okay. Pick the inside face of the wall, and then move the magenta line to the opposite face of the wall.

FIGURE 6.16 Pick the magenta lines in the numbered order illustrated in the figure.

You can still access most of the basic editing commands such as Trim, Split, and Offset while you are creating the floor boundary.

  TIP   Hopefully you do not get an error stating that lines are overlapping. If you do, keep going with the Trim command. Also, you may need to investigate each corner. You may also want to consider that you may have accidentally placed double lines along a wall.

Once Revit allows you to finish the sketch, your east wing and corridor should have a slab underneath it, as shown in Figure 6.17.

FIGURE 6.17 The two slabs under the east wing and the corridor

It is time to add a slab under the east wing. Of course, there will be a numbered list of instructions to go by, but go ahead and try it on your own. Only look at the directions if you get lost!

1. Zoom in on the west wing.

2. On the Home tab, select the Floor button.

3. In the Create Floor Boundary tab, click the Pick Walls button.

4. Pick the exterior walls of the west wing.

5. Trim any gaps or overlaps that may occur in the corners. Also, pay special attention to the radial entry. It can be tricky.

6. Click Finish Floor.

Your west wing should look like Figure 6.18, which is looking at the bottom of the building from a 3D view.

Now that we have a nice slab on the first floor, it is time to add some more slabs to the rest of the levels. The trick with the slabs on upper levels is the fact that they need to extend into the core of the walls. This is where Revit can get sticky. Follow along with the next section, and let's work this out together.

FIGURE 6.18 Adding a slab to the east wing

Building a Floor by Layers

As mentioned in the previous section, the term layer does not equate to AutoCAD's layer. It does, however, equate to layers of materials used to design a floor system. In Revit Architecture, when you create a floor system you can do it in the mind-set of how a floor is actually constructed. You can also specify which material in the floor is going to stop at an exterior wall and which will pass through to the core.

In this section, you are going to build on your experience of creating a floor. Now that you have the concrete slab in place, we will start adding materials to create a floor finish.

To begin, open the file you have been following along with.
If you did not complete the previous chapter, go to the book's web page at **www.sybex.com/go/revit2010ner**. From there you can browse to Chapter 6 and find the file called NER-20.rvt.

The objective of this procedure is to create a floor system with a structure and a finish material. You will also design the floor to interrupt the exterior framing, while letting the brick façade pass from grade to parapet. Let's get started:

1. In the Project Browser, go to the Level 2 floor plan. (Remember not to go to the Level 2 ceiling plan.)

2. In the View Control bar (located at the bottom of the view window), be sure that the detail level is set to Fine.

3. On the Home tab, click the Floor button.

4. On the Create Floor Boundary tab, click the Floor Properties button.

5. In the Element Properties dialog, click the Edit Type… button.

6. Click the Duplicate button.

7. Call the new floor **6" concrete with 1" Terrazzo** (see Figure 6.19).

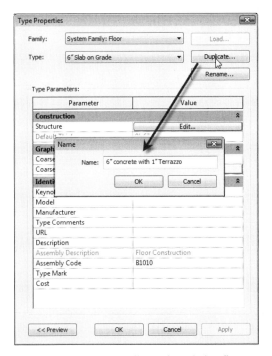

FIGURE 6.19 Duplicate the existing floor.

8. Click OK.

9. In the Structure row, click the Edit button, as shown in Figure 6.20.

FIGURE 6.20 Click the Edit button in the Structure row.

You are now in the Edit Assembly dialog, as you were in the previous procedure. The objective now is to add 1" terrazzo flooring to the top of the 6" of concrete.

Adding a Layer

Now it's time to add the additional material. To do so, you need to understand how the Edit Assembly dialog is broken down. Since we want to add a material to the top of the slab, we need to click above the concrete and insert a new layer, as follows:

1. In the Layer field, you will see three rows. Each of the three rows has a corresponding number. Click on the number 1. This is the top row that reads Core Boundary Layers Above (see Figure 6.21).

2. Underneath the Layers field, you will see an Insert button, as shown in Figure 6.21. Click it.

FIGURE 6.21 Inserting a new layer for the terrazzo

3. The new layer is added. You will now see that the field is divided into columns. The first column is the Function column. Currently it says that the Function is Structure. You will see that this cell is a drop box containing the other available functions. Click the drop box arrow and select Finish 1 [4] (see Figure 6.22).

FIGURE 6.22 Choosing a layer function

4. Click into the Material cell.

5. Click the [...] button.

6. In the Materials dialog, find Terrazzo from the material list to the left. Click OK.

7. In the Thickness column, add 1". Make sure you are typing 1 inch, not 1 foot (see Figure 6.23).

8. To the far right of the rows in the Layers field are Variable check boxes. Click Variable for the Structure row, as shown in Figure 6.23. This will enable you to slope the slab if need be. Only the layer that is set to be variable will actually slope.

FIGURE 6.23 The completed layers for the floor system

9. At the bottom of the Edit Assembly dialog is a Preview button indicating that you can reveal a graphic displaying the floor, as shown in Figure 6.24. Click it. Once you do, you will be able to see your floor in a sectional view.

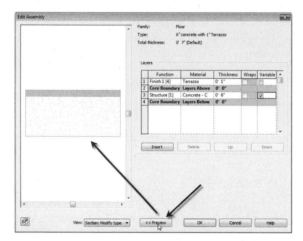

FIGURE 6.24   You can see the floor in section as it is being built.

10. Click OK twice.

11. Click OK one more time to get back to the model.

Great job. You now have a floor with a material on it! The next step is to place it into the model.

With the new floor created, you can now place it into the model. Remember that you are in the second floor. When you place the slab, you want it to extend directly into the wall core. To do so, follow along:

1. Click the Pick Walls button on the Draw Panel. You are going to pick every exterior wall in the west wing except for the radial wall.

2. Start picking walls, as shown in Figure 6.25. *Do not* pick the radial wall at the west entry.

3. On the Draw panel, select the Lines button.

4. Draw a line from the endpoint of the magenta line at the north wall of the east entry (#1 in Figure 6.26), to the endpoint of the magenta line in the south wall (#2 in Figure 6.26).

FIGURE 6.25 Pick the core center line of the exterior walls except for the radial east wall.

FIGURE 6.26 Sketching a line for the west portion of the entry slab

5. On the Create Floor Boundary tab, click Finish Floor.

6. Revit will start asking you questions. The first one is asking you if you want to attach the walls that go up to Level 2 to the bottom of the floor. You *do* want to do this. This will cut the walls down to meet the bottom of the floor. Any change in the floor's thickness will alter the tops of the wall. Click Yes, as shown in Figure 6.27.

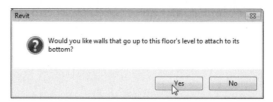

FIGURE 6.27 Click Yes to attach the walls to the floor's bottom.

7. The next message pertains to the exterior walls. Revit is asking if you would like to cut the section out of the walls where the slab is intersecting. In this case you do, so click Yes in the message box shown in Figure 6.28.

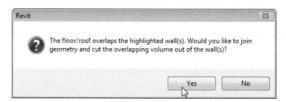

FIGURE 6.28 Click Yes if you want to cut overlapping volumes out of the exterior walls.

 N O T E As these messages come up, Revit usually does a good job of highlighting the items in the model it is addressing in these messages. Get into the habit of looking past the messages to see what items in the model are being highlighted.

With the second floor in place, you can now add it to the floors above. To do so, you can use the Copy/Paste Aligned feature you used in Chapter 3. Try to do this on your own. If you don't remember how, or skipped Chapter 3, follow these steps:

1. Select the floor in Level 2. (It is easiest to select the floor at the west edge.)

2. On the Modify Floors tab, pick the Copy button on the clipboard panel, as shown in Figure 6.29.

FIGURE 6.29 Click the Copy to Clipboard button.

3. Go to the default 3D view, as shown in Figure 6.30.

4. On the Clipboard panel, click Paste Aligned ➤ Select Levels as shown in Figure 6.30.

A good indication that you have successfully copied the floor to the clipboard is the fact that the Paste aligned icon directly to the right of the Copy icon will become activated.

FIGURE 6.30 Paste Levels by Name

5. The Select Levels dialog appears, where you will choose which levels you want to paste your floor. Choose Levels 3, 4, and 5, as shown in Figure 6.31.

6. Click OK. The floors will be pasted to the specified levels, as shown in Figure 6.32.

FIGURE 6.31 Select the levels where you want the slab to be copied to.

FIGURE 6.32 The completed floor placement

Notice that the fifth-level floor is not joined to any of the walls. This is because, when you pasted the floor to this level, Revit did not prompt you to cut the overlapping geometry from the exterior walls. To fix this, follow these steps:

1. After the floors have been pasted, select the fifth-level floor, as shown in Figure 6.33.

2. On the Modify Floors tab, select the Edit Boundary button.

3. On the On the Edit Boundary tab, Select finish Floor.

4. Select Yes to attach the walls that go up to this floor's bottom.

5. Select Yes to cut the overlapping volume out of the walls. Figure 6.33 shows that the walls are now being cut by the slab.

FIGURE 6.33 The fifth floor is now cutting the walls.

6. Repeat steps 1 through 6 for floors 4 and 3.

7. Save the model.

Not too bad. You have a full building of floors placed. Now it is time to drill in to these floors (literally) and see how you can make them perform to your specifications.

The first task in the next section is to create different floor materials for a few specific areas such as the restrooms. The second task is to pitch the restroom floors to floor drains.

Splitting the Floor's Materials

If you have a floor that includes a slab, then one single material of, say, vinyl composition tile (VCT) to the entire surface, won't that cause a problem in the restrooms? Better yet, suppose the floor is carpeted? Carpet just never seems to perform well around a toilet!

The goal of this procedure is to create a new material layer for the first floor slab, and then specify a new material for the restrooms:

1. In the Project Browser, go to the Level 1 floor plan, and zoom into an area similar to the area shown in Figure 6.34.

2. Pick a window around the corner of the building, as shown in Figure 6.34.

3. On the Options bar, select the Filter button (see Figure 6.34).

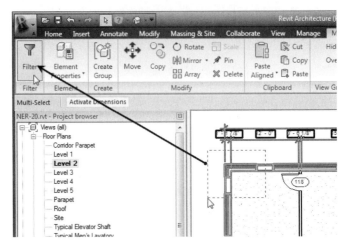

FIGURE 6.34 To select the slab, it is going to be easier to pick an entire area and filter the floor.

4. In the Filter dialog, select the Check None button, as shown in Figure 6.35.

5. Check the Floors option (see Figure 6.35).

FIGURE 6.35 Uncheck all of the elements, and then check Floors.

6. With the floor selected, click the Element Properties button on the Modify Floors tab.

7. Click Edit Type….

8. Click Rename.

9. Call the floor 6" Slab on Grade with 1" Finish.

10. Click OK.

11. Click the Edit button in the Structure row, as shown in Figure 6.36.

FIGURE 6.36 Edit the structure of the slab.

12. In the Edit Assembly dialog, select the Boundary above the Structure layer, as shown in Figure 6.37.

13. Click the Insert button (see Figure 6.37).

FIGURE 6.37 Adding a new layer

14. Call the function **Finish 1 [4]**.

15. Click in the Material cell.

16. Click the […] button.

17. Find the material in the menu called Carpet 1 and click OK.

18. Give the material a thickness of 1".

19. Click the Variable check box in the Structure row, as shown in Figure 6.38.

FIGURE 6.38 The new material is added.

20. Click OK twice.

21. Press Esc.

Now that you have experience adding a new material layer to the floor (you have done it twice in this chapter), you can specify a different material for the various rooms.

Split and Paint

This is a two-part procedure. The first thing you must do to specify an alternate material in a specific area is to split the floor's face. Then you can add (or paint) the desired material to that area.

The objective of the next procedure is to add an alternate material to the restrooms:

1. Zoom in on the lavatory, as shown in Figure 6.39.

2. On the Edit Face panel of the Modify tab, select the Split Face button, as shown in 6.39.

FIGURE 6.39 The Split Face button is located on the Edit Face panel of the Modify tab.

3. Move your cursor into the lavatory area, as shown in Figure 6.40.

4. Notice there is a little square at your cursor. Hover your cursor over the wall shown in Figure 6.40. You should get a tooltip telling you that you are directly over the floor. Once you see this indication, pick the floor.

FIGURE 6.40 Find the edge of the floor.

5. Once the floor is selected, you need to draw three lines around the inside face of the lavatory walls. To do so, on the Sketch bar make sure the Lines button is checked.

6. Draw the three lines as shown in Figure 6.41 (you may have to trim and extend the lines).

WARNING   Because of the fact that the line you are splitting is up against the edge of the slab (as shown in Figure 6.41), the actual floor's edge serves as one of the split lines. When you are adding the three additional lines, you *must* be snapped to the edge of the floor. There can be no overlaps or gaps.

FIGURE 6.41 Place the three split lines around the perimeter of the lavatory.

7. On the Sketch bar, click Finish Sketch.

8. The lavatory area should now be split.

Although it appears as if nothing happened, it just means you can't see it. The next step will change the material of the region. At this point it will become obvious that there is a different material.

With the floor split, it is time to add the new material to this room. This procedure is almost like adding a hatch to an area as if in AutoCAD:

1. On the Modify tab, click the paint icon, as shown in Figure 6.42.

2. The Type Selector will now become active. Select Ceramic Tile - 4" Blue from the menu, as shown in Figure 6.42.

FIGURE 6.42 The paint icon on the Tools toolbar

3. Move your cursor over the region you just created. Notice the material icon next to your cursor, as shown in Figure 6.43.

FIGURE 6.43 Filling the region with the new material

4. Once you see the perimeter of the small region you created around the inside of the lavatory, pick a spot. The area will fill with the new material (see Figure 6.44).

FIGURE 6.44 The completed lavatory

5. Do the same thing to the lavatory north of the corridor. If you get stuck, go back through the steps.

6. Save your model.

Now that splitting the face of the floor is out of the way, it is time to create a pitched floor situation. In some cases, this is an easy procedure. In others, it is not.

Pitching a Floor to a Floor Drain

Sure, it is the responsibility of the plumbing engineer to specify what floor drains to use, but it is generally the responsibility of the architect to specify where the floor drain needs to be, and the pitch of the floor.

That being said, let's move on to creating a pitched floor area in the restrooms. Since there are five floors to work with, let's go up to the second floor and start pitching some slabs!

The objective of the next procedure is to add points in the surface of the slab in order to pitch to a drain:

1. In the Project Browser, double-click on the Level 2 floor plan (make sure you aren't in the Level 2 ceiling plan).

2. Zoom in on the lavatory areas, as shown in Figure 6.45.

3. Select the floor.

PICKING FLOORS CAN BE PICKY

Selecting the floor can always throw people! As you'll recall, to select the floor you literally have to pick a window around multiple items, then isolate the slab in the Filter dialog. This will still be your process here. Whenever the book says to "select" an item, use all of the selection methods you have gained experience with in the previous procedures and chapters.

4. Now that the floor is selected, notice on the Modify Floors tab that you have the choices shown in Figure 6.45. Click the button Add Split Line (see Figure 6.45).

5. Draw lines along the finished inside face of the lavatory, as shown in Figure 6.45. As always, there can be no gaps or overlaps.

N O T E   Yes, it is true that the snapping feature is tedious at best when you're using the Add Ridges and Valleys command. Be patient. You will need to basically get as close to the face of the wall as possible before you pick the point. This is one case where you will need to eyeball the exact pick points.

F I G U R E   6 . 4 5   Draw a split frame around the inside of the lavatory, as shown here.

With the split lines drawn, you have isolated the lavatory area from the rest of the floor. This will enable you to pitch the floor in this area without affecting the rest of the floor. The pitch will only extend as far as the split lines.

To create a drop in the floor, follow these steps:

1. On the Home tab, select the Model Lines button, as shown in Figure 6.46.

2. Draw the line from the midpoint of the restroom's right wall, to the left 3'–0", as shown in Figure 6.46.

FIGURE 6.46 Draw a line to establish the point where the floor will slope to.

3. Press Esc.

4. Select the floor. (Remember the filter.)

5. On the Modify Floors tab, select the Add Point button, as shown in Figure 6.47.

6. Pick the endpoint of the line you just drew, as shown in Figure 6.47.

7. Press Esc once. This will put you in the Modify Sub elements mode. You will know you are in this mode by the icon next to your pointer, as shown in Figure 6.48.

FIGURE 6.47 Pick the endpoint of the line.

---

8. Pick the point you just placed into the model. It will turn red, and a blue elevation will appear. As you know, any blue item is modifiable. Click the 0'–0" value, and change it to –1" (minus one inch).

9. Press Enter. Revit will drop that area of the floor and add the slope lines as if you drafted them in.

10. Press Esc twice.

11. Delete the line you drew as a guideline.

12. Save the model.
    See Figure 6.49. Does your floor look like this? If not, go back and see where you went wrong.

13. Repeat the steps to add a pitch to the lavatory north of the corridor.

14. Save the model (see Figure 6.50).

FIGURE 6.48 Dropping the elevation of the drain down 1" from the surface of the floor

FIGURE 6.49 The final slab in the restroom

Now that you have experience in creating and placing floors, as well as being able to pitch a floor in a specific area, it is time to look at one more item: shaft openings.

CAN I ERASE THIS AND START OVER?

There often will be times where you just need to clear the entire slab and start again. You can do this simply by selecting the floor and clicking the Reset Shape button on the Options bar, as shown here.

FIGURE 6.50 Both lavatories are now pitched and ready to have fixtures added to them.

Creating Shaft Openings

To create a shaft opening, all you are doing is creating a void through your model. This void, however, can conform to walls that are set in the model. The elevator shaft walls, for instance, will define the outside edge of our shaft opening. You may notice that the floors we added to the model are indiscriminately running uninterrupted straight through the shafts. We need to void the floor. Also, the good thing about creating a shaft opening is that if another floor is created, it will be cut out of the shaft automatically.

To get started, open the file you have been following along with. If you did not complete the previous procedure, go to the book's web page at **www.sybex.com/go/revit2010ner**. From there you can browse to Chapter 6 and find the file called NER-21.rvt.

The first thing we need to do is to create two more levels. We need a subterranean level (T.O. Footing) and a penthouse level to extend the elevator shaft up through:

1. In the Project Browser, go to the South Elevation.

2. On the Datum panel of the Home tab, click the Level button.

3. On the Draw panel, select the Pick Lines button, and set an offset of 10'–0".

4. Hover your cursor over Level 1. Make sure the alignment line is below Level 1. Once you see the alignment line, pick Level 1. You now have a new level at –10'–0".

5. Click the Modify button on the Design bar to terminate the command.

6. Pick the level that is set to –10'–0" and rename it to **T.O. Footing**.

7. Click Yes when Revit prompts you to rename corresponding views (see Figure 6.51).

> To select all of the CMU walls, you can simply select only one, right-click, and click Select All Instances. Be careful, though; if there are other CMU walls of the same type in the model, they will become selected as well.

The next step is to select the CMU elevator shaft walls and modify their properties so that the bottoms are extended down to the top of the footing and the tops are extended to the penthouse level:

1. Go to a 3D view.

2. Select all of the CMU walls. Remember to press and hold the Ctrl key as you are selecting the walls.

3. Once you have all of the CMU walls selected, click the Element Properties button on the Modify Walls tab.

4. Under the Instance Parameters, set Base Constraint to T.O. Footing, as shown in Figure 6.52.

5. Click OK.

FIGURE 6.51 Adding a new Top of Footing level

FIGURE 6.52 Click Element Properties, and then change the base to T.O. Footing.

With the bottom established at the correct level, it is time to add the shaft:

1. Go to the Level 1 floor plan (note that it does not matter which floor you are actually in when you place a shaft opening).

2. On the Modify tab, click the Opening ➤ Shaft Opening button as shown in Figure 6.53.

FIGURE 6.53 Select the Shaft opening command from the Modeling tab on the Design bar.

3. On the Create Shaft Opening Sketch tab, click Pick Walls, as shown in Figure 6.54.

FIGURE 6.54 Adding the magenta lines to form the shaft opening to the outside of the CMU walls

4. Pick the walls shown in Figure 6.54. Notice that you can have more than one shaft opening in the same command.

5. Use the Lines button on the Sketch bar to draw the line across the inside face of the exterior wall.

6. Use the Trim command to clean up any corners (see Figure 6.54).

Now that the perimeter has been established, it is time to establish which floors this opening will extend to. Just because we picked the CMU walls, this does not mean that a base and a top height have been established.

1. On the Create Shaft Opening Sketch tab, click the Properties button, as shown in Figure 6.55.

2. Set the Top Offset to –1'-0" (this keeps the roof from having two giant square holes in it).

3. Set Base Constraint to T.O. Footing.

4. Set Top Constraint to Up to Level: Roof.

5. Click OK. Figure 6.55 shows the settings.

FIGURE 6.55 Setting the properties of the shaft opening

6. On the Create Shaft Opening Sketch tab, click the Symbolic Lines button. This will allow you to sketch an opening graphic into the shaft.

7. Draw an "X" in both openings, as shown in Figure 6.56.

FIGURE 6.56 You can add any "drafting" symbolic lines you deem necessary.

8. Click Finish Opening.

Notice the floor is now voided from the openings. Go to a 3D view and look down the shafts. They are wide open, as shown in Figure 6.57.

 N O T E   A shaft opening will only void floors and roofs. Any other geometry such as walls and structural framing will not be voided. You need to modify these elements on a piece-by-piece basis.

Now that you know how to pitch floors, you can begin using Revit for its unique capabilities. Also, you are going to be better prepared to move into the next chapter, which focuses on creating roofs.

FIGURE 6.57 The completed shafts as seen in 3D

Are You Experienced?

Now You Can...

- ☑ add a floor to your model by using the building's footprint as a guide by picking the walls and by drawing lines

- ☑ add additional floors to higher levels by using the Copy/Paste Aligned method of quickly repeating the geometry up through the building

- ☑ add a specific, alternate material to different parts of the floor by using the Split Face command in conjunction with the paint materials function

- ☑ split a floor into segments, and add additional points in which to set a negative elevation to allow for pitching to floor drains

- ☑ create a shaft opening that will cut out any new floor slab. You also can use symbolic lines within the opening to indicate that there is an opening within the shaft

Roofs

Roofs come in all shapes and sizes. Given the nature of roofs, there is a lot to think about when you are placing a roof onto your building. If it is a flat roof, pitch is definitely a consideration. Drainage to roof drains or scuppers is another consideration as well. But how about pitched roofs? Now we are in an entirely new realm of options, pitches, slopes, and everything else you can throw at a roof design. Also, there are always dormers that no pitched roof can live without! Do the dormers align with the eaves, or are they set back from the building?

This book can't address every situation you are going to run into with a roof system, but it will expose you to the tools needed to tackle these situations yourself. The techniques we will be employing in this chapter will start with the concept of adding a roof to the model by using the actual floor plan footprint. As with floors, we will also be building the roof's composition for use in schedules, quantities, and material takeoffs.

Placing Roofs by Footprint

The command you'll probably use most often when working with roofs is the one to place a roof by footprint. Essentially, we will be creating a roof by using the outline of the building in plan view. There are three roof types you can place by using a footprint:

▶ You can place a flat roof (okay, no roof is actually flat, but you get the point).

▶ You can place a gable roof where two sides are sloped and the ends are left open.

▶ You can place a hip roof where all sides are sloped.

The reason these are the only options while placing a roof by footprint is because you are looking at the roof in plan, which limits your ability to place a roof with non-uniform geometry. Later in the book, we will explore doing just that, but for now let's start with placing a flat roof using the footprint of the west wing.

Flat Roofs by Footprint

To begin, open the file you have been following along with. If you did not complete the previous chapter, go to the book's web page at **www.sybex.com/go/revit2010ner**. From there you can browse to Chapter 7 and find the file called NER-22.rvt.

The objective of this procedure is to create a flat roof by outlining the building's geometry in the plan:

1. In the Project Browser, double-click on the Roof view in the Floor Plans section (be careful not to click on Roof in the Ceiling plans).

2. Zoom in to the west wing.

3. Type VP to access the View Properties dialog.

4. Find the Underlay row, and select None from the menu, as shown in Figure 7.1.

FIGURE 7.1 Changing the view's underlay to None

5. Click OK.

6. On the Home tab, click Roof ➤ Roof by Footprint, as shown in Figure 7.2.

7. On the Create Roof Footprint tab, be sure the Pick Walls button on the Draw panel is checked, as shown in Figure 7.3.

8. On the Options bar, uncheck Defines Slope, as shown in Figure 7.3.

FIGURE 7.2 Clicking Roof by Footprint on the Basics tab of the Design bar

9. In the Options bar, make sure the overhang is set to 0.

10. Uncheck Extend into Wall Core (if it is checked).

11. Hover your pointer over the leftmost vertical wall. Notice it highlights. Once you see the wall highlight, press the Tab key on your keyboard. Notice that all the perimeter walls highlight. Once they do, pick (left-click) anywhere along the wall. This will place a magenta sketch line at the perimeter of the building (see Figure 7.3).

FIGURE 7.3 Adding a sketch line to the perimeter of the building by highlighting one wall and pressing Tab

12. On the Create Roof Footprint tab, click Finish Roof.

13. Go to a 3D view, as shown in Figure 7.4.

FIGURE 7.4 The roof has been added. We still have a lot of work to do, though.

With the roof added, step 1 is out of the way. Now we need to create a roof system. You will do this the same way you created your floor system in Chapter 6.

Creating a Flat Roof System

Although this system can be used for a pitched roof often enough, a flat roof system will slightly differ. In Revit Architecture, there are two ways to look at a roofing system. One way is to create it using all of the typical roof materials and to create a large space for the structural framing. This book recommends not doing that. Creating a roof using only the roofing components is necessary, but adding the structure will lead to conflicts when the actual structural model is linked with the architectural model. Also, it is hard for the architect to guess what the depth of the structural framing is going to be. In Revit, you want each component to be as literal and as true to the model as possible. The second way, as we are about to explore, is to build the roof in a literal sense — that is, create the roof as it would sit on the structural framing by others.

The objective of this procedure is to create a roof system by adding layers of materials:

1. Select the roof. (If you are having trouble selecting the roof, remember the Filter tool.)

2. On the Modify Roofs tab, click the Element Properties button.

3. Click Edit Type…

4. Click Duplicate…

5. Call the new roof system 4" **Insulated Concrete Roof**.

6. Click OK.

7. Click the Edit button in the Structure row.

8. Change the material of Structure 1 to Concrete - Cast-in-Place Lightweight Concrete. (You do this by clicking in the cell and by clicking the […] button. You can then select the material from the menu.)

9. Change the structure thickness to 4" (see Figure 7.5).

10. Insert a new layer above the core boundary. (You do this by clicking on the core boundary row, and clicking the Insert button below the Layers section, as shown in Figure 7.5.)

11. Change the function of the new layer to Thermal / Air layer [3].

12. Click in the Material cell.

13. Click the […] button to open the Materials dialog.

14. Select Insulation / Thermal Barriers - Rigid Insulation for the material.

15. Click OK.

16. Change the thickness to 4".

17. Click the Variable button. When we modify the roof, this insulation layer will warp, allowing us to specify roof drain locations.

18. Insert a new layer above the insulation.

19. Give it a function of Finish 1 [4].

20. Select Roofing - EPDM Membrane.

21. Click OK.

22. Change the thickness to ¼" (see Figure 7.5).

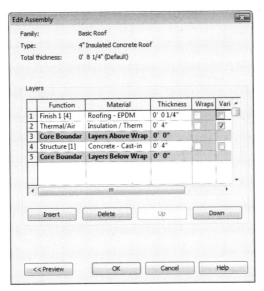

FIGURE 7.5 The complete roof system

TAKE A LOOK

It is always a good idea to keep the preview window open during the modification of the roof system. If you look toward the bottom of the Edit Assembly dialog, you will see a preview button, as shown in the following illustration. Click it, and you will be able to see the roof as it is being constructed.

23. Click OK twice.

24. Click OK again to get back to the model.

25. Press Esc.

Phew! That was a long procedure. It was worth it, though. You will be using this process a lot in Revit Architecture.

For the next procedure, we will add some roof drain locations, and then taper the insulation to drain to these locations.

Tapering a Flat Roof

If you went through the floor procedure in Chapter 6, you will see that the process is similar to pitching a floor. You may have also noticed that creating a roof system is identical to creating a floor system.

To taper the roof insulation, you must first divide the roof into peaks and valleys, and then specify the drain locations based on the centering of these locations:

1. In the Project Browser, make sure you are in the Roof floor plan.

2. Select the roof. (You may have to use the filter here.)

T I P   Even when you do successfully select the roof, you may not be able to tell. The roof doesn't seem to highlight. When you have the roof selected, the Options bar will show the modify icons. Also, look in the Type Selector — it should read Basic Roof : 4" Insulated Concrete Roof.

3. With the roof selected, select the "Create Split Lines" button shown in Figure 7.6.

4. Draw a line from the points shown in Figure 7.6.

5. Press Esc.

6. Select the roof.

T I P   One really nice thing about modifying the roof is now, to select the roof, all you need to do is pick one of the ridgelines and the roof is selected.

7. To activate the points in the roof, click the button in Figure 7.7. This will allow you to modify the points you have picked already.

FIGURE 7.6 Start splitting the radial portion of the roof.

FIGURE 7.7 Click the button shown here to activate the points in the subassembly of the roof.

8. Click the Add Point button, as shown in Figure 7.8.

9. Add two points at the midpoints shown in Figure 7.8.

10. Click the Add Split Line button and draw a ridge across the entire length of the building from point 1 to point 2, as shown in Figure 7.9.

11. Press Esc twice; then, on the Home tab, click Ref Plane ➤ Draw Ref plane, as shown in Figure 7.10.

12. Draw four reference planes spaced approximately the same as in Figure 7.10.

FIGURE 7.8 Adding two points

FIGURE 7.9 Draw a new ridge from the two points shown here.

13. On the Home tab, click the Aligned Dimension button.

FIGURE 7.10 Add a dimension string to the reference planes shown here.

14. Add a dimension string starting at the exterior wall to the left and ending at the exterior wall to the right, as shown in Figure 7.10.

15. Click the blue EQ icon. This will equally constrain the reference planes.

16. Press Esc to terminate the command.

17. Select the roof.

18. Click the Add Split Lines, as shown in Figure 7.11.

19. Draw four ridges at the intersections of the reference planes, as shown in Figure 7.11.

20. Press Esc

21. On the Annotate tab, click the Detail Lines button as shown in Figure 7.12.

22. Draw a diagonal line from the two points shown in Figure 7.12.

FIGURE 7.11 The ridges are in. All that is left is to create some points and start tapering the roof.

23. Press Esc, and then select the roof.

24. Pick the Add Point button

25. Pick the midpoint of the diagonal line.

26. Press Esc twice to clear the command.

27. Select the roof. Notice there is a node where you picked the point. To access the node, pick the Modify Sub Elements button on the Options bar, as shown in Figure 7.13.

28. Pick the point that you just added. Notice there is a blue elevation that shows up, as shown in Figure 7.14. Click the elevation, and type –3".

29. Press Esc twice.

FIGURE 7.12 Adding a temporary line, then picking a point to pitch the insulation to

FIGURE 7.13 Click the Modify Sub Elements button to gain access to the points on the roof.

FIGURE 7.14 Click the point to taper the roof to this point.

This will taper the insulation only in this bay, as shown in Figure 7.15. The objective now is to do the same thing for every bay. Since you cannot copy a point, you need to move the temporary line to the next bay and add a new point.

FIGURE 7.15 The tapers are in place.

Follow along to create another taper:

1. Move the diagonal line (that you drew as a reference) to the next bay to the right.

2. Select the slab.

3. Click Add Points.

4. Add a point to the midpoint of the line.

5. Type –3" in the blue elevation. The roof tapers.

6. Move the line to the next bay and repeat the process.

 N O T E   Remember as you are adding additional lines in this section that the book is merely recommending that you use the Move tool. At this point, you have enough experience to either draw the lines in or use any tool you have learned up to this point.

7. Complete every bay.

8. Add points to the radial area as well.

9. Your roof should look like Figure 7.16 when you have finished.

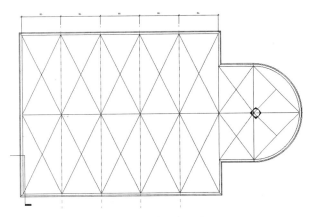

FIGURE 7.16 The completed roof

To further investigate how this roof is working, and to see what the benefits are to doing it this way rather than drafting the lines in, let's cut a section through the roof and see how the detail will look:

1. On the Basics tab of the Design bar, click the Section button.

2. Add a section through the roof, as shown in Figure 7.17.

FIGURE 7.17   Add a section through the roof at this point.

3. On the Options bar, click the Element Properties button.

4. Change View Scale to 3/4" = 1'–0".

5. Change the detail level to Fine.

6. Change the View Name option to Roof Taper Section (see Figure 7.18).

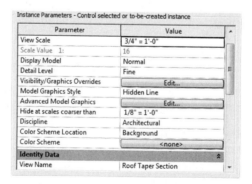

FIGURE 7.18   Changing the element properties of the section

7. Click OK.

8. Double-click on the section head (or you can find the section called Roof Taper Section in the Project Browser).

9. Adjust the crop region so you are only looking at the roof area, as shown in Figure 7.19.

FIGURE 7.19 By adding the points to the roof, you now have an almost perfect section.

THE PROOF IS IN THE ROOF!

This is a perfect example of why the Revit approach to design documentation is the way to go. Although the sloping of the slab may have seemed tedious, in reality it didn't take much longer than it would have if you had drafted those lines in a CAD application. But now, to produce a section, all you need to do is cut one. Also, if you change the location, or the depth of the roof pitch, your lines in plan will be accurate as well as your section.

This concludes modeling a flat roof. We can now move on to creating a pitched roof. Again, although these types of roofs can be easy to add in the beginning, there will be more work required to get them exactly the way you want them.

Pitched Roofs by Footprint

We'll add a pitched roof in an identical manner in which we added the flat roof. The only real difference is the fact that each magenta sketch line will require more attention before you finish the sketch. But, after what you have just been through with tapering the roof's insulation, this will be a cakewalk.

The area of the building where the pitched roof will occur will be over the corridor. The problem with the corridor is the fact that we used a wall system with a parapet cap. This is not the best wall system to receive a pitched roof. The first procedure will involve changing this to a simpler wall system:

1. Go to a 3D view of the model.

2. Select the six corridor walls, as shown in Figure 7.20.

FIGURE 7.20 Select these six walls to be modified.

3. On the Modify Walls tab, select the Element Properties button.

4. Click the Edit Type... button.

5. Click the Duplicate button.

6. Call the new wall system **Exterior - Brick and CMU on MTL. Stud (No Parapet)**.

7. In the Structure row, click the Edit button.

8. In the Edit Assembly dialog, make sure the Preview button has been checked, as shown in Figure 7.21.

9. Click the Sweeps button, as shown in Figure 7.21.

10. In the Sweeps dialog, you will see there are three sweeps to deal with. The top sweep is the parapet cap. Select the Sweep #1 (parapet cap), and click the Delete button, as shown in Figure 7.22.

11. Click OK three times.

12. Click OK one more time to get back to the model.

Your corridor walls should look exactly the same but are now void of the concrete parapet cap.

FIGURE 7.21 Without the preview checked on, you will not be able to modify the parapet sweep.

Remember, your preview will need to be in Section : Modify Type for all of the buttons to be active.

FIGURE 7.22 Deleting the parapet cap sweep

NOTE Although you have pretty good experience with walls up to this point, Chapter 16, "Advanced Wall Topics," is dedicated to the advanced concepts and creation of wall systems.

It's now time to add the roof to the corridor. Since the walls that our roof is going to bear on are now correct, the rest is going to be a snap!

1. Go to the Level 3 floor plan. (This is the roof level for our corridor.)

2. On the Home tab, select Roof ➤ By Footprint.

3. On the Draw panel, make sure the Pick Walls button is selected.

4. On the Options bar, make sure the Defines Slope button is checked, as shown in Figure 7.23.

5. Type 1'–0" in the Overhang field.

6. Pick the six walls that comprise the corridor, as shown in Figure 7.23.

FIGURE 7.23 Pick these walls for the roof's footprint.

With the "easy" walls out of the way, it is now time to create the gable ends. You should still be in the Pick Walls mode. This is okay, but there are a couple things you need to change on the Options bar:

1. Click the Boundary Lines button on the Draw Panel, as shown in Figure 7.24.

2. On the Draw panel again, click the Pick Lines button.

As you are picking the walls, notice that you now have an overhang. This overhang obviously needs to extend to the outside of the walls. Just be conscious of this as you are picking the walls and watch your alignment lines as you proceed.

3. On the Options bar, uncheck Defines Slope.

4. For the offset, enter 0 (see Figure 7.24).

5. Pick the west wall on the east wing, as shown in Figure 7.24.

FIGURE 7.24 You must pick lines to trace the terminating walls of the roof.

It's cleanup time! Of course the magenta lines are overlapping at the long walls. This is okay — you are an expert at the Trim command by now, especially in Sketch mode:

1. On the Tools toolbar, select the Trim command, as shown in Figure 7.25.

2. On the Options bar, select the Corner Trim button.

3. Trim the intersections that overlap. There are going to be four of them (see Figure 7.25).

4. On the Finish Roof Sketch, click Finish Roof.

FIGURE 7.25 Use the Trim command in conjunction with the roof sketch.

One ugly roof, huh? Welcome to the world of pitched roofs in Revit. We will get the roof we want — it is just going to take having to add two roofs here. You will get this, but it is going to involve patience and trial and error!

To fix this roof, you simply have to make two separate roofs and join them together. This is going to be a common procedure for the more complicated roof systems in Revit.

1. Select the roof.

2. On the Modify Roofs tab, click the Edit Footprint button, as shown in Figure 7.26.

FIGURE 7.26 Select the roof and click the Edit Footprint button.

3. Delete every line, other than the three shown in Figure 7.27.

FIGURE 7.27 Keep these three lines.

4. On the Draw panel, click the Lines button.

5. Draw a diagonal line from the endpoints of the two lines, as shown in Figure 7.28.

FIGURE 7.28 Draw a diagonal line as shown.

6. On the Modify Roofs ➤ Edit Footprint tab, click Finish Roof.

7. The roof will display. It still looks funny, but we will take care of that by altering the view range.

8. Start the Roof ➤ Roof by Footprint command again on the Home tab.

9. On your own, sketch the roof shown in Figure 7.29. Make sure the lines along the walls are defining a slope. The lines that represent the ends of the roof do not slope.

10. To add the line that matches the roof to the right, make sure you have the Boundary Line button selected on the Draw panel and that you have Pick Lines selected as well. Now, simply pick the roof to the right, and the line will appear.

11. Review Figure 7.29 to see if your sketch matches. You should have six lines total, and the right and the left ends should not have a slope.

If you accidentally added a line with (or without) a slope, that's fine. You can change it. First, press Esc (to clear the command), and then select the line that needs to be changed. On the Options bar, you can check (or uncheck) Define Slope.

FIGURE 7.29 The new outline of the second roof

12. On the Modify Roofs ➤ Edit Footprint tab, click Finish Roof.

13. Go to a 3D view. Does your roof look like Figure 7.30?

FIGURE 7.30 The corridor roof in 3D

The walls need some help! They are indiscriminately poking up through the roof. You can change this, but it is going to take some wall cleanup. The first thing you need to do is force the walls to have a mitered join at the 45° intersections. The following procedure will show you how:

1. Go to the Level 1 floor plan.

2. Zoom into the wall intersection, as shown in Figure 7.31.

3. On the Modify tab, click the Wall Joins button, as shown in Figure 7.31.

4. Move your cursor over the intersection. You will see a box form around the corner. Once you see this box, pick the wall.

5. On the Options bar, click the Mitered radio button, as shown in Figure 7.31. Notice the walls are now joined at a miter.

6. Perform this procedure at all four corners.

When you have suc-
cessfully mitered a
corner and are ready
to move to the next,
there is nothing indi-
cating that you can
safely pick another
corner. You do not
need it. Once you
see that the walls
are at a miter, you
can pick the next
intersection. When
you have finished all
four, just press Esc.

FIGURE 7.31 Modifying the wall's corners

You can now attach the tops of the walls to the bottom of the roof:

1. Go back to a 3D view and select one of the corridor walls.

2. On the Options bar, notice there is an option to attach the Top/Base of the wall, as shown in Figure 7.32. Click the Attach button.

You don't always
have to modify the
wall's mitering. This
is a special situation
where the corners
will not attach to the
roofs properly unless
you do so.

FIGURE 7.32 Attaching the top or the base

3. Pick the roof that the wall is under. You will see that the wall no longer sticks up past the roof.

4. Do steps 1 through 3 for each corridor wall. When you are finished, your corridor should be spanking nice, like Figure 7.33.

FIGURE 7.33 The completed corridor roof

BUT I GOT THIS WARNING!

Sometimes Revit does not like your "hacking" up its perfectly fine walls. The warning shown here is a very common one and has no effect on the model. You can just ignore it.

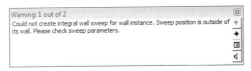

Viewing a Sloped Roof in Plan

Back in Level 3 (the level in which the corridor roof resides), we are having a view problem: the roof is only showing up to the cut plane for that level. This just cannot be. There is a procedure to correct this called a *plan region*:

1. Go to the Level 3 floor plan.

2. On the view tab, click the Plan region button, as shown in Figure 7.34.

FIGURE 7.34 Using a plan region allows you to alter the view range in a specified area of a plan.

3. On the Draw panel, select the Rectangle button, as shown in Figure 7.35.

4. Draw a rectangle around the corridor, as shown in Figure 7.35. Be sure to snap to the exact points where the corridor walls meet the taller walls on the east and west wings.

FIGURE 7.35 Creating the four lines that form the perimeter of the plan region

5. On the Sketch bar, click the Region Properties button.

6. In the View Range row, click the Edit button.

7. In the View Range dialog, set the upper limit to Unlimited and the cut plane to 35'–0", as shown in Figure 7.36.

FIGURE 7.36 Setting the view range for the plan region

8. Click OK twice.

9. On the Sketch bar, click Finish Sketch.

10. You can now see the roof in its entirety, as shown in Figure 7.37.

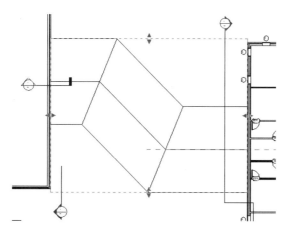

FIGURE 7.37 The finished roof plan

There is one more kind of roof to add. It will be a flat roof that has a slope in one single direction. Although you can do this with simply creating a roof with one edge specified as a pitch, there will be times where you will want a roof sloped at an odd direction that can't be handled by simply angling a roof edge.

Creating a Sloping Roof

To begin, we are going to be capping off the east wing of our building. The exterior walls being used for the perimeter need to be altered. You are already a pro at this, so let's start right there:

1. Go to a 3D view.

2. Select the east wing exterior walls, as shown in Figure 7.38.

3. On the Options bar, click the Type Selector drop-down and select Exterior - Brick and CMU on MTL. Stud (No Parapet). See Figure 7.38.

FIGURE 7.38 Changing the walls to Exterior - Brick and CMU on MTL. Stud (No Parapet)

4. In the Project Browser, go to the East Roof floor plan.

5. On the Home tab, select Roof ➤ Roof by Footprint.

6. On the Draw panel, select the Pick Walls button.

7. On the Options bar, uncheck Defines Slope.

8. Type 1'–0" for the Overhang value.

9. Move your cursor over a wall. Make sure the overhang alignment line is facing outside of the walls to the exterior.

10. Press the Tab Key on your keyboard. All of the walls will be selected.

11. Pick the wall. The magenta lines are completely drawn in. Your sketch should look like Figure 7.39.

FIGURE 7.39 The perimeter of the roof is set.

Now it is time to set the slope. The objective here is to slope the roof starting at the northwest corner (as the low point) and ending at the southeast corner (the high point). This is done by adding a slope arrow:

1. On the Draw panel, select the Slope Arrow button, as shown in Figure 7.40.

FIGURE 7.40 Click the Slope arrow button on the Sketch bar,

2. Pick the two points shown in Figure 7.41, starting with the upper right and ending with the lower-left corner.

3. Press Esc.

4. Select the slope arrow you just added to the model.

FIGURE 7.41 Adding the slope arrow

5. On the Draw panel, click the Properties button.

6. In the Properties dialog, under Constraints change Specify to Slope.

7. Under Dimensions, change the slope to 3" / 12" (see Figure 7.42).

8. Click OK.

9. Click Finish Roof on the Modify Roofs ➢ Edit Footprints tab.

Again, we have a view range issue. You can only see the corner of the roof that sits below the cut plane. You can change that with the view range:

1. Type VP to open the View Properties dialog.

2. Scroll down the list until you arrive at the View Range row. Once you do, click the Edit button.

3. In the View Range dialog, under Primary Range set Top to Unlimited.

4. Set the cut plane increment to 40'–0" (see Figure 7.43).

FIGURE 7.42 Changing the slope arrow properties

FIGURE 7.43 Setting the view range

5. Click OK twice. You can now see the entire roof.

6. Go to a 3D view. You now have a cool, sloping roof, as shown in Figure 7.44.

FIGURE 7.44 The sloping roof

Of course there is a wall issue. You can attach most of the walls to the roof simply by selecting them and attaching the tops. You will, however, have to modify the profile for one wall:

1. In the 3D view, select all of the exterior east wing walls, excluding the one on the west side that is south of the corridor (you can see it in Figure 7.45).

2. On the Modify walls tab, select Attach.

3. Pick Top from Options bar (it is all the way to the left).

4. Pick the sloping roof (see Figure 7.45).

5. In the Project Browser, go to the section called East Corridor Section.

6. Select the wall that does not attach to the roof.

7. On the Options bar, click Edit Profile.

8. Trace the roof. Be sure you delete the magenta line that established the top of the wall.

9. On the Sketch toolbar, click Finish Sketch. You now have all of the walls joined to the roof.

10. Save the model.

FIGURE 7.45 Attaching the tops of the walls to the sloping roof

The next item to tackle will be creating a roof by extrusion. This is where you can really design a custom roof.

Roofs by Extrusion

Creating a roof by extrusion is almost always done in an elevation or a section view. The concept here is to create unique geometry that cannot be accomplished by simply using a footprint in plan. A barrel vault or an eyebrow dormer comes to mind, but there are literally thousands of combinations that will influence how our roofs are going to be designed.

To get started, the last roof left to be placed is the south jog in the east wing of the model. This is the perfect area for a funky roof!

The first thing to do is to change the three walls defining the jog to the Exterior - Brick and CMU on MTL. Stud (No Parapet) wall type we have been switching our walls to:

1. Go to a 3D view.

2. Select the three walls that comprise the jog in the south wall, as shown in Figure 7.46.

3. From the Change Element Type menu on the Modify walls tab, switch these walls to Exterior - Brick and CMU on MTL. Stud (No Parapet), as shown in Figure 7.46.

FIGURE 7.46 Changing the wall types as we have been doing all along

Once you place the elevation, you will have no idea where the view is extended to. Is it to the end of the building? You just don't know. If you pick the elevation arrow (the part of the elevation marker), you can then grip-edit the elevation to see what you need.

▶

4. Go to the Level 1 floor plan.

5. On the View tab, select the Elevation button.

6. On the Element panel, be sure the elevation is an Exterior elevation (you are given the choice in the Change Element Type menu).

7. Place the elevation as shown in Figure 7.47.

8. Pick the view extents (the blue grips at the ends of the elevation), and drag them in so you can only see the east wing.

9. Make sure you pull the view depth window back to see the wall beyond (see Figure 7.47).

10. With the elevation still selected, click the Element Properties button on the Modify Views tab.

11. Change the scale to $\frac{1}{2}$" = 1'–0".

12. Change the detail level to Fine.

13. Change the view name to **South Entry Elevation**.

14. Click OK.

15. On the Home tab, select the Ref Plane ➢ Pick Existing Line / Edge button.

FIGURE 7.47 Adjusting the view

17. Set the Offset to 1'–6".

18. Pick the south-most wall, and offset the reference plane away from the building (see Figure 7.48).

FIGURE 7.48 Adding a reference plane

19. Press Esc twice to clear the command.

20. Select the reference plane.

21. On the Modify Reference Planes Tab, click the Element Properties button.

22. In the Element Properties dialog, change the name to **South Entry Overhang**.

23. Click OK.

24. Open the elevation called South Entry Elevation.

The importance of that reference plane you just added becomes obvious at this point. You needed to establish a clear starting point for the roof you are about to add. Since the roof is going to be added in an elevation, Revit does not know where to start the extrusion. This reference plane will serve as that starting point.

1. On the Home tab, select the Roof ➢ Roof by Extrusion command, as shown in Figure 7.49.

FIGURE 7.49 The Roof ➢ Roof by Extrusion command

2. Once you start the command, Revit will ask you to specify a reference plane. Select Reference Plane: South Entry Overhang from the Name drop-down list, as shown in Figure 7.50.

3. Click OK.

4. In the next dialog, change the Level setting to Level 3, and click OK.

5. In the Home tab, select Ref Plane ➢ Draw Reference Plane, as shown in Figure 7.51

FIGURE 7.50 Selecting the South Entry Overhang reference plane

---

6. Offset a reference plane 3'–0" to the left and to the right of the exterior walls, as shown in Figure 7.51.

7. Offset a reference plane 4'–0" up from the top of the wall, as shown in Figure 7.51.

FIGURE 7.51 Adding reference planes to use as construction lines

8. On the Sketch bar, click the Properties button.

9. In the Create Extrusion Roof Profile tab, click the Roof Properties dialog, then click Edit Type…

10. Click Duplicate.

11. Call it **Canopy Roof**.

> While you are in Sketch mode, when I tell you to click the Properties button, you need to click the Properties button on the *Sketch* bar, not on the *Options* bar. They are two different properties.

12. Click the Edit button in the Structure row.

13. In the Edit Assembly dialog, change the structure thickness to 4", as shown in Figure 7.52.

FIGURE 7.52 Changing the thickness of the canopy roof

14. Click OK twice.

15. Click OK one more time to get back to the model.

Now it's time to put the actual roof into the model. So far we have been using great discipline in terms of setting reference planes and creating a separate roof for this canopy. Try to make this a habit!

1. On the Draw panel, click the Start-End-Midpoint Arc button, as shown in Figure 7.53.

2. Draw an arc from the points shown in the image.

TIP When you are adding a roof by extrusion, you only need to draw one line. The 4" thickness is defined in the actual roof you are using. Once you click Finish Sketch, the 4" thickness will be added to the bottom.

FIGURE 7.53 Drawing an arc, which will define the outside face of the roof

3. Click the Roof Properties button.

4. Set the Extrusion End to be –2'–0", as shown in Figure 7.54.

FIGURE 7.54 Setting the extrusion end

5. Click OK.

6. Click Finish Roof

7. Go to a 3D view. Your roof should look like Figure 7.55.

FIGURE 7.55 The almost completed canopy roof

There is just one thing left to do — and it is pretty obvious: we need to attach the roof to the wall. This can be done in one command:

1. On the Modify tab, click the Join/Unjoin roof button, as shown in Figure 7.56.

2. Pick the top, back arc on the canopy roof, as shown in Figure 7.56.

3. Pick the wall that the roof needs to terminate into (see Figure 7.56).

Picking the wall is easier said than done, mostly because it is hard to tell whether you are picking the correct wall. Simply hover your pointer over the wall until the entire face become highlighted. Once you see this, pick the wall. The roof will then extend to the wall.

FIGURE 7.56 Picking the roof and the wall to join the two together

4. Your roof should look like Figure 7.57. Select the three walls below the roof.

FIGURE 7.57 The now completed canopy

5. On the Options bar, click the Attach button.

6. Select the canopy roof.

The walls are now joined to the roof, as shown in Figure 7.58.

FIGURE 7.58 The walls are now attached to the roof.

All of the conventional roofing systems have been added. It is now time to move on to adding some dormers. This will simply be a collection of the tools you have gained experience with up to this point.

Adding a Roof Dormer

The best way to add a roof dormer is to modify an existing roof. We certainly have plenty of those in this model, so there should be no shortage of roof surfaces we can use to chop up into dormers.

To begin adding a roof dormer, follow along:

1. Go to the Level 3 floor plan.

2. Zoom in on the corridor roof.

3. Select the corridor roof, as shown in Figure 7.59.

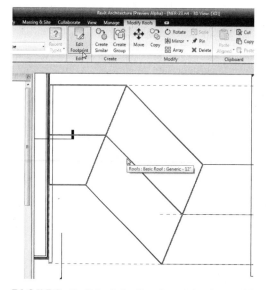

FIGURE 7.59 Selecting the roof to be modified

4. On the Modify Roofs tab, click the Edit Footprint button.

You are now in the Sketch mode for this roof.

It is time to start modifying this roof. This procedure is reminiscent of climbing up on an actual roof and adding a dormer:

1. On the Tools toolbar, select the Split button, as shown in Figure 7.60.

2. On the Options bar, uncheck Delete Inner Segment.

3. Pick two points on the roof edge, as shown in Figure 7.60. The two points are an even 4'–0" in from each edge.

4. Press Esc twice.

FIGURE 7.60 Splitting the line into three pieces

5. Select the middle line.

6. On the Options bar, uncheck Defines Slope.

Now that the length of the dormer has been established, you need to indicate to Revit that you want it to be a gable end dormer. You do this by adding slope arrows:

1. On the Draw panel, click the Slope Arrow button.

2. For the first point of the slope arrow, click the intersection of the first point you split (#1 in Figure 7.60).

3. For the second point of the slope arrow, pick the midpoint of the middle line (see Figure 7.61).

4. Add a second slope arrow coming from the opposite side of the ridgeline, as shown in Figure 7.62.

5. Press Esc twice.

FIGURE 7.61 Adding the first slope arrow

FIGURE 7.62 Adding a second slope arrow

6. Select both slope arrows.

7. On the Options bar, click the Element Properties button.

8. Under Constraints, change Specify to Slope.

9. Under Dimensions, keep the slope at 9" / 12" (see Figure 7.63).

10. Click OK.

11. Click Finish Roof.

12. Go to a 3D view to check out the dormer. It should look identical to Figure 7.64.

Parameter	Value
Constraints	
Specify	Slope
Level at Tail	Default
Height Offset at Tail	0' 0"
Level at Head	Default
Height Offset at Head	10' 0"
Dimensions	
Slope	9" / 12"
Length	13' 10 139/256"

Instance Parameters - Control selected or to-be-created instance

FIGURE 7.63 Changing the values of the slope arrows

Adding roof dormers takes some practice to become efficient. If you do not feel confident that you can do a roof dormer on your own, feel free to either go back through the procedure or find another place in the building to add a second dormer.

FIGURE 7.64 The completed roof dormer

NOTE Notice in the 3D view that the wall followed the modification in the roof. This is because you attached the wall to the roof back when you added the roof to the corridor. The walls have no choice but to comply!

Are You Experienced?

Now You Can...

☑ place different types of roofs, including flat roofs, pitched roofs, and unconventional, sloping roofs, using the footprint of your building

☑ analyze tricky areas, and make multiple roofs if needed instead of relying on a single roof to flex and conform to the situation at hand

☑ edit wall joins to allow walls to attach to roofs after they are created

☑ design different roof systems based on their functionality

☑ create a tapered roof plan using a variable material in the roof system

☑ create a roof by extrusion by setting work planes and using them to lay out a custom roof

☑ create a roof dormer by editing an existing roof and adding slope arrows to indicate a gable end

CHAPTER 8

Structural Items

- ▶ Adding structural grids
- ▶ Creating structural framing
- ▶ Creating structural foundations
- ▶ Understanding structural views

Well, we can't avoid this topic forever. Since we need to consider our structure from pretty much the beginning of the project, I had better add it to the first half of the book before we get too carried away!

Also, since Revit has entire books on this subject alone, this book will address only the structural items available to people using Revit Architecture. If you are a structural engineer or structural designer, it is recommended that you use Revit Structure. It is an application that is just as powerful as Revit Architecture, only it is geared toward structural engineering.

Now, that being said, the two applications share the same file extension (.rvt) and can be opened and modified directly from one application to the other with absolutely no issues.

This chapter will delve into the structural world using the functions available that have been blended in with the architectural tools.

The first item we are going to tackle is usually the first item in the model: structural grids. Although structural grids are added line by line, you will soon discover that these grids are just as "smart" as the rest of Revit.

Structural Grids

The starting point for "all things structural" is most certainly the grid. In Revit Architecture, you will find quickly that placing a structural grid into a model is not a complicated task. Grids are essentially placed one line at a time. Those lines you are placing, however, have intelligence. For example, if you place a vertical grid line called "A" and then place a horizontal grid line called "1" that intersects with A, you will have a grid location. If you place a column at that intersection, the column will assume a new property called Location. That location is … you guessed it: A1.

Let's get started. To begin, open the file you have been following along with. If you did not complete the previous chapter, go to the book's web page at **www.sybex.com/go/revit2010ner**. From there you can browse to Chapter 8 and find the file called NER-23.rvt.

Placing a Grid

Placing a grid means drawing grid lines in one by one. This task sounds tedious, but it is a welcome change from other applications that force you to create an entire, rectangular grid that you have to keep picking at until it resembles your layout. Grids are like snowflakes: no two are the same.

1. In the Project Browser, go to the Level 1 floor plan. (Make sure you aren't in the Level 1 ceiling plan.)

2. Zoom in to the west wing's radial entry.

3. On the Datum panel of the Home tab, click the Grid button, as shown in Figure 8.1.

FIGURE 8.1 Click the Grid button on the Datum panel of the Home tab.

4. On the Draw panel of the Place Grid tab, click the Pick Lines button, as shown in Figure 8.2.

5. Pick the core center line of the north wall, as shown in Figure 8.2.

FIGURE 8.2 Your first column grid

6. The column bubble needs to be moved. Press Esc (to clear the command), and select the column line. Notice the round blue grip, similar to Figure 8.3.

7. Pick that big blue grip, and drag the column bubble to the right about 15'–0", as shown in Figure 8.4.

8. On the Home tab, select the Grid button again.

FIGURE 8.3 Examine the column grid grips.

Notice these are the
same levels: a col-
umn grid has similar
functionality to lev-
els, right down to
the grips.

FIGURE 8.4 Dragging the column bubble to the right

9. On the Draw panel, select the Pick Lines button.

10. Pick the core center line of the 6⅛" wall that terminates at the exterior wall, as shown in Figure 8.5.

11. Drag the right end of the line to align with grid 1. Once you move
your line to the length of grid 1, pick the second point. An alignment
line will appear.

TIP   Alignment lines, however useful, can be tricky to get to display.
The percentage of your zoom has an effect. If you are not getting the alignment lines, simply zoom back (or in) a small amount and they will appear.

12. On the right side of grid 2, there is a blue box. Pick it. It will turn the
grid head on.

13. On the left side of grid 2, you will see that there is a grid bubble. You
will also see the same blue checkbox. Click the checkbox to turn the
grid head off at this location.

FIGURE 8.5 Adding the second grid line

14. Press Esc.

Being able to pick lines is certainly an advantage, but you are not always going to be in the situation where you have geometry in place to do so. In the following procedure, you will add grid 3 by picking two points:

1. Select the Grid button from the Home tab.

2. On the Draw panel, be sure the line icon is selected, as shown in Figure 8.6. (It will be by default.)

3. Pick a point along the center reference plane, as shown in Figure 8.6.

4. Pick a second point in alignment with grid 2 (see Figure 8.6).

FIGURE 8.6 Adding grid 3 at the center of the building

5. Add grids 4 and 5 to the exact opposite ends of the west wing (see Figure 8.7).

FIGURE 8.7 The completed horizontal grids

With grid lines, you can still copy, rotate, move, and mirror. Remember this when you are placing grids.

We need to add two more grids at 45° angles. This will be as easy as drawing lines. The objective here is to manipulate the grids to read the appropriate numbering.

1. On the Home tab, select the Grid button.

2. Pick the center of the radial wall, as shown in Figure 8.8.

3. Draw the line at a 45° angle until you are beyond the radial wall, as shown in Figure 8.8.

4. Rename the grid line to **2.1**.

5. Draw another gridline at a 45° angle in the opposite direction.

6. Renumber it to read **3.9**. See Figure 8.8.

N O T E   In many instances, you will encounter elevation markers and other annotation items that get in the way. You can move these items, but be careful. After you move an item, open the referring view to make sure you did not disturb anything.

FIGURE 8.8 Adding two additional grids and renumbering them

We are going to need two more horizontal column lines that span the length of the building. We will number these lines as **2.10** and **3.1**. The lines will run centered on the corridor walls. To do this, you will use the pick lines icon on the Draw panel.

1. On the Home tab, click the Grid button.

2. On the Draw panel, click the pick lines icon, as shown in Figure 8.9.

3. Pick the core center line of the north corridor wall, as shown in Figure 8.9.

4. Pick the blue grip at the end of the line and stretch it to align with the already placed bubbles, as shown in Figure 8.10.

5. Click the Show Bubble button.

6. Rename the grid to 2.10 (see Figure 8.10).

7. Zoom to the other end of the grid line and uncheck the bubble.

8. Repeat the process for the south corridor wall, adding an additional gridline numbered 3.1, as shown in Figure 8.11.

FIGURE 8.9 Adding a column line to the north corridor wall

FIGURE 8.10 Drag the line, and turn the bubble on so you can rename the grid to 2.10.

FIGURE 8.11 Adding the grids along the corridor walls

The grids are laying out okay, but it looks like some adjustments should be made to move the bubbles apart a little. You can do this by adding an elbow to the grid's end.

Adding Elbows

As with levels, you can add a "break" in the line of the grid, allowing you to make adjustments as if the grid was an arm with an elbow.

1. Select grid 2.10.

2. You will see several blue grips appear. Pick the one that appears as a break line, as shown in Figure 8.12.

FIGURE 8.12 Click the Add Elbow button after selecting the grid.

3. Once you pick this break line, it adds an elbow to your grid line, as shown in Figure 8.13.

N O T E   Notice that the bubble was broken, and it was moved up and out of the way. This will not always happen. In most cases, the grid will probably move in the wrong direction. You can then select the blue grips and move the bubble in the direction you intended.

4. Repeat the procedure for grid 3.1. Your grids should now look like Figure 8.13.

FIGURE 8.13 The cleaned-up grid bubbles

5. Save the model.

It is now time to add the vertical grids. This will be a simple process until we get to the radial entry area. At that point there will need to be some additional manipulating of the grid.

Adding Vertical Grids

The only real issue with starting to add the vertical grids is the numbering versus lettering issue. It is a problem because Revit will continue the sequencing from the horizontal grids. Make sure that, when you add your first grid, you renumber (or rename) the first occurrence of the grid.

The objective of the next procedure is to create a grid pattern running vertically across the view:

1. Zoom out so you can see the entire west wing, as shown in Figure 8.14.

2. On the Home tab, click the Grid button.

3. On the Draw panel of the Place Grid tab, click the pick lines icon, as shown in Figure 8.14.

4. Pick the core center line of the east exterior wall of the west wing, as shown in Figure 8.14.

FIGURE 8.14 Adding the first vertical grid by picking the core center line of the exterior wall

5. Once you pick the wall, the grid is added. It will not be the name or number you want. We will change that. But first, pick the round blue grip and drag the bubble up past the dimensions, as shown in Figure 8.15.

6. Press Esc.

7. Select the new vertical grid.

8. Click in the bubble and rename it to **A**, as shown in Figure 8.16.

FIGURE 8.15   Dragging the new bubble out of the wall

FIGURE 8.16   The grid is now named A.

It is now time to make duplications of this grid. Since you have an arsenal of modify commands under your belt, it becomes obvious that the best way to make duplications of this grid is to copy it, as shown in the following steps:

1. Select grid A.

2. On the Modify toolbar, select the Copy button, as shown in Figure 8.17.

3. On the Options bar, make sure the Multiple checkbox is selected, as shown in Figure 8.17.

4. Pick a base point along the grid line within the wall, as shown in Figure 8.17.

5. Copy grid A to the wall center lines, as shown in Figure 8.17. Notice that the gridlines will autonumber as you go.

FIGURE 8.17 Copying the grid line to the other walls

6. Press Esc.

7. Start the Grid command again.

8. On the Draw panel, be sure the Line icon is picked.

9. Pick a start point at the endpoint of the radial wall where it intersects with the straight wall, as shown in Figure 8.18.

10. Pick the second point in line with the adjacent grid bubbles (see Figure 8.18).

11. Pick the grip on the bottom of the line, and drag it down past the south part of the radial wall.

The next step is to add the grid to the radial entry area. This will not be as easy as simply picking a wall's center line. The trick here will be to establish a reference point to place the grid, and subsequently, a column.

FIGURE 8.18 Adding grid F

Adding a Radial Grid Line

Sometimes, you have to think out of the box. Literally. The radial west entry wing is just that. A box. Now that we have radial geometry to contend with, we need to add a radial grid, as follows:

1. Zoom in on the radial entry of the west wing.

2. Click the Grid button on the Home tab.

3. On the Draw panel, select the line icon, as shown in Figure 8.19.

4. Type in an offset of 6" (still on the Options bar).

5. Pick the finished inside face of the radial wall, as shown in Figure 8.19.

6. The actual grid bubble lands in a congested area. Fix this by adding an elbow and adjusting the bubbles, as shown in Figure 8.20.

I think you get the picture on adding grids. The next procedure is to start adding columns to these grid intersections. To do so, we will start exploring a brand-new tab on the Design bar called the Structural tab.

FIGURE 8.19 Adding a grid line offset from the finish inside face

FIGURE 8.20 Add a bubble to the radial grid line and make the adjustments shown here.

Adding Structural Columns

The hard part is over. Determining where to put the columns is harder than physically placing them in the model. But, of course there are rules to follow, and rules that need to be bent in order to accomplish the results we need to see.

This next series of procedures will include adding structural components into the model and placing framing systems in areas where a structural engineer may defer to the architect for structural integrity given their design intent.

To begin, open the file you have been following along with. If you did not complete the previous section, go to the book's web page at **www.sybex.com/go/revit2010ner**. From there you can browse to Chapter 8 and find the file called NER-24.rvt.

To add columns to the model, follow this procedure:

1. In the Project Browser, go to the Level 1 floor plan.

2. Zoom into the radial entry area in the west wing.

3. On the Home tab, click Column ➢ Structural Column, as shown in Figure 8.21.

FIGURE 8.21 The Structural Column button on the Structural tab of the Design bar

4. You will probably not have any structural columns loaded into the model. If you get the message shown in Figure 8.22, click Yes to browse for a structural column.

5. Browse to Imperial Library ➢ Structural ➢ Columns ➢ Steel.

6. In the Steel directory, browse to HSS-Hollow Structural Section-Column.rfa.

7. Double click on HSS-Hollow Structural Section-Column.rfa; you will get a dialog allowing you to select the type, as shown in Figure 8.23.

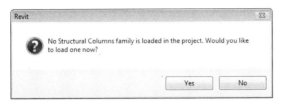

FIGURE 8.22 Click Yes to load a structural column.

8. Select the HSS 6×6×⁵⁄₈ column.

FIGURE 8.23 Select HSS-Hollow Structural Section-Column.rfa and use the 6×6×⁵⁄₈ type.

9. Click OK.

10. On the Options bar, make sure the height is set to Roof, as shown in Figure 8.24.

11. Place the column on the grid intersection F-1.

12. Press Esc.

13. Click the Column ➤ Structural Column button on the Home tab.

14. Place a column at grid intersection F-2. Before you place this column, be sure the height is set to Roof.

15. Place another column at grid intersection F-G (see Figure 8.25).

16. Select the column on the inside of the building (Column F-G).

FIGURE 8.24 Place the column on grid intersection F-1.

FIGURE 8.25 Placing two additional columns

17. On the Options bar, click the Element Properties button.

18. For Top Level, select Roof, as shown in Figure 8.26.

FIGURE 8.26 Set the column's top to extend to the roof.

N O T E   Also notice that the Column Location is set to F-G. This is important because if the column is offset from one of these lines, it will still be
considered at that column location except there will be an offset dimension.

19. Click OK.

20. Mirror the three columns to the opposite side of the entry using column line 3 as the reference plane.

21. Save the model.

It's time to start adding some full height columns at the rest of the grid locations. You will start with the radial grid, and then place the rest of the columns
in the walls of the exterior and the corridor:

1. On the Home tab, click the Column ➤ Structural Column button.

2. On the Options bar, be sure the height is set to Roof.

3. Hover your cursor over grid intersection G-2.1. Notice that you can
see the column, but it is at the wrong orientation.

4. Press the Tab key on your keyboard, and the column will rotate to be
aligned with the grid, as shown in Figure 8.27.

5. Once the column is aligned, pick the intersection. The column is
placed.

6. Repeat the steps for columns 3 and 3.9.

FIGURE 8.27 Placing a column at an angle

It's time now to start placing columns in the main part of the building. Place a column at every grid location. Note that you will have to stretch the column lines to the left side of the building. You should also turn the grid bubbles on at the left side of the building, as shown in Figure 8.28.

FIGURE 8.28 The grids should be extended and the bubbles turned on at each end.

To add columns "by intersection," follow these steps:

1. Start the Structural Column command.

2. On the Place Structural Column tab, select the On Grids button on the Multiple panel button, as shown in Figure 8.29.

FIGURE 8.29 Place On Grids

3. Pick a window around the rectangular portion of the west wing, as shown in Figure 8.30.

FIGURE 8.30 Picking a window where the columns will be placed

4. Notice the Grid Intersection tab now changes to allow you to either finish or cancel. Once you have the window placed, click the Finish Selection on the Multiple Selection panel, as shown in Figure 8.30.

5. Press Esc.

There are quite a few columns placed. Some of these columns will need to be moved, including the four columns in the corridor area. Revit will still locate these columns at a grid intersection, except it will add the offset in the column's properties.

To move the columns and create a column offset, follow these steps:

1. Zoom into the middle of the west wing at the corridor intersection.

2. Select the two columns at the left of the corridor, as shown in Figure 8.31.

3. Move the columns 4'–0" to the left (see Figure 8.31).

FIGURE 8.31 Moving the columns to the left 4'–0"

4. Repeat the same procedure for the other two columns (see Figure 8.32).

5. Zoom into the door shown in Figure 8.32.

6. Move the column to the left 4'–0".

7. Save the model.

FIGURE 8.32 Making adjustments like this will happen quite a bit.

That's enough columns for now. It's time to move on to adding some structural framing. The main areas that framing will be added to are in the canopy areas surrounding the east entry of the east wing.

Structural Framing

Although most structural framing will not be done in Revit Architecture, there are a few areas where you will need to add some framing. Canopies with light structural framing are certainly one area that could call for the architect to wander over to the structural side of the fence.

To begin, open the file you have been following along with. If you did not complete the previous section, go to the book's web page at **www.sybex.com/go/revit2010ner**. From there you can browse to Chapter 8 and find the file called NER-24.rvt.

To start adding structural framing:

1. In the Project Browser, go to the Level 2 floor plan.

2. Zoom in to the radial entry area.

3. Notice you cannot see the exterior column. Adjust the view range for this view to see the item.

4. Type **VP** to open the View Properties dialog.

5. Scroll down to the View Range row, and click the Edit button.

6. In the Primary range, set the bottom to –1'–0".

7. For View Depth, set the level to –1'–0" (see Figure 8.33).

FIGURE 8.33 Setting the view range so you can see 1'–0" below the level

8. Click OK twice. You can now see the column.

It is now time to place the structural framing. Make sure you are zoomed into northwest corner of the west wing.

1. On the Structure panel of the Home tab, select the Beam button, as shown in Figure 8.34.

FIGURE 8.34 Click the Beam button on the Structure panel of the Home tab.

2. If you get the message stating that no structural framing component is loaded into the model, click Yes.

3. Browse to Structural ➤ Framing ➤ Steel.

4. Select HSS-Hollow Structural Section.rfa.

5. In the Type dialog, select HSS 6×6×⁵⁄₈, and click OK.

6. Pick the first point at the column to the left that is buried within the corner of the wall.

7. Pick the second point at the exterior column, as shown in Figure 8.35.

8. With the Beam command still running, pick the exterior column (F-1), then column F-2, as shown in Figure 8.36.

9. Press Esc.

FIGURE 8.35 Adding the beam requires picking two columns.

FIGURE 8.36 Adding the second beam

10. Start the Beam command again.

11. Draw a beam 6" of the finish face of the wall starting at the top beam, ending in the wall, as shown in Figure 8.37.

FIGURE 8.37 Adding a beam 6" off the face of the wall to the center of the beam

 N O T E Revit will not like that you are bearing a beam on a nonbearing wall. When you are asked to make this wall bearing, click Make Wall Bearing.

12. Draw another beam from the left to the right 6" off the finish face of the wall, as shown in Figure 8.38.

FIGURE 8.38 Completing the framing for the canopy

13. Save the model.

It is now time to add some filler beams. In Revit Architecture, you have the ability to add a beam system that is controlled by a specified spacing. Once the system is in place, you can control the properties for the duration of the project.

Adding a Beam System

Although adding beam systems is much more crucial in Revit Structure, it does have its usefulness in Revit Architecture as well. Having the ability to equally space a framing system can be quite advantageous.

To create a beam system, follow along with this procedure:

1. On the Structure panel of the Home tab, click the Beam ➤ Beam System button, as shown in Figure 8.39.

FIGURE 8.39 The Beam System button

2. On the Draw panel, click the Pick Supports button, as shown in Figure 8.40.

3. Pick the two HSS members that form the canopy, as shown in Figure 8.40.

FIGURE 8.40 Picking the four beams as the supports of the beam system

NOTE   The support you pick first determines the direction that the beams will run in. Notice the double lines in the horizontal beam? This indicates the direction of the beam system. If you want to change this direction, click the Direction button on the Draw panel.

4. On the Edit panel, click the Trim button, as shown in Figure 8.41.

5. Trim the overlapping corners of the magenta sketch lines. See Figure 8.41.

FIGURE 8.41   Cleaning up the corners of the sketch by using the Trim command

6. On the Element tab, select the Beam System properties button.

7. Change the layout rule to Maximum Spacing.

8. Change the spacing to 4'-0", as shown in Figure 8.42.

FIGURE 8.42 Changing the properties to reflect a 4'–0" maximum spacing

9. Click OK.

10. To the far right of the Create Beam System tab, click the Finish Beam System button. Your framing should look like Figure 8.43.

FIGURE 8.43 The framing at the canopy

11. Mirror the canopy to the other side of the radial entry. Be careful not to accidentally mirror the columns.

12. You will receive the same message about bearing a structural member on a nonstructural wall. Click the Make Wall Bearing button.

By using the Beam System command, you can easily add multiple occurrences of framing members quite quickly. There will be, however, cases where you need nonuniform members on a different plane, such as lateral bracing.

Adding Bracing

It would be nice to add a rod to the top of this canopy at an angle. You can accomplish this by using the Brace command.

To use the Brace command, let's first add the rod family to our model:

1. To load the rod family, click the Component ➤ Load from Library button on the Home tab.

2. Browse to Structural ➤ Framing ➤ Steel, and open the file called Round Bar.rfa.

3. Now that the file is loaded, go to the north elevation in the Project Browser.

4. In the north elevation, change the detail level to Fine and Model Graphics Style to Shading with Edges.

5. Zoom in on the west canopy.

6. On the Structure panel of the Home tab, click the Brace button, as shown in Figure 8.44.

FIGURE 8.44 Click the Brace button on the Structural tab.

7. Once you select the Brace button, Revit will display a dialog asking you to specify a work plane. In the Pick a Plane menu, select Grid 1, as shown in Figure 8.45.

8. Verify that Round Bar: 1" is the current framing member in the Type Selector on the Options bar.

9. Draw a diagonal bar, as shown in Figure 8.46.

10. Go to the south elevation.

11. Change the detail level to Fine and Model Graphics Style to Shading with Edges.

12. On the Structure panel of the Home tab, click the Brace button.

FIGURE 8.45   Specifying Grid 1 as the working plane for the bracing

FIGURE 8.46   Adding the rod at an angle

13. Choose Grid: F as the work plane.

14. Draw a diagonal rod similar to the one in Figure 8.47.

FIGURE 8.47   Adding the second rod to the canopy

15. Mirror the rods to the other canopy. You can stay in the south elevation to do so.

 N O T E   **If you receive a warning about a circular reference chain, simply click Unjoin Elements.**

16. Save the model.

That pretty much covers it for framing. The next item to learn about will bring us underground into the foundation. Although the structural engineer will usually specify the foundation system, architects must have access to foundation tools to place concrete foundation walls as well as strip and isolate footings and piers. The next section will address these topics.

Foundation Systems

The first question that arises while addressing structural foundations is "What if the architect places a foundation in the model, then the structural engineer places one in their model?"

What will happen is the structural engineer will use a method called Copy/Monitor whereas the engineer takes the architect's foundation and makes it their own. The engineer is then free to alter the foundation. This method will be addressed fully in Chapter 20, "Importing and Coordinating Revit Models."

The first topic in this section will focus on creating foundation walls. Although adding this type of wall is similar to adding architectural walls, there are a few things you want to look out for.

Foundation Walls

For now, let's add a foundation and deal with coordination later. The task before us here is to create a foundation wall constructed of 18" of solid concrete. To proceed, follow along with the procedure.

1. Go to the Level 1 floor plan.

2. Click the Wall ≻ Structural wall button on the Home tab, as shown in Figure 8.48.

3. In the change Element Type menu on the Place Structural wall tab, select : Generic 8" Masonry.

4. On the Element panel, click the Element Properties button.

5. Click the Edit Type button.

6. Click the Duplicate button.

7. Name the new wall **18" Concrete**.

8. Click OK, then click the Edit button.

9. In the wall function row, select Foundation from the drop-down list, as shown in Figure 8.48.

FIGURE 8.48 Changing the wall function to Foundation

10. Just under the wall function row is the Coarse Scale Fill Pattern row. Change the hatch to Concrete by clicking the [...] button and selecting Concrete from the menu. Click OK.

11. Click the Edit button in the Structure row.

12. In the second row in the layers chart, click in the Material cell.

13. Click the [...] button.

14. Find Concrete - Cast-in-Place Concrete.

15. Click OK.

16. Change the thickness to 1'–6" (see Figure 8.49).

FIGURE 8.49 Changing the thickness

17. Click OK twice.

18. Click OK one more time to get back to the model.

19. Press Esc.

The reason we press Esc and basically bailed out at the last second is the fact that we are about to place a wall underneath this level. This view is currently set to not show anything below this level, forcing us to alter the view range.

To modify the view range, follow these steps:

1. Type VP to open the View Properties dialog.

2. Scroll down to View Range.

3. For Primary Range, set the bottom to –1'–0".

4. For View Depth, set Level to –1'–0".

5. Click OK twice.

6. Click the Wall ➢ Structural Wall button from the Home tab.

7. On the Draw panel, click the pick lines icon.

8. Make sure that Depth is set to T.O. Foundation on the Options bar.

9. Pick the core center line of the exterior wall, as shown in Figure 8.50.

10. Keep repeating picking the exterior walls in all three sections of the model.

Your 3D model should look like Figure 8.51. Get into the habit of viewing the model in 3D — especially when you can't see exactly where the walls are being placed in plan.

FIGURE 8.50 Pick the core center line of every exterior wall in the entire model. This includes the corridor as well as the east wing.

FIGURE 8.51 The foundation walls

Now we can travel into the ground and check out how our walls are joining. Some cleanup will be involved:

1. In the Project Browser, find the T.O. Footing floor plan and double-click it.

2. Zoom into the west wing area where the south elevator meets the foundation wall. There is an issue: the walls are funky, as shown in Figure 8.52.

FIGURE 8.52 The walls are not behaving as we would like them to.

3. Select the masonry elevator shaft wall.

4. On the blue grip, right-click and select Disallow Join, as shown in Figure 8.53.

5. Click the grip on the masonry wall, and drag it back to the outside face of the corner, as shown in Figure 8.53.

6. The masonry wall to the right needs to be joined to the foundation wall. To do this, click the Join Geometry button on the Modify toolbar, as shown in Figure 8.53.

7. Pick the foundation wall.

8. Pick the masonry wall. The masonry wall is now notched back for the foundation.

9. Repeat the procedure for the north elevator. The condition may be slightly different than the south elevator, but the process to fix it will be the same.

FIGURE 8.53 Disallowing the wall's join will enable the foundation walls to terminate as expected.

Moving to the east wing, there is one wall we need to fix. The command we will have to use is the Split command:

1. Zoom in on the area, as shown in Figure 8.54.

2. On the Modify tab, click the Split button, as shown in Figure 8.54.

3. On the Options bar, click the Delete Inner Segment checkbox. See Figure 8.54.

Now that the foundation walls are in place, it is time to think about what these walls are bearing on. Revit Architecture has tools to add footings to the bottom of these walls.

Adding Structural Footings

If you are going to as far as placing structural foundation walls, you might as well continue on and place footings underneath them, right? Luckily this is not a difficult task.

FIGURE 8.54 Splitting the foundation wall to follow the profile of the wall above

Before we start adding the structural footings to the plan, we need to first deal with the fact that, by default, this view is not set up to see any objects that are physically below its level. To correct this, we will need to make alterations to the view range of this specific plan.

1. Make sure you are still in the T.O. footing plan, and type **VP** to open the View Properties dialog.

2. Go to the View Range row and click Edit.

3. Set the Primary Range Bottom to Unlimited.

4. Set the View Depth Level to Unlimited, as shown in Figure 8.55.

5. Click OK twice.

FIGURE 8.55 Again with the View Range!

6. On the Structure panel of the Home tab, click the Foundation ➤ Wall foundation button, as shown in Figure 8.56.

FIGURE 8.56 Choosing Foundation ➤ Wall Foundation

In the Element panel on the Place Wall foundation tab, notice it says Bearing Footing - 36" x 12". This is a little big for our purposes, so let's make a new one:

1. On the Element panel, click the Element Properties icon.

2. Click Edit Type.

3. Click Duplicate.

4. Call the new footing element **Bearing Footing - 30" x 12"**.

5. Click OK.

6. Change the width to 2'–6", as shown in Figure 8.57.

Just because this specific foundation is labeled *Wall* does not mean it is a wall. It is labeled *Wall* because it is a continuous (strip) footing that has a wall bearing on it.

FIGURE 8.57 Changing the width to 2'–6"

7. Click OK.

8. Click OK again to get back to the model.

9. Start picking walls. This footing will be centered underneath each wall you pick.

10. When you are done picking the walls, go to a 3D view to make sure you have all of the foundations covered, as shown in Figure 8.58.

If you hover your cursor over a wall and press the Tab key, Revit will select all connecting walls, allowing you to add the bearing footing in literally two clicks.

FIGURE 8.58 Doing a 3D investigation to see whether the footings are all in place

Once all the footings are in place, you can see that we need to focus on the elevator shafts. Since we need an entire foundation mat underneath the elevators, we can use a structural slab.

Structural Slabs

Structural slabs are basically really thick floors. The one we are about to use is a 12"-thick solid concrete floor. Of course, Revit does not have something this thick already built in the library, so we will take this opportunity to make one:

1. Go to the T.O. Footing floor plan.

2. Zoom into the elevator area.

3. On the Home tab, click Floor ➤ Structural Floor, as shown in Figure 8.59.

4. On the Element panel of the Create Floor Boundary tab, click the Floor Properties button.

FIGURE 8.59 Clicking Floor ➤ Structural Floor

5. Click Edit Type.

6. Click Duplicate.

7. Call the new slab **12" Elevator Slab**.

8. Click OK.

9. Click the Edit button in the Structure row.

10. In the Layers field, change the thickness of the structure to 1'–0", as shown in Figure 8.60.

FIGURE 8.60 Changing the structure thickness

11. Click OK twice.

12. Click OK one more time to get back to the model.

13. On the Draw panel, click the Pick Walls button.

14. On the Options bar, set an offset of 1'–0".

15. Pick the three elevator shaft walls, as shown in Figure 8.61.

16. Set the offset back to 0.

17. Pick the exterior Brick on CMU wall, as shown in Figure 8.61.

FIGURE 8.61 When picking the elevator shaft walls, be sure to include the 1'–0" offset.

18. Set the Offset value back to 0 in the Options bar.

19. Pick the Exterior concrete wall.

Now that the perimeter is set, it is time to start trimming the edges to make sure you have a continuous, closed loop:

1. On the Edit panel, click the Trim button.

2. Trim any overlapping corners, as shown in Figure 8.62.

3. On the Floor panel to the right of the Create Floor Boundary tab, click Finish Sketch.

4. Repeat the process for the south elevator.

FIGURE 8.62 Trimming up all of the corners

Your plan should look like Figure 8.63.

FIGURE 8.63 The finished elevator pads

Now that the footings are mostly in place, it is time to think about placing piers and spread footings in the foundation. Luckily, as you are soon to discover, you already know how to do this.

Piers and Spread Footings

Piers and pilasters, simply put, are concrete columns. This is how Revit sees these items, and this is the easiest placement method.

Another nice thing about this part of the lesson is the fact that the grids are in place as well as the steel columns that bear upon them. The only real trick is deciding which plan to put them in.

The objective of the next procedure is to add footings to the bottoms of the structural walls:

1. Remain in the T.O. Footing plan.

2. On the Build panel of the Home tab, click the Column ➤ Structural Column button.

3. On the Place Structural Column tab, click the Load Family button, as shown in Figure 8.64.

4. Browse to Structural ➤ Columns ➤ Concrete.

5. Pick the file called `Concrete-Square-Column.rfa`.

6. Click Open.

7. In the change Element Type menu on the Element panel, find the 24"×24" column.

8. Start placing the columns at the grid intersections, as shown in Figure 8.64.

9. Go to Level 1.

10. Zoom into the corridor.

11. Move the piers under the columns.

12. Do the same for the pier under the doorway, as shown in Figure 8.65.

FIGURE 8.64 Start placing piers.

FIGURE 8.65 Making the necessary adjustments

Now it's time to add the spread footings under the piers. This process will be almost identical to the process we just went through:

1. Go back to the T.O. Footing floor plan.

2. On the Structure panel of the Home tab, select the Foundation ➤ Isolated button, as shown in Figure 8.66

3. No structural foundations are loaded into the project, so click Yes.

4. Browse to Structural ➤ Foundations.

5. Select the file called `Footing-Rectangular.rfa`.

6. Click Open.

7. On the Options bar, click the Element Properties button.

8. Click Edit Type.

9. Click Duplicate.

10. Call the new footing 36" x 36" x 12".

11. Click OK.

12. Change the width to 36".

13. Change the length to 36".

14. Change the thickness to 12".

15. Click OK twice.

16. Add these footings to each pier.

17. Your foundation plan should resemble Figure 8.66.

FIGURE 8.66 The completed foundation

Having a foundation in place in an architectural plan can be a good thing — and it can also be a bad thing. It can be bad because of the fact that structural items are going to start showing up in places you may not want to see them. The last procedure of the chapter will involve isolating the structure from the architecture.

Structural Views

By creating a structural view, you are essentially duplicating an architectural view and hiding the structural items in that view. Sound easy? That is because it is! Just follow these steps:

1. In the Project Browser, right-click on Level 1 and select Duplicate View ➢ Duplicate with Detailing, as shown in Figure 8.67.

FIGURE 8.67 Selecting Duplicate View ➢ Duplicate with Detailing

2. Rename the view called "Copy of Level 1" to **Level 1 Structural Plan**.

3. Right-click on the Level 1 Structural plan and select Properties.

4. In the Discipline category, select Structural from the list, as shown in Figure 8.68.

FIGURE 8.68 Changing the discipline to Structural

5. Click OK.

6. In the Project Browser, right-click on Views All, as shown in Figure 8.69.

7. Click Properties.

FIGURE 8.69 Right-clicking in the Project Browser

8. Change Type to Discipline, as shown in Figure 8.70.

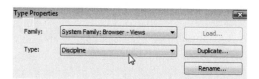

FIGURE 8.70 Changing the type to Discipline

Now the Project Browser is broken down into categories. This will be helpful for large projects with a mix of structure and architecture. Let's add the T.O. Footing plan to the structural category:

1. In the Project Browser, right-click on the T.O. Footing floor plan.

2. Click Properties.

3. Change the discipline to Structural.

This is getting easy! The T.O. Footing plan is now categorized with its structural brethren. Let's go make the Level 1 Architectural plan truly architectural:

1. Open the Level 1 plan (Architectural).

2. Type VP.

3. Scroll down to View Range.

4. Click the Edit button in the View Range row.

5. Change both –1'–0"- increments to 0.

6. Click OK twice.

The foundation information is now gone.

Although the last part of this chapter was short, it is a nice look into the Project Browser and showed how you can start to get organized. If you would like more practice, go into the Project Browser on your own and start organizing it the way you think you would like.

 N O T E   If you need more structural tools than provided within Revit Architecture, or you are, in fact, a structural engineer or designer, you may want to consider purchasing Revit Structure.

Are You Experienced?

Now You Can...

- ☑ place a structural grid in your model using the architectural walls as a reference

- ☑ add additional grids at a radius or by sketch where needed

- ☑ add columns to the gridlines

- ☑ add columns at an offset, keeping the relationship to the grid intersection intact

- ☑ add structural beams to the model

- ☑ add structural beam systems, which can follow on centering rules or equal distance spacing

☑ using the Brace command, create brace framing to be used for both architectural appointments and for actual structural bracing

☑ create entire foundation systems complete with foundation walls, piers strip, and spread footings

☑ organize the Project Browser to show your model broken down into discipline

☑ change a view's discipline to Structural

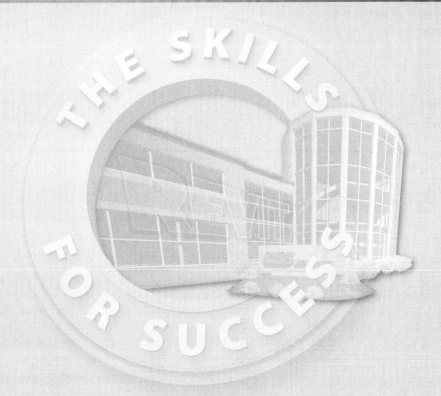

CHAPTER 9

Ceilings and Interiors

▶ Creating ceilings

▶ Creating soffits

▶ Adding components

▶ Specifying wall and floor materials

N ow that the exterior shell is up, and the rooms are basically laid out, it is time to start considering the interiors. As it stands, we have a bunch of rooms with the same wall finish, the same floor finish, and no ceilings to speak of. The restrooms don't have any fixtures, and the rooms are going to be useless without furniture.

Another issue is the fact that we don't have any separate views such as furniture plans or finish plans. This chapter will dive into all of these items — and then some!

Creating Ceilings

Placing a ceiling is quite easy; the hard part is finding the view in which to do it. As you have probably noticed, the Project Browser is broken down into categories. The categories for plans are Floor Plans and Ceiling Plans. While floor plans show the views standing at that level looking down, ceiling plans show the view standing at that level looking up. In Revit, you are looking at a true reflected ceiling plan.

To begin, open the file you have been following along with. If you did not complete the previous chapter, go to the book's web page at **www.sybex.com/go/revit2010ner**. From there you can browse to Chapter 9 and find the file called NER-25.rvt.

1. Go to the Level 1 ceiling plan, as shown in Figure 9.1.

FIGURE 9.1 The Ceiling Plan category

2. On the Home tab, click the Ceiling button, as shown in Figure 9.2.

3. With the Ceiling command active, click into the Change Element Type menu. You should see the same ceiling types as shown in Figure 9.3.

FIGURE 9.2 The Ceiling button on the Modeling tab of the Design bar

FIGURE 9.3 The available ceiling types listed in the Type Selector

4. Choose 2' × 4' ACT System from the Type Selector.

5. Hover your mouse over the room shown in Figure 9.4. Notice the perimeter is outlined in red. This indicates that the ceiling has found at least four walls to use as a layout.

FIGURE 9.4 The ceiling is finding a home.

6. Once you see the red outline, pick a point in the middle of the room. Your ceiling should now look like Figure 9.5.

7. Have at it! Add a ceiling to every room except for the hallway, the bathrooms, and, of course, the elevator shafts, as shown in Figure 9.6.

FIGURE 9.5 The 2×4 tiled ceiling has now been placed.

FIGURE 9.6 Add 2×4 ACT ceilings to the rooms shown here.

 N O T E   If you notice that some of the grids are running in the wrong direction, don't worry. We will change that in a moment.

8. With the Ceiling command still running, select Compound Ceiling : GWB on Metal Stud from the Type Selector.

9. Pick the bathrooms (not the chases) and the hallway.

10. Press Esc.

TRANSFERRING PROJECT STANDARDS

There are going to be times when you do not have the system families you need to carry out the task at hand. Ceiling types seem to be the number 1 system family that falls victim to being inadvertently deleted from a model before it gets used. If you find that you do not have the ceiling types shown in Figure 9.3, do the following:

1. On the Revit Home button, Go to New ➢ Project.

2. In the New Project dialog, click OK to start a new project using the default template.

3. On the View tab, Click Switch Windows to get back to the No Experienced Required project.

4. On the Manage tab, click Transfer Project Standards in the Project Settings panel.

5. In the Select Items to Copy dialog (see the following graphic), click the Check None button.

6. Click Ceiling Types.

7. Click OK.

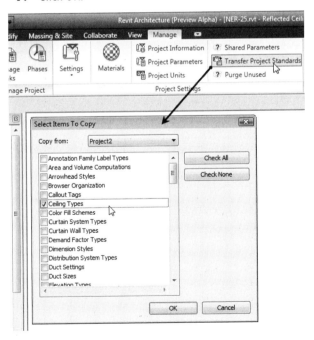

That was just too easy! Too good to be true, right? All right, it is. You always have to make adjustments to this type of item. You probably noticed that you had no control over which direction the grids were running. Also, we have no clue how high these ceilings are. It is time to start modifying the ceilings.

Modifying Ceiling Grids

To be honest, a ceiling consists of nothing more than a basic hatch pattern applied to a material. Actually, everything in Revit is a basic hatch pattern applied to a material. That sure does make it easy to understand!

The one unique thing about hatch patterns in Revit is the fact that you can modify them on screen. That means you can move and rotate a hatch pattern. That also means you can move and rotate a grid pattern. Let's give it a shot:

1. Press Esc to cancel the command you may be in.

2. Pick the grid line, as shown in Figure 9.7 (Make sure you're zoomed in close enough to make the Rotate command active.)

3. On the Modify Ceilings tab, click the Rotate button, as shown in Figure 9.7.

FIGURE 9.7 Select one of the grids, and then click the Rotate button.

4. Rotate the grid 45° by using the two-pick method, as shown in Figure 9.8.

FIGURE 9.8 The rotate process

Your ceiling should now look like Figure 9.9.

FIGURE 9.9 The ceiling at a 45° angle

Rotating a ceiling grid is a good example of the hatch functionality in Revit. You can rotate and move hatch patterns whether they are ceilings, brick, or any other pattern you need to manipulate.

Now that the ceilings are in, let's look at the ceiling's properties before we go too far. As a matter of fact, it is a good idea to investigate the ceiling's element properties before you place it in the model.

Ceiling Element Properties

As I mentioned earlier, ceilings are set up in a similar fashion as floors. So, it stands to reason we are going to see many similar properties.

Before we get started, let's make some modifications to the east wing. The objective of this procedure is to add a hard ceiling with metal framing, gypsum, and a $3/4$" cherry substrate. To do so, however, some of the walls need to be modified:

1. Go to a 3D view of the model.

2. Select the sloped roof that covers the east wing, as shown in Figure 9.10.

3. Right-click.

4. Select Override Graphics in View ➤ By Element (see Figure 9.10).

FIGURE 9.10 Select the roof, and then right-click.

5. In the View-Specific Element Graphics dialog, click the Transparent button in the upper-right corner, as shown in Figure 9.11.

FIGURE 9.11 The View-Specific Element Graphics dialog

6. Click OK. The roof is now transparent.

We did this because some of the walls have to be attached to the roof. It is much easier to do this in a 3D view. But to do so, we need to see the walls that we are going to be working on:

1. Select the wall shown in Figure 9.12.

2. On the Modify Walls tab, select the Attach top button.

3. Pick the roof.

Your wall should look like Figure 9.12.

FIGURE 9.12 Attaching the wall to the roof

The next step is to constrain the partition walls in this area to Level 3. The ceilings we are going to add to these rooms will be much higher than the rest of the building.

1. While still in a 3D view, select the partitions shown in Figure 9.13.

2. On the Modify Walls tab, click the Element Properties button.

3. In the Element Properties dialog, set the Top constraint to Up to: Level 3.

4. Click OK. The walls are now constrained to Level 3.

5. In the Project Browser, go to Level 1 under Ceiling Plans.

FIGURE 9.13 Select the partitions shown here.

The next procedure is a tad off the beaten path but fits squarely within this process. Since we have specified the walls in this area to be of a greater height than the rest of the walls in the model, it is obvious that we are going to be adding ceilings higher than 8'–0". This poses a problem in terms of the Level 1 ceiling plan view range.

Creating a Plan Region

There will be times where you need to set your view range in a specific area that differs from the view range in the plan as a whole. In this example, we will add a ceiling at 14'–6" above the finish floor. If we do this with the current view range settings, Revit will not display the ceiling. If you modify the view range for the entire view, you will see the 14'–6" ceilings, but you will not see the regular 8'–0" ceilings in the rest of the building in that view.

The following procedure will involve creating a region where the view range is different from the view range in Level 1 ceiling plan:

1. In the Project Browser, make sure you are in Level 1 Ceiling Plans.

 WARNING   Double-check to be absolutely sure you are not in a floor plan. You want to be in the ceiling plan!

2. Zoom into the east wing.

3. On the View tab, select the Plan Views ➤ Plan Region button, as shown in Figure 9.14.

FIGURE 9.14 The Plan Region button on the View tab of the Design bar

4. On the Draw panel, click the Rectangle button, as shown in Figure 9.15.

5. Pick a rectangle around the north portion of the east wing, as shown in Figure 9.15.

FIGURE 9.15 Define the limits of the plan region by drawing a rectangle around a specific area.

Notice that the View tab has now switched to the Create Plan Region Boundary tab. We now need to define the view range for this region:

1. On the Element panel, click the Plan Region Properties button.

2. In the Element Properties dialog, click the Edit button in the View Range row.

3. In the View Range dialog, set the Top setting to Level 3.

4. Set the cut plane to 14'–6".

5. Set the bottom to 7'–6".

6. Set the view depth to Level 2 with an offset of 16'–0" (see Figure 9.16).

FIGURE 9.16 Configuring the view range for the crop region

7. Click OK.

8. Click OK again to get back to the model.

9. On the Plan Region panel, click Finish Plan Region.

You now have a plan region. Although it may not seem as though you did anything in the plan, once you place a ceiling at 14'–6" you will be able to see it.

 N O T E   The dotted line you see represents the border of the plan region. Although these borders can get annoying (especially if you start collecting several plan regions), I recommend that you keep them turned on. It is helpful to know where a plan region is in the model, and it is more important for others to know that there is a plan region in that area. Also, these borders will not plot.

With the plan region in place, we can now place a ceiling at a higher distance from finish floor. Since we are going to the trouble of placing a high ceiling, we might as well make the ceiling something special.

Creating a Custom Ceiling

So, what do you do if your ceiling is not an acoustical tile ceiling or a gypsum system? This is Revit! You make a new one.

As mentioned earlier, creating a ceiling is similar to creating a floor or a roof. The properties dialogs are exactly the same. This procedure will guide you through the process of creating a custom ceiling:

1. Be sure you are in the Level 1 ceiling plan, and zoom in on the northeast room.

2. On the Home tab, click the Ceiling button.

3. In the Change Element Type menu, select GWB on Mtl. Stud 4. To the left of the picture of the ceiling is the Element Properties button. Click it (see Figure 9.17).

FIGURE 9.17 Select the GWB on Mtl. Stud ceiling type from the Change Element Type menu, and then click the element properties.

5. In the Element Properties dialog, click the Edit Type button.

6. Click Duplicate.

7. Call the new ceiling **Wood Veneer on Metal framing**.

8. In the Structure row, click the Edit button, as shown in Figure 9.18.

FIGURE 9.18 Click the Edit button in the Structure row to gain access to the ceiling's structural composition.

9. In the Layers field, as shown in Figure 9.19, click on row 4. This is the Finish 2 [5] Gypsum wallboard row.

10. Just below the Layers field is the Insert button. Click it.

11. Click the Down button to move the new row to the bottom.

12. Change the function from Structure to Finish 2 [5].

13. Click into the Material cell and click the [...] button, as shown in Figure 9.19.

FIGURE 9.19 Click the [...] button in the Material column.

14. In the Materials dialog, find Wood - Cherry.

15. Give it a surface pattern of Wood 1.

16. Give it a cut pattern of Plywood, as shown in Figure 9.20.

FIGURE 9.20 Selecting and configuring the material for the ceiling

17. Click OK.

18. Change the thickness to 3/4".

19. Click OK twice.

20. Place the ceiling in the room shown in Figure 9.21.

21. Change Height Offset from Level to 14'–6".

Ceilings : Compound Ceiling : Wood Veneer on Metal framing

FIGURE 9.21   The cherry-veneered plywood ceiling

N O T E   Don't get discouraged if your final result is not the same as Figure 9.21. You took 22 steps to get to this wonderful cherry ceiling; any one of those steps could have gone wrong. Going back through steps and retracing your path is something you may be doing quite a bit.

For the adjacent rooms, add the same ceiling to them. You can keep the same height. You can follow along with these steps, but I encourage you to try to put the ceilings in from memory:

1. In the Project Browser, be sure you are in the Level 1 ceiling plan.

2. On the Home tab, click the Ceiling button.

3. In the Change Element Type menu on the Element panel, find the ceiling called Compound Ceiling : Wood Veneer on Metal Framing.

4. Click the Element Properties button.

5. Set the height above the floor to 14'–6".

6. Click OK.

7. Pick the rooms shown in Figure 9.22.

FIGURE 9.22 The north row of rooms will receive cherry ceilings!

ADDING A CEILING IN EMPTY SPACE

Note that you can add a ceiling to a model if there are no walls defining an enclosed space. To do this, start the Ceiling command in the typical manner by clicking the Sketch button on the Modeling tab of the Design bar, as shown in the following graphic. Once the Ceiling command starts, click the Sketch button on the Options bar. This will allow you to simply draft the ceiling boundaries.

Now that you have experience placing ceilings, and even creating custom ceiling systems, it is time to start adding features. The first items that come to mind are certainly lighting fixtures, but we need to go back even further and figure out how to "cut holes" in the ceilings and add soffits.

Creating Ceiling Openings and Soffits

Unless you are in a residential dwelling, or a prison, you can look up and notice that a ceiling is merely serving as a host for electrical, mechanical, and architectural appointments. Very seldom will you find a ceiling that does not require a modification in some capacity. This section of the chapter will deal with this issue, starting with creating a ceiling opening.

Creating a Ceiling Opening

To begin, open the file you have been following along with.
If you did not complete the previous chapter, go to the book's web page at `www.sybex.com/go/revit2010ner`. From there you can browse to Chapter 9 and find the file called `NER-26.rvt`.

The objective of the next procedure is to cut an opening into a ceiling to later drop a soffit into:

1. Select the Level 1 ceiling plan.

2. Zoom in to the wood ceilings in the east wing, as shown in Figure 9.23.

3. Select the ceiling in the northeast corner of the building, as shown in Figure 9.23.

 T I P   Ceilings can be difficult to select. If you hover your cursor over the ceiling, you will see it highlight. If the wall or some other overlapping geometry highlights instead, tap the Tab key on your keyboard to filter through until you find the ceiling. Once the ceiling highlights, pick it.

---

4. Once the ceiling is selected, click the Edit Boundary button on the Modify Ceilings tab, as shown in Figure 9.23. The ceiling pattern disappears and is replaced by a magenta sketch line at the perimeter of the room.

5. Notice also that the Modify Ceilings tab has an additional Edit Boundary tab. On the Home tab, click the Ref Plane ➢ Draw Reference Plane button on the Work Plane panel as shown in Figure 9.24.

6. Draw two reference planes, as shown in Figure 9.24. Be sure to snap to the midpoints of the magenta sketch lines.

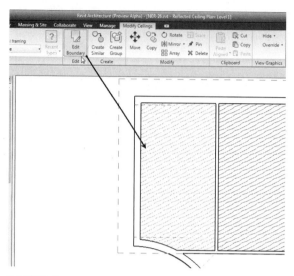

FIGURE 9.23 Click the Edit Boundary button on the Modify Ceilings tab.

FIGURE 9.24 Draw two reference planes to create a center intersection.

7. With the reference planes drawn, click the Lines button on the draw panel of the Modify Ceilings tab, as shown in Figure 9.25.

8. On the Draw panel on the Modify Ceilings tab, click the Boundary Line button. Once you do, you will see an expanded list of sketch choices. Pick the Circle choice, as shown in Figure 9.25.

9. Draw a 4'-0" radius circle at the intersection of the reference planes (see Figure 9.25).

FIGURE 9.25 Sketching a 4'-0" radius circle

10. On the Ceiling panel, click Finish Sketch.

11. Verify that your ceiling looks like Figure 9.26.

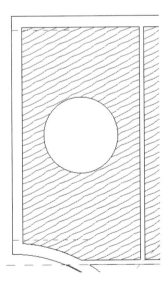

FIGURE 9.26 There's a hole in my ceiling!

With the cutout in place, we need to think about closing this feature with a soffit and, perhaps, another ceiling.

Creating a Soffit

Soffits are nothing more than walls with a base offset. This makes sense if you think about it. If your floor level moves, you certainly want the distance from the finish floor to the bottom of the soffit to remain consistent. This one is going to be easy!

1. On the Home tab, click the Wall button.

2. In the Change Element Type menu, select Basic Wall : Interior: 6⅛" Partition.

3. Click the Element Properties button.

4. Click Edit Type.

5. Click Duplicate.

6. Call the new wall 4½" Soffit.

7. Click OK.

8. Click the Edit button in the Structure row.

9. Delete rows 1 and 7 (the double gypsum layer).

10. Change the gypsum thicknesses to ½".

11. Change the Stud layer to 3½". See Figure 9.27.

FIGURE 9.27 Modify the 6⅛" wall to these dimensions.

12. Click OK twice.

13. In the instance parameters, set Base Offset to 14'–0".

14. Set the top constraint to Level 3 (see Figure 9.28).

15. Click OK.

FIGURE 9.28 Setting the top and bottom constraints

You are now ready to place the soffit. You will add it to the radial hole in the ceiling. Normally, you would need to physically draw the wall using the Arc Sketch function. In this case, you can simply pick the radial portion of the ceiling opening.

1. With the Wall command still running, click the pick lines icon on the Draw panel.

2. Mouse over the radial ceiling opening. Notice a blue alignment line appears. Make sure it is to the inside of the opening, then press the tab button twice.

3. Notice the entire circle is selected, and the blue alignment line is facing the inside of the hole (see Figure 9.29). Once you see this, pick a point to the inside of the hole.

Revit will only allow you to add the wall as a 180° arc. You will need to pick each side of the circle to accomplish a full 360° soffit.

FIGURE 9.29 Creating one cool soffit!

4. Press Esc twice.

Your soffit is complete.

NEVER ASSUME ANYTHING!

They say you should never assume anything, and in this case "they" are right! Let's add a section through this entire row of rooms to gain a perspective on what is going on here.

1. On the View tab, click the Section button.

2. Cut a horizontal section through the entire side of the building, as shown here:

3. Select the section.

4. Click the Element Properties button on the Modify Views tab.

5. Change the detail level to Fine.

6. Change the name to **Section at East Training**. (Yes, these are eventually going to be training rooms.)

7. Click OK.

8. Open the new section. You now have a clear perspective of what is going on with this area.

It is now time to add a secondary ceiling to the inside of the soffit. This procedure will be carried out exactly as it was when you added a ceiling to the entire room.

1. In the Project Browser, go to the Level 1 ceiling plan and zoom in on the ceiling with the soffit.

2. On the Home tab, click the Ceiling button.

3. Select Compound Ceiling : Wood Veneer on Metal Framing.

4. Click the Element Properties button on the Place Ceiling tab.

5. Click Edit Type.

6. Click Duplicate.

7. Call the new ceiling **Mahogany Veneer on Metal Framing.**

8. Click the Edit button in the Structure row.

9. Click in the bottom layer, and click the [...] button to change the material, as shown in Figure 9.30.

FIGURE 9.30 Click the [...] button to change the material.

10. In the Material dialog, find Wood - Mahogany.

11. Change the surface pattern to Wood-2.

12. Change the cut pattern to Plywood, as shown in Figure 9.31.

13. Click OK twice.

14. Click OK one more time to get back to the instance parameters.

15. Change the height offset from Level to 14'–1".

16. Click OK.

17. Place the ceiling inside the soffit.

FIGURE 9.31 Altering the mahogany

You need to adjust your plan region; it has to be set so the cut plane is either below or equal to 14'–1" so you can see the lower ceiling:

1. Pick the dotted rectangle surrounding the rooms. This is the plan region.

2. On the Modify Plan Region tab, click the View Range button.

3. Change the offset for the cut plane to 14'–1", as shown in Figure 9.32.

FIGURE 9.32 Changing the cut plane to 14'–1"

4. Click OK.

Your ceiling plan should look like Figure 9.33.

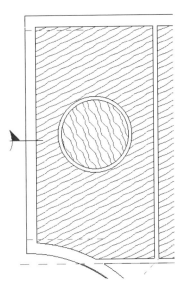

FIGURE 9.33 The completed ceiling

We are getting there with this ceiling, that's for sure! The only thing left is to add some light fixtures.

Adding Light Fixtures to Ceilings

Adding lighting fixtures to a Revit Architecture model is not a difficult task, but there are a few guidelines you must follow to achieve success in installing lighting. For example, you must work with the Options bar to find a face in which to insert the component:

1. In the Project Browser, go to the Level 1 ceiling plan where you have been adding the wood ceilings.

2. On the Home tab, click the Component ➤ Load from Library button, as shown in Figure 9.34.

3. Browse to Imperial Library ➤ Lighting Fixtures.

4. Open the file called Pendant Light - Disk.rfa.

5. Place the light approximately as shown in Figure 9.35.

FIGURE 9.34 Click the Component button on the Basics tab of the Design bar.

 N O T E   There are no snaps when you are trying to place most components. You will have to place the fixture and then move it into position. Needless to say, this is an extra step.

6. Move the light to the center of the radial soffit. This time, you can use snaps (see Figure 9.35).

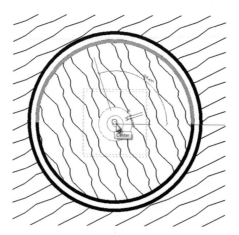

FIGURE 9.35 Move the fixture to the correct location.

7. Open the Section at East Training building section. Notice the light fixture is in the exact location you expected it to be.

 N O T E   If you have directly skipped to this part of the chapter, open the file called NER-27.rfa. You will have to delete the fixtures that are in place, but you will still have the views you need.

8. Select the fixture.

9. Click the Copy button on the Modify Lighting Fixtures tab, as shown in Figure 9.36.

10. On the Options bar, be sure the Multiple button is checked.

11. Copy the fixture 3'–0" to the right and 3'–0" to the left (see Figure 9.36).

FIGURE 9.36 Copying the fixtures in the section

YIKES, THIS ISN'T TO OUR STANDARDS!

Yes, the default line thicknesses are hideous. In Chapter 23, "BIM Standards," we will deal with line thicknesses. For now, you can click the thin lines icon to scale back the thicknesses of the lines, as shown here:

The main point of having you open a section to copy the fixtures is to illustrate that you are now in a fully modeling environment. When you switch back to plan, you will see that the fixtures have been moved. In later chapters, you will learn that this will also add line items to schedules.

Now, let's make some more fixtures:

1. In the Project Browser, go to the Level 1 ceiling plan.

2. Zoom in on the radial soffit. You will see the two new fixtures.

3. Select the right and left fixtures.

4. Click the Rotate command on the Modify Lighting Fixtures tab.

5. On the Options bar, make sure Copy is checked.

6. Rotate the fixtures 90° to create a total of five fixtures, as shown in Figure 9.37.

FIGURE 9.37 You are now copying and rotating as if you were in flat, 2D AutoCAD.

 N O T E   Notice that the fixtures overlap the gypsum soffit. This is because you are actually standing on Level 1 looking up. Revit Architecture has finally taken the confusion out of the reflected ceiling plan mystery.

Now that you have experience dealing with ceilings, it is time to start working on some interior design. Ceilings are a part of this, but what about wall treatments, trims, and architectural millwork? These items will be covered in the next section.

Interior Design

Congratulations! You have arrived at possibly the most difficult subject when it comes to 3D modeling. Why is that? Well, for starters, this is the area where nothing is easy in terms of shape and configuration. For example, suppose you want a crown molding at the ceiling where it intersects the walls. And suppose you need the same crown at the radial soffit! Of course the floors and walls are not the same material, and you need to add furniture as well.

I can go on and on listing the complications we are going to face here, so let's just jump in. The first part of the process will be to add plumbing fixtures.

Adding Plumbing Fixtures and Furniture

Adding a desk follows the same procedure as adding a light fixture. Notice, though, when you added the light fixture it just "knew" that it was supposed to be hosted by the ceiling. It is important to note that most furniture is not hosted by a floor; it is actually hosted by a level. This becomes very important if you have a floor system offset from a level. Your furniture will ignore the floor and stick to the level it is associated with.

To begin, we will have to knock off the less glamorous but all-too-important task of adding bathroom fixtures:

1. In the Project Browser, go to the Level 1 floor plan (floor plan, not ceiling plan).

2. Zoom in on the lavatory area, as shown in Figure 9.38.

3. As you can see there is a callout of this area. Double-click on the callout bubble to open the view called Typical Men's Lavatory.

N O T E   Now that you are more experienced with Revit, I think it almost goes without saying that it is a good thing that we had named this view to something understandable at this stage in the game.

4. With the Typical Men's Lavatory callout opened, we can start adding some fixtures. In the Home tab, click the Component ➤ Load from Library button.

5. In the Imperial Library directory, browse to the Plumbing Fixtures folder.

6. Select the file called Toilet-Commercial-Wall-3D.rfa and click Open.

FIGURE 9.38 The lavatory area

7. In the Type Selector, make sure the 19" Seat Height-type toilet is selected.

8. Place it along the north wall approximately 6" from the east wall, as shown in Figure 9.39.

FIGURE 9.39 Place the 19" Seat Height toilet 6" from the east wall, along the north wall.

One issue here is the fact that this is not a military barracks from the 1960s — we need some stalls. Unfortunately Revit does not provide any out of the box, but this book you bought does! To add some toilet stalls to the model, go to the book's web page at **www.sybex.com/go/revit2010ner**. From there you can browse to Chapter 9 and find the files called:

▶ Toilet Stall-Accessible-Front-3D.rfa

▶ Toilet Stall-Accessible-Side-3D.rfa

▶ Toilet Stall-Braced-3D.rfa

▶ Grab Bar.rfa

▶ Double Sink - Round.rfa

Once you locate the files, download them to the location where all of your Revit families are kept. Then follow along with the procedure:

1. On the Home tab, click Component ➤ Load From Library.

2. Browse to the location where the new families are kept and select them. They are now loaded into your project.

3. On the Home tab, click the Component button.

4. Select Toilet Stall Accessible Front-3D-60×60 Clear.

5. Pick the corner of the bathroom, as shown in Figure 9.40.

FIGURE 9.40 Placing the accessible stall

TIP If you are having difficulties placing the stall directly in the corner, place it at any location along the north wall, then move it to the corner so it looks like Figure 9.40.

The next step is to copy the toilet and add another stall. It would be nice if the family just fit, but this is not a perfect world!

1. Copy the toilet to the right 6'-2½".

2. On the Home tab, select the Component button.

3. Select Toilet Stall Braced - 3D : 36"×60" Clear from the Change Element Type menu.

4. Click the Element Properties button on the Modify Specialty Equipment tab.

5. Click Edit Type.

6. Click Duplicate.

7. Change the name to **59" x 60" Clear**.

8. Click OK.

9. At the very bottom of the dialog, change the width to 4'–11".

10. Click OK twice.

11. Place the stall in the model (see Figure 9.41).

FIGURE 9.41 The two toilets in place

T I P   You may have to press the spacebar as you are placing the stall to flip it into the correct position. Again, if you are having difficulties placing the stall directly in the corner, you can place it along the north wall at any location, and then either align or move the stall into the correct position.

With the toilets and the stalls in place, you need to add a grab bar to the accessible stall. This is the same situation as before in which Revit does not provide this content. You need to either make this component yourself or use the one from the book that you downloaded with the bathroom stalls.

To add a grab bar, follow these steps:

1. Zoom in on the accessible stall, as shown in Figure 9.42.

2. Click the Component button.

3. Select Grab Bar : 4'–0" Length.

4. Place along the wall, as shown in Figure 9.42.

 N O T E   As you are placing the grab bar, it will look like it is going to be embedded into the studs of the wall. Don't worry. Once you pick the point where you want it, it will move to the finished face of the wall.

F I G U R E   9 . 4 2 Adding the Grab Bar family to the wall

T I P   Remember, although it kind of feels like we are just sticking "blocks" into our model, these are all 3D parametric parts. This grab bar, for all you know, is 6'–0" above the ground or sitting on the floor. To adjust this, you do not have to cut a section or go to a 3D view. You can simply select the grab bar, click the Element Properties button, and set Elevation to 2'–6".

Since we are in the men's room, it is time to add some urinals. We will be able to fit two in before we start getting too close to the sink area:

1. On the Home tab, click the Component ➤ Load from Library button.

2. Browse to Plumbing Fixtures.

3. Select the file called Urinal-Wall-3D.rfa.

4. Click Open.

5. Place two urinals about 1'–0" away from the front of the stall, with a 2'–0" space between the two, as shown in Figure 9.43.

FIGURE 9.43 Adding the urinals to the men's room

What a relief to get those urinals in! The next step is to get a sink in with two stations installed into the bathroom. To do this, you can use the double sink you loaded from the book's website.

1. On the Home tab, click the Component button.

2. In the Change Element Type menu, find the family called Double Sink - Round : 24" Depth.

3. Place it into the corner, as shown in Figure 9.44.

FIGURE 9.44 Placing the double sink

Because the women's room is the same size, there will be two stalls and a sink. Create the mirrored layout as shown in Figure 9.45.

Of course the sink will come in at the wrong rotation. By now you know that you can tap the spacebar twice to orient the sink in the correct direction.

If you mirror the stalls, they will go "haywire." You will need to add them separately.

FIGURE 9.45 Completing the women's room

Now that the first floor bathrooms are done, let's move over to some of the actual rooms and offices to furnish these rooms. The first thing we need to do is to add lighting to the ceilings.

Adding Parabolic Troffers

As you are starting to see, the procedure for adding a component does not change based on the component you are adding. This is great news. Adding a troffer, however, is slightly different. You do need to be in a ceiling plan, and you do need to specify the face of the ceiling.

At this point you may be good enough at adding these fixtures to simply look at the following figures and add the lights yourself. Or, if you desire a little help, follow along with these steps:

1. In the Project Browser, go to Level 1 Ceiling Plan. (Notice that we are going to a ceiling plan right now, not a floor plan.)

2. Zoom in on the northeast corner of the west wing, as shown in Figure 9.46.

3. On the Home tab, click the Component ➤ Load from Library button.

4. Browse to the Lighting Fixtures folder.

5. Select the file called Troffer Light - 2×4 Parabolic.rfa.

6. Click Open.

7. Place it in your ceiling, as shown in Figure 9.46.

8. Click the Align button on the Modify tab, as shown in Figure 9.47.

9. Align the light fixture to the grid.

10. Copy the light to the location shown in Figure 9.48.

11. Add lights to the rest of the rooms in the west wing, as shown in Figure 9.48.

With the lights added to the suspended ceilings, we need to illuminate the corridors. This can be done by adding a set of wall-mounted sconces, as follows:

1. Select the Level 1 floor plan.

2. On the Home tab, click the Component ➤ Load from Library button.

3. Browse to the Lighting Fixtures folder.

4. Select the file called Sconce Light - Uplight.rfa.

FIGURE 9.46 Placing a light in a ceiling. You will be aligning it to the grid in a moment.

FIGURE 9.47 Aligning the fixture to the grid

FIGURE 9.48 Adding lights to the rest of the ceilings

5. Add it to the corridor wall, as shown in Figure 9.49.

FIGURE 9.49 Adding a sconce

6. Add the sconces to the walls of the hallways as appropriate, as shown in Figure 9.50.

7. In the Project Browser, double-click on the 3D view called East Wing Corridor Perspective. This will give you a good idea of how the up-lighting influences the corridor (see Figure 9.51).

FIGURE 9.50 Copying the sconce to the other hallway walls

FIGURE 9.51 Looking at the hallway in a perspective view

Well, that corridor is looking great! It's time now to start looking into the offices, and also to see if we can get a kitchen area completed.

Adding Casework and Furniture

Adding casework and furniture is the easiest part of this chapter — that is, if you like the casework and furniture that comes right out of the Revit box. Something tells me that this is not going to be adequate. For this chapter, we will be using the out-of-the box items, but in Chapter 17, we will make some custom millwork families.

To add some office furniture, follow along:

1. Select the Level 1 floor plan.

2. Zoom into the northwest corner office, as shown in Figure 9.52.

3. On the Home tab, click the Component ➢ Load from Library button.

4. Browse to the Furniture folder and select the following five items:

> ▶ Cabinet-File 5 Drawer.rfa
>
> ▶ Chair-Executive.rfa
>
> ▶ Credenza.rfa
>
> ▶ Entertainment Center.rfa
>
> ▶ Shelving.rfa

5. Click Open.

6. In the Change Element Type menu, select Credenza : 72"×24".

7. Place the credenza desk into the room, as shown in Figure 9.52.

FIGURE 9.52 Placing the credenza desk into the first office

8. Click the Component button again.

9. From the Change Element Type menu, select Chair Executive and place it behind the desk, as shown in Figure 9.53.

10. Click the Component button.

11. Select the Entertainment Center : 96"×84"×0" and place it in the corner, as shown in Figure 9.53.

12. Click the Component button again.

13. Place four 36" shelving units across the south wall, as shown in Figure 9.53.

FIGURE 9.53 Adding furniture to the office

At this point, it is a good idea to take a perspective shot at this office to see if this space is developing the way you were envisioning. Although you may never put this perspective view onto a construction document, it is still a great idea to see what is going on:

1. On the View tab, select the 3D View ➢ Camera button.

2. Pick a point in the northwest corner.

3. Pick a second point beyond the southeast corner, as shown in Figure 9.54.

4. In the Project Browser, right-click on the new 3D view and call it **Perspective of Corner Office.**

5. You can turn on your shading with edges, and even the shadows, if you need to do so. Remember, however, shadows are unnecessary and will slow down the view dramatically (see Figure 9.55).

FIGURE 9.54 Adding a camera (perspective view) to the corner office

FIGURE 9.55 The perspective of the corner office

It's time for a kitchen! This is such a nice office, there seems to be a need for a break area right outside. We would not want our executive to have to walk very far for a cup of coffee or a snack.

To get started, we'll load some countertops and cabinets:

1. On the Basics tab of the Design bar, click the Component ➤ Load from Library button.

2. Browse to the Casework folder.

3. Open the Domestic Kitchen folder.

4. Select the following families:

> ▶ Base Cabinet-2 Bin.rfa

> ▶ Base Cabinet-Double Door & 2 Drawer.rfa

> ▶ Base Cabinet-Double Door Sink Unit.rfa

> ▶ Base Cabinet-Single Door & Drawer.rfa

> ▶ Counter Top-L Shaped w Sink Hole 2.rfa

> ▶ Upper Cabinet-Double Door-Wall.rfa

5. Click Open.

6. Add the countertop, as shown in Figure 9.56.

FIGURE 9.56 Adding the countertop

7. Press Esc twice.

8. Select the countertop.

9. Select the stretch arrows and stretch the leg of the counter to the end of the wall, as shown in Figure 9.57.

FIGURE 9.57 Lengthening the counter leg to meet the corner of the wall

10. Add the Base Cabinet-Double Door Sink Unit under the sink.

11. Align the base unit under the sink.

You now have a counter and a sink base. The problem is, you have no idea how high these items are or what they really look like! That's okay — this is Revit. What we need to do is create two elevations looking at these items, as follows:

1. On the Create panel on the View tab, click the Elevation button.

2. Add an interior elevation looking north, as shown in Figure 9.58.

3. Select the square marker and turn on the elevation looking east (see Figure 9.58).

4. Rename the north elevation to **Kitchen North**.

5. Rename the east elevation to **Kitchen East**.

With the elevations in, we can now flip back and forth to make sure we are putting the items in the right places, and to get a good idea of how out cabinet run is looking.

Elevations : Elevation : Elevation 1

FIGURE 9.58 Adding elevations to aid in design

The remainder of the procedure will involve adding the rest of the cabinets. Let's do it!

1. On the Home tab, click the Component button.

2. From the Change Element Type menu, select Base Cabinet - Single Door : 24".

3. Place the base cabinet to the right of the sink cabinet.

4. Select the Kitchen North Elevation. Does your elevation look like Figure 9.59?

5. Go back to the Level 1 floor plan.

6. Place a base cabinet Double Drawer and Two Door : 36" in the position shown in Figure 9.60.

7. Select the Kitchen East elevation.

FIGURE 9.59 The elevation of the cabinet run

FIGURE 9.60 Placing the 36" double drawer, two-door base cabinet

8. Move the base cabinet so there is a 1" counter overhang, as shown in Figure 9.61.

9. Copy the base cabinet to the right three times (see Figure 9.61).

10. Click the Component button.

11. Find Base Cabinet : Filler.

12. Click the Element Properties button.

FIGURE 9.61 The base cabinets are filling the run.

13. Click Edit Type.

14. Click Duplicate.

15. Change the name to **Filler - 1'–1"** and click OK.

16. Change the depth to 1'–1".

17. Click OK twice.

18. Insert the base filler into the model, as shown in Figure 9.62.

FIGURE 9.62 The base filler

19. Select the filler.

20. Click the Element Properties button.

21. Change the width to 3/4".

22. Click OK.

23. Add another Base Cabinet : Filler - 1'–1" to the opposite cabinet to create the corner, as shown in Figure 9.63.

FIGURE 9.63 The completed corner

The bases are done! It is time to add some wall cabinets to the kitchen. I think at this point you will have enough experience to go on your own to populate the rest of your building as you see fit!

1. On the Home tab, click the Component button.

2. In the Type Selector, select Upper Cabinet-Double-Door-Wall : 36".

3. Place the wall cabinet in the model, as shown in Figure 9.64. (Don't worry too much about aligning it to the cabinet below. We will align it in elevation.)

FIGURE 9.64 Adding the wall cabinet

4. Open the Kitchen East elevation.

5. Click the Align on the Modify tab button.

6. Align the wall cabinet to the base cabinet, as shown in Figure 9.65.

FIGURE 9.65 Aligning the wall to the base

7. Copy the wall cabinet to the right three times.

8. Save the model.

Your cabinets should look like Figure 9.66.

FIGURE 9.66 The finished east wall of the kitchen

Now that the kitchen is in place, it would be nice to add a tile floor only to that area. You can accomplish this without having to add extra floors to the model. You can simply split the face of the floor that is already there, and add an additional material.

Adding Alternate Floor Materials

Carpeting does not perform well in kitchens. This is information we know. What we don't know is how to accomplish adding tile to a carpeted floor system without having to cut the existing floor and start piecing in sections of alternate materials. The following procedure will guide you through the steps:

1. Select the Split Face button on the Modify tab, as shown in Figure 9.67.

2. Select the entire floor. This may require finding the edge of the floor along an exterior wall (see Figure 9.67).

FIGURE 9.67 Click the Split Face button and select the slab edge.

3. Using the line icon on the Draw panel, draw a continuous line around the area, shown in Figure 9.68.

N O T E   Remember, you cannot have any overlapping lines or gaps while adding your magenta sketch lines.

4. On the Create Split Face Boundary tab, click Finish Split Face.

Although it does not seem like it, you have split the kitchen from the rest of the floor. Next you'll apply a material to the kitchen. The first step will be to create a suitable material to use.

FIGURE 9.68 Drawing the perimeter of the alternate floor material

Creating a Tile Material

There is one tile material in this model, but it would be beneficial to create a new one with 12" square tiles. This procedure will take the place of using hatching in a conventional drafting situation.

Follow along with this procedure to create a new material:

1. On the Manage tab, click the Materials button, as shown in Figure 9.69.

FIGURE 9.69 Choose Materials Manage tab.

2. In the Materials dialog, scroll down, and select Ceramic Tile - 4" Blue.

3. At the bottom of the dialog, click the Duplicate button, as shown in Figure 9.70.

4. Call the new material Clay Tile - 12" Beige.

5. Change the Pantone color to Pantone 465 C.

6. Change Surface Pattern to 12" Tile (see Figure 9.70).

FIGURE 9.70 Changing the tile appearance

7. Click the Render Appearance tab, as shown in Figure 9.71.

8. In the Render Appearance Based On field, click the Replace button.

9. Select Ceramic Tile Mosaic Beige (see Figure 9.71).

10. Click OK.

The new material is locked, loaded, and ready to spill onto the floor! To do this, you literally are going to use a paint bucket to apply the new material to the kitchen. Follow along:

1. Click the paint material icon, as shown in Figure 9.72.

2. Select Clay Tile - 12" Beige from the Type Selector, as shown in Figure 9.72.

3. Put your paint bucket icon over the edge of the kitchen floor until the region becomes highlighted.

4. Once the region becomes highlighted, pick the floor. Your new tile will appear (see Figure 9.72).

FIGURE 9.71 Adding a texture and .bmp mapping to your new kitchen floor

FIGURE 9.72 The new tile floor

Phew! You are gaining a good amount of experience in terms of adding components and making the interior of the building conform to your design. If you think about it, we have done nothing here that is out of the ordinary. We are simply replacing everyday drafting routines with modeling routines. What a way to go!

Since there is quite a bit of building left, go ahead and load this model up with components. If you get stuck anywhere, go back and find the procedure that pertains to your problem.

Are You Experienced?

Now You Can...

☑ add ceilings to a room as well as create new ceilings and modify them to suit your needs

☑ transfer ceilings from other projects using the Transfer Project Standards function

☑ add soffits to your model by using a typical wall and offsetting the base

☑ create a plan region so you can see elements at different elevations without disturbing the rest of the view

☑ add components such as bathroom fixtures, office furniture, and lighting to your model

☑ create subregions in which to specify an alternate flooring. This allows you to avoid hatching.

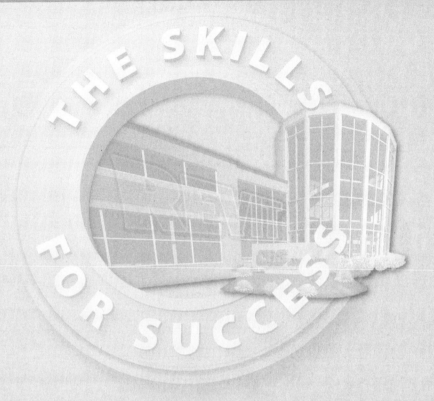

THE SKILLS FOR SUCCESS

Stairs, Ramps, and Railings

▶ Creating stairs using the Rise/Run function

▶ Creating custom winding stairs

▶ Creating railings

▶ Creating ramps

A whole chapter just for stairs, ramps, and railings? You bet! If you think about it, there could be a million combinations of stair and railing systems. As a matter of fact, you very seldom see two sets of stairs exactly the same. Kind of like a snowflake, isn't it? Okay, it's nothing like a snowflake! But you get the point.

To start off, this chapter will address the makings of a staircase, from commercial to a more residential feel with wood members, balusters, and spindles. During this procedure, you will see how Revit brings stairs together. Once we create a common staircase, we will move on to winding stairs, custom railings, and of course, ramps.

Creating Stairs Using the Rise/Run Function

Before we begin, I should mention that there are some features about stairs in Revit that you are going to love, and there are some features (or lack of features) that you are not going to love. As you are creating these stairs, keep in mind that there is no way Revit is going to be able to provide enough functionality to re-create every type of stair you may encounter.

 N O T E   **Throughout this book, you will have the opportunity to download from the book's website custom families that I have created.**

In this section, we will focus on creating a staircase using the traditional Rise/Run method. Then we'll discuss modifying the actual boundary of the stairs, which allows us to create a more unique shape than out of the box.

To begin, open the file you have been following along with. If you did not complete the previous chapter, go to the book's web page at www.sybex.com/go/revit2010ner. From there you can browse to Chapter 10 and find the file called NER-27.rvt.

The objective of the following procedure is to create a staircase using the Rise/Run method:

1. In the Project Browser, go to the Level 2 floor plan.

2. Zoom in on the radial entry in the west wing, as shown in Figure 10.1.

3. On the Circulation panel of the Home tab, click the Stairs button, as shown in Figure 10.1.

FIGURE 10.1 Click the Stairs button on the Circulation panel of the Home tab.

4. In the Create Stairs Sketch tab, click the Stairs Properties button, as shown in Figure 10.2.

FIGURE 10.2 Click the Stair Properties button on the Create Stair Sketch tab.

5. In the Element Properties dialog, change the Base Level to Level 1.

6. Change Top Level to Level 2.

7. Change Multistory Top Level to Level 5 (see Figure 10.3).

NOTE By setting the base to Level 1 and the top to Level 2, you are giving Revit the dimensions it needs to calculate the rise of the stairs. When you add the multistory height, Revit will take the calculation from Levels 1 and 2, then bring it up to the additional floors.

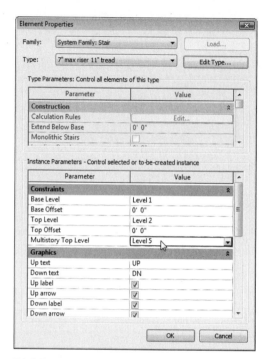

FIGURE 10.3 Changing the element properties of the stairs

8. Click OK.

9. To the left of the Create Stairs Sketch tab, be sure that Run is selected.

10. Pick the intersection of the floor edge and the grid 3.1 for the first point of the stairs. This spot is labeled "1" in Figure 10.4.

11. Move your cursor to the right. You will be able to see a faint display indicating that you have a certain amount of risers created and a certain amount remaining.

12. Once you see that nine risers have been created, with nine risers remaining, pick the spot labeled "2" in Figure 10.4.

13. Move your cursor straight up until you get to the grid intersection labeled "3" in Figure 10.4. Once you see this, pick the third point.

14. Move your cursor to the left all the way past the floor landing. Revit reports that you have 18 created, 0 remaining (see Figure 10.5).

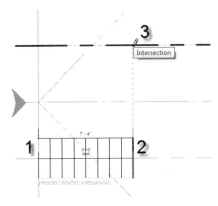

FIGURE 10.4 Adding the "L" shape to the stairs

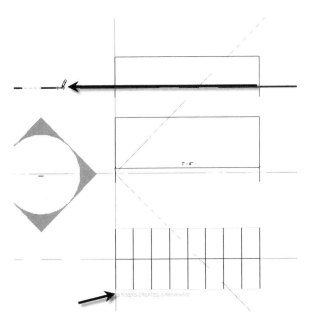

FIGURE 10.5 Make sure your cursor is way past the end of the stairs.

15. Once you see the second flight completed, pick the last point. Revit will draw both flights as well as the landing (see Figure 10.6).

FIGURE 10.6 The stairs have been laid out.

With the basic layout completed, it is time to take a look at the perimeter of the stairs. If you are looking for any architectural design outside of the basic "box" that you get when you place a staircase, you want to edit the boundary.

Boundaries

With the main stairs in place and laid out, you can now start modifying the profile. Given that this is a five-tiered, multilevel staircase, the boundary will be somewhat limited, but not to the point where we can't make something pop out of our design.

To modify the boundary, follow along:

1. On the Create Stairs Sketch tab, click the Boundary button, as shown in Figure 10.7.

FIGURE 10.7 The Boundary button on the Sketch bar

2. On the Draw panel, click the Start-End-Midpoint Arc button, as shown in Figure 10.8.

3. Draw an arc on the outside of the landing at an 8'–0" radius, as shown in Figure 10.8.

FIGURE 10.8 Add an 8'–0" radius to the outside of the landing.

With the radius drawn in, it is important to pause at this point. What we have here is an extra line. Similar to sketching a floor, if you have any overlapping line segments or gaps, Revit will not let you continue. Also, if you have any extra lines, Revit will not let you continue.

Let's clean up the stairs:

1. Press the Esc key twice and then select the straight green line at the outside of the landing.

2. Press the Delete key on your keyboard. The line is removed.

Your stairs should look exactly like Figure 10.9.

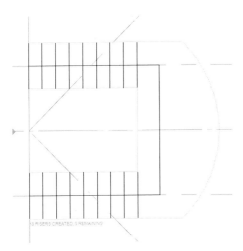

FIGURE 10.9 The completed boundary

With the boundary in place, it is time to select the railing system we are going to use. Out of the box, Revit only provides four choices. We will select one of those choices for this staircase, but will add to the list later on in this chapter.

Adding Railings

Revit provides only four railing systems as a default. You can choose one of these four railings to apply to the staircase during the Sketch mode of the stairs.

Follow along with this procedure to apply a railing to the stairs:

1. On the Create Stairs Sketch tab, click the Railings Type button, as shown in Figure 10.10.

FIGURE 10.10 Click the Railings Type button

2. In the Railings Type dialog, select Handrail – Pipe, as shown in Figure 10.11.

FIGURE 10.11 Select Handrail - Pipe in the Railings Type dialog.

3. Click OK.

With the railings in place, we are on our way to completing this staircase. As a matter of fact, round 1 seems to be done. To complete the stairs, just click Finish Sketch on the Create Stairs Sketch tab. Your stairs should look like Figure 10.12.

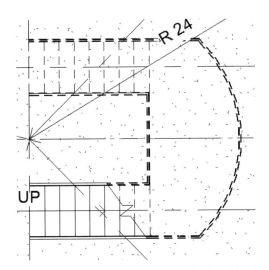

FIGURE 10.12 The stairs as displayed in plan

Normally, when you are dealing with a large, multistory staircase, you should check it out in 3D to make sure all went off as planned. This specific case is no exception!

1. Click the 3D button on the Quick Access toolbar.

2. In the 3D view, focus on the radial entry.

3. Select the radial wall and right-click.

4. From the context menu, select Hide in View ➤ Elements.

You should now examine your stairs (see Figure 10.13).

Here's a problem: the railing just stops dead at the stringer. This may have been acceptable practice around the time, say, when the wheel was still on the drawing boards. We need some kind of ADA compliance here at the bottom of the stairs. To accomplish this, follow along with the next procedure.

To begin, go to the book's web page at **www.sybex.com/go/revit2010ner**. From there you can browse to Chapter 10 and find the file called ADA-Pipe. You can then download it to your computer. Now perform the following steps:

1. On the Home tab, click the Component button ➤ Load from Library.

2. Browse to the directory where you stashed the family you just downloaded, and load the ADA-Pipe.rfa into your model.

FIGURE 10.13 The stairs in 3D with the radial entry "peeled back"

3. Go to the Level 1 floor plan.

4. Zoom in on the bottom of the stairs.

5. On the Work Plane panel of the Home tab, click Ref Plane ➤ Pick Existing Line/Edge, as shown in Figure 10.14.

6. Offset a reference plane 9½" to the left of the bottom riser, as shown in Figure 10.14.

7. Draw another reference plane from the center line of the bottom railing to the left about 2'–0" (see Figure 10.14).

8. On the Home tab, click the Component button.

9. In the Change Element Type menu, select ADA - Pipe.

10. Press the spacebar once to rotate the family into place.

11. Place the family at the intersection of the two reference planes, as shown in Figure 10.15.

FIGURE 10.14 Add two reference planes as indicated.

FIGURE 10.15 Inserting the ADA - Pipe family to the intersection

Extending the Railings

You have just added a family to finish off the stairs at the bottoms. The next step is to extend the railings on the stairs to meet the new family. There is one obstacle in the way, though: the railing on the stairs already has an ending post. The trick is to remove the "Revit-provided" ending post, and replace it with the "Sybex-provided" ADA post you just loaded into your model.

The objective of the next procedure is to extend the railings on the stairs to the ADA posts you just added to the model.

1. In plan, select the bottom railing, as shown in Figure 10.16. Make sure you are not selecting the stairs.

FIGURE 10.16 Select the railing, not the stairs.

2. On the Modify Railings tab, click the Element Properties button.

3. Click Edit Type.

4. Click Duplicate.

5. Call the new railing **Entry Stair Railing**.

6. Click OK.

7. In the Baluster Placement row, click the Edit button, as shown in Figure 10.17.

FIGURE 10.17 Click Edit next to Baluster Placement.

At the bottom of the Edit Baluster Placement dialog, you'll see a Posts category. Within the Posts category is a chance to place a post at the start, ending, or corner of the railing:

1. For the Start setting, select None from the list, as shown in Figure 10.18.

FIGURE 10.18 Set the start of the railing to None. This will remove the post that Revit provides only at the end of this railing.

2. Click OK twice.

3. Click OK one more time to get back to the model.

4. Select the railing on the inside of the stairs.

5. From the Change Element Type menu on the Element panel, select Entry Stair Railing.

It's time to stretch the railing on the stairs to meet up with the family. This procedure is best done in the plan view, where you can see exactly how far you need to stretch the railing:

1. Select the bottom railing.

2. On the Modify Railings tab, click the Edit Path button.

3. Click the Align button on the Modify Railings ➢ Edit Path tab, as shown in Figure 10.19.

4. For the first alignment, pick the back edge of the family you loaded, as shown in Figure 10.19.

5. Now, pick the magenta railing line. (When you hover over the magenta line, you will see an endpoint icon. Once you do, click it.) The magenta line will extend to the family (see Figure 10.19).

6. Click Finish Sketch.

7. Go to a 3D view to make sure the railings align (see Figure 10.20).

Notice that the line seems off center. Don't worry about this — it will line up when you finish the sketch.

FIGURE 10.19 Aligning the end of the railing to the new family

FIGURE 10.20 Check out the railing in 3D to ensure proper alignment.

It would be nice if this were the only place that this railing extension needed to go. The rest of the procedure will step you through the process of adding this extension to the inside railing and then copying it up to the other levels:

1. Copy the ADA - Pipe family up to the inside railing. Make sure you go straight up, as shown in Figure 10.21.

2. Select the inside railing.

3. On the Modify Railings tab, click the Edit Path button.

4. Click the Align button.

5. Align the magenta line with the ADA - Pipe family, as shown in Figure 10.21.

FIGURE 10.21 Copying and aligning the inner railing to the ADA family

6. Select both families.

7. On the Modify Generic Models tab, click the Copy button on the Clipboard panel.

8. Choose Paste Aligned ➤ Select Levels, as shown in Figure 10.22.

9. Pick Levels 2, 3, and 4.

Does your staircase look like Figure 10.22?

It's getting close, but it seems as though there is nothing keeping people from falling off the second, third, fourth, and fifth levels! I don't know about you, but I think this is the perfect place to put a separate railing and tie it into the stair railing.

FIGURE 10.22 The copied families

Landing Railings

Railings, of course, can be drawn independently from a stair. Tying the railing into the stair, however, requires a little more patience. That being said, it starts to become obvious that Revit reflects the real world when it comes to railings. If you have a railing that is difficult to build, it is probably going to be difficult to model. Also, if you arrive at an intersection that cannot be physically accomplished in the field, then guess what? You will struggle trying to get it into Revit.

To add some railings at the landings and tie them into the stair railings, follow these steps:

1. In the Project Browser, go to the Level 2 floor plan.

2. On the Home tab, click the Railing button, as shown in Figure 10.23.

3. Click the Railing Properties button on the Element panel.

FIGURE 10.23 Click the Railing button on the circulation panel of the Home tab.

4. Make sure that Type is set to Handrail Pipe.

5. Click OK.

6. On the Draw panel, make sure the pick lines icon is selected.

7. Change the offset to 8½".

8. Pick the front edge of the floor, as shown in Figure 10.24. The railing should now be set back from the edge of the landing with an 8½" clearance.

9. The magenta line is going to be way too long. Select it and drag the grip down to the point shown in Figure 10.24.

10. At the bottom of the railing, select the grip and drag it out of the wall as well (see Figure 10.24).

 N O T E You can only have one continuous railing at a time. If there are gaps in the railing, it won't work. For example, the second floor is going to need three separate railings.

11. On the Create Railing Path tab, click the Railing Properties button.

12. Click Edit Type.

13. Click Duplicate.

14. Call the new railing **Landing Handrail**.

15. Click OK.

16. In the Baluster Placement row, click the Edit button.

17. In the Posts field, change the start and end post to None (as shown in Figure 10.25).

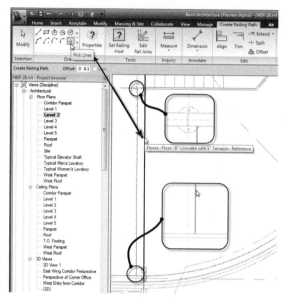

FIGURE 10.24 Adding the first railing segment

18. Also, just above the Posts field, change the pattern to Center (again, see Figure 10.25).

FIGURE 10.25 Configuring the railing for the landing

19. Click OK twice.

20. Click OK one more time to get back to the model.

21. On the Railing panel, click Finish Railing.

Your railing needs to be centered on the reference plane. It may or may not be. If it is not, select the railing. You will see a blue flip grip (double-arrow grip) in the middle of the railing. Pick it, and your railing will flip (see Figure 10.26).

FIGURE 10.26 The railing centered on the reference plane

The next step is to create a railing between the two stair sections. This can be a tad tricky, but once you get the progression, I think you will see why it needs to be done in the following manner:

1. On the Home tab, click the Railing button.

2. In the Create Railing Path tab, click the Railing Properties button.

3. Make sure the type is Landing Handrail, and click OK.

4. Using the same 8½" offset, draw the sketch of the railing as shown in Figure 10.27.

5. Click Finish Railing.

6. If you need to flip the railing, select it, and then click the blue flip grip that appears in the middle of the railing (see Figure 10.28).

FIGURE 10.27 Adding the railing to the middle of the stair landing

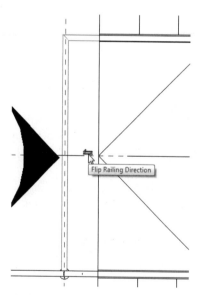

FIGURE 10.28 The finished railing

Now that the two railings are in place, you can use basic editing commands to create an occurrence of the railing on the other side of the stairs. You can either mirror the railing on your own, or if you wish, you can follow along with these steps:

1. Select the south railing, as shown in Figure 10.29.

2. Click the Mirror ➢ Pick Mirror Axis button on the Modify Railings tab.

3. For the reference, pick the center reference plane.

4. Make sure the railing is abutting the north wall.

FIGURE 10.29 Mirroring the railing to the north side of the stairs

5. Select the north railing, as shown in Figure 10.30.

6. On the Modify Railings tab, click the Edit Path button.

7. Draw a connecting piece, as shown in Figure 10.30.

8. Once the railing is sketched in, click the Finish Railing button on the Railing panel to the right.

At this point, it is a good idea to check out your railing in 3D because we are about to copy it to the levels above.

It the railing is backward after you finish the sketch, you can select the flip arrow after you select the railing.

To mirror an item, you can also select the object you wish to mirror, then type MM at the keyboard. This will start the Mirror command.

FIGURE 10.30 Adding the connecting piece to the railing

ALIGNING THE RAILING

If you are having trouble aligning the railing to the correct point of the stair railing, click the thin lines icon on the View tab shown here:

It's copy time! The next objective is to copy these three railings up to the next three levels. You can proceed on your own and use Copy/Paste Aligned, or you can follow along with this procedure:

1. In the Project Browser, go to the Level 2 floor plan.

2. Select the three railings you added to Level 2.

3. On the Modify Railings tab, click the Copy button on the Clipboard panel.

4. Click Paste Aligned ➢ Select Levels.

5. Select Levels 3, 4, and 5.

6. In the Project Browser, go to Level 5.

7. Delete the bottom (south) railing.

8. Select the smaller, middle railing, as shown in Figure 10.31.

9. On the Modify Railings tabs bar, click the Edit Path button.

10. Extend the line down to the south wall, as shown in Figure 10.31.

FIGURE 10.31 Extending the railing to complete Level 5

11. On the Railing panel, click Finish Railing.

12. Save the model.

13. Check out the model in 3D (see Figure 10.32).

Phew! We have built a set of stairs. The good thing is that it's one sweet stair-case. The bad thing is we used all the default layouts and materials. It's time to get into some more complicated shapes and styles.

FIGURE 10.32 The entry stairs and railing

Remember, if you want to get the front radial wall out of the way, you can right-click it, and choose Hide in View ➢ Hide Element. This command will hide the wall in this view. Just remember that when you need it turned back on, you must unhide the element.

Creating a Winding Staircase

Before we get started here, this staircase will be created using the separate stair components. You can try to do a winding staircase using the Run function similar to the one we did earlier, but in many cases (especially when you run into an existing staircase in either a renovation project or an addition), you may just need to draft the stairs, then model over the top of the drafting lines. What? Drafting in Revit? Of course. How else can you expect to get anything done?

The first thing we will need to do is make modifications to the floor in a specific area to create a landing, as follows:

1. In the Project Browser, go to the Level 2 floor plan.

2. Zoom in on the area between the corridor and the east wing, as shown in Figure 10.33.

3. Select the Level 2 floor in the west wing.

4. Once the floor is selected, click the Edit Boundary button on the Edit panel of the Modify Floors tab.

5. Sketch a landing that is 8'–0" long × 7'–10" wide, as shown in Figure 10.33.

You may have to pick a window around the entire area, and then click the Filter button on the Options bar. From there, you can select only floors.

FIGURE 10.33 Create a landing as shown here. We will add a door in a moment.

6. Once the landing is added in, click Finish Sketch on the Sketch bar. If you are asked to attach the walls to the bottom of the floor, click Yes.

With the landing in place, we can now copy a door up to this level. To do this, we will go to the first floor and copy the door that resides there. You can do this on your own, or you can follow along with the procedure:

1. In the Project Browser, go to the Level 1 floor plan.

2. Select the door that is there (see Figure 10.34).

3. Copy the door to the clipboard (Click Copy on the clipboard panel).

4. Choose paste Aligned ➢ Select Levels.

5. Select Level 2 and click OK.

6. In the Project Browser, go back to Level 2. The door and the landing are now in place. (You can look ahead to Figure 10.36 to see the results.)

FIGURE 10.34 Copying the first floor door to the clipboard and pasting it to level 2

With the landing and the door in place, we can now create a winding set of stairs. The first item is to simply lay out the shape in plan using simple drafting lines. The second step is to model over these lines we add using various stair tools, as follows:

1. Select the Annotate tab.

2. Click the Detail Lines button, as shown in Figure 10.35.

FIGURE 10.35 Click the Detail Lines button on the Annotate tab.

3. On the Draw panel, click the Start - End - Midpoint Arc button, as shown in Figure 10.36.

4. For the first point of the arc, pick the midpoint of the landing, as shown in Figure 10.36.

5. Move your cursor down and at 135° from the first point picked.

6. Extend your cursor 11'–0", as shown in Figure 10.36.

FIGURE 10.36 With the Start-End-Midpoint Arc, first start at the midpoint of the landing, then go southeast at an angle of 135° and a distance of 11'-0".

7. To form the arc, move your cursor to the right until the radius snaps into place. Once it does, pick the point, as shown in Figure 10.37.

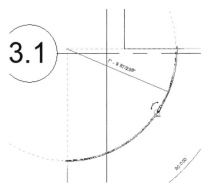

FIGURE 10.37 Pick the third point to form the arc. It will be tangent upon the first two points you picked.

8. Press Esc.

9. Start the Detail Lines command again.

10. On the Options bar, click the pick lines icon.

11. Again, on the Options bar, add an increment of 2'–0" to the Offset field (see Figure 10.38).

12. Offset the center arc to the right, then to the left, forming a 4'–0" overall winder, as shown in Figure 10.38.

FIGURE 10.38 Adding two more arcs based on the centerline of the first

13. Press Esc.

14. Draw a straight line at each end of the arcs, as shown in Figure 10.39.

Okay, take a breather. Compare the examples in the book to what you have. Are we close? If not, go back and investigate.

 N O T E   Get used to this drafting thing; it is still very much a part of BIM, regardless if people say you can't draft in Revit!

FIGURE 10.39 Adding two straight lines at each end of the arcs

The next step is to make an array of the straight lines we just added. These lines will wind up being our guidelines for our risers.

    1. Select the smaller arc, as shown in Figure 10.40.

FIGURE 10.40 Selecting the smaller arc

    2. On the Modify Lines tab, click the Element Properties button.

3. In the instance parameters, check on Center Mark Visible.

4. Click OK.

5. Select the line at the left end of the arcs, as shown in Figure 10.41.

6. Click the Array button on the Modify Lines tab, as shown in Figure 10.41.

7. On the Options bar, be sure that Radial Array is selected.

8. Make sure Group and Associate is checked on.

9. Type 18 for the number.

10. Click Move to Last.

11. Once these are set, pick and drag the blue icon to the center point you turned on earlier (see Figure 10.41).

12. Pick a point along the first line (the one on the bottom left).

13. Pick the second point along the upper-right line.

FIGURE 10.41 Arraying the line to create your own treads

Your array should now be complete. Compare your linework to Figure 10.42.

FIGURE 10.42 The stairs are taking shape.

It's time to start modeling the stairs. This procedure will be nothing more than tracing the lines you have already added to the model. To do this, we are going to utilize the tools available that we have not touched in the previous staircase, as follows:

1. On the Home tab, click the Stairs button.

2. In the Create Stairs Sketch tab, click the Stairs Properties button.

3. Change Base Level to Level 1.

4. Change Top Level to Level 2.

5. Click Edit Type.

6. Click Duplicate.

7. Call the stairs **Corridor Entry Stairs**.

8. Click OK.

9. For the Tread material, click in the field where it says <Default>.

10. You will see an […] button. Click it.

11. Choose Wood - Cherry for the tread material.

12. For the riser material, do the same.

13. For the stringer material, select Wood - Mahogany (see Figure 10.43).

14. Under the Treads category, select Front, Left and Right for Apply Nosing Profile.

15. In the Stringers category, select Match Level for Trim Stringers at Top (see Figure 10.43).

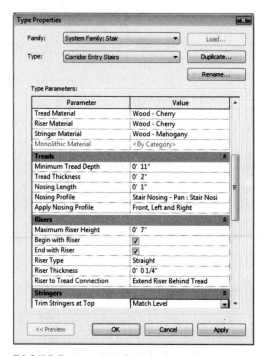

FIGURE 10.43 Customizing the stairs

16. Click OK twice.

17. Click OK to get back to the model.

It's now time to add the stairs to the model. To do this, we will first sketch the boundary:

1. On the Create Stair Sketch tab, click the Boundary button, as shown in Figure 10.44.

2. On the Draw panel, click the pick lines icon.

3. Pick the two arcs defining the outside of the stairs. You will see green arcs copied directly on top of them.

FIGURE 10.44 Clicking the Boundary button

4. On the Draw panel, click the Riser button, as shown in Figure 10.45.

FIGURE 10.45 Clicking the Riser button

5. On the Draw panel, click the pick lines icon.

6. Pick all of the lines you arrayed. This includes the bottom and the top lines (see Figure 10.46).

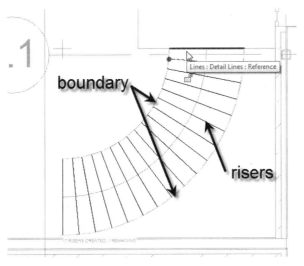

FIGURE 10.46 Pick the detail lines to lay over the actual stair components.

7. Click Finish Stairs on the Stairs panel.

With the stairs "roughed in," we need to get a better look at them. By using the default 3D view, we will have to turn way too many items off in order to see the stairs we are working on. Let's add a perspective view just to see what's going on here!

If you are confident in adding your own perspective view, go ahead and put one in, and name it **East Entry from Corridor.** If not, follow along with the procedure:

1. In the Project Browser, go to the Level 1 floor plan.

2. On the View tab pick the 3D ➤ Camera button.

3. Pick the first point shown in Figure 10.47.

4. Pick the second point shown in Figure 10.47.

5. In the Project Browser, find the new 3D view, and rename it to **West Entry from Corridor.**

6. In the Perspective view, turn on Shading with Edges (this is located at the View Control bar at the bottom of the view).

FIGURE 10.47 Adding the perspective view

Now that we have a perspective on our stairs, there are multiple issues with the railing. The first, more prominent issue is the fact that the railings seem to be floating. This occurs when the stringers are switched from closed to open. Revit still thinks there is a stringer underneath the railings. We will need to move the railings in 2" to fix this problem.

Making Railing Adjustments

Yes, we have been making railing adjustments this entire chapter. Get used to constantly having to do this for each unique situation. This staircase requires us to add some posts back into the railing so it can stop and end at the stringer. But, first let's move the railing back onto the actual treads:

1. Go to the Level 2 floor plan.

2. Select the top railing, as shown in Figure 10.48.

3. On the Modify Railings tab, click Edit Path.

4. Click the Offset button on the Edit panel, as shown in Figure 10.48.

5. In the Offset field in the Options bar, type 2".

6. Deselect the Copy option.

7. Offset the railing into the stairs 2", as shown in Figure 10.48.

FIGURE 10.48 Offset the railing in 2".

8. Click Finish Sketch.

9. Select the other railing.

10. Click the Edit button on the Options bar.

11. Offset the railing in 2".

12. Click Finish Sketch.

Since these railings will not extend past the stringers, it is okay to add posts back to the beginning and the ends of the railings:

1. Select both railings.

2. In the Change Element Type menu, select Railing : Handrail - Pipe.

3. Go to the perspective view. Does your stair and railing system look like Figure 10.49?

FIGURE 10.49 The almost completed stairs

The next series of steps will involve mirroring the stairs to the other side of the landing. Then, of course, we need to add a landing railing so people don't just walk out the door and off the ledge.

1. Go to Level 2 in the Project Browser.

2. Select the stairs and the railings.

N O T E   To select only the stairs and the railings, you can pick a window around the entire set of lines, groups railings, and stairs. From there, you can click the Filter button on the Options bar, and select only stairs and railings.

3. On the Modify Stairs tab, click the Mirror ➤ Pick Mirror Axis button, as shown in Figure 10.50.

4. Pick the center reference plane (I told you this thing would come in handy).

Your stairs are now mirrored to the other side of the landing, as shown in Figure 10.50.

FIGURE 10.50 The mirrored stairs

It's time to tie in the railings. If you are feeling up to the challenge, try it on your own using the landing railing you used in the front entry stairs. If not, just follow along with these steps:

1. On the Home tab, click the Railing button.

2. In the Create Railing Path tab, click the Railing Properties button.

3. Change the type to Landing Handrail (if it is not already). See Figure 10.51.

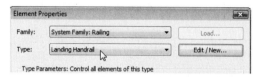

FIGURE 10.51 Setting the landing handrail

4. Click OK.

5. On the Draw panel, click the pick lines icon, as shown in Figure 10.52.

6. Set the offset at 4".

7. Pick the landing lines to offset in the railing, as shown in Figure 10.52.

FIGURE 10.52 Adding the railings to the landing

8. Once the offsets are complete, click the Line icon on the Draw panel, as shown in Figure 10.53.

9. Make sure the offset is set to 0.

10. Draw the lines extending from the stair railing to the landing railing, as shown in Figure 10.53.

11. Trim the corners so your railings look like Figure 10.53.

FIGURE 10.53 Connecting the landing railing to the stair railing

12. On the Railing panel, click Finish Railing.

13. You may have to flip the railing by selecting it, then clicking the Flip arrow. Your railing should look like Figure 10.54.

FIGURE 10.54 The railing at the front of the landing

14. Add two more railings between the stairs and the brick wall. Your stairs should look like Figure 10.55.

FIGURE 10.55 The completed landing

▶

Remember, you must only do one railing at a time. If you try to do more than one continuous line, Revit will not let you continue.

Great! We are getting there. Now it is time to see how a staircase and the accompanying railings come together. For example, it sure would be nice to have a railing with spindles, or better yet, panels added to them. Also, a nice half-round bull nose would improve our staircase. The next section will focus on this concept.

Stair and Railing Families

Similar to the model as a whole, stairs and railings are comprised of separate families that come together to form the overall unit. Although stairs and railings are considered a system family (a family that resides only in the model), they still heavily rely on families to create the entire element.

The next procedure will involve loading separate families into the model, then utilizing them in a new set of stairs and railings we will create in the east wing.

1. In the Project Browser, go to the Level 3 floor plan.

2. Zoom in on the east wing.

3. On the Home tab, click the Floor button.

4. On the Create Floor Boundary tab, click the Floor Properties button to the right of the ribbon

5. Select the 6" concrete with 1" Terrazzo floor system, as shown in Figure 10.56.

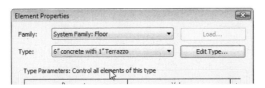

FIGURE 10.56 You must add a floor at the Level 3 floor plan for the stairs to have a landing.

6. Click OK.

7. On the Draw panel, click the Pick Walls button.

8. Pick the walls, as shown in Figure 10.57. Make sure the lines are set to the core center line. (Again, see Figure 10.57.)

9. When picking the south wall, set the offset to 5'–0" in the Options bar, as shown in Figure 10.57.

FIGURE 10.57 Adding the floor outline to the walls. Be sure to offset the line 5'–0" from the south wall. This will be the stair landing.

TIP Although I have said this about 20 times, make sure you have no gaps or overlapping lines. Use the Trim command to clean up the lines to look like Figure 10.57.

10. Once the sketch lines are in place, click Finish Floor on the floor panel to the right of the ribbon.

11. Revit will ask you if you want to attach the walls that go up to this floor's bottom. Click Yes.

12. Next Revit will ask you if you want to cut the overlapping volume out of the walls. Click Yes again.

Your floor is now in place. The next item we will tackle is creating a completely custom railing system.

Creating a Custom Railing System

It's now time to load the components that will comprise our stairs. Although Revit makes an attempt to supply you with some families, you will be downloading the families included with this book by going to the book's web page at **www.sybex.com/go/revit2010ner**. From there you can browse to Chapter 10 and find the following files:

▶ 6210 (2-5_8).rfa

▶ landing.rfa

▶ post.rfa

▶ raised panels.rfa

▶ spindle.rfa

▶ stair nosing.rfa

To get started, we need to load the families into our model so they are available when it comes time to assemble our new railing. If you remember how to do this, go ahead and load all the families that you just downloaded from the web page. If you need some assistance, follow along with the procedure:

1. On the Home tab, click Component ➤ Load from Library.

2. Find the files that you downloaded from the web page.

3. Once you have found the files we listed, click Open to load them.

4. Save the model.

The next step will be to actually create a new railing and add some of these items to it:

1. In the Project Browser, find the Families category and expand it, as shown in Figure 10.58.

2. Find the Railings category and expand it.

3. Find Handrail - Rectangular and double-click it (see Figure 10.58).

FIGURE 10.58 The railing family called Handrail - Rectangular

4. Click Duplicate.

5. Call the new railing **Wood railing with Spindles**.

6. Click OK.

7. In the Rail Structure row, click the Edit button.

8. In the Rails chart, change Name to **Handrail**, as shown in Figure 10.59.

9. Change the profile to **6210 (2-5_8): 2⁵/₈"**.

10. Change the Material to Wood - Cherry by clicking on the [...] button and browsing for the wood material. See Figure 10.59.

FIGURE 10.59 Changing the rail. Note that you can add as many rails as you wish. In this case, we are only adding one.

11. Click OK.

12. Click the Edit button in the Baluster Placement row.

13. In the Main Pattern, change the Baluster pattern to Spindle 1" (see Figure 10.60).

FIGURE 10.60 Adding the spindle to the main pattern

14. Just below the main pattern area is the Use Baluster per Tread on Stairs option. Click it, as shown in Figure 10.61.

15. To the right, you will see a field that says Balusters per Tread. Specify two balusters per tread (see Figure 10.61).

16. In the bottommost field is the Posts category. Change each of the three posts to None. Our spindles are all we need (see Figure 10.61).

FIGURE 10.61 Specifying two balusters per tread and no actual posts

17. Click OK twice.

You may or may not have noticed that we did not get the opportunity to change the baluster's material as we did with the railing. This action must be done in the family itself, as follows:

1. In the Project Browser, you will see a category called Spindle just below the railings, as shown in Figure 10.62. Expand Spindle to expose the 1" spindle.

2. Once you see the 1", double-click on it to open its element Properties dialog.

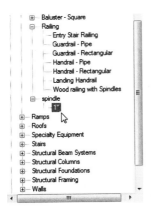

FIGURE 10.62 Finding the Spindle : 1" family to access the material

3. In the Element Properties dialog, find the Material row and click the […] button. This will appear when you click into the field that says <By Category>.

4. Change the material to Wood - Cherry.

5. Click OK.

This completes the railing. Once we add it to the stairs, however, there will certainly be some required "tweaking." The next step is to customize the stairs themselves.

Creating Custom Stairs

Since this is the third staircase we have created in the same chapter, you certainly have gained some experience regarding the placement of stairs and railings into the Revit model. You are also becoming familiar with the stair and railings dialogs. This last procedure will tie all of that together.

Let's create that staircase:

1. On the Home tab, click the Stair button.

2. On the Create Stair Sketch tab, click the Stair Properties button to the right of the ribbon.

3. Click Edit Type

4. Click Duplicate.

5. Call the new staircase **Custom Bull Nose Stairs**.

6. Click OK.

7. In the type parameters, under Construction, turn on the toggle for Monolithic, as shown in Figure 10.63.

8. Moving down the list, change the Monolithic material to Wood - Mahogany.

9. Change the Nosing Profile to Stair Nosing : Stair Nosing (see Figure 10.63).

10. Under the Risers category, change the riser thickness to 3/4".

11. For the Riser to Tread connection, extend the Tread Under Riser. See Figure 10.63.

FIGURE 10.63 Configuring the stairs. As you can see, you have quite a few options.

12. Click OK.

It is time to configure some of the layout properties. These will allow us to calculate the rise/run count as well as some basic offsets we will need.

1. Set Base Level to Level 1.

2. Set Base Offset to 6⅝", as shown in Figure 10.64.

3. Set Top Level to Level 3. (Yes, this is going to be one long staircase!)

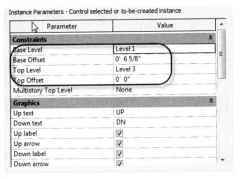

FIGURE 10.64 The base value is set to 6⅝".

4. Click OK.

The next step is to place this monster into the model. Although we did not specify a multistory staircase, we will need multiple landings to give our visitors a breather as they travel up the stairs. This layout will require a little more care in the initial planning stage.

1. On the Home tab, click the Ref Plane ➤ Pick Existing Line / Edge button, as shown in Figure 10.65.

2. Offset a grid, as shown in Figure 10.65.

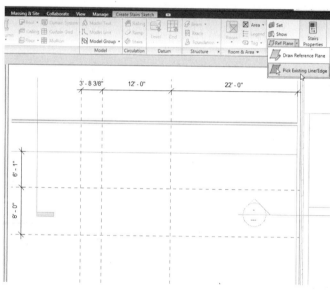

The nice thing about using reference planes while in Sketch mode is the fact that they will disappear once you finish the sketch. If you need to go back and edit the stair, the reference planes will appear again!

FIGURE 10.65 Use these dimensions to lay out the center lines of the stairs.

3. On the Create Stair Sketch tab, click the Run button.

4. Draw your stairs as shown in Figure 10.66. (Pick the points as the figure is sequenced.)

5. Once the points have been picked, click Finish Stairs. Your plan should look like Figure 10.67.

FIGURE 10.66 Picking the intersections of the reference planes to determine where the stairs will be going

FIGURE 10.67 The stairs in place

Remember how the railings seemed to be floating when we opened the stringers in the entry staircase? We are going to have the same issue here. The next procedure is to move the railings in 2" in plan so there is adequate bearing on the stairs:

1. In plan, select the top railing, as shown in Figure 10.68.

2. On the Modify Railings tab, click Edit Path.

3. On the Edit panel, click the Offset button, as shown in Figure 10.68.

4. On the Options bar, enter 2" into the Offset field.

5. Uncheck Copy.

6. Hover your cursor over one of the magenta sketch lines and press the Tab key. This will select the entire railing line.

7. Make sure the dotted alignment line is facing the inside, as shown in Figure 10.68. (If it is not, press the spacebar to flip it.)

FIGURE 10.68 Offset the railing line down 2" from the original location.

8. Once the railing is offset in, click Finish Railing.

9. Repeat the procedure on the other railing.

10. Go to a 3D view to check out the stairs. They should resemble Figure 10.69.

FIGURE 10.69 The stairs as shown in 3D. Notice the nice bull nose and the railings.

The next step (pun intended) is to add a landing to the bottom of the stairs. This requires creating a family. Although we will cover creating families in Chapter 17, this one has been created, and you have downloaded the families needed to create this step in the stairs.

Adding a Custom Landing

The reason we left the 6⅝" offset for the bottom tread is because we need to introduce our own version of what that bottom tread should look like. As mentioned before, this family has been loaded. If not, go to **www.sybex.com/go/revit2010ner**. From there you can browse to Chapter 10 and find the files called Landing.rfa and Post.rfa. Once these families are loaded, proceed with these steps:

1. In the Project Browser, go to the Level 1 floor plan.

2. On the Home tab, click the Component button.

3. Find the component called Landing in the Change Element Type menu.

4. As you are inserting the family, press the Tab key to rotate the landing into the correct position.

5. Place the landing under the last tread at the point shown in Figure 10.70.

FIGURE 10.70 Placing the landing

6. Press Esc.

7. Select the landing.

8. On the Modify Generic Models tab, click the Element Properties button.

9. In the type parameters, change the tread material to Wood - Cherry.

10. Change the base material to Wood - Mahogany and click OK (see Figure 10.71).

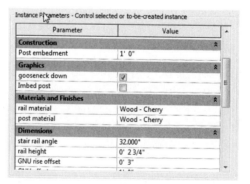

FIGURE 10.71 Changing the landing material to match the theme of the staircase

The next remaining item is to add a post.

Adding a Gooseneck

In this style of railing system, it would be nice to have a gooseneck that will catch the railing as it slopes downward and spiral it into the post. Of course Revit does not have families for this already built, but this book sure does! You should have downloaded the post family earlier in this chapter, but if you did not, go to the book's website at **www.sybex.com/go/revit2010ner**. From there you can browse to Chapter 10 and find the file called Post.rfa. Once it is downloaded and loaded into the model, follow these steps:

1. In the Project Browser, go to the Level 1 floor plan and zoom in on the landing area, as shown in Figure 10.72.

2. On the Home tab, click the Component button.

3. In the Change Element Type menu, select Post with Gooseneck.

4. As you are placing the post, press the spacebar twice to flip it into the correct orientation.

5. Place it on the landing slightly away from the stair railing, as shown in Figure 10.72.

FIGURE 10.72 Place the post with the gooseneck as shown here.

6. Once the post is placed, select it and click the Element Properties button on the Element panel.

7. Change the offset to $6^{5}/_{8}$".

8. Click OK.

 N O T E   If the end of the post seems to be clipped in plan, you need to adjust the view range in the Element Properties dialog. Right now, the 4'–0" clip plane may be a tad too low. To fix this, type **VP**, then find the View Range row. In the View Range dialog, adjust the cut plane to 4'–6".

---

9. Select the post again (if it is not still selected).

10. Click the Move button.

11. Move it from the midpoint of the post's end to the midpoint of the stair railing's end, as shown in Figure 10.73.

FIGURE 10.73 Moving the post to align with the stair railing

12. Select the post again.

13. Click the Element Properties button on the Element panel.

14. In the Materials and Finishes category, change materials for both the rail and the post to Wood - Cherry.

15. Click OK.

16. Mirror the post to the other railing.

In 3D, your landing should now look like Figure 10.74.

FIGURE 10.74 The completed landing

Adding a Railing

It's now time to add the railing to the Level 3 balcony. Compared to that landing we just did, this is going to be a snap! If you feel as though you have the experience required to add your own landing railing, go ahead and take a shot! If not, just follow along with the procedure:

1. In the Project Browser, go to Level 3.

2. Zoom in on the stairs.

3. Right click one of the railings on the stairs and pick Create Similar.

4. Sketch a railing that is 4" in from the face of the landing, as shown in Figure 10.75.

5. Make sure you have a "leg" tied into the stair railing, as shown in Figure 10.75.

6. On the Railing panel, click Finish Railing.

7. Repeat the procedure on the other end (see Figure 10.76).

FIGURE 10.75 Adding the railing. This process is becoming old hat!

NOTE   To repeat the procedure on the other end, you can either mirror the railing you just put in, then edit it to reach the far end of the landing, or you can start the Railing command and do it again. I recommend mirroring the railing, selecting the new railing, and then selecting Edit Path from the Modify Railings tab. You can then grip-edit the right end to meet the wall. This ensures you the railing will be aligned with the railing on the stair.

FIGURE 10.76 Both railings are in place.

The last step is to add a raised panel stile and rail system along the third floor wall.

Adding a Raised Panel Stile and Rail System

The first thing we will need to do is to add an entrance to the large Level 3 training room. The corridor will then receive a custom raised panel line-based family.

1. In the Project Browser, go to the Level 3 floor plan.

2. On the Home tab, click the Door button.

3. From the Change Element Type menu in the Element panel, select the Single-Raised Panel with Sidelights : 36" x 84".

4. Place it in the corridor wall aligned with the stairs, as shown in Figure 10.77.

5. Copy the door to the right 10'-0" to the right, as shown in Figure 10.77.

6. On the View tab, click the Elevation button.

7. In the Change Element Type menu, click the Interior elevation choice.

8. Pick a point, as shown in Figure 10.77.

FIGURE 10.77 Pick the point as shown for the elevation.

9. In the Project Browser, right-click on the new elevation and rename it to **East Wing Balcony Elevation**.

10. Open the East Wing Balcony Elevation.

11. Stretch the crop region so you can see the entire east wing.

12. On the View Control toolbar, change the model graphics style to Wireframe, as shown in Figure 10.78.

13. On the Home tab, click the Component button.

14. On the Placement panel, click Place on Face.

15. In the Change Element Type menu on the Element panel, select the raised panels family.

    If you do not have the raised panel family, you can download it at **www.sybex.com/go/revit2010ner**. From there you can browse to

Chapter 10 and find the file called `Raised Panel.rfa`. Once it is downloaded and loaded in to the model, proceed with the next step.

FIGURE 10.78 Picking the far wall to establish a work plane

16. Pick the base point, labeled #1, in Figure 10.79.

17. Pick the second point, labeled #2, in Figure 10.79.

FIGURE 10.79 Adding the line-based raised panel family

N O T E   If you just can't seem to be able to pick the points specified in Figure 10.79, go ahead and pick two points close to the area indicated in the figure. Once you place the line-based family, you can select it and grip-edit the ends to extend to the wall's edges as shown in the figure.

18. Start the Component command again, and add the raised panel family between the two doors and to the right. This will complete the raised panels for this level.

19. Select all of the raised panel families on this floor (remember to hold the Ctrl key to add to the selection).

20. On the Modify Casework tab, click the Element Properties button to the left of the ribbon.

21. In the Material Finishes category, change the Panel material to Wood - Cherry.

22. Change Frame Material to Wood - Mahogany. See Figure 10.80.

FIGURE 10.80 The finished raised panel, line-based family

Wow! That was quite a bit on stairs. If you take anything away from this chapter, take away the knowledge that stairs are not going to come easy, but you can create any staircase if you approach it knowing you are going to need to create families.

The last section of this chapter will focus on adding ramps to the model. As far as Revit procedures go, ramps are the kid sister to stairs.

Adding Ramps

When you think of ramps in Revit, think of a one-tread, one-rise staircase at a 1/12 pitch. Ramps are placed in the model exactly the same as a stair. You still have the run method, and you can still sketch the ramp using a boundary.

That being said, let's start placing a ramp in your model:

1. In the Project Browser, go to the Level 1 floor plan.

2. Zoom in on the radial entry of the west wing at grid intersection F-5 (see Figure 10.81).

3. The first thing we need to do is to create a flat landing, so on the Home tab, click the Floor button.

4. On the Create Floor Boundary tab, click the Floor Properties button.

5. From the Type menu, select Generic - 12".

6. Click Edit/New.

7. Click Duplicate.

8. Call the new floor **Exterior Concrete Slab.**

9. Click OK.

10. Click the Edit button in the Structure row.

11. Change the Structure [1] material to Concrete - Cast-in-Place Concrete.

12. Change the thickness to 6".

13. Click OK twice.

14. Click OK one more time to get back to the model.

15. Place the concrete at the points shown in Figure 10.81.

 WARNING   Make sure you are using the Lines mode and are picking the outside face of brick. That extra line represents the water table above this floor's level.

FIGURE 10.81 Sketching the slab perimeter

16. Once the slab is in place, click the Finish Sketch button on the Sketch bar.

17. Click No for the next dialog.

Now it is time for the ramp. We will set the ramp's properties for the top to Level 1, and the bottom is also going to be at Level 1 but with an offset.

1. On the Home tab, click the Ramp button, as shown in Figure 10.82.

FIGURE 10.82 Clicking the Ramp button on the home tab

2. On the Create Ramp Sketch tab, click the Ramp Properties button.

3. Click Edit Type.

4. Click Duplicate.

5. Call the new ramp **Exterior Concrete Ramp**.

6. Click OK.

7. Give it a 6" thickness.

8. For the Ramp Material, click the [...] button and specify Concrete - Cast-in-Place Concrete, as shown in Figure 10.83.

9. Notice the maximum incline length is set to the ADA standard of 30'-0".

10. In the Other category, notice the slope is set to 1/12.

11. Click OK.

12. In the instance parameters, set Base Level to Level 1.

13. Set Top Level to Level 1.

14. Set Base Offset to –2'–6", as shown in Figure 10.84.

15. Set the width to 5'–0" (see Figure 10.84).

16. Click OK.

17. On the Draw panel, click the Run button.

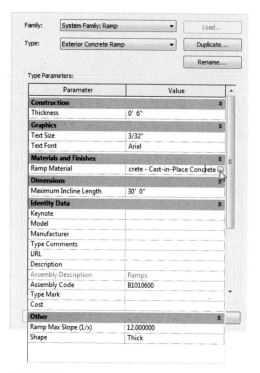

FIGURE 10.83 Modify the type parameters as shown here.

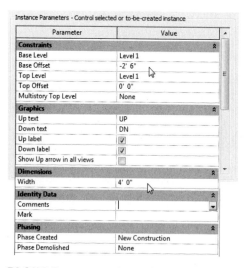

FIGURE 10.84 Setting the instance parameters

18. In the model, click the first point for the ramp similar to the point shown in Figure 10.85. (You will have to just place the point near the midpoint. Revit does not allow you to snap while in this Sketch mode for some reason.)

19. Move your cursor down the view (in a southerly direction) 15'–0" (you will see the temporary dimension), as shown in Figure 10.85.

FIGURE 10.85 Pick the first point on the landing, then move your cursor down 15'–0".

20. Pick a point about 6'–0" away from the end of the ramp in alignment with the right boundary, as shown in Figure 10.86. Once the second point is picked, it should say in the view "30'u of inclined ramp created, 0 remaining."

21. Move your cursor to the right until the ramp stops (see Figure 10.86).

22. On the Create Ramp Sketch tab, click the Railings Type button.

23. Select Handrail - Pipe.

24. Click OK.

25. Click Finish ramp.

26. Select the entire ramp (including the railing).

27. Move the ramp from the midpoint of the top of the ramp to the midpoint of the landing slab.

FIGURE 10.86 The second leg of the ramp

It is best if you keep moving your cursor past the ramp, even knowing the end of the ramp has stopped. This will ensure that the entire ramp has been put in place.

One problem you may notice immediately is the fact that the ramp is sloping in the wrong direction. Also, we need to tie the railings into the slab. If you would like to pick around and see how to do these things on your own, go right ahead. If you would rather go through the procedure, proceed with step 1:

1. Select the ramp.

2. Notice a small blue arrow. Pick it — this will flip the direction of the ramp.

3. On the Home tab, click the Railing button.

4. Click the Railing Properties button and change the type to Handrail - Pipe, and click OK.

5. Draw a railing in 8" from the slab edge, as shown in Figure 10.87.

6. Mirror the slab, the ramp, and the railing to the other side of the building.

7. Save the model.

Creating ramps will be a necessary evil in almost every project. Some will be easier than others, and at times they may try your patience. Keep at it and before long you will have the experience you need to feel confident.

FIGURE 10.87 Adding the railing just as you have been doing this entire chapter

FIGURE 10.88 The two ramps

Are You Experienced?

Now You Can...

☑ create stairs in the conventional method by using the Run command to generate the height and length you need

☑ create stairs by first laying out the geometry by placing linework in the model, then tracing over the lines with the stair components

☑ determine the difference between the boundary and the riser when you need to sketch the stair profile

☑ load necessary components used to customize stairs and railings such as railing types, spindles, posts, and landings

☑ use each separate component and access them in the Project Browser to place materials

☑ configure railings bases on the baluster placement and the railing placement as used in the element properties of the railing

☑ determine how to tie a railing into a stair railing by using offsets and by aligning the railing sketch with the stairs

☑ add a line-based raised panel family to complete millwork items

☑ create ramp landings and create the actual ramp

☑ determine the length of the ramp based on the rise and run of the slope

CHAPTER 11

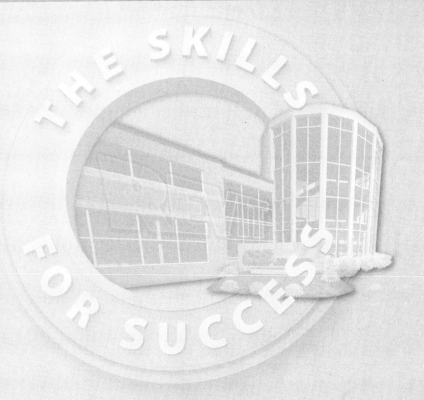

Schedules and Tags

To begin, I want to clarify something specific to the people who have been using AutoCAD Architecture: you do not need to tag an item in order for it to appear in a schedule in Revit Architecture. You can't really just draft a schedule either. But this is not a bad situation to be in. Say, for example, you have a typical door schedule. Wouldn't it be nice to just add a door to the model and have that door automatically show up in the schedule?

Revit allows you to instantly schedule an item based on the fact that we are now using a full database. A door, for example, already has most of the information you need built into it. Didn't it seem funny that when you placed a door in the model it was automatically tagged with a sequential door number? This is the power of BIM. We are now going beyond 3D.

Schedules do not stop just at doors and windows in Revit. You can schedule almost any item that goes into the model. Along with schedules comes the ability to quantify materials and square footages. You can even create a schedule for the sole purpose of changing items in the model. In Revit, it is always a two-way street.

The first topic we will tackle is creating the most common of the schedules in architecture: the door schedule. Once you get this procedure down, you will be off and running.

Creating Schedules

The good news is you have most of the information you need to create a multitude of schedules. The bad news is the Revit-produced schedules are not going to look like your company's schedules at all. Before we go further, it is important to note that some of you will be able to get a perfect duplication of your companies' standard schedules; some of you will not. Those of you who will not have to get as close as possible to your standards, and at that point know that sometimes the cost of doing BIM is not in the pocket but at the plotter as well.

Given that, let's get started. I do think you are going to find creating and using schedules a wonderful experience. You are about to learn how you are going to save hours upon hours of work, all the while maintaining 100 percent accuracy.

Adding Fields to a Schedule

To begin, open the file you have been following along with.

If you did not complete the previous chapter, go to the book's web page at **www.sybex.com/go/revit2010ner**. From there you can browse to Chapter 11 and find the file called NER-28.rvt. The following procedure is going to focus on creating a door schedule. Grab a cup of coffee or a power drink, and follow along!

1. In the Project Browser, go to Level 1 floor plan.

2. On the Create panel of the View tab, click the Schedules ➤ Schedule / Quantities button, as shown in Figure 11.1.

FIGURE 11.1 Click the Schedule/Quantities button on the View tab.

3. The next dialog, as shown in Figure 11.2, allows you to choose which item you would like to schedule. Select Doors and click OK.

FIGURE 11.2 Select Doors and then click OK.

4. The next dialog allows you to add the fields (parameters) required for your schedule. The first field you will add is the Mark. To do this, find

Mark in the area to the left, and click the Add? button in the middle of the dialog, as shown in Figure 11.3.

5. Once this field is added, add the following fields using the same method:

▶ Height

▶ Width

▶ Level

▶ Door Finish

▶ Door Hardware Group

▶ Frame Finish

▶ Frame Jamb Type

▶ Comments

See Figure 11.3.

FIGURE 11.3 Adding the fields to produce a door schedule

6. Click OK. Your schedule should be similar to Figure 11.4.

Door Schedule								
Mark	Height	Width	Level	Door Finish	Door Hardware Group	Frame Finish	Frame Jamb Type	Comments
101	7'-0"	3'-0"	Level 1					
102	7'-0"	3'-0"	Level 1					
103	7'-0"	6'-0"	Level 1					
104	7'-0"	6'-0"	Level 1					
105	7'-0"	3'-0"	Level 1					
105A	7'-0"	3'-0"	Level 1					
106	7'-0"	3'-0"	Level 1					
106A	7'-0"	3'-0"	Level 1					
100B	7'-0"	3'-0"	Level 1					
100C	7'-0"	6'-0"	Level 1					
100D	7'-0"	6'-0"	Level 1					
100A	7'-0"	6'-0"	Level 1					
100E	7'-0"	3'-0"	Level 2					
100F	7'-0"	3'-0"	Level 2					
100G	7'-0"	3'-0"	Level 2					
100H	7'-0"	3'-0"	Level 2					
100I	7'-0"	6'-0"	Level 2					
100J	7'-0"	3'-0"	Level 3					
100K	7'-0"	3'-0"	Level 3					
100L	7'-0"	3'-0"	Level 3					
100M	7'-0"	3'-0"	Level 3					
100N	7'-0"	6'-0"	Level 3					
100O	7'-0"	3'-0"	Level 4					
100P	7'-0"	3'-0"	Level 4					
100Q	7'-0"	3'-0"	Level 4					
100R	7'-0"	3'-0"	Level 4					
100S	7'-0"	6'-0"	Level 4					
100T	7'-0"	3'-0"	Level 5					
100U	7'-0"	3'-0"	Level 5					
100V	7'-0"	3'-0"	Level 5					
100W	7'-0"	3'-0"	Level 5					
100X	7'-0"	6'-0"	Level 5					
107	7'-0"	3'-0"	Level 1					
108	7'-0"	3'-0"	Level 1					
109	7'-0"	3'-0"	Level 1					
110	7'-0"	3'-0"	Level 1					
111	7'-0"	3'-0"	Level 1					
112	7'-0"	3'-0"	Level 1					
113	7'-0"	6'-0"	Level 1					

FIGURE 11.4 The door schedule up to this point

The next step is to start organizing our data in a format in which we would like it to be displayed. We have a long way to go, but when we are done, this schedule can be used over and over again.

 N O T E It is noteworthy to mention at this point that a schedule does not have to be placed on a drawing sheet. Many times you will produce a schedule to simply manipulate data without having to search for it in the model.

Sorting and Grouping

Since Revit is a database, let's think of building a schedule as simply creating a query in a database, because that's exactly what we are doing. By creating a sort, we can start to see our doors in groups and have a tangible understating of where we are. Let's get started.

1. In the Project Browser, you will see a category called Schedule/ Quantities. Open the Schedule/Quantities group and open the Door schedule. (This procedure applies if you are not already in the schedule).

2. In the schedule, right-click any cell and select View Properties, as shown in Figure 11.5.

FIGURE 11.5 Right-click the schedule to go to View Properties.

3. In the Element Properties dialog, you will see a category called Other. Click the Edit button in the Sorting/Grouping row, as shown in Figure 11.6.

FIGURE 11.6 Click the Edit button in the Sorting/Grouping row.

4. On the Sorting/Grouping tab, set Sort By to Level.

5. Check the Header option.

6. Check the Footer option.

7. Select Title, Count, and Totals from the Sort By drop-down list (see Figure 11.7).

8. Click OK.

9. Click OK again to get back to the schedule layout.

10. Save the model.

FIGURE 11.7 Sorting the schedule by level

The next step is to get the header information grouped the way we would like it. Most schedules include groups such as Door Frame and Hardware. We will create similar groupings.

Controlling Headers

Although this step is not crucial to producing an accurate, readable schedule, it is important in the attempt to get this Revit-produced schedule to look like the schedule you have been using for years in CAD. The objective of this procedure is to combine the header content into smaller groups under their own header, similar to what you can do in a spreadsheet.

To start in with controlling the schedule headers, follow these steps:

1. In the Project Browser, open the Door schedule (if you do not already have it open).

    At the top of the schedule is the title (Door Schedule) and the header (which includes Mark, Height, Width, and Level, among others), as shown in Figure 11.8. Focus your attention here.

2. The goal is to combine Mark, Height, and Width into a group under one header called DOOR INFORMATION. To do this, click on the Width cell and drag your cursor to the left. You are selecting all three cells.

3. Once the cells are selected, click the Group button on the Options bar.

T I P   Sometimes when you are picking the first cell to do this task, you will accidentally click into the cell. You do not want this. If this keeps happening, click into the Width cell, and then click just below the cell into the gray area. This selects the cell the way you want it. You can now pick and drag your cursor to the left to highlight all the cells.

F I G U R E 1 1 . 8 Click and drag across the three cells as shown. This will activate the Group button on the Options bar.

4. Click into the new cell and type **DOOR INFORMATION**.

It would be nice if the defaults in Revit were all caps, but they are not. The next procedure will rename some of the headers. This will not change any values.

1. Click in the Mark header and change it to **NUMBER**.

2. Click into Height and change it to **HEIGHT**.

3. Click into Width and change it to **WIDTH**. See Figure 11.9.

DOOR INFORMATION			
NUMBER	HEIGHT	WIDTH	Level
Level 1			
101	7' - 0"	3' - 0"	Level 1
102	7' - 0"	3' - 0"	Level 1
103	7' - 0"	6' - 0"	Level 1

F I G U R E 1 1 . 9 Add the new header and change the descriptions as shown here.

4. Change the Level header to FLOOR as shown in Figure 11.10.

5. Change the rest of the headers to uppercase. This includes the Door Schedule title, as shown in Figure 11.10.

6. Select the cells DOOR HARDWARE to DOOR FINISH.

7. On the Options bar, click the Group button.

8. Call the new header **DOOR**.

9. Remove the word DOOR from the cell DOOR FINISH and DOOR HARDWARE GROUP. (See Figure 11.10.)

10. Highlight FRAME FINISH and FRAME JAMB TYPE.

11. Click the Group button on the Options bar.

12. Call the new header **FRAME**. See Figure 11.10.

DOOR SCHEDULE								
DOOR INFORMATION				DOOR		FRAME		
NUMBER	HEIGHT	WIDTH	FLOOR	DOOR FINISH	DOOR HARWARE GROUP	FRAME FINISH	FRAME JAMB TYPE	COMMENTS
Level 1								
101	7' - 0"	3' - 0"	Level 1					
102	7' - 0"	3' - 0"	Level 1					
103	7' - 0"	6' - 0"	Level 1					

FIGURE 11.10 The groups are now complete.

Now it is time to start filling out some of the blank fields. This is where you can increase productivity by using schedules. Instead of going door by door in the model, you have a list of every door right in front of you!

Modifying Elements in a Schedule

In Revit, data flows in multiple directions. By creating a schedule, the data from the doors flowed into the schedule to populate it. Now, we are going to ask Revit to collect data inputted into the schedule to flow into the doors.

To learn how to populate the schedule, follow along with the procedure.

1. In the Project Browser, open DOOR SCHEDULE (if it is not opened already).

 N O T E   Note that Door Schedule is now **DOOR SCHEDULE** in the Project Browser. This is because you renamed the title in the schedule — proof that we are dealing with bi-directional information.

2. Click into the DOOR FINISH cell for door number 101, as shown in Figure 11.11.

3. Type PT (for paint), as shown in Figure 11.11.

4. Click in the DOOR FINISH cell just below the one you just changed.

5. Notice there is a menu arrow. Click it, and notice that PT is in the list. Click PT. (See Figure 11.11.)

DOOR INFORMATION					
NUMBER	HEIGHT	WIDTH	FLOOR	DOOR FINISH	
Level 1					
101	7' - 0"	3' - 0"	Level 1	PT	
102	7' - 0"	3' - 0"	Level 1	PT	
103	7' - 0"	6' - 0"	Level 1	PT	
104	7' - 0"	6' - 0"	Level 1		
105	7' - 0"	3' - 0"	Level 1		

FIGURE 11.11 Once you start filling out the fields in a schedule, the items will become available in the list for future use.

6. Save the model.

Now, let's see how this affected the actual doors in the model, and perhaps find a door that needs to be tagged with a WD (wood) finish:

1. In the Project Browser, open the Level 1 floor plan.

2. Zoom in on the door between the corridor and the east wing, as shown in Figure 11.12.

3. Select the door.

4. On the Modify Doors tab, click the Element Properties button.

5. In the instance parameters, scroll down to the Other category and find Door finish.

6. Click in the field, and type **WD**, as shown in Figure 11.12.

FIGURE 11.12 Changing the property of an element in the model does the same thing as changing the element in the schedule.

If you click the menu drop-down arrow in the Door Finish field, you will see that PT is available. The schedules and the actual doors are "linked" together.

7. Click OK.

8. Open the door schedule. Notice that door number 100B has a WD finish.

9. Save the model.

USING THE SCHEDULE TO FIND A COMPONENT

There may be cases where you are filling out the schedule, and you are not sure which item you are looking at. The fact that schedules are "live" means that you can find a component from the schedule. To do this, follow the procedure:

1. In the schedule, right-click on door number 114.

2. Select Show, as shown here:

Notice that Revit zooms in on the door, and even gives you choices to find other views as well:

3. Click Close.

4. Close the view and go back to the schedule.

In the interest of not getting carried away with the mundane process of filling out the entire schedule, note that this process is applicable for every field within this type of schedule. The main takeaway point is the fact that you can populate a schedule by either changing the data in the schedule itself or by finding the scheduled component and changing it there.

The next step is to further modify the appearance of the schedule we are working on. We can then start using this schedule to narrow in on a specific grouping of doors to change them based on a filter.

Modifying the Schedule's Appearance

As it stands, not everyone uses the same fonts, headers, and linework around the border of the schedule. Although this next procedure won't really be evident until Chapter 14 ("Creating Sheets and Printing"), it is applicable at this point in the book.

The objective of this procedure is to examine what font this schedule is using as well as the line weights and spacing applied to the schedule. To learn how to adjust the appearance of a schedule, follow along with the procedure:

1. In the Project Browser, open the DOOR SCHEDULE (if it is not opened already).

2. Right-click in any area, and select View Properties.

3. Click the Edit button for Appearance.

4. On the Appearance tab, you will see two categories: Graphics and Text. In the Graphics category, click Outlines and select Medium Lines, as shown in Figure 11.13.

5. In the Text category, make sure Show Title and Show Headers are checked on (see Figure 11.13).

6. Click OK twice.

Your schedule will not change one bit! What we have done is create a situation where the appearance of the schedule won't be apparent until you literally drag it onto a drawing sheet.

FIGURE 11.13 Configuring the schedule's appearance

HEY, THIS LOOKS FAMILIAR

You may or may not have noticed that each time you go to the View Properties
of the schedule and click the Edit button next to a corresponding row (in this
case it was the Appearance row), you are only jumping to a specific tab. Each
schedule category can be accessed in one dialog, as shown here:

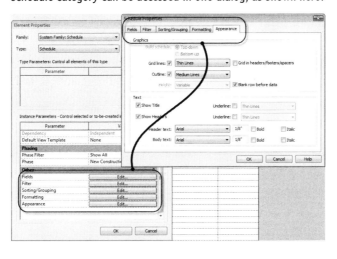

Adding a Schedule to a Sheet

Although adding a schedule to a sheet is a topic for another chapter (Chapter 14), the process is so easy, we are going to go ahead and do it right now. Not to let the cat out of the bag or anything, but you are going to enjoy how sheets come together in Revit. Perform the following steps:

1. In the Project Browser, find the Sheets (All) category, as shown in Figure 11.14. Coincidentally it is located directly below DOOR SCHEDULE.

2. Right-click Sheets, as shown in Figure 11.14.

3. Select New Sheet (see Figure 11.14).

FIGURE 11.14 Creating a new sheet

4. In the next dialog, click the Load button. This will allow you to go find a title block. Although we have not made a title block yet, Revit has a directory with some samples you can use to get started. See Figure 11.15.

FIGURE 11.15 Finding a title block for your use

5. Browse to the Titleblocks directory. It is a folder contained within the Imperial Library directory.

6. Select the file called E1 30 x 42 Horizontal.rfa.

7. Click Open.

8. Back in the Select a Titleblock dialog, select E1 30 x 42 Horizontal, and click OK.

You now have a blank title block, as shown in Figure 11.16.

FIGURE 11.16 You now have a sheet ready to be populated.

The next objective is to click and drag the schedule onto the sheet. If the schedule fits, this is literally the easiest thing to do in Revit.

1. In the Project Browser, find DOOR SCHEDULE.

2. Click it, but do not double-click it. You want to pick it and hold down the pick icon.

3. With the pick (left) icon pressed, drag the schedule onto the sheet. You can place it anywhere you see fit (see Figure 11.17).

4. Once you have moved your cursor to the correct position, pick the place on the sheet. If the bottom hangs over the sheet, that's okay — we will fix it in a minute.

5. Press the Esc key.

6. Select the schedule.

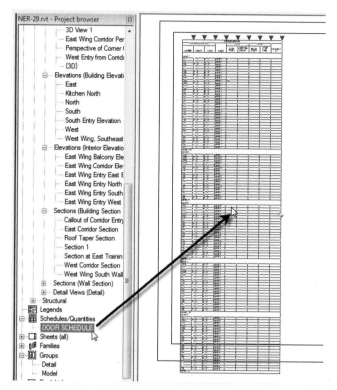

FIGURE 11.17 Clicking and dragging the schedule onto the sheet

7. Notice the blue break grips that are located halfway up the schedule? These are the same types of grips that are used in grids, levels, and sections. Pick one, as shown in Figure 11.18.

8. With the schedule split in two, you can see that it will fit onto the sheet quite nicely. With the schedule still selected, notice there is a blue grip at the bottom of the left portion of the schedule, as shown in Figure 11.19. Pick the grip. Notice you can slide the schedule so it moves up and down evenly.

9. Zoom in on the top of the schedule, as shown in Figure 11.20, and select the schedule.

10. Notice you have blue triangle-shaped icons at each cell in the title and the header. Pick the one on the Comments column and drag it to the right. The comments header will now be readable.

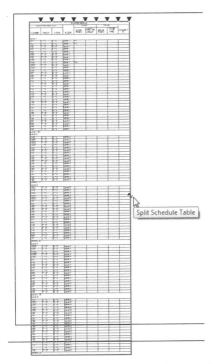

FIGURE 11.18 You can split the schedule into two (or more) sections.

FIGURE 11.19 You can make further adjustments to the schedule by picking the round blue grip.

FIGURE 11.20 Pick the triangle grip to give the Comments field some more room.

When you have a schedule split like this, any adjustment you make to a column will be reflected in the other half of the schedule. You do not have to make the same adjustment twice to the Comments column.

We can make two more adjustments to the schedule once it has been placed onto a sheet. This involves the rotation and joining the two columns back together again.

1. Select the schedule (if it is not already open).

   Notice that on the Modify Schedule Graphics tab, there is a Rotation on Sheet menu, as shown in Figure 11.21. You do not need to change the rotation — just note that it is there.

2. Also notice that there is a blue move grip, as shown in Figure 11.21, which is located in the middle of the two schedule columns. If you pick one and drag the column back over the top of the other, they will automatically join back together (see Figure 11.21).

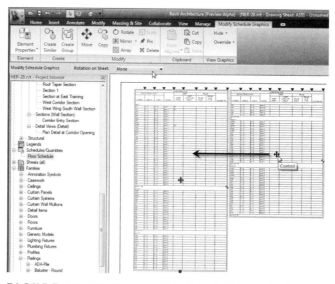

FIGURE 11.21 You can rotate the schedule on the sheet, and you can also join the columns back together if you need to.

3. Save the model.

Just to nail the concept down, let's create a window schedule now. If you like, go ahead on your own and make one yourself. You can then compare it to the one in the book when you have finished to see if you got it. If you would rather go step by step, that's fine too! Just follow along:

1. On the View tab, click the Schedules ➢ Schedule/Quantities button.

2. In the next dialog, select Windows and click OK.

3. In the Schedule Properties dialog, add the following fields:

   ▶ Type Mark

   ▶ Type

   ▶ Width

   ▶ Height

   ▶ Sill Height

   ▶ Level

   See Figure 11.22.

FIGURE 11.22 Adding fields to the schedule

4. Go to the Sorting/Grouping tab, as shown in Figure 11.23.

5. Sort by Type Mark.

6. Add a footer, with Title, Count, and Totals selected.

7. Sort by Level.

8. Check the Grand Totals option.

9. Select Title, Count, and Totals.

10. Check the Itemize Every Instance option (see Figure 11.23).

FIGURE 11.23 Specify the settings shown here.

11. Click OK.

12. Click OK again to get to the schedule and to see the results.

You may run into a situation where you would like to sort items based on a field but would not like to actually display that field. You do have this ability, as follows:

1. Right-click in the Level column, as shown in Figure 11.24.

2. Select Hide Column(s).

FIGURE 11.24 You can hide a column but still have Revit sort the schedule based on the hidden information.

3. Save the model.

N O T E   It is worth noting that a schedule can be created before any information is added to the model. This schedule can then be added to a sheet and the entire file can be saved as a template. Whenever you start a new project, these schedules will start filling themselves out and will already be on sheets!

Phew! I think you get the picture. If you like, feel free to create a bunch of schedules on your own. Practice does make perfect.

Let's venture now into creating a material takeoff. It would be a shame to have all of these computations go unused!

Creating Material Takeoffs

Creating a material takeoff is similar to creating a schedule. The only difference is the fact that we are now breaking components down and scheduling the smaller pieces. For example, we could get a schedule of all of the doors in the model. That we know; we just did that. But with a material takeoff, we can now quantify the square footage of door panels or glass within the doors. To take it a step further, we can do material takeoffs of walls, floors, and any other building component we see fit to quantify.

The objective of this procedure is to create three different material takeoffs: one for the walls, one for the floors, and one for the roofs. Let's get started:

1. On the View tab, click Schedule ➢ material takeoff as shown in Figure 11.25.

FIGURE 11.25 To add a new material takeoff, you must go to the View tab.

2. In the New Material Takeoff dialog, select Walls, as shown in Figure 11.26.

FIGURE 11.26 Select Walls in the New Material Takeoff dialog.

3. Click OK.

4. In the next dialog, add the following fields:

▶ Material: Area

▶ Material: Name

▶ Count

See Figure 11.27.

FIGURE 11.27 Adding the materials

5. Go to the Sorting/Grouping tab.

6. Sort by Material: Name.

7. Add a footer.

8. Choose Title, Count, and Totals from the menu, as shown in Figure 11.28.

9. Check the Blank Line option.

10. At the bottom of the dialog, check Grand Totals.

11. Choose Title, Count, and Totals from the menu.

12. Select the option Itemize Every Instance (see Figure 11.28).

FIGURE 11.28 Configuring the parameters for the schedule

13. Click OK twice.

The next step is to start taking some totals on our own. The first thing we can do is to have Revit automatically format a column to produce an independent total; then we can break this takeoff out and drill in to more specific line-item type totals.

1. Right-click in any field and select View Properties.

2. Click the Edit button next to the Formatting row to bring up the dialog shown in Figure 11.29.

3. In the field to the left, select Material: Area, as shown in Figure 11.29.

4. To the bottom right, check Calculate Totals, as shown in Figure 11.29.

FIGURE 11.29 In the Formatting tab, you can specify Calculate Totals for the Material : Area column.

5. Click OK twice.

You now have a total square footage at the bottom of your takeoff groups, as shown in Figure 11.30.

Wall Material Takeoff			
Material: Area	Material: Name	Count	Plywood cou
3988 SF	Air Barrier - Air Infiltration Barrier	1	83.083333
3663 SF	Air Barrier - Air Infiltration Barrier	1	76.309896
4288 SF	Air Barrier - Air Infiltration Barrier	1	89.330729
537 SF	Air Barrier - Air Infiltration Barrier	1	11.180556
831 SF	Air Barrier - Air Infiltration Barrier	1	17.314453
574 SF	Air Barrier - Air Infiltration Barrier	1	11.958333
871 SF	Air Barrier - Air Infiltration Barrier	1	18.148438
3921 SF	Air Barrier - Air Infiltration Barrier	1	81.681409
532 SF	Air Barrier - Air Infiltration Barrier	1	11.076535
771 SF	Air Barrier - Air Infiltration Barrier	1	16.062288
715 SF	Air Barrier - Air Infiltration Barrier	1	14.898688
525 SF	Air Barrier - Air Infiltration Barrier	1	10.946615
813 SF	Air Barrier - Air Infiltration Barrier	1	16.930244
3008 SF	Air Barrier - Air Infiltration Barrier	1	62.67589
1104 SF	Air Barrier - Air Infiltration Barrier	1	22.994919
2405 SF	Air Barrier - Air Infiltration Barrier	1	50.098002
1336 SF	Air Barrier - Air Infiltration Barrier	1	27.824629
3731 SF	Air Barrier - Air Infiltration Barrier	1	77.719887
1616 SF	Air Barrier - Air Infiltration Barrier	1	33.66556
295 SF	Air Barrier - Air Infiltration Barrier	1	6.156136
849 SF	Air Barrier - Air Infiltration Barrier	1	17.691708
646 SF	Air Barrier - Air Infiltration Barrier	1	13.449251
646 SF	Air Barrier - Air Infiltration Barrier	1	13.449251
605 SF	Air Barrier - Air Infiltration Barrier	1	12.59957
38268 SF			

FIGURE 11.30 The total square footage is being calculated.

The next step is to break this takeoff down to smaller, more specific takeoffs. Once we do this, we can provide our own calculations based on almost any formula we need.

Creating a Calculated Value Field

The objective here is to create separate schedules for Plywood and Gypsum by adding a new variable to the schedule that contains a formula that we create. Yes, it is as hard as it sounds, but once you get used to this, it won't be so bad! Perform the following steps:

1. In the Project Browser, right-click on the Wall Material Takeoff, and select Duplicate View ➤ Duplicate, as shown in Figure 11.31.

FIGURE 11.31 Duplicating the schedule

2. Right-click on the new view and select Rename.

3. Rename it to **Plywood Takeoff**.

4. Double-click on Plywood Takeoff to open the view.

5. Right-click in the view window and select View Properties.

6. Click the Edit button in the Filter row.

7. Filter by Material : Name

8. In the menu to the right, select Equals from the list.

9. In the field below Material : Name, select Wood - Sheathing - Plywood (see Figure 11.32).

FIGURE 11.32 Filter based on material

10. Click OK twice.

Your takeoff should look like Figure 11.33.

Plywood Takeoff		
Material: Area	Material: Name	Count
3878 SF	Wood - Sheathing - plywood	1
3576 SF	Wood - Sheathing - plywood	1
4178 SF	Wood - Sheathing - plywood	1
526 SF	Wood - Sheathing - plywood	1
822 SF	Wood - Sheathing - plywood	1
545 SF	Wood - Sheathing - plywood	1
842 SF	Wood - Sheathing - plywood	1
3831 SF	Wood - Sheathing - plywood	1
517 SF	Wood - Sheathing - plywood	1
761 SF	Wood - Sheathing - plywood	1
700 SF	Wood - Sheathing - plywood	1
515 SF	Wood - Sheathing - plywood	1
797 SF	Wood - Sheathing - plywood	1
2955 SF	Wood - Sheathing - plywood	1
1088 SF	Wood - Sheathing - plywood	1
2372 SF	Wood - Sheathing - plywood	1
1320 SF	Wood - Sheathing - plywood	1
3684 SF	Wood - Sheathing - plywood	1
1589 SF	Wood - Sheathing - plywood	1
286 SF	Wood - Sheathing - plywood	1
845 SF	Wood - Sheathing - plywood	1
640 SF	Wood - Sheathing - plywood	1
640 SF	Wood - Sheathing - plywood	1
587 SF	Wood - Sheathing - plywood	1
37493 SF		
37493 SF		

FIGURE 11.33 The takeoff is filtered based only on plywood.

The next step is to break down the plywood into 4×8 sheets. We will need to add a formula based on the square footage given by Revit divided by 32 square feet to come up with the plywood totals.

1. Open the Plywood Takeoff in the Project Browser (if it is not already).

2. Right-click in the view, and select View Properties.

3. In the Element Properties dialog, click the Edit button in the Fields row.

4. On the Fields tab in the Schedule Properties dialog, click the Calculated Value button in the middle of the dialog, as shown in Figure 11.34.

FIGURE 11.34 Click the Calculated Value button in the middle of the dialog.

5. For the name, enter **Number of Sheets**.

6. Make sure Discipline is set to Common.

7. Make sure Type is set to Number (see Figure 11.35).

8. Add the following formula: **Material: Area / 32 SF**.

9. Click OK.

10. Click the Formatting tab, as shown in Figure 11.36.

11. Select the new field called Number of Sheets.

You must type the fields being used exactly as they are displayed. For example, the Field **Material: Area** must be typed exactly like that. This pertains to caps as well. All formulas in Revit are case sensitive.

FIGURE 11.35 Change the calculated values to the values shown here.

12. Under the Field Formatting section, click Calculate Totals, as shown in Figure 11.36.

FIGURE 11.36 Click the Calculate Totals option.

13. Click the Field Format button.

14. Uncheck Use Default Settings, as shown in Figure 11.37.

15. Change the units to Fixed.

16. Make sure the rounding is to 0 decimal places.

17. Click Use Digit Grouping (see Figure 11.37).

18. Click OK.

19. Go to the Sorting/Grouping tab.

20. At the bottom, deselect the Grand Totals option.

21. Click OK twice.

FIGURE 11.37 Overriding the units to allow this field to round

Your material takeoff should resemble Figure 11.38.

Plywood Takeoff			
Material: Area	Material: Name	Count	Number of Sheets
3878 SF	Wood - Sheathing - plywood	1	121
3576 SF	Wood - Sheathing - plywood	1	112
4178 SF	Wood - Sheathing - plywood	1	131
526 SF	Wood - Sheathing - plywood	1	16
822 SF	Wood - Sheathing - plywood	1	26
545 SF	Wood - Sheathing - plywood	1	17
842 SF	Wood - Sheathing - plywood	1	26
3831 SF	Wood - Sheathing - plywood	1	120
517 SF	Wood - Sheathing - plywood	1	16
761 SF	Wood - Sheathing - plywood	1	24
700 SF	Wood - Sheathing - plywood	1	22
515 SF	Wood - Sheathing - plywood	1	16
797 SF	Wood - Sheathing - plywood	1	25
2955 SF	Wood - Sheathing - plywood	1	92
1088 SF	Wood - Sheathing - plywood	1	34
2372 SF	Wood - Sheathing - plywood	1	74
1320 SF	Wood - Sheathing - plywood	1	41
3684 SF	Wood - Sheathing - plywood	1	115
1589 SF	Wood - Sheathing - plywood	1	50
286 SF	Wood - Sheathing - plywood	1	9
845 SF	Wood - Sheathing - plywood	1	26
640 SF	Wood - Sheathing - plywood	1	20
640 SF	Wood - Sheathing - plywood	1	20
587 SF	Wood - Sheathing - plywood	1	18
37493 SF			1,172

FIGURE 11.38 The finished Plywood material takeoff

Wow! Not too bad for only drawing a bunch of walls. As you can see, using the scheduling/material takeoff feature of Revit adds value to using this application. Well, the value does not stop there. We can use the same functionality to create legends and drawing keys as well.

Creating Key Legends

Here's the problem with Revit. At some point, you are going to need to add a component to the model that is not associated with anything. Say, for example, you have a door that you would like to put on a sheet with the door schedule. You sure don't want that door included in the schedule, and you sure don't want to have to draw a wall just to display it. This is where creating a key schedule comes into play.

Adding Legend Components

The objective of the following procedure is to create a key legend adding elevations of doors that are used in the model. As it stands, a legend can mean any number of things. It could be just a list of abbreviations; it could be a comprehensive numbering system keyed off the model itself; or it could be a graphical representation of items that have already been placed into the model for further detailing and coordinating. Another special aspect of legends is the fact that a single legend may need to be duplicated on multiple sheets within a drawing set. You don't know it yet, but this is a problem for Revit. By creating a legend, however, you are going to be able to get around this.

The objective of the following procedure is to create a door type legend:

1. On the View tab, click the Legends ➤ Legend button, as shown in Figure 11.39.

FIGURE 11.39 Click the Legends ➤ Legend button on the View tab.

2. The next dialog wants you to specify a scale. Choose ¼" = 1'–0". This is fine for now (see Figure 11.40).

3. Call the view **Door Type Legend**.

4. Click OK.

FIGURE 11.40 Choose ¼" = 1'-0".

Congratulations! You now have a blank screen. This is actually a good thing, though. Think of it as a clean slate where you can draft, add components, and just throw together a legend.

OTHER FUNCTIONS HAVE BEEN ACTIVATED

Without knowing it, you have made some tools available that we have not explored yet. You are going to start to learn that Revit knows the type of view you happen to be in. Some commands are available in one view but they may not be in the next. Keep this in mind as you venture through Revit and become frustrated that a command is not working. You usually just need to switch views.

The next step is to start adding some components. You will need to go to the Annotate tab for this.

1. Go to the Detail panel of the annotate tab.

2. Click the Component ➤ Legend Component button, as shown in Figure 11.41.

FIGURE 11.41 Clicking the Legend Component button

3. In the Options bar, choose Doors : Single - Raised panel with Sidelights : 36"×84", as shown in Figure 11.42.

4. Change the view to Elevation : Front.

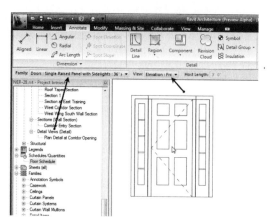

FIGURE 11.42 Changing the options for the legend

5. Pick a point to place the elevation.

6. With the command still running, you can place another instance. This changes the view to Floor Plan. Place another instance of the door just above the elevation, as shown in Figure 11.43.

7. In the Options bar be sure the host length is set to 6'–0" (see Figure 11.43).

8. With the command still running, place a Door : Double Flush to the right of the first door. Make sure View is set to Elevation : Front.

9. Place the corresponding plan view just above the door. Make sure Host Length is set to 6'–0".

10. Place a bi-fold door just to the right of the second door, with a plan view to the top.

11. Set the top's host length to 6'–0" (see Figure 11.44).

FIGURE 11.43 Place two instances of the same door for the legend.

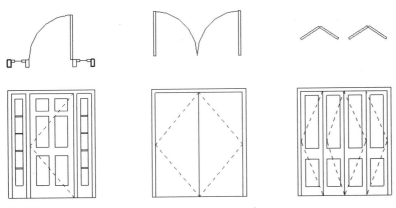

FIGURE 11.44 The three doors in the legend

The next step is to add some text in an attempt to label the doors. These items cannot be labeled, which can be a disadvantage to "breaking away from the model." This is basically a dumb sheet.

    1. On the Text panel, click the Text button.

    2. Make sure the text style is Text $3/32$" and that the leader is set to None, as shown in Figure 11.45.

3. Place some text centered under each door elevation, and label the doors A, B, and C (see Figure 11.45).

FIGURE 11.45 Placing the text underneath the doors

4. Save the model.

It is nice to have accurate "blocks" available based on what you have added to your model up to this point. By using the Revit method of building a legend like this, you are removed from the horror of stealing old legends from other jobs. I think we all know what a nightmare this turns into when they are not accurate. Plus, in Revit, you have a library of the doors you are using right at your fingertips. They do not have to be managed or updated constantly. They will always be there, and they will always be accurate.

The next step is to create a symbol legend — that is, we need to make a sheet which contains all of our typical symbols. This task will be carried out in a similar manner.

Adding Symbols to a Legend

As mentioned earlier, this task will be similar to the creation of the door legend. The only difference is you will be adding your typical symbols as they appear on the sheets. Every company has a sheet like this. I'm sure yours does too.

The first objective is to create this legend from scratch using the Revit tools. The second objective is to import your legend from CAD (which I'm sure you have). Once you complete the two procedures, you can decide which is best for your firm.

Using the Revit Symbols

To use the Revit-provided symbols, you are going to create a new legend view, and you will use the Annotate tab to insert the typical components. If you are feeling brave, go ahead and make a Symbol key on your own. You can follow the figures to make sure you are adding the expected components. If you would rather follow along with the procedure, let's get started:

1. On the View tab, Legends ➢ Legend button.

2. Set the scale to ¼" = 1'–0".

3. Call the new legend **Symbol Legend**.

4. Click OK.

5. On the Detail panel of the Annotate tab, click the Symbol button, as shown in Figure 11.46.

FIGURE 11.46 Click the Symbol button on the Annotate tab.

6. In the Change Element Type menu, click Callout Head, as shown in Figure 11.47.

7. Place the callout head into the view as shown in Figure 11.47.

8. With the Symbol command still running, place a door tag directly underneath the callout head, as shown in Figure 11.48.

9. Place a Room Tag with Area.

10. Place a View Title (see Figure 11.48).

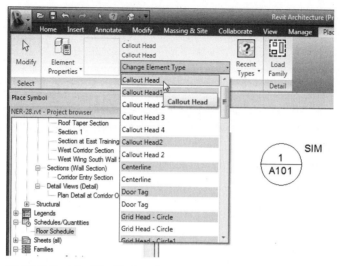

FIGURE 11.47 Placing the callout head

SIM
1
A101

(101)

Room name

| 101 |

150 SF

 View Name
1/8" = 1'-0"

FIGURE 11.48 Populating the legend

The next step is to add some notes indicating what it is we just added to the legend. Again, you will not be tagging the items — you are merely placing text and leaders.

1. On the Text panel, click the Text button.

2. On the Place Text tab, click the One Segment button, as shown in Figure 11.49.

3. Pick two points for the leader, and type **TYPICAL CALLOUT** (see Figure 11.49).

FIGURE 11.49 Adding the text to the legend

4. Add the following notes to the rest of the symbols:

> TYPICAL DOOR TAG
>
> TYPICAL ROOM TAG
>
> TYPICAL VIEW TITLE

See Figure 11.50.

FIGURE 11.50 Adding descriptive text

The next step is to place a box around the items and then draw three equal lines to make a grid. This is done by strictly drafting lines, as the following procedure will show:

1. On the Annotate tab, click the Detail Line button, as shown in Figure 11.51.

FIGURE 11.51 Click the Detail Line button on the Annotate tab.

2. In the Options bar, be sure Thin Lines is selected, as shown in Figure 11.52.

3. On the Draw panel, click Rectangle, as shown in Figure 11.52.

4. Draw a rectangle around the symbols and the text (see Figure 11.52).

FIGURE 11.52 Adding the linework around the symbols and text

5. Click the Detail Lines button again.

6. On the Draw panel, click the Lines button.

7. Draw three horizontal lines in the box. They do not have to be equal distances but still should separate the symbols.

8. Place a dimension string starting at the top of the rectangle, to the second line, to the third, to the fourth, then to the bottom of the rectangle.

9. Click the EQ button on the Dimension string.

10. Move the symbols and the text to the proper positions (see Figure 11.53).

FIGURE 11.53 Draw the horizontal lines shown, then equally constrain them using the Dimension command.

11. Delete the dimensions.

12. Click Unconstrain in the next dialog.

13. Save the model.

Now that you have experience with creating legends using strictly Revit components and lines, it is time to investigate how we can use premade AutoCAD legends as an import.

Importing AutoCAD Legends

Just because you have switched to Revit does not mean that you are going to be throwing away over a decade of work regarding typical details and legends. Revit accepts AutoCAD and MicroStation .dwg and .dgn files just fine. Of course, there will be some "tweaking," but once you get the process down, I think you are going to rely heavily on this functionality.

The objective of the following procedure is to create a new legend view, and then import an existing AutoCAD legend into the view. To get started, you will need to go to the book's web page at **www.sybex.com/go/revit2010ner**. From there you can browse to Chapter 11 and find the file called `Interior Partition Legend.dwg`. You can then place the drawing file on your system in a place where you can retrieve it later. Now perform the following steps:

1. On the View tab, click the Legends ➤ Legend button.

2. Call the new legend **Interior Partition Legend**.

3. Make the scale 1"–1'–0" (one inch equals one foot).

4. On the Insert tab, click Import CAD.

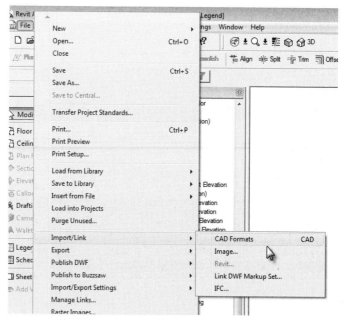

FIGURE 11.54 Importing CAD formats

5. Find the AutoCAD `.dwg` file called `Interior Partition Legend.dwg`.

 WARNING   Do not click Open until instructed to do so. There are several items we need to look at in the import dialog that have a crucial effect on the imported graphics.

6. At the bottom of the Import/Link CAD Formats dialog, notice you have a few choices:

Colors Change this to Black and White.

Layers Make sure this is set to All. We will be able to manipulate the AutoCAD layers after we bring the DWG file into Revit.

Import Units This should be set to Auto-Detect. In Chapter 18, we will import a site. At that point, we will have to modify this choice, but for now, leave it as Auto-Detect.

Positioning Leave this as Auto - Center - to - Center.

See Figure 11.55.

FIGURE 11.55 The Import CAD Formats dialog. Be deliberate when importing a CAD file by choosing the Options at the bottom of the dialog.

7. Click Open.

Once the CAD file has been imported, it will be zoomed off the view so you cannot see it. Follow the procedure to zoom the CAD import into view and manipulate the data:

1. Type **ZA** (to zoom all).

2. You can now see the import. Once the import is in view, select it.

3. On the Options bar, click the Query button, as shown in Figure 11.56.

4. Select the line shown in Figure 11.56.

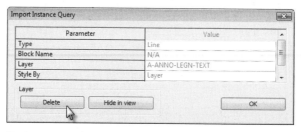

FIGURE 11.56 Click the Query button on the Options bar.

5. Once you select the line, Revit will report information back to you about that line. You are also given the chance to delete the layer. Click Delete, as shown in Figure 11.57.

FIGURE 11.57 You can query items in the CAD import. You can also delete items.

6. Click OK. All of the lines on that layer are gone.

W A R N I N G   Be careful when you do this. Revit is not like AutoCAD. When you delete a layer in Revit, the layer is deleted and any object that happens to be on that layer is deleted as well. You could easily delete objects inadvertently.

7. Press Esc twice.

The next step is to fix some of the text that didn't quite wrap correctly. What we will need to do is explode the import so it is broken down into Revit lines and objects.

1. Select the import again.

2. On the Modify Interior Partition Legend.dwg tab, click Explode ➤ Full Explode, as shown in Figure 11.58.

FIGURE 11.58 Click the Full Explode button on the Options bar.

 N O T E   The difference between Full Explode and Partial Explode is that a partial explode will break the import down to the next level of blocks. For example, if there was a block included in the drawing file, such as a column bubble, the explode would break down the import but leave the column bubble as a block. When you do a full explode, you are exploding every object in the import — blocks and all.

3. Select the text UNDERSIDE OF STRUCTURE.

4. Pick the grip to the right, and drag the text box to the left until the text wraps into the correct position, as shown in Figure 11.59.

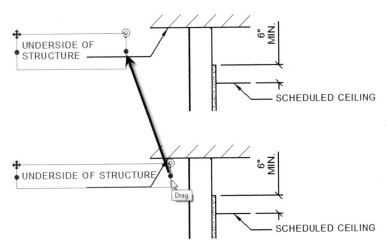

FIGURE 11.59 Fixing the improperly wrapped text

5. Do the same for the other details that have text improperly wrapped.

6. Save the model.

 N O T E   You may ask, "How did Revit know what line weights to use for my import?" This is a great question. There are import/export settings you can configure that will translate AutoCAD colors to Revit line weights. If you are using standard AIA layering, you will have very little problem with this translation. If not, you may have some work to do. In Chapter 12 we will be configuring this file.

Now that you have experience with keys, it is time to move on to addressing how tags work in Revit and why they are addressed along with schedules.

Adding Tags

Now that you are halfway through the book, you will find that some subject matter has been brushed over in the past. Tags are certainly no exception to this. They simply cannot be avoided since they come in automatically with most items. But there is a mystery surrounding them. Where do they come from, how does Revit know what tag to associate with what element, and how the heck do you make Revit's tags look like your tags?

One thing about tags that makes them special is the fact that they almost can be seen as a "window" looking into the item itself. A tag allows you to pull a parameter out of an item and put that parameter onto the drawing in a physical sense. Given that, tags are how we label things!

To start, let's concentrate on the simple and then move to the more complex. First you'll learn how to add a tag that did not get added automatically.

Adding Tags Individually

As you may have noticed, not everything we placed in the model received a tag — especially many of the doors and windows that we copied to different floors. The objective of the following procedures is to add tags to individual objects. The first type of tag will be By Category.

Tags by Category

Tagging an item by category simply means that, when you start the Tag command, it will look for an entire object to tag with the loaded tag that was created specifically for that object.

1. In the Project Browser, go to the Level 2 floor plan.

2. Zoom in on the area where the corridor meets the east wing, as shown in Figure 11.60.

FIGURE 11.60 The area where the corridor meets the east wing

3. On the Tag panel of the Annotate tab, click the Tag by Category button, as shown in Figure 11.61.

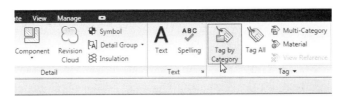

FIGURE 11.61 Click Tag by Category on the Annotate tab.

4. On the Options bar, uncheck the Leader option, as shown in Figure 11.62.

5. Pick the door shown in Figure 11.62. Your tag is added.

FIGURE 11.62 Tag the door shown here. Be sure you deselect Leader on the Options bar.

Adding tags to doors is a straightforward concept. Keep in mind, however, doors and windows are certainly not the only "taggable" items in Revit.

Tagging Walls

Tagging walls is almost as automatic as tagging doors and windows. The only difference is that when you tag a wall, the tag will initially be blank.

To learn how to tag a wall, follow along with the procedure:

1. In the Project Browser, go to the Level 2 floor plan.

2. Zoom in on the east wing.

3. Click the Tag by Category button.

4. Pick the wall indicated in Figure 11.63.

FIGURE 11.63 Picking one of the corridor partitions to tag

5. Many times, you will not have a tag loaded for this specific type of item. When that situation occurs, you will get the message shown in Figure 11.64. Click Yes to load the tag.

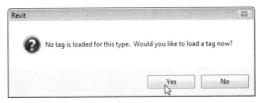

FIGURE 11.64 When you try to tag an item that does not have the specific tag type loaded into the model, you get this dialog prompting you to load the tag.

6. Select Annotations ➤ Architectural ➤ Wall Tag.rfa.

7. Click Open.

8. On the Options bar, click the Leader button so that the tag is leadered into the wall.

9. At the bottom row of the Tag panel, you will see a pull down arrow. Pick the Loaded tags button (see Figure 11.65).

FIGURE 11.65 Click the arrow, then select Loaded Tags.

10. In the Tags dialog, scroll down to Walls, as shown in Figure 11.66.

11. In the Loaded Tags cell for Walls, pick Wall Tag : ½".

12. Click OK.

13. Pick the wall again. You now have a wall tag.

14. Press Esc.

15. Select the new wall tag (it will be blank).

16. Notice the blue items. Click the blue question mark in the tag.

The Loaded Tags dialog controls the default tag that will be applied to all objects in the model. You can also access this dialog by selecting Settings ➤ Annotations ➤ Loaded Tags.

FIGURE 11.66 Changing the default tag for walls to Wall Tag: ½".

17. Call it **MC-1**, as shown in Figure 11.67.

18. Click OK to the warning that you are changing a type parameter.

FIGURE 11.67 Adding the wall tag data

19. Press Esc.

20. Click Tag by Category on the Annotate tab.

21. Pick any other corridor partition in the floor. Notice this time the tag is automatically placed with the appropriate MC-1 tag filled out.

But Where Is That Information Stored?

When you modify this type of tag, it is generally the type mark that carried this data. To see where the type mark is, select any one of the interior partitions, and click the Element Properties button on the Options bar. Then click Edit Type. In the type parameters, you can scroll down to find the type mark, as shown here:

This information is also tied into the schedule. As you are selecting fields to add to the schedule, you are selecting from the same list that Revit used to tag items in the model. This is the definition of BIM: the right information is used in the right places.

Suppose you would like to tag a number of the same items in one shot? Revit will allow you to do this by using the Tag All Not Tagged command.

Using the Tag All Command

This command is a favorite among Revit users. One of the most common examples of using this command is when you Copy/Paste Aligned multiple items to higher-level floors. You will almost always miss a few tags, or even all of the tags. This is where Tag All comes into play.

The objective of this next procedure is to find the Tag All Not Tagged feature and tag many items in one shot.

1. In the Project Browser, go to the Level 4 floor plan.

2. Notice that many doors and windows are not tagged. (If, for some reason, all of the doors and windows are tagged, select the tags and delete them for this procedure.)

3. On the Annotate tab, click the Tag All button, as shown in Figure 11.68.

FIGURE 11.68 The Tag All button on the Annotate tab

4. In the Tag All dialog, click Door Tags.

5. Hold the Ctrl key and select Windows. This indicates that every door and window in the view is about to receive a tag.

6. Make sure the All Objects in Current View radio button is selected (see Figure 11.69).

FIGURE 11.69 Selecting door and window tags

7. Click Apply.

8. Click OK.

It almost goes without saying that Tag All is quite a valuable tool. Another valuable tool is the ability to reach into a component and tag specific material within the component itself.

Tagging by Material

Tagging by Material could be one of the most underused commands in all of Revit. The reason is most people think of a tag as, well, a tag — some kind of box with some abbreviations or letters in it. That's too bad, because we can also use tags as a means to place notes. Tagging an item's material is one way of doing just that.

The objective of the following procedure is to create a material description, then place a tag pursuant to that note:

1. In the Project Browser, go to the Level 1 floor plan.

2. Zoom in on the kitchen area.

3. On the Tag panel of the Annotate tab, click the Material button, as shown in Figure 11.70.

FIGURE 11.70 Click the Material button on the Tag panel Material.

4. You will probably get the message stating that no material tag is loaded into the model. If so, click the Yes button to load one.

5. Browse to Annotations ➢ Architectural ➢ Material Tag.rfa.

6. Click Open.

7. Place your cursor over the tile floor as shown in Figure 11.71. Notice the tag says Interior Finish. This is the default description that we will change in just a moment. Once you see this, pick a point on the tile floor, then place the note to the right, as shown in Figure 11.71.

8. Press Esc.

FIGURE 11.71 Placing the Interior Finish note

8. Select the tag.

9. On the Modify Material Tags tab, click the Element Properties button.

10. Click Edit Type.

11. Change the leader arrowhead to Arrow Filled 15 Degree, as shown in Figure 11.72.

FIGURE 11.72 Changing the leader arrowhead is one of the first things you will probably have to do.

12. Click OK.

13. Click OK again to reveal the leader. Yes, that looks much better.

The next objective is to change what the tag says. Since we added that tag by specifying material, it is time to check out the materials to see exactly where this note came from.

1. On the Manage tab, click the Materials button as shown in Figure 11.73.

FIGURE 11.73 Select Settings ➢ Materials.

2. Find the material called Clay Tile - 12" Beige, as shown in Figure 11.74, and select it. (We made it earlier when we were doing the floors in Chapter 6.)

3. To the right of the Materials dialog, you will see four tabs: Graphics, Render Appearance, Identity, and Physical. Click the Identity tab, as shown in Figure 11.74.

4. In the Descriptive Information section, click the Description field and type **CLAY TILE IN KITCHENS, TYP** (see Figure 11.74).

FIGURE 11.74 Changing the description of the material can result in "automatic" notation of your model.

5. Click OK. See Figure 11.75 to check the changed material tag.

You can see that any time you use this material, it can be notated with the same text. This also works in sections, elevations, and enlarged plans. If you decide to change the note in the materials, it will update every occurrence in the entire model.

FIGURE 11.75 The material is now tagged with a leadered note.

The next topic we'll explore is where these tags are coming from and how we can create our own. Notation and symbols are the basis for maintaining CAD standards. If you simply use the examples given to you by Revit, you will have a set of drawings that look very generic and will immediately turn off your design team.

Creating Custom Tags

As mentioned before, templates very much drive how Revit works. Creating families is a prime example of this. To create a custom tag, you must first create a family and then load it into your drawing. The tag we will create is a casework tag. Revit does provide one, but ours needs to be smaller (based on scale), and it needs a box surrounding it.

To learn how to create a custom tag from scratch, follow along:

   1. On the Revit Home button, click New ➢ Family.

   2. Browse to the Annotations folder.

   3. Select the file called Generic Tag.rft.

   4. Click Open.

Welcome to the Family Editor! The first thing you may notice is the large block of text in the middle of the view that says, "Note: Use Settings Family

Categories to set the tag's category. Insertion point is at intersection of ref planes. Delete this note before using."

This is a great note, and we need to start by taking its advice:

1. Select the note, and click the Delete button (or press the Delete key on your keyboard).

2. Click the Family Category and Parameters button, as shown in Figure 11.76.

FIGURE 11.76 Pick the Family Category and Parameters button.

3. In the Family Category and Parameters dialog, select Casework Tags, as shown in Figure 11.77.

FIGURE 11.77 Select Casework Tags.

4. Click OK.

The next thing you notice is that the ribbon has changed. The only items available are designed to aid you in the creation of a family. There are many buttons that we will get to in Chapter 17, "Families," but for now, we are interested in the Label button.

1. In the Annotate panel on the Create tab, click the Label button, as shown in Figure 11.78.

FIGURE 11.78 Click the Label button on the Create tab.

2. Click the Element Properties button on the Element panel, as shown in Figure 11.79.

FIGURE 11.79 Click the Element Properties button.

3. Click Edit Type.

4. Click Duplicate.

5. Call the new label $1/16$".

6. Click OK.

7. In the Text category, change the Text Height to $1/16$".

8. Change the Width Factor to .8.

9. Click OK twice.

10. In the model, place the tag directly on the intersection of the reference planes, as shown in Figure 11.80.

11. In the Edit Label dialog, select Type Mark from the list to the left.

FIGURE 11.80 Placing the tag onto the reference plane intersection.

12. In the middle of the Edit Label dialog is an Add Label button. Click it. The Type Mark label should show up in the right field, as shown in Figure 11.81.

FIGURE 11.81 Adding the Type Mark label

13. Click OK.

14. Press Esc twice (or click the Modify button on the Quick access toolbar).

The label has been added. It's small but it's there. The next step is to draw a rectangle around this text. The following procedure describes how:

1. On the Create tab, click the Line button, as shown in Figure 11.82.

FIGURE 11.82 Click the Line button to start sketching the box.

2. On the Draw panel, click the pick lines icon.

3. On the Options bar, change the Offset value to $^{1}/_{16}$".

4. Offset the horizontal reference plane up $^{1}/_{16}$" and down $^{1}/_{16}$", as shown in Figure 11.83.

FIGURE 11.83 Offsetting the horizontal reference plane up $^{1}/_{16}$" and down $^{1}/_{16}$"

5. In the Options bar, change the Offset value to $^{1}/_{8}$".

6. Offset the vertical reference plane to the left and to the right $^{1}/_{8}$", as shown in Figure 11.84.

7. On the Modify tab, click the Trim button.

8. Trim the four corners so your screen resembles Figure 11.84.

FIGURE 11.84 Create the box as shown here.

9. Press Esc.

10. Save the file as Casework Tag.rfa. Make sure you save the file in a location where will you will be able to locate it at a later date.

11. On the Family Editor panel, click the Load into Projects button, as shown in Figure 11.85.

FIGURE 11.85 Loading the family into your project

WHICH ONE DO I CHOOSE?

If you have more than one model open (other than this family), you will see a dialog asking you to select the file you wish to load the family into. If this happens, simply select NER-28.rvt (or the file you are working on) as shown here:

With the new tag loaded into the project, we can now use it. Since it is a casework tag, we need to find some casework to label, as follows:

1. In the Project Browser, go to the elevation called Kitchen North. You can also go to the Level 1 floor plan, and zoom in on the kitchen. From there, you can double-click on the elevation marker pointing at the north leg of the kitchen.

2. Zoom in on the cabinets, as shown in Figure 11.86.

3. On the Tag panel on the Annotate tab, click the Tag by Category button.

4. On the Options bar, uncheck Leader.

5. Pick the base cabinet with two doors and one drawer, as shown in Figure 11.86.

FIGURE 11.86 Picking the base cabinet with two doors and one drawer

6. Once you pick the cabinet, move the tag underneath.

7. Select the tag.

8. Select the question mark within the tag.

9. Rename it to B2D1D, as shown in Figure 11.87.

FIGURE 11.87 Renaming the tag

Because this is an annotation family, the size will change with the fluctuation of the scale. If you change the scale from ⅛" to ¼", the tag will shrink by half. To do this, follow along with the procedure.

1. In the View Control toolbar, change the scale from ⅛" to ¼", as shown in Figure 11.88.

2. Move the tag up so it is closer to the cabinet.

3. Add another tag to the cabinet to the right.

4. Call it **B1D** (see Figure 11.88).

FIGURE 11.88 Change the scale to ¼" = 1'-0" and add a second tag to the base cabinets as shown.

As you can see, this is a huge step above inserting a block in a 2D drafting application and filling out an attribute that has nothing to do with the actual element it is labeling. Plus the scaling feature works wonders when it comes time to creating elevations and enlarged views.

The next topic to explore is creating a tag that will work in any situation we need…sort of a multipurpose tag.

Multicategory Tags

If you think about it, we used a door tag for the doors, a window tag for the windows, and a wall tag for the walls. Jeepers! How many different tags are we going to need to complete a set of construction documents? Well, in Revit, you can create what is called a multicategory tag. This will be the same tag (aesthetically) that identifies a common property in any element.

Unfortunately, Revit does not provide a sample multicategory tag, so we will just have to make one. The objective of the next set of procedures is to create a new multicategory tag, then use it on various furniture items.

As mentioned earlier, any new family should be created by using a template. This will ensure you that you are using the correct data, so the family will behave as expected. This is what we are doing right now:

1. Click the Revit Home button, and then go to New ➤ Family.

2. In the `Annotations` folder, locate the file called `Multi-Category Tag.rft`.

3. Open the `Multi-Category Tag.rft` template.

4. Since we have started the family by using a template, the ribbon has changed. On the Annotate panel, click the Label button.

5. Pick the point at the intersection of the two reference planes.

6. In the Edit Label dialog, add the Family Name and Type Name parameters, as shown in Figure 11.89.

7. In the Family Name row, click the Break checkbox (see Figure 11.89).

FIGURE 11.89 This time you are actually adding two parameters. By clicking the Break button, you are telling Revit to "stack" the parameters.

8. Click OK.

9. Go to the Revit Home button, and select Save As. Place it somewhere you can find it later.

10. Call the new tag **Multi-Category tag**.

11. On the Family Editor panel, click Load into Projects.

12. In the NER-28 project, go to Level 1, and zoom in on the northwest office in the west wing.

13. On the Annotate tab, click the Multi-Category button on the Tag panel as shown in Figure 11.90.

FIGURE 11.90 Choose Multi-Category on the Tag panel.

14. On the Element panel, click the Element Properties button.

15. Click Edit Type.

16. For the Leader Arrowhead, select Arrow Filled 15 Degree.

17. Click OK twice.

18. On the Options bar, click Leader, as shown in Figure 11.91.

19. Hover your pointer over the furniture items in the room shown in Figure 11.91. Notice the tag is reporting the information for any item you mouse over. Pick the entertainment unit to the left of the room.

20. With the grips on the tag, move it out of the way, and adjust the leader so it looks like Figure 11.91.

21. Add another tag to the credenza located on the north wall. Adjust this tag as well (see Figure 11.91).

22. Add one more to the shelving on the south wall of the room, and adjust the leader so it looks acceptable (again, see Figure 11.91).

FIGURE 11.91 Add the Multi-Category tag to the entertainment unit as shown. Make sure you adjust the tag to show the information unobscured.

Using multicategory tags is a great way to label a model. It is nice because you do not need a specific tag for the various elements. These items could have been different types of furniture and casework. As long as they have a family name and a type name, the label tag will work!

Another way to record items in a model is by adding keynoting. This procedure is done in conjunction with a schedule. The last section of this chapter will focus on this procedure.

Keynoting

Keynoting has been used in construction documents dating back to the Pharaohs. Okay, maybe not that far back, but you get the point. Revit does a nice job in terms of tracking keynotes. The only issue is the fact that nothing comes pre-keynoted in Revit. That is, a keynote value needs to be assigned to each item. If your company uses keynoting, you will have to assign a keynote to every item in Revit in your template.

That being said, let's break down keynoting and start learning how to add keynotes to your model. There are three different types of keynotes you can add to a model: keynote by element, material, and user. The first type of keynote is keynoting by element, which we will jump right to.

Keynoting by Element

Keynoting by element means you simply select an object and place the keynoted text. This procedure is the same as when you tagged an object, except this time the information you are reporting is actually a CSI formatted keynote.

To use the keynoting by element function, follow this procedure:

1. In the Project Browser, go to the Level 1 floor plan.

2. Zoom in on a hallway sconce lighting fixture.

3. On the Tag panel of the Annotate tab, select Keynote> Element, as shown in Figure 11.92.

 N O T E   If no keynote tag is loaded, click Yes in the subsequent dialog and browse to Annotations ➤ Keynote Tag.rfa.

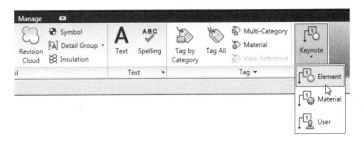

F I G U R E   1 1 . 9 2 Select Keynote ➤ Element.

4. On the Options bar, click the Change Element Type menu and click Keynote Tag: Keynote Text, as shown in Figure 11.93.

F I G U R E   1 1 . 9 3 Choose Keynote Tag: Keynote Text [f1193.tif]

N O T E At this point, it is up to you to determine which style of keynoting your firm uses. Do you keynote the plans with the CSI number, with the Key-note description, or with a combination of the number and the description? Either way, we will be making a keynote schedule with these items in a list.

5. On the Element panel, click the Element Properties button.

6. Click Edit Type.

7. Change the Leader Arrowhead to Arrow Filled 15 Degree.

8. Click OK.

9. Click OK again to get back to the model.

10. Pick the wall sconce shown in Figure 11.94.

11. Pick a second point for the leader line.

12. Pick a third point to place the keynote text (see Figure 11.94).

FIGURE 11.94 Placing the leadered keynote

Since there has been no keynote assigned to this family, it is time to specify one now. The nice thing about the way Revit allows you to specify keynoting information is that you can either assign the information through the Element Properties dialog or you can simply place a keynote tag, and Revit will prompt you to specify the information that does not exist.

Once you pick the third point, Revit will provide you with the keynote menu shown in Figure 11.95. Follow these steps to place the keynote value into the sconce family:

1. Scroll to Division 26 Electrical.

2. Go to the group 26 51 00 Interior Lighting.

3. Go to group 26 51 00.B2 Wall Mounted Incandescent Fixture, as shown in Figure 11.95.

FIGURE 11.95 Selecting the proper keynote value for the sconce

4. Click OK.

5. Drag the text to the right to see the arrow and the note clearly.

SO, WHERE IS THIS INFORMATION COMING FROM?

Now that the information has been added to the tag, you can see where it is stored in the Element Properties dialog.

1.   Select a sconce.

2.   On the Modify Lighting Fixtures tab, click the Element Properties button.

3.   Click Edit Type.

4.   Scroll down to the Keynote field. Notice it now contains information, as shown here:

6. On the Tag panel of the Annotate tab, select Keynote ➤ Element again.

7. Pick another wall sconce and place the keynote. Notice this tag is consistent throughout.

Now that you have experience keynoting by element, it is time to reach into the materials and see how we can apply a keynote value in this capacity.

Keynoting by Material

Similar to keynoting by element, you can tag material with a keynote as well. It is good practice to use the Material dialog to assign keynotes.

To assign keynotes to a material, follow these steps:

1. On the Manage tab, click the Materials button.

2. In the Materials dialog, find Wood-Cherry, as shown in Figure 11.96.

3. To the right of the dialog, click the Identity tab, as shown in Figure 11.96.

4. At the bottom of the dialog in the Annotation information, click the […] button next to the keynote field (see Figure 11.96).

FIGURE 11.96 Browsing for a new keynote

5. Go to division 6 Woods, Plastics and Composites.

6. Go to 06 40 00 Architectural Woodwork.

7. Select 06 40 00.A2 Wood Laminate (see Figure 11.97).

8. Click OK.

9. Click OK again.

10. Go to the Level 1 floor plan.

11. Zoom into the stairs in the east wing.

12. On the Tag panel of the Annotate tab, click Keynote ➤ Material.

FIGURE 11.97   Finding 06 40 00.A2 Wood Laminate

13. Pick the stair landing's surface.

14. Place the keynote as shown in Figure 11.98.

FIGURE 11.98   Placing the material keynote

Now that you have experience adding a keynote value to material, it is time to buckle down and assign keynotes to all of your materials. It is also important to note that, as your firm develops more materials, you need to be diligent in adding keynotes to the new materials as they are created.

The next style of keynoting allows you to specify an alternate keynote to an element. To begin, we will physically open the keynote text file and add some custom notes.

Keynoting by User

There are going to be times where a completely custom keynote will be required. Although you should try to stick to the CSI formatting, there will always be reasons to add your own. To do so, the first thing we need to look at is how to customize the Keynote list.

1. Save your model, and close out of Revit Architecture completely.

2. Open the file C:\ProgramData\Autodesk\RAC 2010\Imperial Library\RevitKeynotes_Imperial_2004.txt.

 W A R N I N G   Before you start typing anything, you need to know that, when you need a separator between texts, you must press the Tab key. If not, the code won't work.

---

3. Scroll down the list until you find the note: 06 43 00.B1→³/₄" Plywood Treads And Risers→06 43 00.

4. Click in the end of the note, press Enter to start a new line, and add the row 06 43 00.B2→Custom Hardwood Stairs→06 43 00 (see Figure 11.99).

```
06 22 00.A5      1x5 Wood Trim    06 22 00
06 22 00.A6      1x6 Wood Trim    06 22 00
06 22 00.A7      1x8 Wood Trim    06 22 00
06 22 00.A8      1x10 Wood Trim   06 22 00
06 22 00.A9      1x12 Wood Trim   06 22 00
06 40 00         Architectural Woodwork  Division 06
06 40 00.A1      Plastic Laminate          06 40 00
06 40 00.A2      Wood Laminate    06 40 00
06 40 00.A3      Metal Laminate   06 40 00
06 43 00         Wood Stairs and Railings        Division 06
06 43 00.A1      2x_ Stringer      06 43 00
06 43 00.A2      2x12 Stringer     06 43 00
06 43 00.B1      3/4" Plywood Treads And Risers   06 43 00
06 43 00.B2      Custom Hardwood Stairs           06 43 00  I
06 43 00.C1      1 3/8" x 2 1/2" Rail Cap          06 43 00
06 43 00.C2      1 1/2" Round Rail        06 43 00
06 43 00.C3      1 9/16" x 3 3/8" Rail Cap         06 43 00
06 43 00.C4      1 3/4" x 3 3/8" Rail Cap          06 43 00
06 43 00.D1      5/16" x 3 1/4" Stair Nosing       06 43 00
06 43 00.D2      3/4" x 3 1/4" Stair Nosing        06 43 00
06 46 00         Wood Trim        Division 06
06 46 00.A1      3/4" x 5 7/8" Crown Molding       06 46 00
```

FIGURE 11.99 Adding the row 06 43 00.B2→Custom Hardwood Stairs→06 43 00

5. Save the file.

6. Open Revit Architecture.

7. Open your file.

8. In the Project Browser, go to Level 1 (floor plan).

9. On the Tag panel of the Annotate tab, click Keynote ➤ User

10. Pick the stairs, as shown in Figure 11.100.

FIGURE 11.100 Picking the stairs to place the keynote

11. In the Select Keynote dialog, your new keynote will be at the top of the list, as shown in Figure 11.101.

12. Pick the new keynote.

13. Click OK.

The stairs now have a custom keynote.

Now that we have every kind of tag imaginable placed in our model, we need to create one more schedule to close the chapter: a keynote schedule.

FIGURE 11.101 The new keynote

Creating Keynote Legends

Creating keynote legends is similar to creating a schedule. Sometimes there is a fine line between what a schedule is and what a legend is. Keynotes seem to almost fall between these two concepts. Either way, follow this procedure to create a keynote legend:

1. On the View tab, click Legends ➤ Keynote Legend.

2. The name Keynote Legend is fine, so click OK at this dialog.

3. In the Keynote Legend dialog, only two fields are available, and they are both added to the schedule. All you need to do is click OK, and the schedule has been created (see Figure 11.102).

Keynote Legend	
Key Value	Keynote Text
06 40 00.	Wood Laminate
06 43 00.	Custom Hardwood Stairs
26 51 00.	Wall Mounted Incandescent Fixture

FIGURE 11.102 The new keynote schedule

Well, that was easy! As mentioned before, if the data is there, it is not hard to create a query such as this to display the information.

One more item to address is where Revit looks for information regarding keynotes: in the Settings listings.

Keynote Settings

To find the keynote settings, follow these steps:

1. On the Tag panel of the Annotate tab, click the drop down arrow on the bottom of the panel. This will allow you to click the Keynote Settings button as shown in Figure 11.103.

FIGURE 11.103 Settings ➢ Keynoting displays where the keynotes are configured.

Although we are not going to change anything, it is noteworthy that the default path is by library location. This is desired, because when you upgrade Revit and you have a custom keynote file, you can move it to the same directory, and Revit will read it into the model.

By specifying by project, this means there will only be one keynote legend. If you specify by sheet, you can then drag the legend onto multiple sheets and only the keynotes that are visible on that specific sheet will be included in the legend. We will cover this in further detail in Chapter 14.

This concludes Chapter 11. As you noticed, there are many items that can be tagged, keynoted, and scheduled. If you feel as though you could use more practice, go ahead and create some more schedules, tags, and keynotes!

Are You Experienced?

Now You Can...

- ☑ **create several different types of schedules**

- ☑ **add custom fields to the schedules that calculate values**

- ☑ **create material takeoffs that give you up-to-the-second information as you add items to the model**

- ☑ **create legends by using a blank view, and basically drafting items into the model**

- ☑ **import AutoCAD-generated data to create a legend that looks exactly like your CAD did**

- ☑ **create drawing sheets, add a schedule, and manipulate a schedule to fit on the sheet**

- ☑ **add tags to the model in addition to the tags that were automatically added when you placed the components**

- ☑ **place tags that "reach into" a component and display different materials**

- ☑ **create custom tags in which to display any information you choose**

- ☑ **create keynotes and keynote schedules**

- ☑ **modify the default Keynote.txt file found in your system program files**

CHAPTER 12

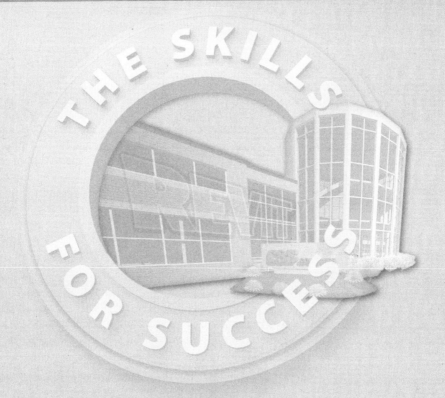

Detailing

- ▶ Working with line weights
- ▶ Drafting on top of a Revit-generated detail
- ▶ Creating filled regions
- ▶ Adding repeating details
- ▶ Adding and creating detail components
- ▶ Annotating details
- ▶ Drafting your own lines
- ▶ Importing CAD

Simply put, Revit will only be used by you as a schematic design application if this portion of the program, detailing, will not work. It is imperative that you are able to detail in Revit efficiently. When firms fail in the attempt to use Revit, this is the area in which that failure occurs. If fact, many of you have bought this book may only to jump to this chapter. And why is that? It is because many people (this author included) buy into the concept of really cool 3D perspectives and one-button modeling.

Once we get Revit, we find out immediately that the real hurdle involved in getting it to work lies in the detailing. Sure, you can cut sections and create callouts, but how do you add that fine level of detailing needed to produce a set of documents that you are willing to stamp and sign? This chapter addresses the issues surrounding detailing.

Working with Line Weights

The first thing that comes to mind when dealing with CAD standards is line weights, right? In AutoCAD it's layers, in MicroStation it's levels, but on paper it is line weights that control 75 percent of our company's standards. As you will learn in this chapter, Revit can be a good 2D drafting application as well. As we learn how to control our line weights in the 3D elements, we can also control line weights, well, line by line.

To begin, open the file you have been following along with. If you did not complete the previous chapter, go to the book's web page at **www.sybex.com/go/revit2010ner**. From there you can browse to Chapter 12 and find the file called NER-29.rvt.

The objective of this procedure is to format the line weighs and to see where, and how, they are being read by Revit.

1. In the Project Browser, open the section called Roof Taper Section.

2. Notice the perimeter of the walls and the roof are extremely heavy in contrast to the finer lines that divide the submaterials. This is what we are going to change. On the Project Settings panel of the Manage tab, click Settings ≻ Object Styles, as shown in Figure 12.1.

3. In the Object Styles dialog, you will see a list of every object category available in Revit. The first items we want to change are the roofs. In the category column, scroll down until you see Roofs, as shown in Figure 12.2.

Glancing up at the headers that describe the columns, you will see the Line Weight column. This column is divided into two sections: Projection and Cut. The Projection column controls the line weights of objects as they are viewed in plan or elevation. The Cut column controls the line weights as they are shown in section. So, to reiterate, "Projection" means plan and elevation. "Cut" means section. Our objective is to modify the line weight for both the cut and the projection of the floor.

FIGURE 12.1 The Settings ➤ Object Styles command

4. In the roofs row, change the Cut value to 3, as shown in Figure 12.2.

5. Click the plus sign next to Roofs to expand the category.

6. Notice all of the subelements are shown, and you can control the line weights accordingly. Change the cut of Fascias to 3.

7. Change the cut for Gutters to 3

8. Change the cut for Roof Soffits to 3 (again, see Figure 12.2).

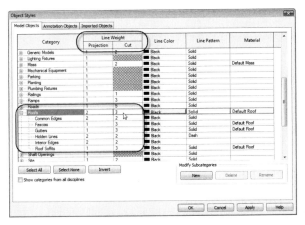

FIGURE 12.2 Changing the object properties

9. Find Floors, and change the cut line weight to 3.

10. Find Walls, and change the cut line weight to 3.

11. Click OK (see Figure 12.3).

FIGURE 12.3 Your section's outline should start looking a lot better.

IT'S TEMPLATE TIME!

Many of the procedures we cover here in the first section of this chapter lend themselves well to the topic of standards and templates. Changing the line weights of objects needs to be done in a Revit template. BIM management and templates are discussed in full in Chapter 23 "BIM Management."

Now we can start adding our own items to the section. The next group of procedures focuses on inserting and creating detail components to use in the sections.

Drafting on Top of the Detail

As mentioned before, Revit provides a good number of 2D details that we can insert at any time. When Revit does not have the component we need, we can always create one. It is not that hard to do.

In this section, we will physically create a detail. The procedures we will apply consist of adding detail components, linework, filled regions, and some good old-fashioned drafting!

Using Predefined Detail Components

The first procedure focuses on inserting predefined detail components. The great thing about this is the fact that you do not have to do anything that you have not done repeatedly throughout this book — it's just a matter of finding the right button to get it all started.

1. Make sure you are still in the detail called Roof Taper Section.

2. On the Detail panel of the Annotate tab, click Detail Component ➢ Load from Library, as shown in Figure 12.4.

FIGURE 12.4 Click Detail Component ➢ Load from Library on the Detail panel of the Annotate tab.

3. On the Options bar, click the Load button.

4. Browse to the Detail Components directory. (It is located in the Imperial Library directory.)

5. Open the Div 01-General folder.

6. Click the file called Break Line.rfa.

7. Click Open.

8. In the Type Selector, be sure that Break Line is selected, as shown in Figure 12.5.

9. Press your spacebar twice. (This will flip the break line into the correct orientation.)

10. Pick a point similar to the point shown in Figure 12.5.

FIGURE 12.5 Placing the break line and flipping the component

The next step is to simply start drafting. As mentioned earlier, you are only going to get so far with 3D modeling before you have to take matters into your own hands and simply draft. The way we can approach this in Revit is to take the parts of the detail we want to keep and hide the rest. Once portions of the detail are hidden, it is time to start adding our own ingredients such as detail components and good old-fashioned lines.

THIS FLIPPIN' BREAK LINE IS BACKWARD!

If you forgot to flip the break line as you were inserting it and it is now masking the wrong region, that's okay. Simply press Esc, and then select the break line. Now you can press the spacebar twice to flip the break line, as shown here:

Masking Regions

To "hide" portions of the detail, Revit has added a nice little feature called a masking region. Instead of wrestling around with items you ultimately have little or no control over, you can hide these items to make way for your detailing.

To learn how to apply a masking region, follow these steps:

1. Make sure you are still in the detail called Roof Taper Section.

2. On the Detail panel of the Annotate tab, click Region ➢ Masking Region, as shown in Figure 12.6.

FIGURE 12.6 Click Region ➢ Masking Region.

3. On the Sketch bar, click the Lines button, as shown in Figure 12.7.

4. On the Options bar, there are some choices available in the Type Selector menu. Choose Invisible Lines, as shown in Figure 12.7.

 N O T E   By selecting Invisible Lines, you ensure that the perimeter of the masking region will not be visible once you exit the Sketch mode.

5. Again on the Options bar, click the Rectangle button.

6. Draw a rectangle at the approximate points shown in Figure 12.7.

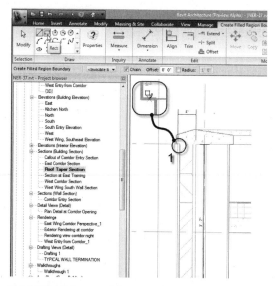

FIGURE 12.7 Click the Rectangle button on the Options bar and place a masking region as shown.

7. Once the rectangle is placed, click the Finish Sketch button on the Sketch bar.

The area is now masked. The problem is, though, some areas such as the break line are a little *too* masked. The next procedure will step through changing the display order of a detail's objects:

1. Select the break line, as shown in Figure 12.8.

2. On the Modify Details tab, notice a row of buttons pertaining to the display order. Click the Bring to Front button, as shown in Figure 12.8.

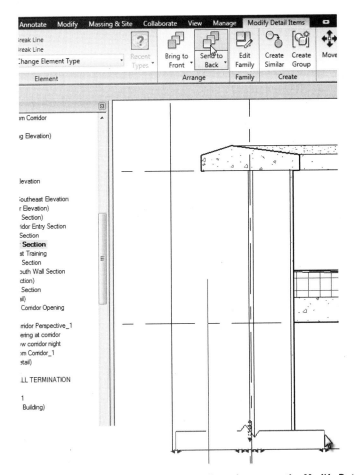

FIGURE 12.8 Click the Bring to Front button on the Modify Details tab after selecting the break line.

Your detail should now look like Figure 12.9.

FIGURE 12.9 The detail with the completed masking region

The next step is to add a brick face. Yes, Revit did show the brick before we masked it, but we need to show coursing, as well as how the façade is tied back to the wall. To do this, we will use a function called a repeating detail.

Repeating Details

Revit has a procedure that allows you to add a detail component as a group. You do this by basically drawing a line, and Revit adds the detail in an array based on the points you pick.

To learn how to add a repeating detail, follow this procedure:

1. On the Detail panel of the Annotate tab, select Detail ≻ Repeating Detail, as shown in Figure 12.10.

FIGURE 12.10 Click Repeating Detail.

2. On the Options bar, choose Repeating Detail : Brick from the Type Selector, as shown in Figure 12.11.

3. Pick the point labeled 1, as shown in Figure 12.11.

 T I P Picking that point is going to be a little harder now that it's not there! The objective is to draw an actual façade based on the existing points where the Revit-generated brick once resided. When you hover your mouse over where the brick was, you will see the masked detail appear, as shown in Figure 12.11. Once it appears, you will see the point you need to pick.

4. Once you pick the first point, move your cursor down the view.

5. Notice the brick is facing the wrong side. Press the spacebar to flip the brick into the wall, as shown in Figure 12.11.

6. Pick the point labeled "2," as shown in Figure 12.11.

FIGURE 12.11 Add the repeating detail based on the points shown here.

Your detail should look like Figure 12.12.

The next step is to keep going with the repeating detail. The problem we are faced with here is the fact that we need to deal with the soldier course that is in the exterior wall. We can add that in a moment. What we need to do in this instance is to complete the brick down past the break line.

FIGURE 12.12 The first repeating detail

If you feel like you are getting the hang of adding this repeating brick detail, go ahead and add the second repeating detail (when done, it should look like Figure 12.14 at the end of these steps). If you would like some instruction, follow along:

1. Click the Repeating Detail button on the Detail panel on the Annotate tab.

2. Pick the point 1, as shown in Figure 12.13.

3. Press the spacebar.

4. Pick the point 2, as shown in Figure 12.13. Make sure you pick the second point well past the break line, or the brick will stop short.

5. Press Esc. Look at Figure 12.14. Does your detail look the same?

6. Select the break line

7. On the Arrange panel, click the Bring to Front button. The repeating detail is now behind the break line.

The next step is to add the soldier course. This will be done in the same way as when you added the break line. In this respect, Revit offers a good library broken down into the CSI format.

> Remember, you can add a second repeating brick detail by right-clicking on the first one you added and selecting Create Similar.

FIGURE 12.13 Picking two points

FIGURE 12.14 The bricks are being placed.

To add the soldier course, follow along with the procedure:

1. On the Detail panel on the Annotate tab, click Component ≻ Load from Library.

2. Browse to the `Detail Components` folder.

T I P   If you have not noticed, when you click the Component ≻ Load from Library, you *always* go to the `Detail Components` folder. This may go without saying, but it took a few months for this author to understand this simple concept.

3. Go to the `Div 04-Masonry` folder.

4. Go to the `041200-Clay Unit Masonry` folder.

5. Select the `Bricks-Top.rfa` file.

6. Click Open.

7. Once the file is loaded, select Bricks-Top : Standard 3/8" joint from the Type Selector, as shown in Figure 12.15.

8. Press the spacebar once to flip the detail to a vertical plane.

9. Place the detail as shown in Figure 12.15. As you are placing the detail, you will notice that Revit will snap it into the proper position.

FIGURE 12.15 Placing the Bricks-Top : Standard 3/8" joint detail component

Well, the soldier course is in place, but that fat line weight is horrendous! It would be nice if everything that came out of the Revit box looked nice and met our specifications, but alas, that is not the case. It is time to modify this component to make it look presentable.

Modifying a Detail Component

Right about now is when every CAD/BIM manager around the globe raises an eyebrow — for good reason. Revit allows you to modify a component by actually opening the file! But don't worry; you have to issue a Save As to save the detail. If even this is a concern, we will be addressing proven BIM management methods in the last chapter (Chapter 23) of this book. For now, just follow along, and we will talk about management later.

The objective of the following procedure is to create a texture on the brick detail and to use a line weight that the user can control in the model.

1. If you still have a command running, click the Modify button at the top of the Drafting tab on the Design bar, or press the Esc key.

2. Select the Bricks-Top family.

3. On the Modify Detail Items tab, click the Edit Family button, as shown in Figure 12.16.

4. The next dialog asks you if you want to open this file to edit it. Click Yes.

FIGURE 12.16 Click Yes to open Bricks-Tops for editing after selecting the Bricks-Top family

The detail component family is now open. It is time to operate, Doctor. The next set of procedures will focus on modifying the linework of the brick and adding what is called a filled region.

Modifying Filled Regions

A filled region is similar in nature to a masking region in that you proceed in applying both in the same manner. A filled region, however, contains a hatch pattern that is visible when the region is completed. This is how we hatch in Revit. It takes the place of the conventional hatch command found in AutoCAD and MicroStation.

The objective of the next procedure is to modify the filled region that comprises the brick. We are also going to use the region's outline to define the perimeter and the texture of the brick itself.

1. Select one of the heavy lines that comprise the outline of the brick, as shown in Figure 12.17. Revit will indicate that this is a filled region, as revealed in the tooltip that appears when you hover your pointer over one of the boundaries.

2. On the Detail panel of the Modify Detail Items tab, click the Edit Boundary button, as shown in Figure 12.17.

FIGURE 12.17 Click the Edit Boundary button on the Detail panel after selecting the filled region.

3. Select the top and bottom lines (the long horizontal lines) and delete them as shown in Figure 12.18.

4. Select the left and the right lines. In the Type Selector on the Options bar, select Detail Items, as shown in Figure 12.18.

FIGURE 12.18 Deleting the two horizontal lines and placing the two vertical lines on the Detail Items line type

 N O T E   As you may notice, manipulating lines is almost identical to AutoCAD in terms of the process in changing a line's "layer." You select the line, then change that line's line type in the Type Selector.

5. On the Draw panel, select the Line button, as shown in Figure 12.19.

6. On the Options bar, select Detail Items from the Type Selector.

7. Draw a series of jagged lines, as shown in Figure 12.19.

8. Do the same for the bottom. Your brick should now look like Figure 12.19.

FIGURE 12.19 Adding a texture to the brick family

9. Once you have finished sketching the texture in, click the Region Properties button on the Element panel.

10. Click Edit Type.

11. Change the background from Opaque to Transparent, as shown in Figure 12.20.

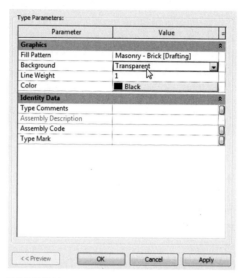

FIGURE 12.20 Changing the background to Transparent

12. Click OK.

13. Click OK again to get back to the model.

14. Click Finish Region on the Region panel.

15. Select the mortar joint to the left of the brick, as shown in Figure 12.21.

16. On the Detail panel, click the Edit Boundary button.

17. Select the arced lines.

18. Place them on Detail Items, as shown in Figure 12.21.

19. On the Region panel, click Finish Region, and your brick should look like Figure 12.22.

NOTE   By putting all of the lines on the Detail Items line type, you are telling Revit that you do not want to specify a specific line weight here, but rather let the user specify the line weight by changing the Detail Items in the Object Properties dialog after you load the detail back into the model.

FIGURE 12.21 Editing the mortar joint filled region and then placing the lines on Detail Items

FIGURE 12.22 The brick is looking the way you want it to.

The next step is to add a shading underneath the brick pattern. To do this, we will create an entirely new filled region and add it to the brick by tracing over the existing filled region.

1. On the Detail panel of the Design tab, click the Filled Region button, as shown in Figure 12.23.

FIGURE 12.23 Click the Filled Region button on the Detail panel.

2. On the Element tab, click the Region Properties button.

3. In the Type list, change the Type to Solid Fill - Black, as shown in Figure 12.24.

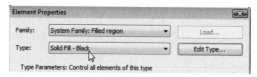

FIGURE 12.24 Changing the region to Solid Fill - Black

4. Click Edit Type.

5. Click Duplicate....

6. Call the new region **Light Shade**.

7. Click OK.

8. In the Fill Pattern row, click into the Solid Fill [Drafting] field. You will see a [...] button in the right corner. Click it.

9. Notice that you can select any hatch pattern you wish. Make sure Solid Fill is selected, as shown in Figure 12.25, and click OK.

FIGURE 12.25 Select the Solid Fill pattern and click OK.

10. In the Color row, you will see a button that is labeled Black. It also has a little black box icon included. Pick the black box.

11. In the Color dialog, click the Gray tile, as shown in Figure 12.26. (The color is actually RGB 192-192-192.)

FIGURE 12.26 Selecting the gray color (RGB 192-192-192)

12. Click OK twice.

13. Click OK one more time to get back to the model.

14. On the Design bar, click the Lines button, as shown in Figure 12.27.

15. On the Draw panel, click the Pick Lines button, as shown in Figure 12.27.

16. Hover your cursor over one of the jagged lines of the brick face, and press the Tab key.

17. Once you press Tab, all of the lines you are trying to trace are highlighted. Once the lines are all highlighted, pick any one of the lines, as shown in Figure 12.27. Revit will draw the region based on these points.

18. On the Region panel, click Finish Region. Your brick should look like Figure 12.28.

19. Once the Filled Region is in place, select it.

20. On the Options bar, click the Send to Back button, as shown in Figure 12.29.

You may find that nothing is happening when you press Tab. If this is the case, click into the view in any location. Revit just needs to focus on the view. You can also hold down the wheel button on your mouse to pan a little. This will also switch the focus from the Options bar to the view window.

FIGURE 12.27 Press Tab to select the chain of lines, as shown here.

FIGURE 12.28 The solid pattern will wash out the previous pattern. We will fix this in a moment.

FIGURE 12.29 Sending the light shade to the back

21. Press Esc. Your brick should now look like Figure 12.30.

FIGURE 12.30 The finished brick

22. Click the Save icon.

WHERE DO I WANT TO SAVE THIS?

Great question. Notice that when you clicked the Save icon, Revit did not just save over the original file. You are forced to do a Save As. You have one of three choices here:

▶ If the file is not write protected and you have administrative access to the original folder, you can simply save over the original file. (Do I need to mention that you had better make sure this is what you want to do?)

▶ Save it as a different file altogether in either the same directory or somewhere else.

▶ Do not save it at all and load it into your project. Revit will still update the project with the changes even if you did not save the family file.

You can even close out of the family file and not save any changes. Your model will still hold the changes. If you choose to edit the file at a later date, you can select the family in the model and click Edit Family. Revit will open a copy of the modified family.

23. Save the file to a separate location other than the root folder. The file is also available at the book's web page: **www.sybex.com/go/revit2010ner**. From there you can browse to Chapter 12 and find the file called Bricks-Top.rfa.

24. On the Family Editor panel on the Create tab, click the Load into Project button, as shown in Figure 12.31.

FIGURE 12.31 Click Load into Projects.

25. Click Yes to overwrite the family, but do not check the Overwrite Parameter Values of Existing Types. Just click OK without checking anything else.

26. Go back to your model to verify that your detail looks like Figure 12.32.

FIGURE 12.32 The new soldier brick in the model

27. Save the model.

The next group of procedures focuses on editing the bricks that are used in the repeating detail. We certainly want the same face texture, and it would be nice if there was a mortar joint between them.

Before we modify the bricks, let's explore how a repeating detail is created. The objective of the next procedure is to discover how a repeating detail works and how we can create a new one.

1. Make sure you are in the detail called Roof Taper Section.

2. Select one of the repeating details, as shown in Figure 12.33.

3. On the Element panel, click the Element Properties button, as shown in Figure 12.33.

FIGURE 12.33 Click the Element Properties button after selecting one of the brick repeating details.

4. In the Element Properties dialog, click the Edit Type button.

5. Click into the Detail list. Notice that every detail component listed in your model is available. The detail component being used here is Brick Standard : Running Section.

Notice also that you can change the spacing and the patterns of how the repeating detail will perform.

6. Click OK twice.

The next objective is to modify the specific detail component that the repeating detail is using. To do so, we must add an instance of the detail component (in this case it is Brick Standard : Running Section) and then edit the family. Once we load it back into the model, the repeating detail will be up to date.

If you would like to give it a shot and do it on your own, go ahead. Make your section look like Figure 12.36 at the end of this series of steps. If you would rather have some guidance, follow along:

1. On the Detail panel of the Annotate tab, click Detail ➤ Detail Component.

2. In the Type Selector, pick the Brick Standard : Running Section detail component. (Remember, this was the component that we discovered the repeating detail was using.)

3. Place the detail component off to the side of the wall, as shown in Figure 12.34.

FIGURE 12.34 Place the Brick Standard : Running Section detail component off to the side. You are going to later delete this occurrence of the component.

4. Press Esc.

5. Select the Brick Standard : Running Section you just inserted.

6. On the Family panel, click the Edit Family button.

7. Click Yes to open the family Brick Standard.

8. Select the filled region.

9. On the Detail panel, click Edit Boundary.

10. Delete the right and left thick lines.

11. On the Draw panel, click the Lines button.

12. In the Type Selector, click Detail Items.

13. Draw the jagged lines in both sides, as shown in Figure 12.35.

14. Click Finish Region on the Region panel.

15. On the Create tab, click the Lines button.

16. On the Draw panel, click the arc passing through three points button.

17. On the Options bar, be sure Detail Items is chosen from the Type Selector list.

18. Draw an arc on both sides of the brick, as shown in Figure 12.35.

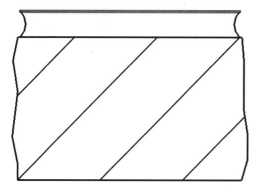

FIGURE 12.35 Draw the textured face while you are in the Edit mode for the filled region. Draw the arcs for the mortar joint using lines.

19. Once you are finished, save the new brick. You can also find this brick at the book's web page in Chapter 12; it's called `Brick Standard.rfa`.

20. In the project, click Yes to overwrite the family.

21. Delete the stray detail component you placed. We were only using it for access to the family.

Compare your detail to that in Figure 12.36.

FIGURE 12.36 The brick actually looks like brick!

The next step is to anchor this façade back to the wall. Two things need to be added. We will first add a structural relief angle above the soldier course, then a brick tieback to a lower course.

1. On the Annotate tab, click Detail ➢ Detail Component.

2. On the Detail panel, click the Load button.

3. Open the Detail Components folder.

4. Go to Div 05-Metals.

5. Go to 051200-Structural Steel Framing.

6. Double-click on the file AISC Angle Shapes-Section.rfa.

7. In the Type list, find L6X4X$^{5}/_{16}$.

8. Click OK. You will have to use the flip grip to flip the instance.

9. Place it into the model as shown in Figure 12.37.

FIGURE 12.37 Placing the L6X4X⁵/₁₆ angle

Of course the line weight is basically a blob, so we must modify the family in order for it to look accurate. The next procedure is almost a review of what we had to do to the bricks.

1. Select the angle.

2. On the Family panel, click Edit Family.

3. In the Family Editor, select the filled region (it is the entire angle), and click Edit Boundary on the Detail panel.

4. Select all of the lines that comprise the perimeter of the angle.

5. In the Type Selector menu, select the Detail Items. (We are switching from heavy lines to Detail Items.)

6. On the Region panel, click Finish Region.

7. On the Family Editor panel, click Load into Projects.

8. Click Yes to overwrite the file.

9. Adjust the angle so it looks like Figure 12.38.

FIGURE 12.38 The angle in place and looking like an angle

The next step is to find a fastener to anchor the angle back to the wall's substrate. There is a problem, however. The type of bolt we need is a lag bolt that is power driven from the exterior into the wall. Revit does not provide one out-of-the-box. Luckily the book you bought does! To find the lag bolt provided with the book, go to the book's web page, browse to Chapter 12, and find the file called A307 Lag_Bolt-Side.rfa.

1. To load the lag bolt into your model, select the Annotate tab, then select Component ➤ Load Family. Browse to the directory where you put the A307 Lag_Bolt-Side.rfa file.

2. With the lag bolt loaded, click Detail ➤ Detail Component on the Annotate tab.

3. Select A307 Lag_Bolt-Side : 3/4" from the Type Selector.

4. Insert the lag bolt into the angle as shown in Figure 12.39.

FIGURE 12.39 Inserting the lag bolt

The next step is to add a corrugated wall tie to the brick below the soldier course. Since the brick is a pretty good distance away from the wall, we will also need to add some wood blocking to the model.

1. On the Detail panel of the Annotate tab, click Detail ➢ Load from Library.

2. Go to the Detail Components folder.

3. Go to Div 06-Wood and Plastic.

4. Go to 061100-Wood Framing.

5. Click the file called Nominal Cut Lumber-Section.rfa.

6. Select the 2×6 type, and click OK.

7. Place the 2×6 into the wall in the wall, as shown in Figure 12.40.

8. Press Esc.

9. Select the blocking you just added and right-click it.

10. Select Override Graphics in View ➤ By Element.

11. In the Projection Lines category, change the weight to 2.

12. Click OK. Your blocking should look like Figure 12.40.

FIGURE 12.40 Adding the wood blocking

The next step is to add the corrugated wall tie. This will be done in the same manner, except that it is located in a different directory.

1. On the Detail panel of the Annotate tab, click Detail ➤ Load from Library.

2. Go to the Detail Components folder.

3. Go to 040500-Common Work Results for Masonry.

4. Go to 040519-Masonry Anchorage and Reinforcing.

5. Select the file called Corrugated Wall Tie-Section.rfa.

6. Place the wall tie into your model, as shown in Figure 12.41.

FIGURE 12.41 Placing the corrugated wall tie

The next step is to add some blocking along the concrete parapet cap. Also, we need additional blocking along the lag bolts. If you would like, go ahead and copy the 2×6 blocking around the model to mimic Figure 12.43 at the end of this series of steps. Or you can follow along:

1. Select the 2×6 blocking.

2. On the Modify Detail Items tab, click the Copy command.

3. Pick the base point of the upper-right corner, as shown in Figure 12.42.

4. Copy the blocking to the point shown in Figure 12.42.

5. Select the new blocking and rotate it into position, as shown in Figure 12.42. (You will have to also nudge the blocking to center it into the wall.)

FIGURE 12.42 Rotating the blocking after copying it

6. Copy the blocking down to double it, as shown in Figure 12.43.

7. Copy the vertical blocking to the positions shown in Figure 12.43 to allow for support of the lag bolts.

8. Select all of the blocking that has the heavy line weight, right-click and choose Override Graphics in View ➤ By Element. Change the projection line weight to 2.

9. Compare your detail to Figure 12.43.

The next type of detail component we will add is a line-based component. The 3/4" void in the middle of the wall is plywood sheathing. You can add the plywood "hatch" in one of two ways. You can just add a filled region that has the plywood hatch built into it, or you can add a detail component.

FIGURE 12.43 Copy the blocking around as shown.

Let's do the latter. To add a line-based detail component, follow along:

1. On the Detail panel of the Annotate tab, click Component ➤ Load from Library.

2. Browse to the Detail Components directory.

3. Go to Div 06-Wood and Plastic.

4. Go to 061600-Sheathing.

5. Double-click the file called Plywood-Section.rfa.

6. In the model, make sure Plywood Section : ¾" is current in the Type Selector.

7. Draw a line from point 1 and point 2, as shown in Figure 12.44.

Your bolt may become obscured by the blocking. This is okay. Simply select the bolt and use the Draw Order tool on the Options bar to bring the bolt to the front.

FIGURE 12.44 Drawing the plywood into the core

8. Once the plywood is drawn in, make sure the bottom is down past the break line. Once it is, select the plywood and choose Send to Back from the Draw Order button on the Modify Detail Items tab.

I think you get the point in terms of adding detail components. One thing we need to do now is figure out how to control the line weight so the outlines of the bricks look a little bolder.

If you remember, some of the detail components were modified based on the line weight of the filled region perimeter. This thickness was taken from Heavy Lines to Detail Items. We need to set the Detail Items to a thickness we can live with.

1. On the Manage tab, select Settings ➢ Object Styles.

2. Scroll down the list until you see Detail Items.

3. Change the Projection line weight to 2, as shown in Figure 12.45.

FIGURE 12.45   Changing the Detail Items Projection line weight to 2

4. Click OK. Your detail now has a bolder perimeter.

> **N O T E**   It is a great idea to plot this detail right now! Although Revit does a nice job of letting you see the contrasting line weights on the screen, it may be a different story at the plotter. Do yourself a favor and make sure this is the line weight you want.

Another item left to explore in terms of adding detail to a view is the simple concept of drawing lines.

Drawing Detail Lines

As mentioned before, in Revit you can simply draw lines. You can only get so far with detail components, and then you need to pick up the pencil and add your lines.

The next set of procedures will focus on adding lines to your model; then we will look deeper into how these lines are created and modified.

1. In the Project Browser, make sure you are in Section : Roof Taper Section.

2. On the Detail panel of the Annotate tab, click the Detail Lines button, as shown in Figure 12.46.

FIGURE 12.46   Click the Detail Lines button on the Drafting tab of the Design bar.

3. In the Type Selector in the Options bar, click Medium Lines, as shown in Figure 12.47.

4. On the Options bar, uncheck the Chain option.

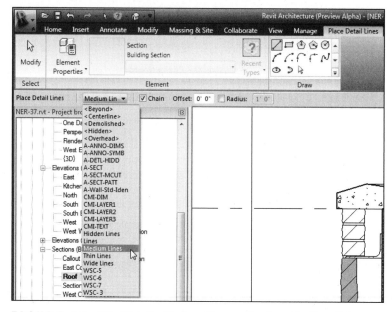

FIGURE 12.47 Click the Medium Lines option from the Type Selector on the Options bar.

 N O T E   Does this seem familiar? If you are used to the AutoCAD method of drafting, this is the same as starting the Line command and choosing the correct layer.

5. Draw a line, as shown in Figure 12.48. Be sure to use your endpoint and perpendicular snaps.

6. With the Line command still running, select the Pick Lines button on the Options bar.

7. Change the Offset to 1½", as shown in Figure 12.49.

8. Offset the line you just drew down 1½", as shown in Figure 12.49.

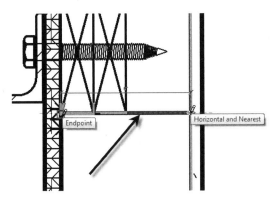

FIGURE 12.48 Drawing a medium line

FIGURE 12.49 Offsetting the line down 1¹/₂" to create a second line

9. With the Line command still running, change to Thin Lines in the Type Selector.

10. In the Draw panel, select the Draw Lines button.

11. Change the offset to 0.

12. Draw the "X" for the blocking, as shown in Figure 12.50.

13. Copy the blocking down to form a double plate, as shown in Figure 12.50.

14. Draw another "X" below the plates to indicate a stud, as shown in Figure 12.50.

FIGURE 12.50 Adding the detail to indicate studs and plates by using detail lines

So, what makes a Medium Line medium and a Thin Line thin? This is a part of Revit that we need to have full control over. After all, your biggest challenge is going to be getting your plotted sheets to match your old CAD plotted sheets. Specifying line weights is crucial.

Specifying Drafting Line Weights

Just like in CAD, you would not dare to draw even a single line if you did not know the proper "layer" it was being drafted on, right? So why should Revit be any different?

The objective of the next procedure is to investigate where the line weights are stored and how they relate to the lines you are drawing:

1. On the Manage tab, choose Settings ➢ Line Styles.

2. In the Line Styles dialog, expand the Lines Category by clicking on the plus sign next to Lines.

    Notice there are some line styles that appear to have been generated in AutoCAD — they were. These line styles were imported when you brought in the legend back in Chapter 11.

3. Click into the Wide Lines category and change the value from 5 to 4, as shown in Figure 12.51.

FIGURE 12.51 Change Wide Lines from 5 to 4.

4. Click OK.

To learn more about setting up line weights and how to establish a good useful template, hop over to Chapter 23. This chapter is dedicated solely to BIM management.

The next item to tackle is the fact that this detail looks naked without any text or dimensions added to it! Although we have applied both of these items in past chapters, we need to use them as they are relevant to detailing.

BUT WHAT DO "5" AND "4" REPRESENT?

In Revit, line weights are sorted from thinnest to heaviest. You can add additional line weights, but I recommend that you stick to the 16 available. To see where these settings are stored, choose Settings ➤ Line Weights. In the Line Weights dialog, notice that numbers 1 through 16 are listed. These numbers represent what you see in the Line Styles dialog. Also notice that the thicker line weights degrade in thickness as the scale is reduced (see the following graphic).

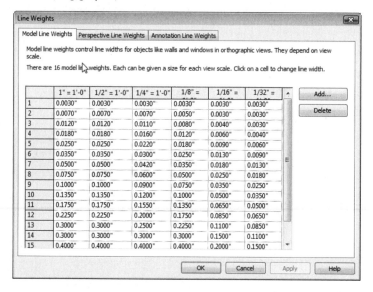

Adding Notes

In Revit, adding notes to a section can take on a whole different meaning than in CAD. You may remember back in Chapter 11 when we were able to specify materials and then tag them in a plan? Well, you can do the same thing right here in Revit.

Or, if you wish, adding notes to a detail can be exactly like it was back in CAD. Sometimes sticking to the tried and true isn't such a bad thing either!

The objective of the next set of procedures will be to add notes by tagging materials, and to add notes by simply leadering in some text.

Adding Notes by Material

Because we have some experience adding information to materials, it would be nice to leverage that experience here. The next procedure will involve going to the material settings and adding a description to the brick that reads BRICK FACADE. Then we will add that tag in the section.

If you are confident you can go and do this on your own. Your finished detail should look like Figure 12.54 at the end of this series of steps. If you would like some instruction, follow along.

1. On the Manage tab, click the Materials button.

2. Find Masonry - Brick in the list to the left, as shown in Figure 12.52.

3. On the right side of the dialog, go to the Identity tag, as shown in Figure 12.52.

4. In the Description, type **BRICK FACADE.**

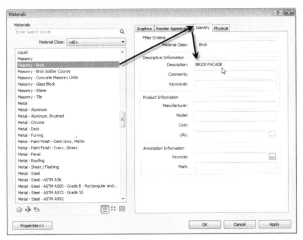

FIGURE 12.52 Changing the Description to BRICK FACADE in the Identity tab

5. Click OK.

6. In the Project Browser, make sure you are in the section Roof Taper Section.

7. On the Annotate tab, click the Material button on the Tag panel, as shown in Figure 12.53.

8. Once you place your cursor over the brick, you will see the tag fill in. Place the tag as shown in Figure 12.54.

FIGURE 12.53 On the Annotate tab, click the Material button on the Tag panel.

FIGURE 12.54 Placing the material tag

Another method of applying a description to a material is to tag the item first and then fill out the tag. If you do so, the material will automatically be identified, and the tag will be filled out the next time you tag the same material.

1. On the Annotate tab, click the Material button on the Tag panel.

2. Place a tag, as shown in Figure 12.55, on the tapered roof insulation. Notice there is nothing but a question mark. This means Revit does not yet have a description for the material.

3. Click the question mark. It turns blue.

4. Click the question mark again and type **TAPERED RIGID INSULATION**. See Figure 12.56.

FIGURE 12.55 Adding a material tag to the insulation

 N O T E When you add a material tag in this manner, you will usually have to move the text to the right or the left to make it readable. In this case, select the text and move it to the right using the drag grip.

FIGURE 12.56 Add the note TAPERED RIGID INSULATION.

Now it's time to just add some free-form notes. The great thing is, we have already done this, and we have gone as far as setting up our own leaders for that text.

Adding Textual Notation

The reason for the duplication of efforts regarding text is to drive home the fact that Revit allows you to add text indiscriminately of the view, and also indiscriminately of the scale. Text in a plan is the same as text in a detail. And we are going to prove it in the next procedure:

1. On the Annotate tab, click the Text button.

2. On the Place text tab, click the Right Justify button, as shown in Figure 12.57.

3. Again, on the Place Text tab, click the Two Segments leader (see Figure 12.57).

4. In the section, pick the first point of the leader at #1 in Figure 12.57.

5. Pick the second point above and to the left of the first point (#2 in Figure 12.57).

6. Pick the third point for the second segment, as shown in Figure 12.57.

FIGURE 12.57 Adding the leadered text

7. Type the note CORRUGATED BRICK TIE ON 2X6 BLOCKING.

8. Click off the text into another part of the model, and your text will justify to the leader.

9. Press Esc.

10. Select the text.

11. Pick the grip to the left, and drag the box to resemble Figure 12.58. Your text will wrap.

12. Save the model.

FIGURE 12.58 Wrapping the text

The most common procedure for adding detail to a model is to do what we have just covered. In other words, take what you can from the model, then add linework and detail components to the view. You will, however, find yourself in the situation where you would rather just draft your detail from scratch. This can be done as well, as you'll see in the next section.

Creating Blank Drafting Views

Over the years, Revit has been labeled as a "poor drafting application." This is unfortunate, because it can be a very good drafting application when given the chance. The only challenge is to figure out where to start!

The objective of the next procedure is to create a blank view, then learn how to simply draw lines:

   1. On the View tab, click the Drafting View button, as shown in Figure 12.59.

FIGURE 12.59 Click the Drafting View button on the View tab.

   2. In the New Drafting View dialog, give the new view a name of **TYPICAL WALL TERMINATION.**

   3. Change the scale to ³⁄₄" = 1'–0" (see Figure 12.60).

FIGURE 12.60 Changing the view name and scale

   4. Click OK.

You are now in a completely blank "canvas." Anything you draw here is truly drafting and is not tied back to the model whatsoever.

The objective of the next procedure is to start adding lines and more detail components. The item we are going to draft is a detail showing a flexible top track of a metal stud partition.

   1. On the Annotate tab, click the Detail Lines button.

   2. In the Options bar, click Medium Lines.

   3. Draw a horizontal line about 4'–7" long, as shown in Figure 12.61.

   4. With the Detail Lines command still running, change the offset in the Options bar to 8".

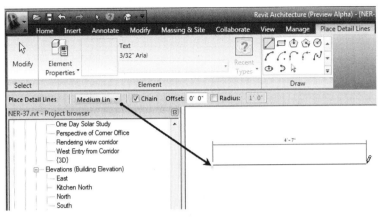

FIGURE 12.61 Drawing a detail line approximately 4'–7"

5. Using the two endpoints of the first line, draw another line below.

GET DOWN THERE!

Remember, if your line is above the first line you drew, press the spacebar, and it will flip the line down below the first, as shown here:

6. Press Esc.

7. Start the Detail Lines command again.

8. On the Place Detail Lines tab, click the Pick Lines button.

9. Again on the Place Detail Lines tab, change the offset to 1½", as shown in Figure 12.62.

10. Offset the bottom line down 1½". Your detail should look like Figure 12.62.

11. With the Detail Lines command still running, click the Line button and set the offset to 3", as shown in Figure 12.63.

FIGURE 12.62 Using Pick Lines and adding an offset of 1½"

12. On the Options bar, make sure the Chain button is checked on.

13. For the first point of the line, pick the midpoint of the bottom line, as shown in Figure 12.63.

14. For the second point of the line, pick a point about 1'–9", straight down as shown in Figure 12.63. (This draws a line offset 3" from the center of the line above.)

15. To draw the other line, pick a point aligned with point 2 (shown as point 3 in Figure 12.63).

16. Pick a point perpendicular to the bottom line (see Figure 12.63).

FIGURE 12.63 By setting an offset of 3", you can draw two lines using a common center line.

17. Press Esc.

18. Compare your lines with that of Figure 12.64.

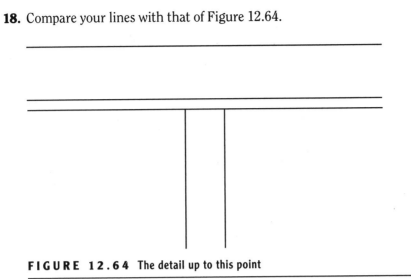

FIGURE 12.64 The detail up to this point

19. Click the Trim button on the Modify tab, as shown in Figure 12.65.

20. Trim the edges of the top of the wall, as shown in Figure 12.65.

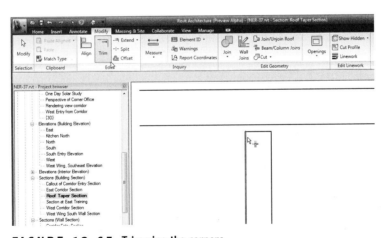

FIGURE 12.65 Trimming the corners

The next step is to add the track to the bottom of the floor. You will do this by creating three wide lines. The trick is you are going to need to do a good amount of offsetting. If you want to explore and try this on your own, go ahead and match Figure 12.68 (at the end of this series of steps) dimensionally. Remember, we are using wide lines for the track.

If you would rather have guidelines, follow these steps:

1. On the Annotate tab, click the Detail Lines button.

2. In the Type Selector menu, click Wide Lines.

3. On the Place Detail Lines tab, click the Pick Lines button.

4. On the Options bar, set the offset to ⅛".

5. Offset the bottom of the floor down ⅛". (It will look like the bottom line simply got thicker, but once we trim it up it will look right.)

6. With the Detail Lines command still running, set the offset to ⅜".

7. Offset the left and the right lines as shown in Figure 12.66.

FIGURE 12.66 Offsetting the heavy lines ⅜" to the right and to the left

8. Offset the bottom of the "floor" down 3".

9. Trim the tops of the left and right thick vertical lines to the thick horizontal line.

10. Trim the bottoms of the thick, vertical lines to the 3" horizontal line, as shown in Figure 12.67.

FIGURE 12.67 Offsetting the thick lines

11. Delete the 3" horizontal line. Your detail should now look like Figure 12.68.

FIGURE 12.68 The top track is now in place.

Now it is time to add the gypsum to both sides of the wall. By using the same method as before, we will simply use thin lines to denote two layers of 5/8" gypsum on both sides of the stud. If you feel as though you are ready to complete this task on your own, go ahead. Your detail should match that of Figure 12.68. (Remember, we are adding two layers of 5/8" gypsum to both sides of the wall, and we are using thin lines to denote this.)

If you would rather have some guidelines to practice with, let's step through the procedure:

1. On the Annotate tab, click the Detail Lines button.

2. Select Thin Lines from the Type Selector.

3. On the Place Detail Lines tab, click the Pick Lines button, as shown in Figure 12.69.

4. Type 5/8" in the Offset field.

5. Offset two lines in from the right and the left, as shown in Figure 12.69.

FIGURE 12.69 Adding the lines for the gypsum

Look at this! The steps are getting shorter. As you can see, we used only the Detail Lines command but yet have successfully offset every line we needed without leaving the command we were running at the time. Who says you can't draft in Revit!

The next procedure will involve adding a filled region to the "floor" Although we don't want to be too specific about what we are calling out here, we do still need some contrasting hatch.

If you would like venture out on your own, try to duplicate Figure 12.71 at the end of this series of steps. You will need to add a filled region using diagonal lines. If you would rather follow the procedure, let's get started.

1. On the Annotate tab, click the Region button.

2. In the Type Selector, click Invisible Lines, as shown in Figure 12.70.

3. On the Sketch bar, click the Region Properties button, as shown in Figure 12.70.

FIGURE 12.70 Click the Region Properties button on the Sketch bar.

4. Click Edit Type.

5. Click Duplicate.

6. Call the new region ROOF.

7. Click OK.

8. Change the Fill Pattern to Diagonal Up-Small [Drafting].

N O T E   Remember to change the Fill pattern by clicking the [...] button after you click in the Material cell. You can then browse to find the pattern you are looking for in the menu.

9. Click OK twice.

10. Click OK one more time to get back to the model.

11. Draw a boundary, as shown in Figure 12.71.

12. Click Finish Region. Your pattern should look like Figure 12.71.

FIGURE 12.71 The detail with the hatching included

This detail is looking good — so good that it would be nice to never have to draw it again. Let's proceed with creating a special group that we can just drag onto another view.

Creating a Detail Group

Groups can be extremely advantageous to the drafting process. Although I mentioned at the start of this section that details and drafting views are not linked to the model, we can still provide some functionality within the details themselves by creating what is called a group. This will give us further control over every instance of this specific detail within the entire model.

The objective of the following procedure is to start create a new group, and add it to another view.

1. Select everything in the view by picking a window.

2. On the Edit toolbar, click the Group button, as shown in Figure 12.72.

FIGURE 12.72 Click the Group button on the Edit toolbar.

3. In the Create Detail group dialog, call the new group **Typical Slip Track**. Click OK.

4. The group has been created. You will see an icon similar to the UCS icon in AutoCAD. This is your origin. Pick the middle grip and drag it to the left corner of the track (where it meets the floor), as shown in Figure 12.73.

5. Save the model.

FIGURE 12.73 Moving the origin to the location shown

With the group created, it is time to add it to another view. Since not every view is showing exactly the same thing, we can alter the group's instance for it to conform to the detail it is being placed into.

The objective of this next procedure is to physically add the new detail group to the Roof Taper Section.

1. In the Project browser, find the Section (Building Section) called Roof Taper Section.

2. On the Annotate tab, click Detail Group ➤ Place Detail Group, as shown in Figure 12.74.

FIGURE 12.74 Click Place Detail Group.

3. Move your cursor over the underside of the roof. Notice you get a snap. This is the origin point of the detail.

4. Pick a point along the bottom of the roof similar to what is shown in Figure 12.75.

TAPERED RIGID INSULATION

FIGURE 12.75 Picking a point along the bottom of the roof to place the group

5. Once the group is placed, press Esc.

The next step is to remove some of the extraneous hatch and lines. You can do this within a group, but you must be careful not to edit the group in a way that affects all other instances.

The objective of the next procedure is to remove the extra lines and hatch from the group.

1. Hover your cursor over the thick line representing the bottom of the floor in the group, as shown in Figure 12.76.

2. Press the Tab key. This allows you to get to the second level of the group and highlight the single line.

3. Pick the line, as shown in Figure 12.76.

4. You will see a small, blur group icon appear. When you hover your mouse over it, it says that you can exclude this member from the group. This is what we want to do, so click the button.

FIGURE 12.76 Excluding an element from the group

5. Repeat the process for the top line.

6. Repeat the process for the hatch.

7. Save the model. Your detail should now look like Figure 12.77.

FIGURE 12.77 The slip track without the extra lines

The next step is to make modifications to the original group to see how each insertion of a group is influenced. This is where the advantage of using groups in a model comes into play.

The objective of the next procedure is to open the original group and modify it. Once the modifications are completed, the other groups will be updated.

1. In the Project Browser, find the TYPICAL WALL TERMINATION view under Drafting Views (Detail) and open it.

2. Select the group.

3. On the Modify Detail Groups tab, click Edit group. You will now see the Edit group panel to the right of the ribbon.

4. On the Drafting tab of the Design bar, click the Insulation button, as shown in Figure 12.78.

FIGURE 12.78 Click the Insulation button on the Drafting tab of the Design bar.

5. Place the insulation starting at the midpoint of the top of the stud and terminate the insulation at the bottom of the stud, as shown in Figure 12.79.

FIGURE 12.79 Drawing the insulation

6. Click the Finish button on the group toolbar, as shown in Figure 12.80.

FIGURE 12.80 Click the Finish button.

7. Open the Roof Taper Section and observe that the insulation has been added.

ALWAYS BE AWARE OF THE PROJECT BROWSER

You can add a group from the Project Browser as well. If you scroll down in the Project Browser, you will see a category called Groups. Expand the Groups category, and you will see the Model category. Expand this, and you will see the Slip Track Group, as shown in the following graphic. All you need to do is click this group and drag it into the model.

So, we are starting to get detailing covered pretty well. There are two issues left to discuss. One is the fact that it would be nice to reference these details from the plan even knowing that they are not physically tied into the model. The second is how we can import CAD into a detail.

Adding a Section to Another View

You already know how to add a section marker in plan. What you may not know is how to tell Revit that you would rather specify the reference.

The objective of the next procedure is to go to the Level 1 ceiling plan and add a section pointing to our drafting view.

1. In the Project Browser, open the Level 1 ceiling plan.

2. Zoom in on the area of the west wing, as shown in Figure 12.81.

3. On the View tab, click the Section button.

4. Before you place the section, look up at the Options bar. There you will see a button labeled Reference Other View. Click it.

5. In the menu to the right of the Reference Other View label, click into the drop-down and select Drafting View: TYPICAL WALL TERMINATION.

6. Place the section into the model, as shown in Figure 12.81.

FIGURE 12.81 Choosing the correct options while placing the section

7. Press Esc.

8. Double-click on the section. It will open your drafting view.

9. Save the model.

W A R N I N G   Be careful here! In AutoCAD and MicroStation, we got used to doing this type of referencing daily. In Revit, your coworkers may not be accustomed to this inaccurate style. Be deliberate when you add sections referring to other views, and try not to do this too often.

With creating a drafting view behind us, it is time to look at our old friend CAD. (Some may say the new acronym is Ctrl Alt Delete.) Regardless of the existing sentiment of CAD, it did get us this far. And we still need it — more so in the drafting capacity. Yes, you can import CAD into a detail.

Importing AutoCAD into a Drafting View

I will go out on a limb and venture to guess that you have a handful of CAD details that you use on a daily basis. The question always is, "What do I do with this pile of details I spent years, and thousands of dollars, to create?" Well, you can still use them.

The objective of the next procedure is to create a new drafting view and import an AutoCAD detail. If you would like, you can attempt to import your own detail, or you can use the file provided. Just go to the book's web page at **www.sybex.com/go/revit2010ner**. From there you can browse to Chapter 12 and find the file called base cabinet.dwg. You can then place it on your system for later retrieval.

The objective of this procedure is to import a CAD detail into a drafting view.

1. In the View tab, click the Drafting View button.

2. In the next dialog, name the new view **TYPICAL BASE CABINET**.

3. Set the scale to $1\frac{1}{2}" = 1'{-}0"$.

4. On the Insert tab, click the Import CAD button.

5. Browse to the location where you placed your CAD file.

6. Select the file, but do not click Open yet.

7. At the bottom of the Import dialog, set Colors to Black and White.

8. Set Layers to All.

9. Set Import Units to Auto Detect.

10. Set Positioning to Auto : Center-to-Center.

11. Click Open.

12. Type ZA. The detail should now be in full view.

13. Select the detail.

14. On the Modify Base Cabinet.dwg tab, click Explode ➤ Full Explode.

15. Select one of the filled regions.

16. Click the Element Properties button on the Modify Detail Items tab.

17. Click Edit Type.

18. Change the fill pattern to Sand - Dense [Drafting].

19. Click OK twice.

USE THE BUILDER BUTTON!

To change the pattern to Sand, make sure you click the [...] button next to the area where it says Solid Fill, as shown in this graphic. From there, you can choose the hatch pattern.

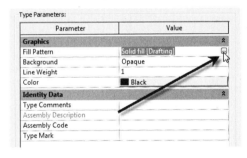

20. Click OK one more time to get back to the model.

21. Make sure your cabinet is hatched properly.

22. Save the model.

As you may notice, the line weights are all one weight. If you would like to address this matter now, jump to Chapter 23 and go to the section on Import/ Export settings.

Up to this point, we have been using detail lines for our drafting. The one issue here is the fact that detail lines are only visible in the specific view you are working in. Suppose you wanted linework to show up both in plan/elevation as well as a 3D view? It is this situation where you want to use the actual "Lines" tool.

Adding 2D and 3D Lines to the Model

Just because we are drafting, this does not mean that we can't do it in a 3D function. There is a tool in Revit that is simply called Lines. This is used to project lines into multiple views. It is applied just like a detail line, only it behaves the same as a Revit 3D family in that you can see it in every view (unless you turn it off).

The objective of the next procedure is to add detail lines to the east sloping roof. They are nothing fancy, but you will quickly get the picture on how to use this feature.

1. In the Project Browser, find the East Roof floor plan and open it.

2. On the Home tab, find the Work Plane panel to the right of the ribbon and click the Set button, as shown in Figure 12.82.

FIGURE 12.82 Click the Set button on the Work Plane panel of the Home tab.

3. In the Work Plane dialog, click the Pick a Plane radio button, as shown in Figure 12.83.

FIGURE 12.83 Click the Pick a Plane radio button.

4. Click OK.

5. Pick the roof, as shown in Figure 12.84.

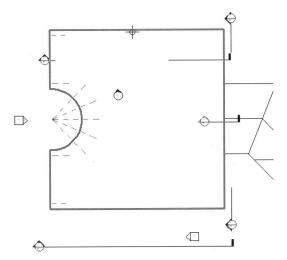

FIGURE 12.84 Pick the roof. Your work plane is now set to slope with the roof. Anything you draw will be on this sloping plane.

6. On the Model panel of the Home tab, click the Model Line button.

7. In the Type Selector menu in the Options bar, click the Medium Lines line type, as shown in Figure 12.85.

FIGURE 12.85 Click the Medium Lines button on the Home tab.

8. On the Draw panel, choose the arc passing through three points button, as shown in Figure 12.87.

9. Draw an arc from the two endpoints shown in Figure 12.86. Make the radius 80'–0".

10. Go to a 3D view. You can still see the arc.

FIGURE 12.86 Drawing an 80'–0" radius arc

It is a good idea to keep this feature in mind. This drafting tool will become quite useful when it comes to sketching in 3D. There are going to be many situations where you are going to use this little nugget!

Are You Experienced?

Now You Can...

- ☑ modify and add line weights to be used in both the 3D and 2D environment

- ☑ add linework in a drafting view as well as a 2D and 3D view

- ☑ create both masking regions as well as filled regions to provide hatching to a model

- ☑ mask an area so you can draft over it

- ☑ add detail components to the model and create repeating details

- ☑ modify detail families to suit your needs

- ☑ Create new Drafting view to draft from "scratch" and import a CAD file into a drafting view.

- ☑ Create a group to be used in multiple drafting views and change the group and update each copy in each view.

CHAPTER 13

THE SKILLS FOR SUCCESS

Creating Specific Views and Match Lines

▶ Duplicating views

▶ Creating dependent views

▶ Creating match lines

A s you are starting to see, Revit is all about the views. In fact, by using Revit, not only are you replacing the application you are using to do your drafting with, but you are replacing your existing file storage system as well. This is largely due to the fact that we are now using one model, and we are simply using views of that model for our project navigation.

That being said, I wanted to dedicate an entire chapter to project navigation. Although you have steadily been gaining experience in this area, there is much more that can be expanded upon to round out your Revit expertise.

The first item we will tackle in this chapter is the process of duplicating a view to create another. Although it is a straightforward procedure, a lot is riding on the hope that you proceed with this function correctly. As you are about to find out, this command is not a simple copy and paste operation.

Duplicating Views

As mentioned in the introduction paragraph, Revit is going to change how you organize a project. You will no longer open a file and save it as another file so you can make changes without affecting the original. As you know, Revit is all-inclusive in terms of "files." Well, there is only one. From there, there are views that reside within the Project Browser.

Of course I am not telling you anything you have not learned. If you have gone through the book from page 1, you will have already gained experience in the creation of views (especially in Chapter 3, "Creating Views"). If you are just jumping to this chapter, you most certainly have had some exposure to the creation of views. The reason this topic is broken into two chapters is to help you gain a more in-depth understanding of how views are manipulated and organized.

Now let's duplicate some views! To begin, open the file you have been following along with. If you did not complete the previous chapter, go to the book's web page at **www.sybex.com/go/revit2010ner**. From there you can browse to Chapter 13 and find the file called NER-30.rvt.

The objective of the following procedure is to create a furniture plan of Level 1, then turn off the furniture on the original Level 1.

1. In the Project Browser, find Level 1 and right-click.

2. Select Duplicate View ➤ Duplicate with Detailing, as shown in Figure 13.1.

3. You now have a view called Copy of Level 1. Right-click on it.

> **The difference between choosing Duplicate with Detailing and just Duplicate is the fact that Duplicate with Detailing will also copy all of the tags and annotations you have in the view being copied. Duplicate will only copy the geometry.**

FIGURE 13.1 Right-clicking on Level 1 in the Project Browser

4. Rename it to **Level 1 Furniture Plan**.

5. Make sure you are still in Level 1. In the Level 1 view window, type VG. This will bring up the Visibility Graphics window.

6. In the Visibility Graphics section, deselect Casework, Furniture, and Furniture Systems.

7. Click OK.

Now, any time you add furniture or casework, it will only show up in the furniture plan. You do not need to deal with a layer or display configuration.

The ability to create a copy of a view and then modify its visibility graphics to display certain items is a critical function that exists within Revit. Another similar task is also available: the ability to create coordinated match line divisions in a model by creating dependent views.

Creating Dependent Views

You create a dependent view in much the same way you duplicate a view. In fact, you are duplicating a view. The function of a dependent view is to "nest" a duplicate of a view within the host view (or the view you are making the duplicate of).

This "nested" view is dependent on the "host" view in terms of visibility graphics and view properties. You can have multiple dependent views categorized under the "host" view. The reason we create dependent views is to add match lines. Yes, you could simply duplicate a view and move its crop region, but having dependent views — as you will see in Chapter 14, "Creating Sheets and Printing" — can be tagged in a specific way for Revit to keep track of the sheets they are on. It is also advantageous to have dependent views based on the fact that your Project Browser becomes much less cluttered without unnecessary floor plans.

The objective of the next procedure is to make a dependent view of Level 1 Floor Plan.

1. In the Project Browser, right-click on the Level 1 floor plan.

2. Select Duplicate View ➤ Duplicate as a Dependent. You now have a view that is nested under Level 1. As you can see, Level 1 is now expanded to show its dependencies.

3. Right-click on Level 1 again.

4. Select Duplicate View ➤ Duplicate as a Dependent. You now have two views nested under Level 1 (see Figure 13.2).

5. Right-click on the Dependent (2) on Level 1 dependent view.

6. Rename it to **Level 1 East**.

7. Rename the other dependent view to **Level 1 West** (see Figure 13.2).

FIGURE 13.2 Creating the two views dependent on Level 1

Now that the views are duplicated and nested within the host view, it is time to divide the Level 1 floor plan. We will do this by adjusting the crop region.

Adjusting the Crop Regions

Every view in Revit has what is called a crop region. If you read Chapter 3, you know this, or you may have enough experience in Revit to realize this fact as well. What you may not know is that crop regions play an important role when your plan is too large to fit on a sheet. All we need to do at this point is to slide the east and the west crop regions to display the correct views.

The objective of the next procedure is to adjust the crop regions to display the appropriate parts of the plan based on the name of the views.

1. Open the Level 1 East dependent view.

2. Select the crop region, as shown in Figure 13.3.

3. Drag the right side of the crop region to the position shown in Figure 13.3.

FIGURE 13.3 Dragging the crop region in the Level 1 west view

4. Open the Level 1 west view.

5. Select the crop region.

6. Drag the left side of the region to the right as shown in Figure 13.4.

STRETCH THAT VIEW

You will notice that there are two stretch grips. One is for the actual crop region, and the other is for the annotation crop region. We will cover what the annotation crop region means in a moment. For now, pick the stretch grip to the inside as shown here:

FIGURE 13.4 Dragging the crop region to the right

7. Select the crop region again if it is not selected already and right-click.

8. Choose Go to Primary View to open the Level 1 floor plan.

9. Once in the Level 1 floor plan, turn on the crop region by clicking the Display Crop Region button on the View Control toolbar, as shown in Figure 13.5.

FIGURE 13.5 Turning on the crop region from the View Control toolbar

Now you can see the area where the match line needs to be drawn. You should have the crop region overlapping in the corridor. If not, drag the crop regions so that they match Figure 13.6.

FIGURE 13.6 Adjusting the crop regions to overlap in the corridor

> **N O T E**   If you would like to turn a dependent view back to an independent view, you can simply right-click on the dependent view and select Convert to Independent View. This will break the "link" to the host view.

Unfortunately, if you have a match line situation in your project, you are going to have to follow this procedure with each floor plan separately. For multifloor projects, this can become time consuming.

As you can see, adjusting the crop region is how you specify which part of the plan is going to show up on your sheet. This poses one issue. If you have text that you would like to lie outside of the crop region — that is, if you have a leadered note pointing to an item within the cropped boundary — you may not see the note. This is where we can adjust the annotation crop region.

Adjusting the Annotation Crop Region

Since the crop region "cuts off" the model at a specified perimeter, what is to become of our text that needs to lie outside of this boundary? This is where the annotation crop region comes in handy. You are always going to have the situation where a leadered piece of text needs to be outside of the geometry it is labeling. We can make adjustments to ensure this can happen.

The objective of the next procedure is to adjust an annotation crop region to clean up a plan.

1. In the Project Browser, find the Level 1 east dependent view and open it.

2. Select the crop region, as shown in Figure 13.7. Notice that there are two perimeters: one is a solid line type, and the other is a dotted line type.

FIGURE 13.7 Select the plan's crop region. Notice there is an additional region on a hidden line type. This is the annotation crop region.

3. In the corridor, there is a dimension that seems to be floating. This is because the crop region is allowing this dimension to show. With the crop region still selected, pick the outside stretch grip (as shown in Figure 13.8) and stretch the annotation crop region in until the dimension disappears.

THE SECOND LINE

If you do not see the second line, follow these steps:

1. Type **VP** in the view window.

2. In the Element Properties dialog, scroll down until you get to the Extents area.

3. Make sure the Annotation Crop option is checked, as shown here:

FIGURE 13.8 Stretching the annotation crop region to the left

N O T E   The annotation crop feature is available in any view. This example used a plan, but you can do the same procedure in a section or an elevation as well.

Now that you understand how to add crop regions and display them appropriately, it is time to add the match line.

Adding Match Lines

In CAD, adding a match line is nothing more than the simple practice of drawing a line. In Revit, adding a match line is nothing more than the simple practice of drawing a line — only in Revit, that line is being drawn in Sketch mode,
and that line can be propagated to other views. Also in Revit, once that line is
placed it does in fact register as having two sides of a model. In Chapter 14, when
we drag our views onto sheets, Revit will know where each side of the model is
in terms of being placed on a sheet.

The objective of the next procedure is to place a match line into the model.

   1. Open the Level 1 floor plan.

   2. On the Sheet Composition panel of the View tab, click the Matchline
       button, as shown in Figure 13.9.

F I G U R E   1 3 . 9   Click the Matchline button on the View tab.

   3. On the Create Match Line Sketch tab, click the Matchline Properties
       button.

   4. Make sure the top and bottom constraints are set to Unlimited.

   5. Click OK.

   6. On the Sketch bar, click Lines button.

   7. Draw the match line as shown in Figure 13.10.

   8. Click Finish Sketch on the Sketch bar.

FIGURE 13.10 Placing the match line

Your match line will now appear as a bold hidden line. Since the physical appearance of a match line never seems to be the same from firm to firm, we can adjust the appearance of the line.

Match Line Appearance

A match line is not an actual "line" by definition but is an object. Therefore, we can control its appearance by using the Object Styles dialog.

The next procedure will focus on changing the appearance of the match line:

1. On the Manage tab, select Settings ➢ Object Styles.

2. Click the Annotation Objects tab, as shown in Figure 13.11.

3. Scroll down until you see Matchline.

4. Click into the Line pattern (the Dash cell).

5. Once you click into the cell, you will see a menu arrow. Click it and select Dash Dot ³⁄₈" (see Figure 13.11).

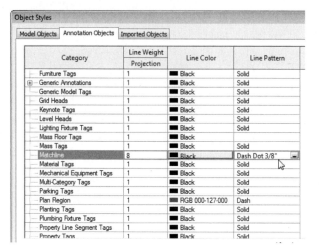

FIGURE 13.11 Changing the match line's line type to Dash Dot ³⁄₈"

6. Click OK. Your match line is now a different line type.

Now that the match line is in place, and the plan is "split" into two halves, it is time to add some annotation labeling the match line.

For the match line annotation, we will simply place a piece of text that says MATCHLINE. But when we are referencing each side of the plan, we will need to add view references.

Adding View References to a Match Line

Once the plan is split, and the match line is in place, we can now tag each side of the match line. When we drag the view onto a drawing sheet, the tag will be filled out with the correct page name. It is important to note, however, that although this process is automatic, it is not fully automatic. You do need to specify the correct view name as you are placing the tag.

The objective of the next procedure is to place a piece of text that says MATCHLINE along the match line, and to add a view reference to each side of the match line.

1. In the Project Browser, open the Level 1 floor plan view.

2. On the Annotate tab, click the Text button, as shown in Figure 13.12.

N O T E   Unfortunately when you are placing text, you cannot rotate the text until after you have added it. In this procedure, simply place the note, rotate it, and then move it into position.

3. On the Place Text tab, you have leader options. Click the No Leader button (the A), as shown in Figure 13.12.

4. Pick a window near the match line for the text.

5. Type the word **MATCHLINE** and click off of the text, as shown in Figure 13.12.

FIGURE 13.12 Typing the text MATCHLINE

6. Select the text (if it is not selected already).

7. Click the rotate grip and rotate the text 90 degrees.

8. Click the move grip, and drag the text over to the match line so it is positioned as shown in Figure 13.13.

9. On the Tag panel of the View tab, click the View Reference button.

10. On the Options bar, you will see a Target view menu. Make sure Floor Plan : Level 1 East is current, as shown in Figure 13.13

11. Pick a point to the left of the match line (see Figure 13.13).

12. With the view Reference command still running, change the Target View to Floor Plan : Level 1 East.

13. Place a view reference to the right of the match line.

14. Press Esc. You are now ready to add these views to a drawing sheet for the next chapter.

FIGURE 13.13 Adding a view reference includes having to choose the correct target view from the Options bar.

One last item to discuss before we close this chapter is how we can create and use settings from a single view once it is determined that these view settings are what we would like to repeat over and over.

Using View Templates

When we created the furniture plan in the beginning of the chapter, we had to go into the Visibility Graphics options to manipulate the data to not show furniture in a specific plan. It would be nice to have settings like these built into a template so we could simply apply that template to a view the next time the situation arose.

The objective of the next procedure is to create a view template and apply it to another view.

1. In the Project Browser, right-click on Level 1.

2. Select Create View Template from View.

3. In the Name dialog, call the template **without furniture or casework**.

4. In the next dialog, Revit allows you to further control the view properties as well as the visibility graphics. Since we don't need to make any further adjustments, click OK.

5. Right-click on Level 2

6. Select Apply View Template.

7. In the View Template dialog, select the without furniture or casework template, as shown in Figure 13.14.

FIGURE 13.14 Selecting the without furniture or casework template

8. Click OK.

As you can see, using view templates are going to help you with maintaining company-wide standards immensely! Use templates as often as possible. For more information on setting up standards, flip to Chapter 23, "BIM Management."

>
> **You can also select multiple items and apply the same template to many plans if so desired.**

Are You Experienced?

Now You Can...

- ☑ create duplicates of views, and tell the difference between duplicating with detailing and simply just duplicating a view

- ☑ create dependent views, allowing separate views to be nested under one host view

- ☑ add match lines and view reference tags

- ☑ create and use view templates

CHAPTER 14

THE SKILLS FOR SUCCESS

Creating Sheets and Printing

▶ Creating and populating sheets

▶ Managing revisions

▶ Creating a cover sheet

▶ Printing a document set

Our deliverable product is a set of construction documents and specifications. So it stands to reason that the application we use to produce these construction documents is at its strongest in this arena. Unfortunately, when you see marketing campaigns related to Revit, all that is shown are huge skyscrapers and realistic renderings. And of course you see the slide that shows the architect handing a model to the contractor, and then the contractor hands it to the owner. Don't get me wrong — all that stuff is good, but it is time to focus on the most powerful feature of Revit Architecture: the ability to create sheets. You would not think this is the standout feature, but when it is 4:30 and the job is going out the door at 5:00, you will never go back to a drafting application after you have used Revit at the 11th hour.

The first part of the chapter will focus on the creation of a sheet, and how to populate it with views. Although you have completed this task back in Chapter 11, "Schedules and Tags," it is time to drill into the ins and outs of sheet creation.

Creating and Populating Sheets

Luckily this part of Revit holds true to form — that is, we still don't have to start setting up different drawings or models to simply reference them together. We are going to create sheets much how we created most of the other views, because that is all a sheet is: a view. But a sheet goes one step further. Look at a sheet as a view that collects other views for the purpose of printing.

The objective of the following procedure is to create a new sheet. To get started, open the model you have been working on. If you missed the previous chapter, go to the book's web page at **www.sybex.com/go/revit2010ner**. From there you can browse to Chapter 14 and find the file called NER-31.rvt.

1. In the Project Browser, scroll down until you see a category called Sheets, as shown in Figure 14.1.

2. Right-click on Sheets and select New Sheet (see Figure 14.1).

3. In the Select Titleblock dialog, select the E1 30×42 : Horizontal title block. (It is probably the only one available.)

4. Click OK.

N O T E   The title block we are using is a standard Autodesk-supplied title block. Later in the chapter, we will look at how to make custom title blocks. Also, your new sheet may be numbered differently from the example in the book. This is okay; we are going to change this in a moment.

FIGURE 14.1 Selecting a new sheet

Congratulations! You now have a blank sheet. The next procedure will involve adding views to the sheet by the click-and-drag method.

1. In the Project Browser, find the dependent view called Level 1 East, as shown in Figure 14.2.

2. Pick (left-click) the view, and hold down the pick (left) button.

3. Drag the view onto the sheet, as shown in Figure 14.2.

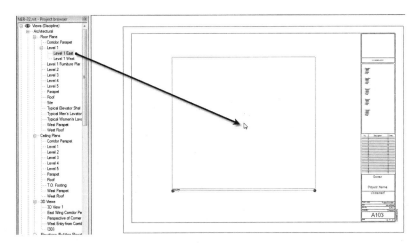

FIGURE 14.2 Dragging the view onto the sheet

4. Once the view is centered in the sheet, let go of the pick button. You will now see the view following your cursor. When you get to a good spot, pick (left click). This will place the view onto the sheet.

This is how you populate a sheet using Revit — quite the departure from CAD. One nice thing is the fact that the title is filled out, and the scale will never be incorrect. The next step is to start renumbering sheets so we can create a logical order.

Sheet Organization

If you have been following along with the book, you will already have a sheet numbered A101. It would be nice if we could give this sheet a new number and start our sequence over again. Revit gives you the ability to do just that.

The objective of the next procedure is to change the sheet numbering and to add more sheets, allowing Revit to sequentially number the sheets as they are created.

1. In the Project Browser, find the sheet A101 Unnamed and right-click.

2. Select Rename, as shown in Figure 14.3.

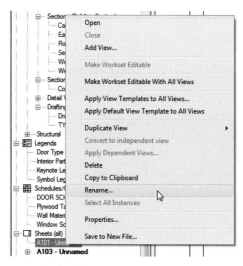

FIGURE 14.3 Renaming the sheet

3. Change the sheet number to A601.

4. Change the name to **SCHEDULES AND GENERAL NOTES**.

5. Click OK.

6. Right-click on sheet A103 (if it is not named A103, it is the only other sheet other than A601, the sheet you just created).

7. Select Rename.

8. Change the number to A101.

9. Change the name to EAST WING PLAN.

10. Click OK.

Your Project Browser should now resemble Figure 14.4.

FIGURE 14.4 The reorganized Project Browser

With the sheets organized, we can now proceed to create more. As we proceed, we will be able to see that not only do the sheets number themselves, but all of the sections, elevations, and callouts will start reading the appropriate sheet designations.

The objective of the next procedure is to create more sheets and to add views to them.

1. Right-click on the word Sheets in the Project Browser.

2. Select New Sheet.

3. Click OK to add the title block.

4. In the Project Browser, find the dependent view called Level 1 West and drag it onto the new sheet.

5. Pick a point on the sheet to place the view.

6. In the Project Browser, double-click on the A101 sheet. Notice that the view reference next to the match line is filled out with the appropriate designation.

7. Double-click on A102 to open the view again.

You may notice in the Project Browser that sheet A102 is still unnamed. The next procedure will describe a different way to rename and renumber a sheet.

> You may also notice that there is a plus sign (+) next to A101. If you expand the tree by clicking on the +, you will be able to see the views that are included on this view. This can prove to be immensely useful because you cannot add a view to another sheet (or the same sheet for that matter) if it is already included in a sheet.

1. With Sheet A102 opened, zoom into the right side of the view, as shown in Figure 14.5.

2. Select the title block. Notice that a few items turn blue. If you remember, any item that turns blue like this in Revit can be modified.

3. Click into the text that says Project Name and type NO EXPERIENCE REQUIRED.

4. Click into the text that says Sheet Name and type **WEST WING PLAN** (see Figure 14.5).

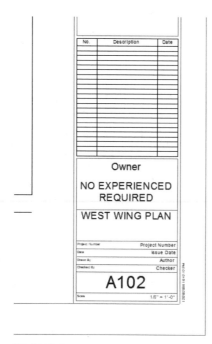

FIGURE 14.5 Changing the title block information

5. Create another sheet.

6. Number it A201.

7. Call it **ENLARGED PLANS**.

8. Drag the following views onto the sheet:

   ▶ Typical Elevator Shaft

   ▶ Typical Men's Lavatory

   ▶ Typical Women's Lavatory

9. Arrange them so they are in a row, as shown in Figure 14.6.

FIGURE 14.6 Creating a sheet and adding views in a row across the bottom of the page

 NOTE Also notice that the title block is filled out. The page number and the sheet name are filled out because we edited these names when we made the sheet, but the project name will appear on every new sheet that we create.

Now that the first floor plans and typical enlarged plans are placed on a sheet, it is time to move on to adding the details that we created.

If you feel as though you have enough experience creating a sheet and adding views, go ahead and proceed on your own. Your new sheet will be numbered A301, called Building Sections, and you will be adding the views East Corridor Section, West Corridor Section, Section at East Training, and West Wing South Wall Section. Your sheet should look like Figure 14.7.

If you would like some assistance in putting the section sheet together, follow along with this procedure:

1. In the Project Browser, right-click on the Sheets category.

2. Select New Sheet (you can glance back to Figure 14.1 if you need visual assistance).

3. Select the E1 30×42 Horizontal Titleblock, and click OK.

4. In the Project Browser, right-click on the new sheet and select Rename.

5. Give the new sheet a number of A301 and a name of BUILDING SECTIONS.

6. In the Project Browser, find the Sections (Building Sections) category.

7. Drag the section called West Corridor Section onto the lower-left corner of the sheet.

8. Drag the section called Section at West Training onto the sheet to the right of the East Corridor Section.

9. Drag the section called West Corridor Section onto the sheet and place it into the upper-left corner. Be sure you align it directly above the West Corridor Section.

10. Drag the section called East Wing South Wall Section to the right of the East Corridor Section and directly above the Section of East Training. Notice the alignment lines will allow you to accurately place the section. Once you have these four sections in place, your sheet A301 should look like Figure 14.7.

FIGURE 14.7 The completed sheet A301

Now that we have created a few sheets, you may be noticing that it would be nice if we could make some adjustments to the view without leaving the sheet. The next section of this chapter will focus on the properties of a viewport and how to make it "live" on the sheet so we can make modifications.

Modifying a Viewport

Wait a second. Isn't a "viewport" an AutoCAD vernacular? Yes, it is. But a viewport in AutoCAD and a viewport in Revit are two different things altogether.

In Revit, when a view is dragged onto a sheet, a linked copy of that view becomes a viewport. This is what you see on the sheet. Any modification that is now made to the original view will immediately be reflected in the viewport, and vice versa. See Figure 14.8 for a graphical representation.

FIGURE 14.8 A representation of the relationship between the original view and the viewport

The objective of the next procedure is to activate a viewport to make modifications on the sheet, and also to explore the element properties of the viewport.

1. Open the sheet A301 (if it is not open already).

2. Zoom in on the viewport East Wing South Entry Section, as shown in Figure 14.9.

3. Select the view.

4. Right-click and select Activate View, as shown in Figure 14.9.

FIGURE 14.9 Activating a viewpoint

N O T E   By activating the view in this manner, you are essentially opening that view. The only difference between physically opening the view in the Project Browser and activating the view on the sheet is that by activating the view on the sheet, you can now see the title block, which will help in terms of layout.

5. With the view activated, you can work on it just as if you had opened it from the Project Browser. Select the crop region, as shown in Figure 14.10.

6. Stretch the top of the crop region up so you can see the entire view.

7. Stretch the bottom of the crop region down to expose the bottom of the section.

FIGURE 14.10   Stretching the crop region so you can see the entire view

8. In the View Control toolbar, select Hide Crop Region.

UNSIGHTLY CROP REGIONS BE GONE!

By selecting Hide Crop region, as shown here, you are simply "cleaning up" the view. As we will explore in this chapter, you can keep the crop region on and tell Revit not to print it.

9. Select Deactivate View.

10. Right-click on the view to the left of the West Wing South Entry Section. It is the view called West Corridor Section.

11. Stretch the crop region down so you can see the entire foundation.

12. Hide the crop region.

13. Right-click and deactivate the view.

With the view widened, it is coming close to the actual title. You can move the viewport or the title independently of one another. The objective of the following procedure will involve moving the viewport up, then moving the view title down to provide some more room.

1. Select the West Wing South Entry Section viewport.

2. Hold down the pick button, and move the entire viewport up. As you are moving the viewport up, an alignment line will appear. This means that the views are physically aligned. Once you see the alignment line, release the pick button.

3. Press Esc.

4. Select the view title, as shown in Figure 14.11.

5. Move it down. As you are moving the view title, it will snap in alignment to the view title to the left, as shown if Figure 14.11.

FIGURE 14.11 You can select the view title independent of the actual viewport.

N O T E   The view titles can also be customized. This procedure, however, falls under the category of BIM management. To learn how to create a new view title, check out Chapter 23, "BIM Management." There is a section dedicated to the creation of a view title.

Now that we have some experience creating sheets and making adjustments to the views and viewports, we can easily create one more sheet that contains sections.

The following procedure will focus on creating a detail sheet. If you feel as though you can create this sheet on your own, go ahead. The sheet will be sheet number A401, it will be named DETAILS, and the views to be added are Corridor Entry Section, Callout of Corridor Entry Section, Roof Taper Section, and TYPICAL WALL TERMINATION. Your finished sheet should look like Figure 14.12.

If you would rather have some assistance, follow along with this procedure:

1. In the Sheets category in the Project Browser, right-click on the Sheets title.

2. Select New Sheet.

3. Number it A401 and name it DETAILS.

4. In the Project Browser, drag the section (Wall Section) called Corridor Entry Section, and place it in the sheet all the way to the right.

5. In the Project Browser, drag the section (Building Section) called Callout of Corridor Entry Section onto the sheet to the top left of the previous section (see Figure 14.12).

6. Drag the section called Roof Taper Section to the bottom left of the first view you added.

7. Drag the view called TYPICAL WALL TERMINATION to the sheet directly to the left (see Figure 14.12).

8. Zoom in on the view title for the Corridor Entry Section, as shown in Figure 14.13.

9. Select the Corridor Entry Section viewport. Notice there are blue grips on the view title.

10. Stretch the grip on the right to the right to extend the line, as shown in Figure 14.13.

11. Save the model.

FIGURE 14.12 Building the A401 DETAILS sheet

FIGURE 14.13 Stretching the view title line to the right via the blue grip

On your own, if you wish, pan and zoom around investigating all of the reference markers. They are starting to fill themselves out based on the sheets that the referring views have been placed on.

NOTE   You can only place one instance of a view on a sheet. You also cannot place a view on multiple sheets. This is Revit's way of keeping track of what view is on a page and which page that view is on. The only type of views that can be placed on more than one sheet is a Legend view. If you would like to place a view on a sheet more than once, you will need to duplicate the view in the Project Browser.

Now that we know how to manipulate a viewport, it is time to take a look at the viewport's element properties. I think you will be glad to see how familiar these properties are.

Viewport Element Properties

Just like anything else in Revit, viewports have associated element properties. All you need to do is select the viewport and click the element properties button on the Options bar.

The objective of the following procedure is to look through the viewport's element properties and to make some minor modifications.

1. Open the view A401 DETAILS (if it is not already).

2. Select the Corridor Entry Section view (the tall section to the right of the sheet).

3. On the Modify Views tab, click the Element Properties button.

 N O T E   Notice that the element properties for the viewport are exactly the same as those for a typical view. When you change the element properties of a viewport, you are actually changing the element properties of the corresponding view.

4. Scroll down the list until you arrive at the Title On sheet, as shown in Figure 14.14.

5. Change the Title on Sheet to **SECTION AT ENTRY CORRIDOR**.

6. Click Edit Type.

7. In the type parameters, you can choose which view title you will be using, or if you want any view title at all. We will be addressing creating custom view titles in Chapter 23, so for now just click OK.

8. Click OK again to get back to the model.

9. Zoom in on the detail and notice that the name has changed.

Notice that when you select the viewport, the name and detail number turn blue. This means that you can change the values right on the sheet.

Now that we have pretty much exhausted creating and manipulating sheets, it is time to explore another sheet function: adding revisions.

Instance Parameters - Control selected or to-be-created instance	
Parameter	Value
Discipline	Architectural
Color Scheme Location	Background
Color Scheme	<none>
Identity Data	
View Name	Corridor Entry Section
Dependency	Independent
Title on Sheet	SECTION AT ENTRY CORRIDOR
Sheet Number	A402
Sheet Name	DETAILS
Referencing Sheet	A101
Referencing Detail	1
Default View Template	None
Extents	

FIGURE 14.14 You can make the title on the sheet different from the view name.

Adding Revisions to a Sheet

An unfortunate reality in producing construction documents is the fact that there will come a time where revisions will need to be performed. In CAD, you normally create a duplicate of the file, save that file into your project directory and then create the revisions. The only real way to keep track of them is to add a "rev cloud" and change the attribute information in the title block. In Revit, however, you are given a revision schedule and the means to keep track of your revisions.

The objective of the next procedure is to add a revision cloud and to populate a schedule that is already built into the sheet.

1. In the Project Browser, open Sheet A101.

2. On the Annotate tab, click the Revision Cloud button, as shown in Figure 14.15. Notice you are now in Sketch mode.

FIGURE 14.15 Click the Revision Cloud button on the Annotate tab.

3. Place a revision cloud around the plan, as shown in Figure 14.16.

 T I P   To get the revision cloud drawn accurately, you must go in a clockwise manner. Unfortunately, if you err in getting the cloud on the sheet, you should probably undo and start over.

FIGURE 14.16 Placing a revision cloud

---

4. On the Create Revision Cloud Sketch tab, click Finish Cloud.

5. On the Annotate tab, click Tag by Category, as shown in Figure 14.17.

6. Pick the revision cloud.

7. You will probably get a dialog stating that you do not have a tag loaded for this category. If you get this dialog, click Yes to load one.

8. Select Annotations ➢ Revision Tag.rfa.

9. Pick the revision cloud. You now have a tagged revision cloud, as shown in Figure 14.17.

FIGURE 14.17 The revision tag has been added to the cloud. Also, notice the title block has Revision 1 added to it.

Zoom closer to the title block. You will also notice that the revision schedule has the first revision added to it. This is because Revit is now keeping track of your revisions.

The next procedure will focus on making modifications to the revision scheme so we can better keep track of the revision schedule.

1. On the View tab, click the small arrow in the lower-right corner of the Sheet Composition panel, as shown in Figure 14.18.

2. In the Sheet Issues/Revisions dialog, change the date to today's date.

3. For the description, type **First Floor Revisions**.

4. Click the Add button, as shown in Figure 14.18.

5. Give the new revision a date in the future.

6. For the description, enter **Revised Sections** (see Figure 14.18).

7. For the numbering, check Per Project.

8. Click OK.

9. In the Project Browser, open the sheet A301 BUILDING SECTIONS.

10. On the Annotate tab, click the Revision Cloud button.

FIGURE 14.18 The Sheet Issues/Revisions dialog

11. Place a cloud around the upper-right detail.

12. On the Sketch bar, click Finish Cloud.

13. Select the cloud you just added.

14. On the Options bar, make sure you have Seq. 2 - Revised Sections selected, as shown in Figure 14.19.

FIGURE 14.19 By selecting the revision cloud, you can specify the sequence from the Options bar.

15. On the Annotate tab, select Tag ➤ By Category.

16. Place the revision tag on the cloud. You may also notice that the schedule is filled with only the appropriate revision pursuant to this sheet.

Now that we have experience with the concept of how sheets and revisions come together, there is one more avenue we need to explore in terms of populating sheet information. You may have noticed that the title blocks are not yet complete. The fields that are not filled out relate to project information that needs to be included on each sheet. This is where project parameters come in.

Addressing Project Parameters

Since Revit is built upon a database, it makes sense that items like Project Name and Project Number are going to be added to the design in a different manner than that of CAD. In CAD, you fill out attributes sheet by sheet, or you simply externally reference a title block with the "sheet information." In Revit, you fill out the project information in one place. The information you add to the database propagates down to the sheets. When, or if, this information changes, it is done quickly and accurately.

The objective of the next procedure is to locate the project parameters and populate the model with the job information.

1. On the Manage tab, click Project Information, as shown in Figure 14.20.

SAVE THAT MODEL!

You may have noticed that a save reminder keeps popping up. Revit likes to ask you if you want to save the model *before* you execute a command. This process has greatly reduced the amount of crashes as compared to AutoCAD. See the following graphic.

2. Click the Edit button next to Energy Data, as shown in Figure 14.20. The resulting dialog allows you to add the project's geographical information as well as energy data. This will allow you to export the information to GBXML as well as provide information so your architectural model can be imported into Revit MEP.

3. Click OK.

4. You can fill out the rest of the information as follows:

  ▶ Project Issue Date: 12/12/09

  ▶ Project Status: 100%

  ▶ Project Name: NO EXPERIENCE REQUIRED

  ▶ Project Number: 20090342

See Figure 14.20.

FIGURE 14.20 Fill out the project data accordingly.

 N O T E   Notice the NO EXPERIENCE REQUIRED text has already been entered. This is because you added it to the appropriate field in the title block. Remember, when you are dealing with Revit, and databases in general, it is a two-way flow of information.

5. Click OK.

6. Open any sheet and examine the title block. All of the information should be filled out.

Now that we are able to populate the information in a sheet, there is one more item to cover quickly before we jump into printing: adding a drawing list.

Generating a Cover Sheet

It goes without saying that this ingenious method of creating and managing sheets would not quite be perfect unless you could generate a sheet list and put it on a cover sheet. Well, this is Revit. Of course you can! The best part about it is you already have the experience necessary to carry out this procedure.

The objective of the next procedure is to create a drawing list and add it to a cover sheet.

1. On the View tab, click Schedules ➢ Drawing List, as shown in Figure 14.21.

FIGURE 14.21 The Drawing List button on the View tab

2. In the Drawing List Properties dialog, add Sheet Number and Sheet Name, as shown in Figure 14.22.

3. Click the Sorting Grouping tab.

4. Sort by Sheet Number.

5. Check Ascending.

6. Click OK.

FIGURE 14.22 Adding Sheet Number and Sheet Name (in that order)

Wow! Creating a schedule is so easy, you will probably be doing this on your lunch break instead of playing Internet games!

For now, let's keep this schedule in the Project Browser and create a cover sheet that we can drag it onto. The objective of the next procedure is to create a new title block family, add it to the project, then drag the drawing list onto the cover.

1. On the Revit Home button, click New ➤ Titleblock, as shown in Figure 14.23.

2. Select E1 - 42 × 30.rft.

3. Click Open.

4. On the Annotate panel of the Create tab, click Label, as shown in Figure 14.24.

5. On the Options bar, click the Element Properties button.

6. Click Edit Type.

7. Click Duplicate.

8. Call the new tag TITLE and click OK.

9. Make sure the Text Font is Arial.

10. Change the Text Size to 1".

11. Click Bold.

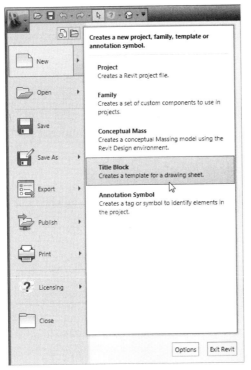

FIGURE 14.23 Creating a new title block

FIGURE 14.24 Selecting Label from the Create tab

12. Click OK twice.

13. On the Options bar, click the Center Justification button.

14. Pick a point in the upper center of the sheet.

Once you place the tag, you will immediately see the Edit Label dialog. This dialog will allow you to add the label you wish. Once this cover sheet is loaded into the project and added to a new sheet, the project information will become populated automatically.

The objective of the next procedure is to fill add the correct tags to the sheet.

1. Find Project Name, and click the Add Parameter(s) to Label button, as shown in Figure 14.25.

FIGURE 14.25 Adding the project name to the label

2. Click OK.

3. Click the label and widen the grips. You may have to adjust the label so it is centered in the sheet, as shown in Figure 14.26.

FIGURE 14.26 Adjusting the label so it is centered in the sheet

4. Click the Revit Home button and then click Save As.

5. Save the file somewhere that makes sense to you. Call it **Title Sheet**.

6. Click Load into Projects.

If you have more than one project opened, you will see a dialog allowing you to choose which project to load the sheet into. If this is the case, choose the No Experience Required project you are working on.

7. In the Project Browser, right-click on Sheets and select New Sheet.

8. In the Select a Titleblock dialog, select Title Sheet.

9. Click OK. You will see your tag is now populated with the project information.

10. In the Project Browser, find the Drawing List (it is in the Schedules/ Quantities category) and drag it onto the sheet.

11. Select the schedule and adjust it so the text is readable. Your title sheet, although not very glorious, should look like Figure 14.27.

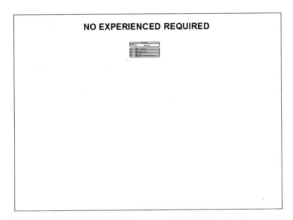

FIGURE 14.27 The completed title sheet

One issue is the actual title sheet is appearing in the schedule as sheet A403, Unnamed. We can change that in the element properties of the sheet:

1. In the Project Browser, right-click on the sheet A403, Unnamed and select Properties. (If it is not A403, it will still be Unnamed, and you can find the appropriate sheet.)

2. In the Element Properties dialog, change the sheet number to **000**.

3. Change the sheet name to **Cover Sheet**.

4. Uncheck Appears in Drawing List.

5. Click OK. The sheet is now named properly for organizational purposes; however, it does not show up in the schedule.

Perfect! We have a handful of sheets. The beauty is that you do not have to leave the model to see how these sheets are shaping up. In Revit, they are always just a click away!

Since we have these sheets, it is time to explore how we send them to the plotter. After all, it is paper construction documents that we are producing.

Printing from Revit Architecture

Luckily, printing is one of the easiest things you are going to be confronted with in Revit. There are, however some dangerous defaults that will have to be considered when printing. I can go out on a limb and say that printing from Revit in some cases is too easy.

The objective of the next procedure is to print a set of drawings. Pay special attention to the warnings, though — they will steer you clear of danger.

1. On the Revit Home button, select Print.

2. For the printer name, select the printer you wish to print to.

3. If printing to a file, you have the choice of combining all the files into one or creating separate files. Choose to combine into one file. If you are not printing to a file, ignore this choice.

4. For Print Range, you can print the current window or a portion of the current window, or you can choose Selected Views/Sheets. Choose Selected Views/Sheets.

T I P   When you choose to print the current window, this means that you are printing the current view. When you choose to print a portion of current window, this means that you are printing the area that you are currently zoomed into. In Revit, you do not pick a window like you do in CAD.

---

5. Click the Select button, as shown in Figure 14.28.

6. At the bottom of the View/Sheet Set dialog, uncheck Views.

7. Now only the sheets are selected. Click on all of the sheets.

8. Click OK.

9. Revit will ask you if you want to save the set for a future print. Click No.

10. In the lower-right corner, you will see a Settings field. Click the Setup button, as shown in Figure 14.29.

FIGURE 14.28 Choosing the options to print the drawings

T I P   Printing from Revit is similar to a paper space model space environment whereas you can simply print a specific view or you can choose to print an entire sheet. The only difference is you are not bothered by scale. The sheets and views are printed at the scale specified in Revit.

FIGURE 14.29 Clicking the Setup button

W A R N I N G   Make a habit of selecting the Setup button before you print. There are some crucial settings in the resulting dialog that need to be verified.

11. For Paper, choose the correct paper size you wish to print to.

12. For the paper placement, choose Center.

13. For Zoom, select Zoom: 100% of Size.

 WARNING   The Fit to Page radio button should never be selected unless you know that you are not plotting to scale. If you would like a reduced set of drawings, you can specify Zoom and then move to a smaller percentage (50% is a half size set).

14. For the options, check Hide Ref/Work Planes.

15. Check Hide Unreferenced View Tags.

16. Hide Scope Boxes.

17. Hide Crop Boundaries.

18. Click OK.

19. Click OK again, and your plot is off.

20. Save the file.

Well, there you have it. The book does not create a sheet for every single view. If you feel like your experience is questionable regarding creating sheets and printing, go ahead and create more sheets, and keep printing away until you feel confident to move on to Chapter 15, "Creating Rooms and Area Plans."

Are You Experienced?

Now You Can...

- ☑ **create sheets by simply dragging views and creating viewports**

- ☑ **configure project parameters to populate the sheets**

- ☑ **create a drawing list**

- ☑ **create a title sheet**

- ☑ **print or plot a sheet set**

CHAPTER 15

Creating Rooms and Area Plans

▶ Creating rooms

▶ Creating areas

▶ Creating color fill plans

▶ Creating room schedules

This chapter brings us to a great point in Revit. We are in a position now where we can start to build on what we have added to our model up to this point. By creating rooms and areas, you are starting to merge the model with the database. In Chapter 15 ("Schedules and Tags") we did the same thing, but by adding rooms and areas we are physically building our construction documents, while at the same time adding crucial information to the model's database.

The first topic we will tackle is the task of creating a room and adding it to the model. The procedures that follow will focus on finding where to launch the room and areas, and the parameters Revit looks for while placing a room into the floor plan.

Creating Rooms

Because of the fact that Revit draws from a database to gather information, the process of "creating" a room boils down to you adding some notes to an already built form. Once the room is placed in the model, Revit will automatically tag it. Contrary to other drafting applications, however, Revit does not rely on the tag for its information. Once a room is in the model, it can either contain or not contain a tag. This is a great way to organize the flow of room information.

To get started, open the model you have been working on. If you missed the previous chapter, go to the book's web page at **www.sybex.com/go/revit2010ner**. From there you can browse to Chapter 15 and find the file called NER-32.rvt.

The objective of the following procedure is to find the Room & Area tab, and to configure and add some rooms to the model.

1. In the Project Browser, find the dependent view called Level 1 West, and open it up.

2. In the Room & Area panel on the Home tab, click the Room button, as shown in Figure 15.1.

FIGURE 15.1 Clicking the Room button on the Room and area panel of the Home tab

If you do not have the Room & Area tab shown, right-click on any tab in the Design bar. You will see a list of tabs that are not currently displayed. Find Room & Area, and select it. You will not have the proper tab displayed on the Design bar.

3. Hover your cursor over the southwest room, as shown in Figure 15.2. Notice that there is an "X" and the outline of a room tag.

4. Once you see the "X" show up, pick a spot in the middle of the four walls.

FIGURE 15.2 When you hover your mouse over the intended area of the room, you will see an indication that Revit has found the bounding edges.

5. Press Esc.

You now have a room added to the model. Of course, it is a nondescript room name with a nondescript room number. The following procedure will correct that. The objective here is to change the room name and number on the screen.

1. Select the room tag that you just added to the model.

N O T E   You may be sick of hearing this by now, but I'll say it again: when you select a component in Revit, the items that turn blue are always editable.

2. Click the "Room" text.

3. Change the name to SOUTHWEST CORNER OFFICE.

4. Click on the room number "1".

5. Change the number to 101 (see Figure 15.3).

FIGURE 15.3 Changing the room name and number to SOUTHWEST CORNER OFFICE, 101

When you are modifying the fields within a tag in Revit, the best method to finalize the data is to simply click on an area away from the tag itself. This will ensure that you do not inadvertently create an additional line in the tag's value.

Now that we have a room in place and it is named properly, we can start cooking in terms of adding additional rooms. This is because Revit will begin to sequentially number the rooms as they are placed into the model.

The objective of the next procedure is to populate the rest of the east wing with rooms.

1. On the Room & Area tab of the Design bar, click the Room button.

T I P   If you get the save reminder, be sure to save the model. In no situation is this ever going to be a bad idea!

2. Place a room in the adjacent area, as shown in Figure 15.4 (we can't quite call this area a room just yet, can we)?

3. Call the room **SOUTHWEST CONFERENCE** (see Figure 15.4).

N O T E   Did you notice that the room tag was trying to align itself with the adjacent tag? This is a fantastic feature in Revit Architecture!

4. On the Room & Area panel of the Home tab, click the Room button again.

5. Place a room in the radial entry area.

6. Rename the room to **WEST ENTRY**.

7. Renumber the room to **001**.

8. Place a room in the south elevator shaft.

9. Rename it to **SOUTHWEST ELEVATOR 010**.

10. Place a room in the north elevator shaft.

11. Rename it to **NORTHWEST ELEVATOR 011**.

12. Place a room in the corridor.

13. Call it **WEST WING CORRIDOR** and number it **100**.

14. Just north of the SOUTHWEST CONFERENCE and SOUTHWEST CORNER OFFICE, place two rooms, each called **GATHERING**. Number them **103** and **104** (See Figure 15.4).

F I G U R E   1 5 . 4   The first floor layout up to this point

16. Zoom over to the east portion of the west addition where the lavatories are.

17. In the north lavatory, add a room named **MEN'S 105**.

18. In the south lavatory, add a room named **WOMEN'S 106**.

I think you are getting the concept of adding rooms! Although we have a good amount of rooms added to the east wing, we need to start adding some plain old offices. The next procedure will involve adding offices to the rest of the spaces in the east wing of Level 1. From there we can look at the room's element properties and figure out how to alter to the room information.

1. Make sure you are in the west wing area of the model, on Level 1.

2. On the Room & Area panel of the Home tab, click the Room button.

3. Pick the large area to the right of the women's lavatory, as shown in Figure 15.5.

4. Rename the room to OFFICE. Change the number to 107.

 N O T E   If the numbering starts to become inconsistent with the examples in the book, that is okay. This will happen from time to time in Revit. You can either accept the differences between the book and your model, or you can simply renumber the rooms to match. Either way, this will not affect the outcome of the procedures.

5. On the Room & Area panel of the Home tab, click the Room button.

6. Add rooms to the rest of the vacant areas. (Skip the Kitchen area and the room to the right of it, as shown in Figure 15.5).

FIGURE 15.5 Adding rooms to the remainder of the spaces

Now that all of the rooms are in (at least in this section of the building), we can start examining the specific element properties to see how we can add functionality and to further populate the database information pertaining to each room.

Configuring Element Properties

Each room is going to have specific properties associated with it. There will be floor finishes and wall finishes as well as ceiling types and finishes. It would be nice if Revit picked up this information by "reading" the walls ceilings, walls, and floors, but it does not. And for a good reason. Imagine having to create a different wall type for each paint color, and then split each partition as it passes through each room. In Revit, you will specify these individual room finishes within the element properties of the room itself.

The objective of the next procedure is to generate additional room information within the element properties of the room.

1. Zoom in on the SOUTHWEST CORNER OFFICE 101 room.

2. Hover your cursor over the room until you see the "X" show up, as you can see in Figure 15.6.

FIGURE 15.6 Hovering the cursor over the room until the "X" appears

 T I P   Any time you wish to view the element properties of a room, you need to click on the actual room, not the room tag. Sometimes selecting the room can be difficult because of the fact that the room itself is invisible until you mouse over it. With some practice, this process will soon become second nature.

3. Once you see the "X" show up, pick the room.

4. On the Modify Rooms tab, click the Element Properties button.

5. In the Element Properties dialog, scroll down to the Identity Data group, as shown in Figure 15.7.

6. Add WD-1 to Base Finish.

7. Add ACT to Ceiling Finish.

8. Add PT to Wall Finish.

9. Add VCT to Floor Finish (see Figure 15.7).

FIGURE 15.7 Adding values to the identity data

10. Click OK.

11. Select the SOUTHWEST CONFERENCE room.

12. On the Modify Rooms tab, click the Element Properties button.

13. Click into the Base Finish field. Notice there is a pull-down menu. Click the arrow and select WD-1, as shown in Figure 15.8.

14. Change the rest of the fields using the previous entries.

15. Click OK.

16. Save the model.

Parameter	Value
Unbounded Height	10' 0"
Volume	Not Computed
Identity Data	⌃
Number	102
Name	SOUTHWEST CONFERENCE
Comments	
Occupancy	
Department	
Base Finish	WD-1
Ceiling Finish	WD-1
Wall Finish	
Floor Finish	
Occupant	

FIGURE 15.8 Once a field has been added to the database, it is available for the rest of the rooms.

Changing a room's elements properties is a simple task. There is, however, one more item to discuss. This pertains to a room that spans multiple floors such as the west entry.

The objective of the next procedure is to change the height of the west entry room's element properties.

1. Zoom in on the west entry area and select the room, as shown in Figure 15.9.

FIGURE 15.9 Selecting the west entry room

If you are having trouble selecting the room, remember, you can pick an entire window around the area and use the Filter button on the Options bar.

2. Click the Element Properties button on the Modify Rooms tab.

3. Change Upper Limit to Roof.

4. Change Limit Offset to 0.

5. Click OK. This will set the west entry to extend from Level 1 to the roof.

Now that we have experience changing the element properties of the rooms, it is time to take a look at the element properties of the actual walls that divide the rooms. Certainly you noticed that when you placed the rooms in the lavatories, the room did not fill the small entry areas. We can correct this by changing the wall's room bounding properties.

Room Bounding Properties

By default, each wall you add to the Revit model will automatically define a room boundary, and this is what we want to see 95 percent of the time. There are some situations, however, where we do not want a wall to separate the room itself. In such cases, we can modify the instance parameters of the wall to disallow the division of the room.

The objective of the following procedure is to "turn off" the room bounding in certain walls.

1. In the West Wing floor plan, zoom in on the lavatory area.

2. Select the wall that divides the Men's toilet area from the Men's lavatory entry area, as shown in Figure 15.10.

FIGURE 15.10 Selecting the partition within the Men's lavatory

3. On the Modify Rooms tab, click the Element Properties button.

4. Scroll down to the Room Bounding row.

5. Uncheck Room Bounding, as shown in Figure 15.11.

FIGURE 15.11 Unchecking Room Bounding

6. Click OK.

7. Repeat the procedure in the Women's lavatory.

8. Save the model.

Having the ability to add rooms and manipulate the information within the Revit database easily gives you a tremendous advantage as you move forward with the rest of the model. Also, that information is relayed into the room's tag, which is automatically added as you place the room into the model.

This concept brings us to our next topic: how to change the actual tag to display the information on the drawings that we desire.

Placing and Manipulating Room Tags

As mentioned earlier, the room tag is merely a vehicle to relay the room's data to the construction documents. As a default, a room tag is added automatically as you place the room into the model. A default room tag is included, but we are not stuck with this room tag.

The objective of the next procedure is to add an alternate room tag to the room, and to open the tag's family editor to investigate the composition of the tag.

1. Zoom into the SOUTHWEST CORNER OFFICE.

2. Select the room tag.

3. In the Element panel on the Modify Room Tags tab, select Room Tag with Area, as shown in Figure 15.12.

FIGURE 15.12 Change the type to reflect a room tag that displays the area.

Now that was just way too easy! Let's take a closer look at what we just did. A room tag is nothing more than the cover sheet we created back in Chapter 14. All we need to do is simply open the file, and place a tag into the family.

To open the tag's Family Editor, follow this procedure:

1. Select the room tag for the SOUTHWEST CORNER OFFICE.

2. On the Modify Room Tags tab, click the Edit Family button.

3. Click Yes to open the file.

4. With the family file open, click on the Room Name piece of text that is visible. (These "pieces of text" are actually tags).

5. On the Modify Label tab, click the Edit Label button.

6. In the Edit Label dialog, the list to the left displays all of the fields that you can easily add to the room tag (see Figure 15.13). Do not change anything and click OK.

FIGURE 15.13 A list of available fields you can add to the room tag

W A R N I N G   If you are modifying the room tag, do yourself and the rest of your design team a huge favor and inform everyone that you are in there modifying your company's standards! Of course you are the CAD manager; set the permissions to this network directory accordingly.

7. Close out of this file without saving any changes.

Now that you know what tag Revit uses while placing a room, and how to manipulate that tag, it is time to tie the tag into something more robust. Since a tag is just a reflection of the room data, we can add another Revit object that does the same thing: a room schedule.

Adding a Room Schedule

Up to this point in our careers we have been adding room information twice, sometimes three times. And why is that? It's because we used to have to fill the tag out in the plan, then fill the same information out in the room schedule. If you were in the unfortunate situation where you had an enlarged plan, then you were adding the information yet again for a third time. Now when you have to change that information you need to do it in multiple places. Now, I'm not saying that Revit will end all of your problems, but it sure will make life easier!

The objective of the next procedure is to create a room schedule. We will then finish filling out the room information from the actual schedule, thus saving time and increasing accuracy.

1. On the View tab, click Schedule and then click the Schedule/ Quantities button, as shown in Figure 15.14.

2. In the New Schedule dialog, select Rooms from the list to the left.

3. Click OK.

4. On the Fields tab, add (in this order):

Number

Name

Base Finish

Floor Finish

Wall Finish

Ceiling Finish

Comments

Level

See Figure 15.14.

FIGURE 15.14 Adding the fields to the schedule

5. Click the Sorting/Grouping tab.

6. Sort by room number.

7. Click OK. Your schedule will look similar to Figure 15.15, with the probable exception of the "Room 0."

FIGURE 15.15 The room schedule

8. With the schedule still open, click into the WEST ENTRY Base Finish cell, and type **WD-2**.

TURNING OFF UNWANTED ROOMS

The schedule in the book has an errant room that really does not belong in the schedule. Because going step by -step through a book does not give you a true feel for a real-world scenario, I can tell you that you will wind up with some misplaced rooms. This is okay, because you can turn them off in the schedule. If you click the Not Placed/Not Enclosed menu, you will see that you can show, hide, or isolate unwanted data. For this example, I will choose Hide to remove the row (See the following graphic).

9. Click into the Floor Finish cell and type **TER** (for Terrazzo).

10. Click into the Wall Finish cell and type **VINYL**.

11. Click into the Ceiling Finish cell and type a hyphen (-).

12. Click into the WEST WING CORRIDOR Base Finish cell. Notice there is a menu arrow, as shown in Figure 15.16. Click it. You now have a choice between two base finishes. Choose WD-2.

13. Change the other values to TER, VINYL, and ACT (see Figure 15.16).

		Room Schedule			
Number	Name	Base Finish	Floor Finish	Wall Finish	Ceiling Fini
001	WEST ENTRY	WD-2	TER	VINYL	-
010	SOUTHWEST ELEVATOR				
011	NORTHWEST ELEVATOR				
100	WEST WING CORRIDOR	WD-2	TER	VINYL	ACT
101	SOUTHWEST CORNER OFFICE	WD-1	VCT	PT	ACT
102	SOUTHWEST CONFERENCE	WD-2			
103	GATHERING				
104	GATHERING				

FIGURE 15.16 Filling out the room schedule

Now that we have the rooms in place and a schedule filled out, it is time to move to a more colorful aspect of adding rooms to the model: adding a color fill plan.

Adding a Color Fill Plan

Another benefit associated with using the rooms feature in Revit is the fact that you can add a color plan at any time, and can virtually create any type of color scheme or pattern scheme you desire. And here's the best part: adding one is so easy it is almost fun!

The objective of the next procedure is to make a duplicate of the West Wing floor plan and to create a color scheme based on room name.

1. Right-click on the Level 1 floor plan view and select Duplicate View ➤ Duplicate, as shown in Figure 15.17.

FIGURE 15.17 Duplicating the view

2. Right-click on the new view and select Rename.

3. Rename it to **Level 1 Color Plan**.

4. Click OK.

5. Open the new plan.

6. In the Room & Area panel of the Home tab, click the Legend button, as shown in Figure 15.18.

7. Once you click the Legend button, you can now place the legend into the model. Place it into the upper-right corner of the view (inside the crop region), as shown in Figure 15.19.

FIGURE 15.18 Clicking the Legend button

8. In the Choose Space Type and Color Scheme dialog, change Space Type to Rooms and Color Scheme to Name (see Figure 15.19).

FIGURE 15.19 Placing the legend and specifying the color scheme

9. Click OK. You now have a nice color plan.

10. Select the actual color scheme legend.

11. Click the Edit Scheme button on the Modify Color Fill Legends tab, as shown in Figure 15.20.

12. Notice you can alter the color and the fill pattern for each room. Once you have investigated this, click OK.

FIGURE 15.20 Proceeding to edit the scheme

Pretty cool concept! One thing you may notice is that the two rooms we skipped are still white. It is time now to take a look at the situation we have here. The problem is, there are no walls dividing the two rooms, but it would be nice to have two separate rooms anyway! To do this, we can add a room separator.

Adding Room Separators

Although it seems like a small issue, this one topic has been known to confuse some people. Within Revit, you can physically draw a room without any walls at all. Or, you can simply draw a "line in the sand" between two rooms that are not separated by an actual wall. This is known as adding a room separator.

The objective of the next procedure is to separate the kitchen from the break room by adding a room separator.

1. In the Level 1 West Color fill plan, zoom in on the area shown in Figure 15.21.

2. On the Room and Area panel of the Home tab, click the Room button.

3. Place a room over the top of the tile flooring, as shown in Figure 15.21.

FIGURE 15.21 Place a room over the tiles (it will spill into the adjacent room).

4. On the Room & Area tab of the Design bar, click the Room Separation button, as shown in Figure 15.22.

5. On the Draw tab, click the pick lines icon.

6. Pick the edge of the flooring, as shown in Figure 15.23.

FIGURE 15.22 Click the Room Separation button on the Room & Area panel of the Home tab.

FIGURE 15.23 Adding the room separation line

7. Press Esc twice.

8. Click the Room button.

9. Place a room to the right of the kitchen area.

10. Change the room to the left to **KITCHEN**.

11. Change the room to the right to **BREAK**.

12. On the Annotate tab, click the Tag All button.

13. Select Room Tags and click OK.

We are really moving along here! We now have a fully coordinated room schedule tied into a room color fill plan that can be modified by simply changing a room tag. How did we ever live without Revit?

The next item to discuss is how to create a gross area plan. The process is similar but slightly more involved than creating a room color plan.

Creating an Area Plan

Almost any job of considerable size will require an area plan at some point in the early development of the project. This normally occurs in the programming phase, but the need for this type of plan can persist well into the later stages of a project.

The objective of the next procedure is to create a separate floor plan, then to divide it up into areas.

1. On the Room & Area panel of the Home tab, select Area and click the Area Plan button, as shown in Figure 15.24.

FIGURE 15.24 Click the Area Plan button.

2. In the New Area Plan dialog, choose Gross Area from the list, and choose Level 1 for the Area Plan Views.

3. Click OK.

4. Click Yes to automatically create area boundaries. You now have a new floor plan with a blue boundary around the perimeter of the entire building.

5. On the Room & Area tab, click the Area Boundary button, as shown in Figure 15.25.

6. Draw a line, as shown in Figure 15.25, separating the corridor from the west wing.

FIGURE 15.25 Drawing the area separator

7. Draw another similar separator between the east wing and the corridor.

 NOTE If your lines are not exactly snapping to the endpoints, this is not that big a deal. Unlike Sketch mode, Revit is much more forgiving when it comes to creating area separations.

8. On the Room & Area tab, click the Area button, as shown in Figure 15.26.

FIGURE 15.26 Click the Area button.

9. Place an area in the west wing, then in the corridor, then in the east wing, as shown in Figure 15.27.

10. Select the tag in the west wing.

11. Rename it to WEST WING.

12. Click the Corridor tag.

13. Rename it to LINK.

14. Click the West Wing tag.

15. Rename it to WEST WING.

16. On the Room & Area panel, click the Legend button.

17. Place the legend in the upper-right corner of the view, as shown in Figure 15.27.

18. In the Choose Space Type and Color Scheme dialog, choose Areas (Gross Building) for Space Type and Gross Building Area for Color Scheme.

19. Click OK.

20. Select the color scheme Legend.

21. Click the Edit Color Scheme button on the Modify Color Scheme Legends tab.

22. For Color, change Area Type to Name.

23. Click OK at the warning.

24. Click OK to return to the model (see Figure 15.27).

25. Save the model.

FIGURE 15.27 The plan is divided into three areas.

Great job! You now have experience with creating area plans. If you feel as though you could use some more practice before you start on a real project, you have five more floors in this model you can work on! You can either go on your own or step back through this chapter's procedures.

Are You Experienced?

Now You Can...

- ☑ add rooms to the model

- ☑ add room separators to the model

- ☑ create color scheme plans

- ☑ create area plans

- ☑ create room schedules

- ☑ update the rooms in the model directly from a room schedule

CHAPTER 16

Advanced Wall Topics

▶ Creating custom compound walls

▶ Creating stacked walls

▶ Creating sweeps and reveals

▶ Creating curtain walls

▶ Creating vertically angled walls

More on walls? Really? It seems as though all we do is walls. Well, that's because our buildings are comprised mainly of walls. As you may have noticed, the exterior walls are compound wall structures with reveals and parapet caps. In the east wing, we have a staircase that is completely unsupported. It would be nice to add a wall to make those stairs less spongy. Given the fact that the east wing is a high-end architectural woodwork area, that wall could use some trims that can be added right to the wall's profile. Also, we have not touched on a curtain wall of any kind whatsoever.

The first item to tackle is how to develop a wall with different materials. The exterior walls we have been using in this model are a prime example of a compound wall. The bottom 3' of the wall consists of concrete block while the rest of the wall is brick. When you cut a section through the wall, you can see that the wall has an airspace as well as a metal stud wall backup.

Creating Compound Walls

Usually these chapters start with a claim that "the following procedure is so easy a caveman could do it" (or something of that nature). The development of compound walls is not the easiest thing you are going to tackle in Revit. This procedure is somewhat touchy, and doing it well takes practice. In this section, we are going to create an interior wall with a wood finish on the bottom along with different wood material on the top. We will also extrude a chair rail along the wall.

To get started, open the model you have been working on. If you missed the previous chapter, go to the book's web page at **www.sybex.com/go/revit2010ner**. From there you can browse to Chapter 16 and find the file called NER-33.rvt.

The objective of the next procedure is to create a compound wall from a basic wall and then add a sweep profile.

1. Open the Level 1 East dependent floor plan.

2. On the Home tab, click the Wall button.

3. In the Change Element Type menu on the Element panel, choose Basic Wall : Generic - 6".

4. On the Place Wall tab, click the Element Properties button.

5. Click Edit Type.

6. Click Duplicate.

7. Call the new wall Stairwell 3 support wall and click OK.

8. Click the Edit button in the Structure row.

9. Click into the Material cell for the Structure row, as shown in Figure 16.1.

10. Click the […] button.

11. In the Materials dialog, find: Wood - Stud Layer, and click OK.

12. Change the thickness to 5½", as shown in Figure 16.1.

FIGURE 16.1 Changing the structure to a 5½" wood stud

13. At the bottom of the Edit assembly dialog is a Preview button. Click it (see Figure 16.2).

14. With the preview open, change the View to Section: Modify Type Attributes.

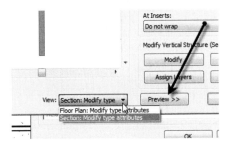

FIGURE 16.2 Changing the view to a section

Adding a preview to the Edit Assembly dialog is not only a nice feature, it is also absolutely necessary to continue with the editing of the wall. As you will soon see, you will not have access to certain buttons without the preview being displayed in a sectional view.

It doesn't seem like we have done much, but we have set the stage to start building our wall. It is time now to focus back on the "layers" field.

Adding "Layers" to the Compound Wall

If you are an AutoCAD veteran, the term "layer" now takes on a different meaning. In Revit the term layer, as it pertains to a wall assembly, means that it is a material layer that will be assigned an actual thickness as well as its own material.

As you can see in Figure 16.3, the Layers field is broken down into two categories: Exterior and Interior. For the following procedure, we will add materials to both the exterior and interior portion of the wall.

To create a new compound wall, follow this procedure:

1. In the Layers field, click on the number 1, as shown in Figure 16.3 (it is the field just above the Lavers Above Wrap row).

FIGURE 16.3 Clicking on row 1 to highlight the entire row

TIP   Note that when you are trying to highlight an entire row in the Layers field, you must click right on the actual number. A small black arrow will appear, indicating that you can click that spot to highlight the entire row.

2. Click the Insert button.

3. Change Function to Finish 1 [4].

4. Click into the Material cell, and click the [...] button.

5. Find Finishes - Interior - Gypsum Wall Board (5/8").

6. Click OK in the Materials dialog.

7. Change Thickness to 5/8".

8. Click on row 4 (Layers Below Wrap).

9. Click the Insert button.

10. Click the Down button, as shown in Figure 16.4. It is located below the Layers field.

11. Change Function to Finish 1 [4].

12. Click into the Material cell, and click the […] button.

13. Find Finishes - Interior - Gypsum Wall Board (⁵/₈").

14. Click OK in the Materials dialog. Your Layers field should resemble Figure 16.4.

Notice that the pre-view is instantly adding the changes to the wall. This interaction will be of great benefit down the road.

FIGURE 16.4 Adding a ⁵/₈" gypsum layer to the interior of the wall

Now that the wall is wrapped with one layer of ⁵/₈" gypsum on each side, it is time to start placing the veneered plywood layers to the exterior of the wall.

The objective of the next procedure is to add a ³/₄" plywood layer to the exterior of the wall.

1. Click on 1 Finish 1 [4] (the top layer).

2. Click Insert.

3. Change the function to Finish 2 [5].

4. Change the material to Wood - Mahogany (it is the mahogany material that has plywood for the cut pattern). Click OK.

5. Change the thickness to ³/₄". Your wall's layers should resemble Figure 16.5.

FIGURE 16.5 Adding the 3/4" mahogany veneered plywood material

6. At the bottom of the dialog, click the OK button.

7. Click Apply.

In the preview, you can hold down the wheel button on your mouse and pan around. You can also wheel in and out to zoom in and out of the preview.

WARNING   By clicking OK, then Apply, you are basically saving your work. In the Edit Assembly dialog, there is no Save or Apply button as you are creating the wall. Also never press Esc. This will cancel every change you have made and will almost certainly result in costly repairs to your computer as you rain blows upon it.

Now it's time to go back in and split the wall materials in two. It would be nice if we could have cherry at the top and mahogany at the bottom. Revit gives you the ability to do this.

Adding New Materials by Splitting a Region

If you want more than one material along the face of a wall, you will use the Split Region command that is imbedded within the Edit Assembly dialog. The objective of the following procedure is to add a new material, then apply it to the top half of the plywood face.

1. Click the Edit button in the Structure row.

2. Click on Layer 1 (the top layer).

3. Click Insert.

4. Make the function Finish 2 [5].

5. For the material, find Wood - Cherry, and click OK. (Do not give it a thickness.)

6. Click the Split Region button, as shown in Figure 16.6.

7. Move your cursor up the plywood face. Notice that your cursor turns into a knife. You will also see a short, horizontal line within the plywood. This indicates where the region will be cut.

N O T E   You are going to find that splitting the correct region can be extremely difficult even if you have done this procedure many times. Make sure you zoom in to the area, take a deep breath, and try it again if you are getting frustrated.

8. Once you see 3'–0" in the temporary dimension, pick the point as shown in Figure 16.6. *Do not press Esc when you are finished!*

FIGURE 16.6 Cutting the plywood at a specific height

You have now split the plywood. The only thing left to do is to apply a new material to the upper region. You can accomplish this by using the Assign Layers button.

Assigning Material to Different Layers

The Assign Layers command will allow you to choose where you would like to assign a layer to. This is quite useful within the context of this dialog because now you are not "stuck" without the ability to just move the layers around the wall as you need. Of course, when you split the wall such as we just did, you will notice that the thickness of the two wood layers are set to 0 and Variable. Revit needs us to assign an alternate layer at this point.

The objective of the following procedure is to assign the cherry layer to the upper portion of the plywood.

1. Pick the Layer 1 row (Wood - Cherry), as shown in Figure 16.7.

2. Click the Assign Layers button, as shown in Figure 16.7.

3. Move your cursor over the upper region of the plywood layer and pick. Cherry is now assigned to the upper portion of the wall, and the layers are now set back to 3/4" (see Figure 16.7).

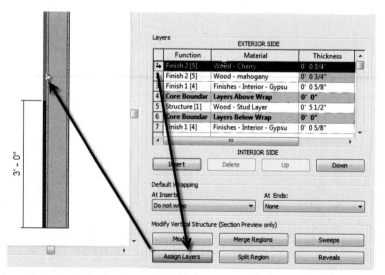

FIGURE 16.7 Assigning the cherry layer to the upper portion of the wall

4. At the bottom of the dialog, click OK.

5. Click Apply.

6. Click the Edit button in the Structure row to get back to the Edit Assembly dialog.

7. Pan to the top of the wall in the display, as shown in Figure 16.8.

8. Click the Modify button, as shown in Figure 16.8.

9. Hover your cursor over the top of the ¾" plywood, as shown in Figure 16.8.

10. Once the top of the plywood becomes highlighted, pick the line.

11. Unlock the blue padlock (see Figure 16.8).

FIGURE 16.8 Unlocking the plywood to enable independent movement once the wall is placed into the model

12. Click OK twice.

13. Click OK one more time to get to the model.

14. Click the Modify button on the Home toolbar.

15. Save the model.

By unlocking the layer, you can now move that layer up or down depending on what you need. Another good example of the usefulness of this functionality is when you need to slide a brick ledge down past a foundation.

Some people find splitting the regions in the Edit Assembly easy while others find it to be more difficult. I found the procedure difficult at first. If you are like me, this will require more practice until you have done a few more walls. Don't worry — it only gets easier as time passes.

Adding an automatic sweep along this wall would be nice. Come to think of it, a nice wood base and a chair rail would finish off this wall perfectly.

Adding Wall Sweeps

The concept of adding a wall sweep is as close to actual construction as you can come without actually setting up a chop saw. That is because, when we want to add a specific profile to sweep along a wall, we need to go outside of the model, find (or create) the profile, and then bring it in to the model. This process is similar to ordering trim and installing it.

The objective of the following procedure is to load a base and a chair rail trim into the model. We will then include these items in the wall we have been working on.

1. On the Build panel of the Home tab, click Component ➤ Load From Library.

2. Go to the Profiles directory.

3. Load the files Base 1.rfa and Casing Profile-2.rfa. (Use Ctrl to select both files.)

4. On the Home tab, click the Wall button.

5. Make sure the current wall is Stairwell 3 Support Wall.

6. Click the Element Properties button on the Options bar.

7. Click Edit Type.

8. Click the Edit button in the Structure row.

9. Click the Sweeps button, as shown in Figure 16.9.

FIGURE 16.9 Adding a sweep to the wall

10. In the Profile dialog, click the Add button, as shown in Figure 16.10.

11. For the Profile use Base 1 : $5\frac{1}{2}$" x $\frac{5}{8}$".

12. For the material, use Wood - Mahogany (the one with the cut pattern that is set to a wood hatch).

13. Click the Add button again.

14. The new profile will be Casing Profile-2 : 5$\frac{1}{2}$" x $^{13}/_{16}$".

15. Set the material to Wood - Mahogany.

16. Set the distance 2' 6$\frac{1}{2}$" from the base, as shown in Figure 16.10.

FIGURE 16.10 Configuring the two sweeps

17. Click OK and zoom in on the wall where the sweeps are so you can confirm they are placed as expected.

18. Click OK again.

19. Make sure Base Offset is set to 0'–0".

20. Click OK one more time to get back to the model.

21. Set the height to Unconnected with a height of 10'–0".

22. Set Loc Line to Finish Face Exterior.

23. Set the offset to –1" (see Figure 16.11).

24. Draw the wall by snapping to the inside of the stringers, as shown in Figure 16.11. You want to go in a clockwise direction, so start with the northern part of the staircase, as illustrated by the "1" in Figure 16.11.

25. On the Edit Geometry panel on the Modify tab, click the Edit Wall Joins button.

26. Using the Wall Joins tool, go to each wall corner and make the join Mitered.

T I P   If you receive a warning stating that a sweep cannot be added, ignore it. This warning is sometimes generated when there is a sweep on the face of a wall.

FIGURE 16.11 Placing the wall clockwise in the model

The wall has been added to the model. Since we are placing it underneath a staircase, there are going to be issues with the actual profile of the wall. This brings us to the next section of this chapter, which guides you through modifying a wall's shape after it has been placed into the model.

Modifying a Wall's Profile In-Place

Although we have touched on this subject back in Chapter 2, "Creating a Model," we are going to take this procedure to the next level. You can make a wall conform to any odd geometric shape you wish if you follow a couple of simple rules and procedures.

The objective of the following procedure is to edit the profile of the new walls to conform to the profile of the stairs.

1. On the View tab, click the Elevation button.

2. Place an interior elevation as shown in Figure 16. 12.

3. Open the elevation.

FIGURE 16.12   Placing an interior elevation

4. Select the wall, as shown in Figure 16.13.

5. On the Options bar, click Edit Profile, as shown in Figure 16.13.

FIGURE 16.13   Select the wall to be modified and click the Edit Profile button.

6. On the Options bar, click the pick lines icon.

7. Pick the underside of the stairs. Follow the profile exactly.

8. Delete the existing top magenta line and the existing left magenta line by selecting them and pressing the Delete key. All you should have left is the profile shown in Figure 16.14.

9. Use the Trim command to clean up all of the corners. Revit will not allow you to continue if you do not. (See Figure 16.14.)

FIGURE 16.14 Cleaning up the lines so they form a continuous loop

10. Click Finish Sketch. Your wall is now trimmed to the underside of the stairs.

 NOTE If your wall does not look right, select the wall again and click Edit Profile. Keep working on it until you are satisfied.

11. Repeat the procedure for each wall under the stairs. Remember to add elevations for each. Your finished walls should look like Figure 16.15.

Now that we can create a compound wall and modify it to fit in an odd place, it is time to learn how to manually add some sweeps.

FIGURE 16.15 The finished walls should follow the profile of the stairs.

Manually Adding Host Sweeps

The problem with the wall scenario that we have created in the previous procedure is the fact that we only have horizontal wall sweeps. Suppose we need some vertical wall sweeps? This is where host sweeps come into play.

A host sweep is exactly like the sweeps we just added to the wall's properties, only by adding a host sweep, we can add them manually.

The objective of the next procedure is to configure and add a host sweep to the model.

1. Go to the elevation shown in Figure 16.16.

2. On the Modelling tab of the Design bar, click Host Sweep and select the Wall Sweep button, as shown in Figure 16.16.

3. On the Place Wall Sweep tab, click the Element Properties button.

4. Click Edit Type.

5. Click Duplicate.

6. Call the new sweep **Chair Rail Sweep.**

FIGURE 16.16 Choosing the Wall Sweep command

7. For the profile, choose Casing Profile-2 : $5\frac{1}{2}$" x $\frac{13}{16}$" from the list, as shown in Figure 16.17.

8. For the material, choose Wood - Mahogany (see Figure 16.17).

FIGURE 16.17 Adding the profile as well as the material to the host sweep

9. Click OK.

10. Click OK again to get back to the model.

11. On the Place Wall Sweep tab, click Vertical on the Profile panel, as shown in Figure 16.17.

12. Make sure your Chair Rail Sweep is current in the Change Element Type menu.

13. Place a vertical rail about 1'–0" in from the right corner, as shown in Figure 16.18.

FIGURE 16.18 Placing the sweep on the corner

N O T E If you are having trouble placing the sweep on the corner, that means that you still need to go to the plan and select Edit Wall Joins from the Tools toolbar. Pick the corner of the walls, and select Mitered from the Options bar. If you need further assistance with this procedure, go back to Chapter 2 and read up on creating mitered wall joins.

14. After the trim is placed, press Esc.

15. Select the vertical trim. Notice there are grips on the top and the bottom. Pick the bottom grip and drag it up to meet the top chair rail, as shown in Figure 16.19.

16. Add another sweep about 3'–0" to the left of the first sweep.

FIGURE 16.19 Dragging the sweep up to the chair rail

17. Once the sweep is in, select it. You will see a temporary dimension appear. Change the dimension to 3'–0".

18. Drag the bottom up.

19. Repeat the procedure so your elevation looks like Figure 16.20.

FIGURE 16.20 The finished south wall of the stairs

20. Add vertical rails at a 3'–0" +/– to the other walls as well. Your walls should look like Figure 16.21.

FIGURE 16.21 The final walls with the sweeps added

So, we can now make modifications to a simple wall in any direction. We have experience adding sweeps to the wall's composition, and we can add sweeps freehand when we need to.

One other type of wall that we should cover before we get to curtain walls is a stacked wall. There will never be a time where you need a compound wall in which the outside face is not in alignment. When we run into this situation, we have to construct an entirely new wall altogether.

Creating Stacked Walls

A stacked wall, simply put, is a wall created by stacking two premade walls together. You can't have a stacked wall without at least two basic walls that you can join together. The good thing about stacked walls is that you can stack as many as you like. I recommend that you use some restraint, though — these walls can start to use up memory if you get too carried away.

The objective of the following procedure is to join three basic walls together to create one stacked wall. The outcome will create an alcove for architectural casework.

1. On the Home tab, click the Wall button.

2. In the Change Element Type menu, select Basic Wall : Interior 6⅛" Partition (2Hr).

3. On the Element panel, click the Element Properties button.

4. Click Edit Type.

5. Click Duplicate.

6. Call it 18" Soffit Wall, and click OK.

7. Change Wrapping at Inserts and Wrapping at Ends to Interior.

8. Click the Edit button in the Structure row.

9. In the Layers field, click on 3 Core Boundary (Layers Above Wrap), and click Insert.

10. Set Function to Structure [1].

11. Set Material to Air Barrier - Air Infiltration.

12. Set Thickness to 8¼".

13. Click Insert (to insert another layer above).

14. Set Function to Substrate [2].

15. Set Material to Metal - Stud Layer.

16. Set Thickness to 3⅝" (see Figure 16.22).

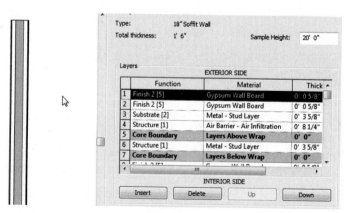

FIGURE 16.22 The walls layers

17. Click OK twice.

18. Click OK one more time to get back to the model.

19. In the Quick Access toolbar, click the Modify button (this clears the Wall command).

Now it's time to start building the stacked wall. Since we have two walls to work with, we can specify them in the Edit Assembly dialog for the stacked wall. The objective of the next procedure is to join the 18" soffit wall with the 6$^{1}/_{6}$" partition wall.

1. On the Home tab, click the Wall button.

2. Scroll down the Change Element Type menu until you arrive at Stacked Wall: Exterior - Brick Over CMU w Metal Stud, and select it.

3. On the Element panel, click the Element Properties button.

4. Click Edit Type.

5. Click Duplicate.

6. Call the new wall **Recessed Wall**, and click OK.

7. Click Edit in the Structure row.

8. For the offset, select Finish Face Interior.

9. In the Types field, change Wall 1 to 18" Soffit Wall.

10. Change Wall 2 to Interior - 6$^{1}/_{8}$" Partition (2Hr).

11. Change Height to 5'–6".

12. Insert a wall below the Interior - 6$^{1}/_{8}$" Partition (2Hr) wall.

13. Change the third wall to 18" Soffit Wall.

14. Change the height to 3'0".

15. At the top of the dialog, change Sample Height to 10'–0" (see Figure 16.23).

16. Click OK twice.

17. Click OK one more time to get back to the model.

18. Draw the wall in the east wing, as shown in Figure 16.24. (If you wish, you can create an elevation, or cut a section through the wall.)

A good way to establish the overall thickness is to look at the top of the Edit Assembly dialog. There you will be able to see the total thickness.

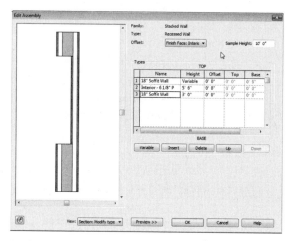

FIGURE 16.23 Creating the stacked wall

FIGURE 16.24 Adding the new stacked wall to the model

With the concept of being able to create a stacked wall behind us, we can now move into the crazy world of curtain walls. Although curtain walls are complex in nature, Revit handles them quite well.

Creating Curtain Walls

The topic of curtain walls brings us away from the conventional mind-set of walls. Curtain walls are related to a conventional wall in the fact that they are placed into the model the same way, but curtain walls have many more restrictions and element properties that must be examined before placement into the model can occur.

Given that, curtain walls also provide the most dramatic effect on your building. As this section will explain in detail, a curtain wall is composed not only of glass and aluminum extrusions. A curtain wall can be constructed from building materials such as brick, CMU, and wood. You can also predefine the materials and the spacing, or you can be creating them grid by grid, depending on your situation.

The first part of this section will focus on adding a predefined curtain system to the model.

Adding a Predefined Curtain Wall

The quickest way to model a curtain wall is to use one that has already been created for you. The great thing about the "out-of-the-box" curtain walls that are provided with Revit is the fact that there are enough instance and type parameters available to make the curtain wall conform to what you need for each situation.

The objective of the next procedure is to add a predefined curtain wall system to the radial west entry wall.

1. In the Project Browser, open the Level 1 West dependent view.

2. Zoom in on the west entry.

3. On the Home tab, click the Wall button.

4. In the Change Element Type menu, select Curtain Wall : Store Front.

5. On the Element panel, click the Element Properties button.

6. Click Edit Type.

7. Click Duplicate.

8. Call the new curtain wall **West Entry** and click OK.

9. Notice that you have many parameters that can be configured. For Vertical Grid Pattern, change the spacing to 4'–0".

10. Check Adjust for Mullion Size.

11. For Horizontal Grid Pattern, change Layout to Maximum Spacing. Also check Adjust for Mullion Size.

12. Click OK.

13. In the instance parameters, change Base Offset to 3'–7".

14. Set Top Constraint to Up to level: Roof.

15. Set Top Offset to –1"–0" (that's minus 1'–0").

16. Click OK.

17. On the Options bar, click the pick lines icon.

18. Pick the radial entry wall, as shown in Figure 16.25. Make sure you are picking the wall center line.

FIGURE 16.25 Picking the radial entry wall to add the curtain wall

19. Go to a 3D view. Your curtain wall should resemble Figure 16.26.

REVIT CAN BE TOUCHY

You may receive a warning that says "Could not create integral reveal for wall instance. Sweep position is outside of its wall. Please check sweep parameters" (see the following graphic). If you do, just click the red X in the upper-right corner of the warning to dismiss it.

FIGURE 16.26 The curtain wall in 3D

The ability to create an automatic curtain wall such as the radial one in the west entry way is quite an advantage when it comes to quickly modeling a curtain system. However, you are not always going to be presented with a perfectly square vertical shape. This is where creating a blank curtain wall comes in handy. You can then add grids and mullions at spaces that are at odd intervals.

Adding a Blank Curtain Wall

A blank curtain wall is nothing but a giant chunk of glass. By adding a blank curtain wall, you are telling Revit "Don't bother spacing the panels, I'll do it myself."

The objective of the next procedure is to create a blank curtain wall and add it to the model. We will then go to an elevational view and edit the profile of the panel.

1. In the Project Browser, open the Level 1 East dependent view.

2. On the Design Work Plane panel of the Home tab, click Ref Plane ≻ Pick Existing Line and click the Edge button.

3. Offset a reference plane 2'–0" from the face of brick, as shown in Figure 16.27.

FIGURE 16.27 Offsetting two reference planes 2'–0" from the face of brick

4. On the Home tab, click the Wall button.

5. In the Change Element Type menu, pick Curtain Wall: Curtain Wall 1 from the list.

6. On the Element panel, pick the Element Properties button.

7. Click Edit Type.

8. Click Duplicate.

9. Call the new curtain system **South East Entry** and click OK.

10. Check the Automatically Embed radio button.

11. Click OK.

12. For the Base Offset, change the value to 0'–0".

13. For Top Constraint, set the value to Up to Level: Level 5.

14. For Top Offset, change the value to 0'–0".

15. Click OK.

16. Draw the wall at the center line of the wall between each reference plane, as shown in Figure 16.28.

FIGURE 16.28 Drawing the curtain wall at the center line of the wall between the two reference planes

17. In the Project Browser, open the elevation South Entry Elevation.

18. In the South Entry Elevation, change Model Graphics Style to Shaded with Edges (this is so we can see the glass wall better).

Now that we have the wall drawn and are looking at the elevation, we can begin to alter the profile and add some curtain grids of our own. The objective of the next procedure is to edit the curtain profile.

1. Select the curtain wall.

2. On the Modify walls tab, click Edit Profile.

3. On the Draw panel, click Lines.

4. Offset the roof down 2'–0", and trim the edges of the curtain wall to the offset line.

5. Delete the horizontal magenta line that is now floating.

6. Click Finish Wall. Your curtain wall's profile should resemble Figure 16.29.

To select the curtain wall, you will have to hover your pointer over an edge. Once the curtain wall's perimeter becomes highlighted, select it.

FIGURE 16.29 The complete curtain wall profile

With the shape of the curtain wall finished, it is time to create some divisions along the vertical and horizontal plane of the wall. In Revit, these are called curtain grids.

Creating Curtain Grids

Because all we have is a single pane of glass, we will need to "dice" this glass up. In this situation, we can start dividing the glass panel by using the Curtain Grid command. Once we have finished, we can add mullions, doors, and even materials to the panels.

The objective of the next procedure is to add curtain grids to the glass panel.

> **1.** On the Build panel of the Home tab, click the Curtain Grid button, as shown in Figure 16.30.

FIGURE 16.30 Click the Curtain Grid button on the Build panel of the Home tab.

> **2.** On the Place Curtain Grid tab, click the All Segments button, as shown in Figure 16.31.

3. Move your cursor up the left side of the curtain wall and pick a horizontal point that is 8'–0" up from the base of the wall, as shown in Figure 16.31.

FIGURE 16.31 Picking a point 8'–0" up from the base of the wall

4. Press Esc.

5. Select the horizontal grid.

6. Click the Copy button on the Modify panel.

7. Copy the grid up 4'–0".

8. Copy the 4' grid up 2'–0".

9. Repeat this pattern until you have reached the top of the wall (see Figure 16.32).

10. Click the Curtain Grid button.

11. Slide your cursor along the base of the panel (notice the grid is extended in a vertical direction).

12. On the Placement panel, click the button for One Grid Segment.

13. Pick the midpoint of the panel. (You should only have segmented the bottom panel.)

14. Press Esc.

15. Select the vertical grid.

16. On the Modify toolbar, click the Move icon.

FIGURE 16.32 Copying the grids to form the custom curtain wall

17. Move the grid to the left 3'–0".

18. Copy the grid to the right 6'–0". Your wall should now look like Figure 16.33.

FIGURE 16.33 Chopping up the panel (note that the levels have been removed for clarity)

Now that the panel is broken up, it is time to start adding some materials. One material you may not think of is an actual door! Yes, in Revit curtain walls, you add a door to a curtain panel as a material.

Adding Materials

Aside from doors, we can add any material that is present in the model. We can even add separate wall systems as well.

The objective of the next procedure is to add a door to the curtain system; then we will add brick belts that fill the 2'–0" sections.

1. On the Home tab, click Component ➤ Load from Library.

2. Browse to Doors, then open the file called Curtain Wall-Store Front-Dbl.rfa.

3. Zoom in to the 6'×8' panel.

4. Hover your cursor to the top of the panel.

5. Press the Tab key twice. The panel will now be highlighted. Once the panel is highlighted, pick it (see Figure 16.34).

FIGURE 16.34 Selecting the 6'×8' panel

6. In the Change Element Type menu, pick Curtain Wall-Store Front-Dbl from the Type Selector. A door now appears in the panel.

7. Select the 2'–0" panel above the door.

8. In the Change Element Type menu, pick Basic Wall : Generic : 12" Masonry.

9. Press Esc.

10. Fill the rest of the 2'–0" bands with the same Generic 12" Masonry.

Hey, This Is Gray!

If the wall is showing up backward (if the wall appears gray), then you need to physically flip the entire curtain wall. To do so, go to the Level 1 East plan and select the curtain wall. Once the wall is selected, you can click the little double arrow in the middle of the wall as shown here. This will flip the direction of the entire curtain wall.

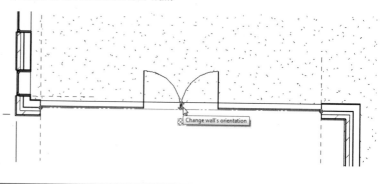

With the panels in place, it is time to start filling in the mullions — which brings us to our next step: adding mullions to the grid.

Adding Mullions to the Grid

The next logical step is to create the mullions that will be attached to the grid we just added. Since we have a few areas where there should not be any mullions, the job becomes more tedious.

The next example could go one of two ways. The first procedure will involve adding mullions "piece by piece," while the second procedure will allow you to add mullions all at once and then delete the mullions you do not need. This procedure will take the latter approach; we'll add the mullions all at once and then remove the superfluous mullions as needed.

1. On the Modelling tab of the Design bar, click the Mullion button, as shown in Figure 16.35.

2. In the Change Element Type menu, choose: Rectangular Mullion : 2.5" × 5" Rectangular.

3. Pick the grid above the door, as shown in Figure 16.36.

FIGURE 16.35 Click the Mullion button on the Modelling tab of the Design bar.

FIGURE 16.36 Placing the 2.5"×5" rectangular mullion above the door

4. Press Esc.

5. Click the Mullion button again.

6. On the Options bar, click All Empty Segments.

7. Pick anywhere on the grid. The mullions have been added to the entire system.

With the mullions added, we have actually gone too far! There is now an aluminum extrusion that separates the CMU from the adjacent brick. The objective of the next procedure is to remove these pieces of mullion.

1. Zoom into an area where the CMU meets the brick, as shown in Figure 16.37.

2. Select the small mullion piece that lies between the brick and the CMU. (You will have to press the Tab key several times to accomplish this.)

FIGURE 16.37 Selecting the mullion

3. With the mullion selected, notice you can either modify the join (as shown in Figure 16.37) or you can press the Delete key and remove the mullion. In this case, delete the mullion.

So, what have we accomplished here? Well, we have embedded a predefined curtain wall to a radial profile, and we have added a curtain system to a giant glass panel by hand. The only thing left to do is to apply a curtain wall to a sloping surface.

Adding a Wall to a Massing Object

Sometimes in architecture, artistic expression is required on a project, such as curved and laterally sloping walls that cannot be accomplished using straight, linear components. Nine times out of 10 some form of expression is going to be added to a project. We need to be able to deal with that in Revit, and we can!

The process involved in adding a sloped wall is to first create a massing object, and then apply the wall to the face of that object. It is almost as easy as it sounds!

The objective of the next procedure is to create a mass along the south entrance of the building.

1. In the Project Browser, open the East Corridor Section.

2. In the East Corridor Section view, turn on the crop region, as shown in Figure 16.38.

FIGURE 16.38 Turning on the Crop region and adjusting the line

3. With the Crop Region still selected, click the Element Properties button on the Modify Views tab, as shown in Figure 16.39.

FIGURE 16.39 The crop region's element properties

4. In the Instance Parameters dialog, scroll down to the Far Clipping row.

5. Click the Clip Without Line button, as shown in Figure 16.40.

6. In the Far Clipping dialog, click the No Clip button (see Figure 16.40).

7. Click OK.

FIGURE 16.40 Adjusting the view's clipping

Now that the view is set up, we can take full advantage. The objective of the next exercise is to place a mass. Once the mass is placed, we can add a wall and a roof to it.

> **1.** On the Massing and Site tab, click the In-Place Mass button, as shown in Figure 16.41.

FIGURE 16.41 Click the In-Place Mass button.

> **2.** If you get the Show Mass dialog, just click OK.

3. Name the mass **South East Entry** and click OK.

4. On the Lines panel, click the arc three points button, as shown in Figure 16.42.

5. You will be prompted to pick a work plane. Pick the far wall, as shown in Figure 16.42.

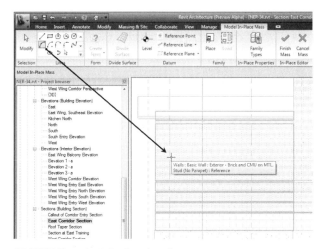

FIGURE 16.42 Starting the mass

6. Draw an arc, as shown in Figure 16.43.

7. On the Lines panel, click the Lines button, and draw three lines forming a box, as shown in Figure 16.43.

FIGURE 16.43 Adding the 3D mass

8. On the Quick Access bar, click the Default 3D view.

9. Zoom in on the perimeter you have sketched and select it, as shown in Figure 16.44.

10. On the Form panel of the Modify In-Place Mass tab, click the Create Form button, as shown in Figure 16.44.

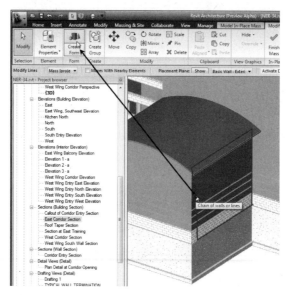

FIGURE 16.44 Click the Create Form button.

11. Pick (left-click) and drag the right-facing arrow so that the mass is in alignment with the corner of the building, as shown in Figure 16.45.

12. Pick the top, front edge of the mass.

13. Click the arrow facing up and drag the edge down, causing a slope. You can eyeball the distance, then type 18' 4 in the temporary dimension, as shown in Figure 16.46.

14. Click Finish Mass.

15. On the Massing and Site tab, click Model by Face ➤ Roof, as shown in Figure 16.47.

16. Pick the top of the mass, as shown in Figure 16.48.

FIGURE 16.45 Dragging the extrusion to the right

FIGURE 16.46 Creating the roof slope

FIGURE 16.47 Click Model by Face ➤ Roof.

17. Once you have picked the top of the mass, click the Create Roof button, as shown in Figure 16.48.

FIGURE 16.48 Creating the roof

18. Press Esc.

19. On the Massing and Site tab, click Model by Face ➤ Curtain System.

20. On the Place Curtain System by Face tab, click the Element Properties button.

21. Click Edit Type.

22. Click Duplicate.

23. Name the new curtain system **Southeast Entry**.

24. Click OK.

25. Change Curtain Panel to System Panel: Glazed.

26. Set Join Condition to Border and Grid 1 Continuous. For the Grid 1 pattern, set Layout to Maximum Spacing.

27. Set Spacing to 3' 0".

28. Repeat the layout and the grid spacing for the Grid 2 pattern.

29. Change all of the mullions to use Rectangular Mullion : 2.5" × 5" rectangular (see Figure 16.49).

FIGURE 16.49 Changing the grid

30. Click OK twice to get back to the model.

The next step is to apply the curtain system to the face(s) of the mass. The objective of the next series of steps is to apply the new curtain system to the front and the left side of the mass.

1. Pick the front face of the mass.

2. Pick the left face of the mass.

3. Click Create System. Your walls should resemble Figure 16.50.

FIGURE 16.50 The new curtain wall

As you can see, we are just at the doorway of massing. Literally. There is no way to get into this little portico we just created. In the next chapter, we will be discussing creating families and will delve much deeper into the massing that comprises Revit Architecture 2010.

Are You Experienced?

Now You Can...

- ☑ create custom compound walls by using the Edit Assembly dialog

- ☑ create stacked walls by joining compound walls together

- ☑ create sweeps in both the walls profile as well as free-form sweeps

- ☑ create curtain walls by using a predefined wall system and from a blank panel

- ☑ create vertically angled walls by applying a curtain system to a massing object

CHAPTER 17

Creating Families

▶ Creating a basic family

▶ Crating a complex family

▶ Creating an in-place family

A s you are probably becoming acutely aware, having the right content is going to make or break a Revit project. I am sure you are also acutely aware that, other than the content that Autodesk has provided and the content you downloaded from this book's web page, you don't have any-where near the amount of content you need to start a project! That being said, it is time to buckle down and dig into how Revit works, and see how having adjustable, parametric families is going to turn you into a Revit fan for life.

The first item we will tackle is how to create a basic family. We will start with the creation of a wall sweep, and then move into creating an arched doorway. As you become fluent with these two basic family types, it's going to be like a ball rolling down a hill!

Creating a Basic Family

Well, you have to start somewhere. To be honest, no good family is "basic," but some are simply easier to create than others. The concept is the same, however.

Essentially a family has three basic components:

Reference planes   Yes, reference planes drive the family. Look at these as the "skeleton" of the family.

Constraints   Constraints are simply dimensions with a parameter associated with them to give the "skeleton" its flexibility.

3D massing   This is locked to the skeleton. We'll call this the "skin." Corny, I know, but it gets the point across.

To get started, we need to figure out where to get started. Any family that is to be inserted into a Revit model needs to start with a template. Choosing the correct template, as you will soon discover, is going to make your life much simpler.

The objective of the next procedure is to start a new family by choosing a template within Revit.

1. Open Revit Architecture.

2. In the Recent Files screen, click the New link in the Families pane to the right (or you can click the Revit Home button and select New ≻ Family).

3. In the Imperial Templates folder (this is where the family templates are stored), select Profile-Hosted.rft, and then click Open.

As mentioned earlier, the first thing you will notice are the reference planes. A good family starts and ends with these. The next thing you will notice is some text. Revit adds some "advice" in each of its family templates. Once you have read the advice, you can delete it. We will do that in a moment, but first let's add some reference planes to the family.

Adding Reference Planes to a Family

The one bad thing about creating a family is the fact that you can get away with making a family without using reference planes at all. This is bad because the family that has been made with no (or not enough) reference planes will be faulty at best. This author has learned that lesson the hard way. Although it may seem redundant to add reference planes, I strongly advise you to use them and use them often.

The objective of the following procedure will be to offset some reference planes to create the wall sweep.

1. On the Datum panel of the Create tab, select Reference Plane ➤ Pick an Existing Line/Edge, as shown in Figure 17.1.

FIGURE 17.1 The Ref Plane button on the Create tab

2. On the Options bar, set the offset to 1'–0".

3. Hover your cursor over the center, vertical reference plane. Once you see the blue reference line appear to the right of the vertical plane (as shown in Figure 17.2), pick the center reference plane. You will now have two vertical reference planes spaced 1'-0" apart.

4. With the Reference Plane command still running, pick the horizontal reference plane and offset it down using the same offset increment of 1'–0". Your family should now resemble Figure 17.3.

These two reference planes represent the actual body of the sweep. We will now add two secondary reference planes for more control over the family.

FIGURE 17.2 Adding a second vertical reference plane

FIGURE 17.3 Adding a second horizontal reference plane downward

The objective of the following procedure is to add two more reference planes to the family.

1. Click Reference Plane ➢ Pick an Existing Line/Edge.

2. Set the Offset to 2".

3. Offset the top horizontal reference plane down.

4. Offset the left vertical reference plane to the right (see Figure 17.4).

FIGURE 17.4 Offsetting two more reference planes

With the reference planes in place, we can now move on to adding some dimensions to the reference planes. Once the dimensions are added, we can then add actual parameters to those dimensions to make our family flexible when we add it to the model.

Adding Dimensions and Parameters to a Family

We are now looking at one of the most outstanding features of Revit. The fact that we can create a parametric component easily, and then allow the end user to change the dimensions, can really put your company into overdrive in terms of pushing BIM through and having success with Revit in general.

The first procedure involves adding dimensions to the reference planes we have already put into place. The second procedure will be to add parameters to the dimensions we have added.

1. On the Dimension panel of the Create tab, click the Aligned Dimension button.

2. Add a horizontal dimension from the left reference plane to the right reference plane. The dimension should be 1'–0".

3. Add a second dimension from the top reference plane to the bottom reference plane. The dimension should be 1'–0".

4. Add a dimension from the left reference plane to the 2" reference plane to the right.

5. Add a dimension from the top reference plane to the reference plane 2" down (see Figure 17.5).

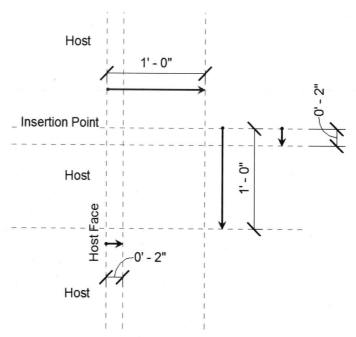

FIGURE 17.5 Adding the dimensions to the reference planes

The next step is to make this family come alive! Since we are in the Family Editor, when you select a dimension you will get a choice to add a label to the dimension. This label is tied to a parameter that can be modified.

To add a label to a dimension, follow these steps:

1. Select the top, horizontal 1'–0" dimension.

2. On the Options bar, click the Label field, and choose Add Parameter (see Figure 17.6).

FIGURE 17.6 Choosing Add Parameter on the Options bar

3. In the Parameter Properties dialog under Parameter Data (as shown in Figure 17.7), type **Width** for the Name.

N O T E   When you add a name to the parameter, you are actually adding part of a formula. There is a chance that this name will be part of a mathematical expression. When naming parameters, be deliberate, and give it some thought. Also, the mathematical expressions built into the parameters are case sensitive. If you are going to capitalize the first letter of each word, be consistent.

4. In the Group Parameter Under field, select Dimensions.

5. Click the Type toggle (see Figure 17.7).

6. Click OK. The parameter is now added to the dimension.

7. Select the 1'–0" vertical dimension.

8. On the Options bar, click the Label field.

FIGURE 17.7 Configuring the parameter

CHOOSING INSTANCE OR TYPE

This decision could be the most important decision you will make when creating family parameters. As you have noticed when you are modifying a family in the model (such as a wall, door, window, and so on), you can either make a change to the one instance of the component you have selected, or you can click Edit / New and change the component globally within the model. This is because, when the parameter was created, either the Instance or the Type toggle has been checked. So, when you are creating a parameter, you need to ask yourself, "Do I want the user to modify only one instance of this family by changing this parameter, or do I want the user to change every instance of this family by changing this parameter?"

Also, to complicate matters, if you plan to use this parameter in a mathematical expression, every parameter in that expression must be of the same type. For example, you cannot add an instance parameter to a type parameter. Revit will not allow it.

9. Select Add Parameter from the menu.

10. For the name, type **Height**.

11. Group the parameter under Dimensions.

12. Make it a type parameter.

13. Click OK.

14. Select the two 2" dimensions.

15. On the Options bar, click the Label menu.

16. Select Add Parameter.

17. For the name, type **Reveal**.

18. Group it under Dimensions.

19. Make it a type parameter.

20. Click OK.

Remember, if you hold the Ctrl key, you can select multiple items. The objective of selecting both of the 2" dimensions is that we are going to create one parameter to put both of the items on it.

Now that the reference planes are in place and the dimensions are set with the parameters, it is time to go behind the scenes and see how these families operate by examining the family types and adding formulas to the parameters.

The Type Properties Dialog

Within the Family Editor lies a powerful dialog that allows you to organize the parameters associated with the family you are creating. The Type Properties dialog also allows you to perform calculations, and to add increments in an attempt to test the "flex" of the family before it is passed into the model.

The objective of the following procedure is to open the Family Types dialog and to configure some parameters.

1. On the Family Properties panel, click the Types button, as shown in Figure 17.8.

FIGURE 17.8 The Types button on the Family Properties panel

2. In the Family Types dialog, click into the Formula cell in the Height row.

3. Type **Width**, and press the Tab key on your keyboard (see Figure 17.9).

FIGURE 17.9 The Height parameter is now constrained to the Width parameter.

4. Click into the Width value (the area in the Width row that has the 1'–0" increment).

5. Change Width from 1'–0" to 6". Notice the Height value changes too.

6. Click OK. The 1'-0" dimensions are reduced to 6".

7. Click the Type Properties button.

8. Change the width back to 1'–0".

9. Click Apply.

10. Click the New button in the Family Types field, as shown in Figure 17.10.

11. Call the new type 12"x12" and click OK (see Figure 17.10).

12. Click the New button again.

13. Call the new type 6"x6", and click OK.

14. Change Width to 6".

15. Change Reveal to 1".

16. Click Apply.

17. Change the type back to 12"×12".

18. Click OK.

19. Click Save and save the family somewhere you will be able to retrieve it later. Name the file Cove sweep.rfa.

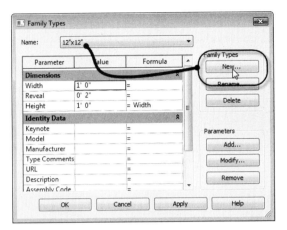

FIGURE 17.10 Creating a new family type

Now that we have the reference planes and the parameters in place, we were able to "flex" the family to make sure that it will work properly once we load it into the project.

The next step is to add the physical lines that comprise the perimeter of the sweep. Given that this was created using the wall sweep template, the actual family is merely going to be a 2D profile. The family won't become a 3D object until we pass it into the model and use it as a wall sweep.

The objective of the next procedure is to draw the perimeter of the cove sweep.

1. On the Detail panel of the Create tab, click the Lines button.

2. Draw a line from the intersection labeled 1 in Figure 17.11 to the intersection labeled 2 in Figure 17.11.

3. Draw a line from point 2 to point 3.

4. Press Esc.

5. Draw a line from point 1 to point 4.

6. Draw a line from point 4 to point 5.

7. On the Options bar, click the arc passing through three points button and draw an arc from point 5 to point 3. Once the two points are snapped in place, move your cursor to the left until the radius snaps into place. Your family should look like Figure 17.11.

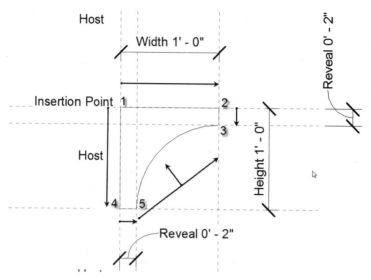

FIGURE 17.11 Drawing the boundary of the profile

IT'S TIME TO FLEX YOUR FAMILY!

Now that the family is complete, you need to go back to the Type Properties dialog, and change the parameters to see where this family will break. This testing is called *flexing* in the Revit world and should be done as often as possible.

With the family completed, it is time to load it into the model and use it as a wall sweep. This is where you get to enjoy the fruits of your labor. To get started, open the building model you have been working on. If you missed the previous chapter, go to the book's web page at **www.sybex.com/go/revit2010ner**. From there you can browse to Chapter 17, and find the file called NER-34.rvt.

1. Open the Cove Sweep file.

2. On the Family Editor panel, click the Load into Project button.

3. In the NER-34 project, select one of the exterior walls in the west wing.

4. Click the Element Properties button on the Element panel.

5. Click Edit Type.

6. Click the Edit button in the Structure row.

7. Make sure the preview is on and that it is showing a section.

8. Click the Sweeps button.

9. In the Wall Sweeps dialog, click the Add button.

10. For the Profile, select Cove Sweep : 12"×12" from the list (notice the 6"×6" is available too).

11. For the material, apply Concrete - Precast Concrete.

12. Set Distance to –1' 4".

13. In the column to the right, make sure it says From Top.

14. In the Side column, make sure the choice is Exterior.

15. Click OK twice.

16. Click OK yet again.

17. Click OK to get back to the model.

18. Zoom in on the walls — there should be a sweep, as shown in Figure 17.12.

FIGURE 17.12 The new precast concrete wall sweep

I think that perhaps you are getting a taste for what you can do with this powerful tool. And as you can see, we are only scratching the surface of the fun we can be having. I think you are ready to try a real family!

The next section of this chapter will be spent creating an opening with a radial header. Think about the lessons learned in the cove sweep, and let's start really digging in.

Creating an Arched Door

Now that the "easy" family is out of the way, it's time to start blending the procedures of creating a parametric frame with actual 3D extrusions and sweeps. These 3D extrusions and sweeps will behave exactly like the cove family we just made. Once you learn how to create one type of family, the lessons you learned will transfer to the next.

This section of the chapter will start with a blank door template and proceed with modifying a wall cut, then move to adding casing, a jamb, and then a door.

The objective of the next procedure is to start a new family and create a door opening with an arched top.

1. Click the Revit Home button and select New ➤ Family.

2. Find the template called Door.rft and click Open.

3. The first thing you will notice is that quite a bit of work has been done for you. This is great, but you don't need all of the items in the template. Select the door jambs, as shown in Figure 17.13, and delete them from either side of the door.

FIGURE 17.13 Deleting the jambs from either side of the door

4. In the Project Browser, find the exterior elevation, under the Elevations (Elevations 1) category, and open it.

5. In this view you will see a wall and an opening. Select the bottom of the opening, as shown in Figure 17.14.

N O T E   The wall that you see is provided by Revit in order for you to design your opening to be flexible with any sized wall in the model after you load this family. Once the door family is in the project, this wall is removed. It is provided merely as a purpose for layout.

6. On the Options bar, click Transparent in Elevation.

7. Next, click the Edit Sketch button on the Openings panel (see Figure 17.14).

FIGURE 17.14 Editing the door opening

8. By clicking Edit Sketch, you are now in Sketch mode. On the Draw panel, click the Start - End - Midpoint arc button, as shown in Figure 17.15.

9. Draw an arc, as shown in Figure 17.15.

10. Delete the leftover top line. Your door opening should be a continuous perimeter.

FIGURE 17.15 Rounding off the door top

11. Click Finish Opening on the Opening by Face panel.

With the opening in place, it is time to start testing! Yes, we need to test the width to see if the actual radial top will behave as expected. Taking the time to do this now is an extremely small concession to the pain of deleting half the family later trying to find what "broke" the family.

The objective of the next, short procedure is to test the width of the opening.

1. Click the Types button on the Family Properties tab.

2. Change the value for Width to 4'–0".

3. Click OK.

4. Verify that the arc did as expected. If it did not, you need to reedit the opening and make sure you are snapped to the correct points.

I told you that would be quick. That is all the time it takes to make sure your family is good to go up to this point.

Now it's time to start adding some components to the family. The first item we will tackle is the door jamb. This will be done by creating a solid form and then a solid extrusion.

Creating a 3D Extrusion Within a Family

Other than the curtain wall we applied to a face of a mass in the previous chapter, we have been working in this massive 3D program without actually doing one single 3D operation. Well, that has come to an end. At some point, you will need to deal with 3D and massing. When it comes to learning families, you will not be able to avoid it.

3D within a family, however, is slightly different than any 3D item you may have created in the past. The wonderful thing about creating 3D items within a family is the fact that these items are fully adjustable after they are created.

The objective of the next procedure is to create a door jamb using solid extrusion. We will then lock the faces of the extrusion to the walls so the family will adapt to any wall thickness when passed into the model.

1. Make sure you are in the exterior elevation.

2. On the Create tab, click Solid ➤ Solid Extrusion.

3. In the Work Plane panel, click the Set button, as shown in Figure 17.16.

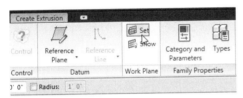

FIGURE 17.16 Click the Set button in the Work Plane panel.

W A R N I N G   Step 3 has you setting the work plane to the face of the wall. *This step is of utmost importance.* If you skip this step, your door will not respond to the change in the wall's thickness once you load it into the model.

4. In the Work Plane dialog, click Pick a Work Plane and click OK.

5. Pick the face of the wall, as shown in Figure 17.17.

6. Now that the work plane has been set, click the pick lines icon on the Draw panel.

7. On the Options bar, check the lock toggle, as shown in Figure 17.18.

8. Pick the inside face of the opening, as shown in Figure 17.18.

FIGURE 17.17 Setting the face of the wall as the work plane

9. Once the inside face is picked, change the offset on the Options bar to 1".

10. Pick the same lines offsetting the inside face of the jamb into the opening 1".

LINE IS TOO SHORT?

You may get an error at some point as you are picking these lines. This is more of a nuisance than anything else. All you need to do is click OK, delete the line(s) that were set into the wrong spot, and redo the same command. You will have more success the second time through.

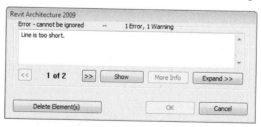

11. Zoom into the bottom of the jambs.

12. Set the offset on the Options bar to 0".

13. Draw a line connecting the bottom of the jambs, as shown in Figure 17.18.

FIGURE 17.18 Picking the frame for the jamb

14. On the Sketch bar, click the Extrusion Properties button.

15. Set the Extrusion End to –3", as shown in Figure 17.19.

16. Click the small button to the right of the Material row, as shown in Figure 17.19.

FIGURE 17.19 Click this button to add a material parameter.

17. Click Add Parameter at the bottom-left corner of the dialog.

18. Name it Jamb Material.

19. Group it under Materials and Finishes.

20. Keep it a type parameter.

21. Click OK.

22. Notice the Material field is no longer active. Click OK again.

What did we just do? By not selecting the actual material in the properties of the extrusion, we created a parameter so users could specify whatever material they deemed necessary. This is a valuable step in family creation. It's called flexibility.

Speaking of flexibility, this jamb is held at a steady 3". This is an incorrect value and will remain static unless we do something about it. We will do so right now. The objective of the next procedure is to align the inside face of the jamb with the inside face of the wall and to lock that alignment in place.

1. Go to a 3D view, and make sure you are "spun around" so you can see the inside face of the wall where the jamb does not align.

2. Click the Align button, as shown in Figure 17.20.

3. On the Options bar, select Wall Faces for the preference.

4. Pick the inside face of the wall.

5. Pick the inside face of the jamb.

6. Click the open padlock icon that appears (see Figure 17.20).

7. Press Esc.

8. Click the Save icon.

9. Save the door into a directory where you will be able to find it.

10. Call it Arched Door.rfa.

11. Make sure your project is open.

12. In the Arched door.rfa file, click Load into Projects.

13. In the model, open the Level 1 East floor plan.

14. On the Home tab, click the Door button.

15. Insert it in the wall, as shown in Figure 17.21. (Do not worry too much about placement.)

FIGURE 17.20 Aligning and locking the inside face of the jamb to the wall

FIGURE 17.21 Adding the family to the project

16. Select the door.

17. On the Modify Doors tab, click the Element Properties button.

18. Click Edit Type and observe the parameters. Look familiar? You created them!

19. Click OK twice.

20. Go back to the door family.

Wow! So this thing actually works. Good deal. The next trick is to add some casing to the outside of the frame. To do so, we will have to use a solid sweep.

Creating a 3D Sweep Within a Family

Going along the same lines (literally) as the extrusion, we can create a situation where we actually sketch a path and extrude a profile along that path. The trick is to make sure that this sweep can flex along with the door.

The objective of the next procedure is to create the door casing by using a 3D sweep.

1. Go to a 3D view (if you are not there already) and position the view so it looks like Figure 17.22.

2. On the Create tab, click Solid ➤ Sweep.

3. On the Mode panel, click the Pick Path button.

4. Pick the inside corner of the jamb starting with the left side, as shown in Figure 17.22.

5. Click Finish Path on the Create Sweep tab.

6. On the Mode panel, click the Select Profile button.

7. On the Options bar, click the Load Profiles button.

8. Go to the Profiles folder and select Casing Profile-2.rfa.

9. Click Open.

10. In the Options bar, click the Profile drop-down and select Casing Profile 2 : 5½" × 3/16" (notice the red dot is now replaced with the actual profile).

11. On the Options bar, type –0'–5¾" for the Y offset. Notice the profile is pushed back onto the wall with a ¼" reveal.

12. On the Create Sweep tab, click the Sweep Properties button.

13. Click the small button to the right of the Material category.

14. Click Add Parameter.

15. Call the parameter Casing Material.

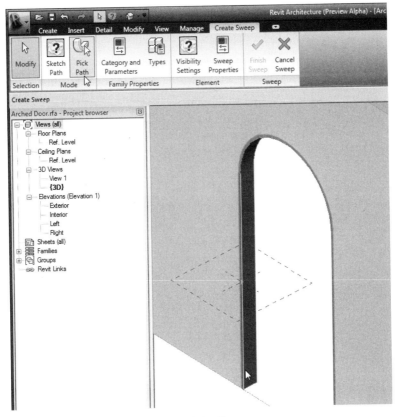

FIGURE 17.22 Picking the path for the sweep

16. Group it under Materials and Finishes.

17. Click OK twice.

18. Click OK again to get back to the model.

19. Click Finish Sweep. Your door should look like Figure 17.23.

20. Repeat steps 1 through 20 on the other side of the door. (Do not try to mirror it. It will not work.)

21. Save the family.

22. Load it into your model.

23. In your model, select the door.

24. Click the Element Properties button.

FIGURE 17.23 The finished sweep

25. Click Edit Type.

26. Change the Width value to 3'–0".

27. Click OK twice.

Your door is still working properly and is looking better!

Let's move forward and start working on adding a door to the family. The biggest challenge here will be the plan swing representation, but with a few new items to learn, this will be no problem.

The objective of the next procedure is to add a door, a stop, and some plan symbolic linework.

1. Open the door family.

2. Go to the exterior elevation.

3. On the Create tab, click Solid ➤ Extrusion.

4. On the Draw panel, click the pick lines icon.

5. Set the offset to $1/8$".

6. Offset the two sides, and the radial top to the inside $1/8$".

7. Set the offset to $1/2$".

8. Offset the bottom up (see Figure 17.24).

9. Trim the bottom corners so the door is one panel.

FIGURE 17.24 Adding the door

10. On the Element tab, click the Extrusion Properties button.

11. For the Extrusion end, type $-1^{3}/8$".

12. For the material, click the button to the right of the Material field, and add a new parameter called **Door Material**.

13. Categorize it under Materials and Finishes.

14. Click OK.

15. Click Finish Sketch.

16. In the Project Browser, go to the plan view.

17. Click the Thin Lines button on the View tab, as shown in Figure 17.25. You door should look like this figure.

FIGURE 17.25 The finished door in plan

18. Load the door into your project. (Click Yes to overwrite the door that is there.) Verify that the door is looking correct.

Now that the door is created, it is time to fix up the plan view. What we need to do is add a door swing. Also, we really don't want to see the door panel in plan, so we can create a view state to turn it off in the plan view.

The objective of the next procedure is to create a door swing and to make the door panel invisible in plan.

1. On the Design bar, click the Symbolic Line button, as shown in Figure 17.26.

FIGURE 17.26 The Symbolic Line button

2. Draw a line straight up from the right corner of the jamb (on the exterior side of the wall) 4'–0", as shown in Figure 17.27.

3. Draw another line to the right 1³⁄₈".

4. Draw another line straight down 4'–0".

5. Draw another line to the right 1³⁄₈" (see Figure 17.27).

6. Pick the Symbolic Lines button again.

FIGURE 17.27 Draw the symbolic door swing as shown.

7. Draw an arc from the left side of the jamb to the top of the symbolic swing as shown in Figure 17.28.

FIGURE 17.28 Drawing the plan swing arc

With the plan swing in place, we can now turn off the actual door panel. This step is quick and painless!

1. Select the door panel.

2. On the Modify Extrusion tab, click the Visibility Settings button on the Form panel.

3. Uncheck Plan/RCP.

4. Uncheck When Cut in Plan/RCP (When Category Permits).

5. Click OK.

6. Save the family.

7. Load it into the model. If it didn't explode, your door is complete!

As you can see, it is not all that difficult to create a family. This topic could be a book within a book. Start experimenting with your own families. If you run into a snag, send me an email at ericaugi@gmail.com, and we can work on it.

The next type of family we will study is one that literally can't be avoided. You are going to find yourself in the situation where you need the surrounding geometry of the model to create the family. This is called an *in-place family*.

Creating an In-Place Family

An in-place family gives you the best of both worlds. When you start the In-Place family command, your model turns into the Family Editor. You can make a family exactly the same way you just did, except that it is native to the model. Many times you will need this flexibility when you have a family you will never use again in any other building. This also gives you the flexibility to create custom content that cannot be created using the conventional Revit commands.

To create an in-place family, follow along with this procedure:

1. Open the model you have been working on.

2. Open the section view called East Wing South Wall Section.

3. On the Home tab, click Component ➤ In-Place, as shown in Figure 17.29.

FIGURE 17.29 The Create button on the Modelling tab

4. Set Category to Doors.

5. Call the new door **West Opening**.

6. Click OK.

7. On the Model In-Place tab, click the Opening button.

8. Pick the brick wall facing you.

9. Sketch an opening, as shown in Figure 17.30.

FIGURE 17.30 The arched opening

10. Click Finish Opening.

11. Go to a 3D view.

12. On the Model In-Place tab, select Solid ≻ Sweep.

13. On the Mode panel, click the Pick Path button.

14. Pick the exterior corners of the opening forming the arc and the two straight lines to either side of the opening (see Figure 17.31).

15. Click Finish Path on the Pick Path tab.

16. In the Project Browser, go to the Level 1 East floor plan.

17. Click the Select Profile button on the Mode panel.

18. On the Options Modify Profile tab, click the Edit Profile button (see Figure 17.32).

19. Sketch the profile, as shown in Figure 17.32.

When you are pick-
ing the lines for the
path, you will find
that you cannot pick
the entire line on
either the two sides
or the arc. All you
need to do is pick
any line on the three
corners, and then
trim them to meet at
the corners.

FIGURE 17.31 Picking the exterior edge for the sweep's path

20. Click Finish Profile.

21. Click the Sweep Properties button.

22. Add a parameter called **Casing Material**.

23. At the bottom of the dialog in the Other category, click the Trajectory Segmentation.

24. Set Maximum Segment Angle to 1.

25. Click OK.

26. Click Finish Sweep.

27. Click Finish Model.

28. Go to a 3D view; your opening should look like Figure 17.33.

The moral of this story is this: when you have a custom situation within the model that cannot be created using the conventional Revit tools, create an in-place family. You should also make it as flexible as possible, and give the user some choices such as materials so anyone can manipulate the family as if Autodesk itself provided it.

FIGURE 17.32 Sketching the profile

FIGURE 17.33 The finished family

Are You Experienced?

Now You Can...

- ☑ create a cove sweep family
- ☑ identify the family template you need to use to start a family
- ☑ create a door family
- ☑ add symbolic lines to a family
- ☑ create an in-place family
- ☑ create sweeps and extrusions
- ☑ create parameters and manipulate and constrain work planes

CHAPTER 18

Site and Topography

- ▶ Adding a site within Revit
- ▶ Importing CAD
- ▶ Adding site components
- ▶ Splitting a surface
- ▶ Creating subregions
- ▶ Grading
- ▶ Rotating to true north

You might be thinking about asking this question, and I think I know the answer. No, there is not a fourth Revit. It would be nice if there was a "Revit Civil" but there is not. So, we are left to our own devices when it comes to adding a site to our model. This is okay, because in many cases Revit is well equipped to take on the challenge. Unfortunately, also in many cases you will find that Revit is dependent upon AutoCAD or MicroStation to provide a real case scenario for a site that can be imported (similar to importing a plan or a detail). This is okay too because Revit provides tools to add a topographic surface to an imported CAD site.

To get started, let's do something easy, and then migrate into the more difficult areas such as importing a CAD file. The first item we will tackle will be to start a site using datum points that you will manually pick using the Toposurface function on the Design bar's Site tab.

Adding a Site Within Revit

The first major function within Revit Architecture when adding a site is the topographic surface. Revit has a separate tab on the Design bar called the Site tab that lets you access this feature.

So, let's get cracking. To get started, open the model you have been working on. If you missed the previous chapter, go to the book's web page at **www.sybex.com/go/revit2010ner**. From there you can browse to Chapter 18 and find the file called NER-35.rvt.

The objective of the next procedure is to add a topographical surface by choosing datum points and elevations.

1. In the Project Browser, find the floor plan called Site and open it.

2. On the Massing and Site tab, click the Toposurface button, as shown in Figure 18.1.

FIGURE 18.1 Clicking the Toposurface button on the Site tab of the Design bar

3. On the Options bar, set the elevation to –6" (that's negative 6").

4. Pick points in a circle around the footprint of the building, as shown in Figure 18.2.

FIGURE 18.2 Adding the first contours

N O T E   Notice that once you clicked the Toposurface button, Revit launched the Sketch mode. The button that is selected by default within the Toposurface Sketch mode is the Points button. This is what we are doing here.

5. With the Points command still running, set the elevation on the Options bar to –1'–0".

6. Pick a circle surrounding the inside contour lines, as shown in Figure 18.3.

7. With the Points command still running, set the elevation on the Options bar to –3'–0".

8. Add a third contour line surrounding the second, as shown in Figure 18.4.

9. On the Element panel, click the Surface Properties button.

10. Click into the Material field, and click the […] button.

11. Choose Site - Grass from the material list and click OK.

12. Click OK again.

13. Click Finish Surface.

14. Go to a 3D view and check out your site, as shown in Figure 18.5.

FIGURE 18.3 Adding the second contour to the site

FIGURE 18.4 Adding the third set of contours

FIGURE 18.5 The toposurface

Next let's see how we can modify a site once it has been created. We will have to deal with the fact that the ramps at the west entry are buried in our site now.

Modifying a Toposurface

Since there will always be the need to make modifications to a toposurface, you will need to learn how to do so. The method is basic. Select the site, click Edit, and away you go!

The objective of the next procedure is to make modifications to the toposurface to allow for the ramps to land on earth.

1. Go back to the Site plan.

2. Zoom in on the west entry area where the ramps are, as shown in Figure 18.6.

3. Select the site (you may have to find an edge).

4. On the Modify Topography tab, click Edit Surface.

5. On the Design bar, click the Place Point button.

6. On the Options bar, set the elevation to –2'–6" (negative 2'–6").

7. Pick a series of points, as shown in Figure 18.6.

8. Click Finish Surface on the Create Topography Surface tab.

9. Go to a 3D view to make sure the ramps are terminating at grade.

10. Save the model.

FIGURE 18.6 Adding the −2'–6" points

Excellent! You are getting the hang of this. The next thing we need to do is create some raised areas (small hills) where we can eventually add some plantings and different materials. The problem is, to create a small hill, we need the site to sharply rise to the new elevation. To achieve this, we have to physically split the surface.

Splitting the Surface

When you need a drastic change in the surface's elevation without influencing the rest of the site, you must split the surface. Just to warn you up front, be deliberate about when and where you do this because you are physically cutting a hole in the surface and adding a secondary toposurface to the void. Although these surfaces can be merged back together, some situations can prove to be difficult to cleanly do this.

The objective of the next procedure is to split the toposurface and create smaller toposurfaces.

1. In the Project Browser, go back to the Site plan.

2. On the Massing and Site tab, click the Split Surface button, as shown in Figure 18.7.

FIGURE 18.7 The Split Surface button

3. Select the toposurface.

4. Zoom in on the corridor area that links the east and the west wings, as shown in Figure 18.8.

5. On the Draw panel, click the Lines button.

6. Sketch a perimeter similar to the one in Figure 18.8.

FIGURE 18.8 The split surface sketch

7. Click Finish Split Surface. You now have a new toposurface.

The beauty of this is now we can manipulate this surface without influencing the main topography. This is the ideal situation for creating bumps and berms.

The objective of the next procedure is to raise this toposurface to an elevation of 4'–0". This will be done by using a point and placing the datum in the middle of the berm.

1. Select the newly formed toposurface as shown in Figure 18.9.

2. Click the Edit Surface button on the Modify Topography tab.

3. On the Tools panel, click the Place Point button.

4. On the Options bar, enter a value of 4'–0" in the Elevation field.

5. Pick three points near the center of the "hill," as shown in Figure 18.9.

FIGURE 18.9 Adding a new datum elevation

Once you have placed the points in the model, you can still pick the points and drag them left and right, as well as up and down. Also, if you look at the site in section or elevation, you can pick the points and drag them up and down too.

6. Click Finish Surface.

7. Go to a 3D view, and pan around so the hill is visible.

8. Select the hill.

9. On the Options bar, click the Element Properties button.

10. In the Material field, click the [...] button.

11. In the Materials dialog, select Site - Earth.

12. Click OK.

13. Click OK again to get back to the model. Your site should resemble Figure 18.10.

N O T E   Yes, you can copy these little "hills" around just like anything else in Revit — I am very glad you asked! After you copy the hills, you can edit them just like any other toposurface.

Well, I think you can see where this is all going. You can work with sites; it is just good to have some kind of procedure. This takes us to our next perplexing situation. Suppose we just wanted to keep the contours and the dips and hills intact, but only want to specify a new material in a subregion of the main topography? Well, you can!

FIGURE 18.10 The raised area of the site

Creating Subregions

The purpose of a subregion is to match two surfaces together so any change in elevation or lateral movement will be reflected within both regions. We need this ability for walks and most roadways. To split the toposurface into subregions, you are giving yourself the freedom of being able to manipulate two different materials within the same datum. Another benefit to creating subregions is that the file size will remain as if there was still one toposurface. If you were to split the surface every time you needed a path or a roadway, your file size would bloat.

The objective of the following procedure is to create a walkway path using the subregion command.

1. Go to the Site plan.

2. Zoom in on the west entry.

3. On the Massing and Site tab, click the Subregion button, as shown in Figure 18.11.

5. On the Draw panel, click the Start End Midpoint Arc button.

6. Draw a path similar to the one shown in Figure 18.12. (It does not have to be exact.)

FIGURE 18.11 The Subregion button

FIGURE 18.12 The subregion as it is being sketched

 N O T E   You cannot cross over and exceed the extents of the original boundary. If you do, Revit will not allow you to finish the sketch. Also, this subregion must form a continuous loop with no gaps or overlapping lines. You will need a straight line at each end of the path.

7. Click Finish Subregion.

8. Select the subregion.

9. On the Modify Topography tab, click the Element Properties button.

10. Change the material to Site - Earth.

11. Create another subregion extending to the bottom ramp. Use your imagination.

12. Go to a 3D view and compare yours with Figure 18.13.

FIGURE 18.13 The sidewalks in 3D

How did you do? If you don't like the line in the sidewalk, you can simply redo the two separate sidewalks and create just one.

Not too shabby! There definitely is something missing from this site, though. It sure would be nice to start adding some trees and plantings. The great thing about adding plantings after you have your topography in place is the fact that any site component added to the model will be hosted by the topography. This means you do not have to determine the elevation!

Adding Site Components

Adding a site component to Revit is no different than adding a desk or a door. A component is a component as far as Revit is concerned. As you have learned, a component is hosted by a system component. For example, when you are inserting a window, there needs to be a wall, or Revit will not allow such a foolish transaction to occur. The same goes for a site component. You need dirt to plant a tree!

The objective of this next procedure is to add various trees and plantings to the Revit model. The first thing we need to do, however, is to load some bushes.

1. On the Home tab, go to Component ➢ Load from Library.

2. Scroll to the Planting directory.

3. Load every file in the directory.

4. In the Project Browser, go to the Site plan.

5. On the Massing and Site tab, click the Site Component button, as shown in Figure 18.14.

FIGURE 18.14 The Site Component button

6. In the Change Element Type menu on the Element panel of the Site Component tab, click the RCP Shrub Boxwood 2'–9", and line your walkway as shown in Figure 18.15.

FIGURE 18.15 Adding the shrubs to the walkway

7. Click the Site component button again.

8. From the Change Element Type menu, select any tree you wish, and plant it on our little hill.

9. Put some shrubs around it.

10. Go to a 3D view and compare it to that shown in Figure 18.16.

FIGURE 18.16 The trees and shrubs on the hill

 N O T E   Now that looks simply horrible! Don't worry. When we move to the next chapter, we will focus on rendering. This is where the trees literally come to life.

Now that you have all of the contours and plantings in place, we need to knock out a small maintenance issue. There is a function that will allow you to automatically add contour labels to the site. This is a great feature within Revit Architecture.

Adding Contour Properties and Labels

Since nothing in Revit Architecture is "dumb," we can take advantage of a topographic surface having some "smarts" as well. Even the contour lines of a site are smart.

The objective of this next procedure is to examine some site settings and throw some labels into the contours. It is a quick set of steps, but important nonetheless.

To examine the Site Settings, run through the following procedure.

1. Click the arrow in the lower-right corner of the Model Site panel, as shown in Figure 18.17.

2. In the Site Settings dialog, you will see a field that contains additional contours. Change the value of 1' 0" to 6", as shown in Figure 18.17.

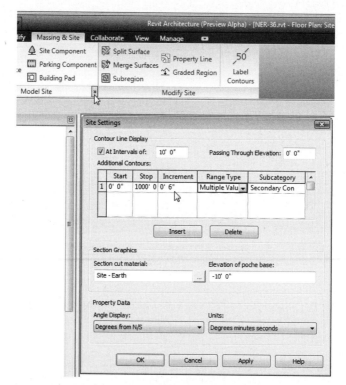

FIGURE 18.17 Changing the additional contour increment

3. Click OK. Notice the contours are tighter.

With the contours in place, it is time to label them. Luckily there is a function in Revit that allows you to do it all in one shot. All you need to do is draw a "line" specifying the alignment of the contours, and let Revit add the labels automatically.

Follow these steps to add contour labels to the site:

1. On the Massing and Site tab, click the Label Contours button, as shown in Figure 18.18.

FIGURE 18.18 The Label Contours button

2. Pick a point to the outside of the toposurface, labeled "1" in Figure 18.19.

3. Pick a second point near the building, labeled "2" in Figure 18.19. Once you pick the second point, the contours are labeled.

FIGURE 18.19 Adding the contour labels

With the site in place, it is time to address a situation that has arisen unbeknownst to you. You see, we never actually defined any areas where we may not want earth to "spill into," such as the basement. This will affect every section that we have. This is okay because we can place what is called a pad to displace the earth in the basement.

Adding Building Pads to Displace Earth

When you have the situation where you need to displace a volume of earth, you will use a tool exclusive to the Site tab to do so. By placing a building pad into your model, you are telling Revit that you want to cut the earth away from this area while still leaving the earth beneath a certain elevation. For example, if you wanted to remove the earth from the basement (which we will actually be doing) but still needed the earth to exist beneath the basement, you must place a building pad.

To place a building pad into the model, follow this procedure:

1. In the Project Browser, go to the T.O. Footing plan. It is located in the Structural category.

2. On the Massing and Site tab, click the Building Pad button, as shown in Figure 18.20.

FIGURE 18.20 The Building Pad button

3. Click the Pad Properties button on the Sketch bar.

4. Click Edit Type.

5. Click Duplicate.

6. Call the pad **Footprint**, and click OK.

7. For the Structure, click the Edit button.

8. Change the thickness to 6".

9. Click OK twice.

10. Change Height Offset From Level to 6".

11. Click OK to get back to the model.

12. Place the pad against the outside of the foundation wall underneath the entire model, as shown in Figure 18.21.

FIGURE 18.21 Place the pad to the outside of the wall.

13. Click Finish Sketch.

14. In the Project Browser, open the West Corridor Section.

15. You can see the pad sitting on top of the footing extending past the wall, as shown in Figure 18.22. Select it.

16. Once the pad is selected, right-click and select Hide in View ➤ Elements.

FIGURE 18.22 Hiding the pad in the view

17. Go to the Model Site panel and click the Settings arrow.

18. In the Section Graphics area, change the Elevation of Poche Base value to –15' 0".

19. Click OK. The earth hatch is now beneath the slab area.

With the pad in place, we can now rest assured that our sections are showing the earth where it is supposed to be.

The next item we will cover is creating a property line. In most conventional drafting applications, this involves nothing more than adding a polyline around the site. In Revit that approach is the same, but the property line can tell you much more about the boundary it is incasing.

Adding a Property Line

If you want to add a property line, Revit provides you with the tool you need. Of course this is Revit here, so we are not just adding a "dumb line" to the model. Once you start the Property Line command, Revit will ask you if you want to create the property line either by using bearing distances or by Sketch (which can be converted to a bearing table after it has been placed).

To add a property line, follow this procedure:

1. In the Project Browser, go to the Site floor plan.

2. In the Massing and Site tab, click the Property Line button, as shown in Figure 18.23.

FIGURE 18.23 The Property Line button

3. In the Property Line Creation dialog that appears, click the Create by Sketching choice.

4. Draw a series of lines around the perimeter, as shown in Figure 18.24.

5. Click Finish Property Line.

6. Select the property line.

7. On the Property Lines panel, click the Edit Table button.

8. Click OK if you get a "are you sure you want to do this" dialog.

9. Save the model.

FIGURE 18.24 Sketching the property line

You now have a table of deed data that can be modified as you see fit.

The next item on the agenda is a powerful tool when it comes to creating a site in Revit. As much as it would be nice to never depend on CAD, most of our topographical information will be coming from the CAD world. Revit has a By Instance function that can utilize this procedure.

Creating a Toposurface by Instance

Creating a toposurface by instance requires that you import a CAD file. Once the CAD file is imported, you can then go to the Toposurface command. Within the Toposurface command is the choice to use an imported instance to "drape" a surface from Revit.

To get started, you can either choose a site that was created in CAD that you may want to experiment with, or you can go to the book's web page at **www.sybex.com/go/revit2010ner**. From there you can browse to Chapter 18 and find the file called contours.dwg.

To use an imported instance to create a toposurface, follow these steps:

1. In Revit, create a brand-new project.

2. Save it as Imported Site.rvt.

3. In the Project Browser, go to the Site plan.

4. In the Insert tab, click the Import CAD button.

5. Browse to the contours.dwg file you downloaded. (If you have your own site .dwg, that's fine too.)

6. Before you click Open, change Colors to Black and White, Layers to All, and Import Units to Feet. Also, change Positioning to Auto - Origin to Origin.

7. Click Open.

8. Type **ZA** to see the entire site.

9. On the Massing and Site tab, click the Toposurface button.

10. On the Sketch bar, click Create from Import ➤ Select Import Instance, as shown in Figure 18.25.

FIGURE 18.25 Select Import Instance command

11. Select the imported CAD file.

12. Uncheck Layer 0 and Defpoints in the Add Points from Selected Layers dialog.

13. Click OK.

14. Click the Surface Properties button on the Create Topography Surface tab.

15. Change Material to Site - Grass.

16. Click OK to get back to the model.

17. Click Finish Surface.

18. Go to a 3D view. Your topography should look like Figure 18.26.

Now that would be a hard toposurface to create entirely within Revit! The next item we need to explore is how to grade a surface giving us areas of cuts and fills. The process itself is straightforward, but as you are about to learn, we need to first deal with what is called project phasing.

FIGURE 18.26 The new toposurface in Revit

Creating a Graded Region

This section of the chapter will focus on creating cuts and fills within a site. We do this by lowering and raising points that already exist within the topography. The problem is, once we are done altering the site, we do not know which part of the site was there before (existing) and which part is new. This means that we have two issues at hand.

The objective of the following procedure is to move the site to an existing phase to prepare it for the grading procedure.

1. Type VG.

2. In the Visibility Graphic Overrides dialog, click the Imported Categories tab.

3. Uncheck contours.dwg.

4. Click OK.

5. Select the toposurface.

6. On the Modify Topography tab, click the Element Properties button.

7. Scroll down to the bottom of the dialog until you see the Phasing category.

8. Change Phase Created to Existing.

9. Click OK.

10. On the Massing and Site tab, click the Graded Region button, as shown in Figure 18.27.

FIGURE 18.27 The Graded Region button

11. In the next dialog, create a new toposurface exactly like the existing one.

12. Select the toposurface.

13. You will get a warning stating that you may not be able to see all of the points. Click the X to close the warning.

14. Type VP (for View Properties).

15. Scroll down to the View Range field, and click the Edit button.

16. Choose Unlimited for both Primary Range: Bottom and View Depth Level.

17. Click OK.

18. Select a window around the center of the site (this will select a bunch of points), as shown in Figure 18.28.

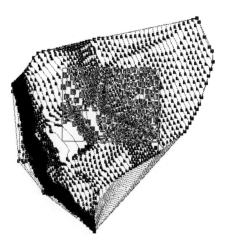

FIGURE 18.28 Selecting a range of points

19. On the Options toolbar, enter a value of 0 for the elevation.

20. Click Finish Surface.

21. Verify that your site appears the same as Figure 18.29.

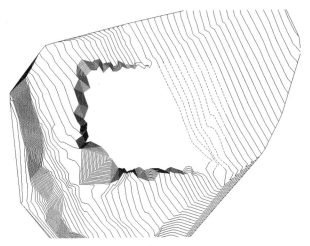

FIGURE 18.29 The site with cuts and fills

22. Save the model and close it.

Now that we know how to create graded regions in a site, it is time to delve into how we can physically rotate a site to true north.

Orientating a Site

How do we rotate a site to true north while keeping the rest of the model positioned in the 0 degree orientation? Well, there is a specific procedure, which you will learn by following along:

1. Open the NER-35.rvt file you have been working on (or any file with a site that you may be using).

2. Type **VP** (for View Properties).

3. Find the Orientation category, and change it from Project North to True North.

4. Click OK.

5. On the Manage tab, click Position ➢ Rotate True North.

6. In the Options bar, type **130** for the CCW Rotation Angle value, as shown in Figure 18.30.

FIGURE 18.30 Rotating the site

7. Go to the Level 1 floor plan; the site will still be oriented to Project North while the site plan is of a different orientation. Of course, now this mind-set makes the "North Wing" and the "East Wing" nomenclature irrelevant to the actual orientation of the site (see Figures 18.31 and 18.32).

 T I P   You must physically reposition the property line based on the northing easting coordinates that were preset. In the future, add the property lines after you rotate the site to true north.

Now that we have accomplished rotating the site, what happens if we need to move the entire model to a datum point recorded from sea level? As it stands, we just started modeling from an elevation of 0. This situation needs to be addressed.

FIGURE 18.31 The site rotated to true north

FIGURE 18.32 The Level 1 floor plan rotated to Project North

The objective of the following procedure is to relocate the datum elevation to 100' 0":

1. In the Project Browser, open the South Elevation.

2. Select one level marker.

3. On the Modify Levels tab, click the Element Properties button.

4. Click Edit Type.

5. For Elevation Base, select Shared.

6. Click OK twice.

7. On the Manage tab, click Position ➤ Relocate Project (see Figure 18.33).

8. Pick the point labeled "1" in Figure 18.33.

9. Move your pointer directly up from the first point.

10. Type 100 (see Figure 18.33).

FIGURE 18.33 Relocating the project

Now that we know how to position our entire model laterally and vertically, we can adapt to whatever condition we need to design to.

Are You Experienced?

Now You Can...

- ☑ add a topographical surface to your site by using points

- ☑ create a topographical surface in your site by using an imported CAD file

- ☑ add site components

- ☑ split and divide a site's topography

- ☑ rotate a project to true north

- ☑ relocate a project's datum elevation

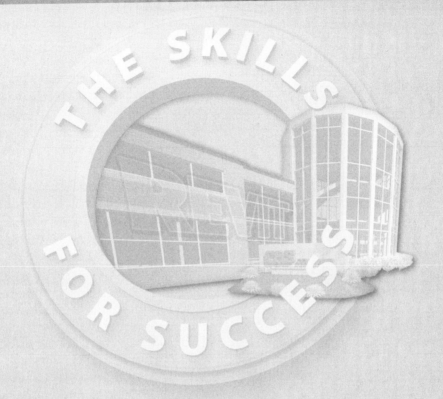

CHAPTER 19

Rendering and Presentation

▶ Rendering exterior scenes

▶ Creating and rendering interior scenes

▶ Saving the rendering

▶ Exporting a rendering

▶ Creating walkthroughs

▶ Creating solar studies

Well, here we are! The chapter you have probably been chomping at the bit to get into — and for good reason! It's the output that we create from this chapter that will make our bosses, and better yet, our clients get behind what we are presenting. Like I always say, none of this software is any good if you can't capture the work to begin with. That being said, this chapter will focus on creating renderings, and show you how to add animations and provide solar studies based on the project's geographical location.

The first item to tackle is how to go about creating an exterior rendering. Just trying to tackle the subject of rendering as a whole would convolute the matter. The thing is, when we create a rendering, lighting obviously plays a major role. Day lighting and artificial lighting are two completely different bears; one will influence the effect of another. For example, if you are rendering an exterior scene, there are bound to be windows. If this rendering appears at night, or at dusk, the interior lights will be turned on.

The objective of the first section of this chapter is to create a rendering from the exterior of the building using day lighting scenes, sky, and shadowing to create the rendering we need.

Creating an Exterior Rendering

In the previous chapter, we completed one of the hardest tasks when it comes to creating a proper exterior rendering: how a building is rotated in terms of true north. It stands to reason that your rendering will not be accurate if you have a glass curtain wall that is facing north but still have sunlight pouring through it. The correct building orientation is crucial, and we have accomplished that part. If you didn't read Chapter 18, you can still proceed with this chapter, but I strongly recommend that you review the last section of Chapter 18 as soon as you get the chance.

To get started, open the model you have been working on. If you missed the previous chapter, go to the book's web page at `www.sybex.com/go/revit2010ner`. From there you can browse to Chapter 19 and find the file called `NER-36.rvt`.

The objective of the first procedure is to create a camera view that we can use for our first rendering. We will then adjust the view controls and look at the sunlight effects.

1. In the Project Browser, open the Level 1 floor plan.

2. Zoom in on the corridor area in the middle of the building.

3. Add some curtain walls to the corridors, as shown in Figure 19.1. (Come on, I know you can do it.) These are Level 1 to Level 3 with a –6" offset from Level 3. You can use the Curtain Wall Storefront.

4. On the View tab, go to 3D view ≻ Camera.

5. Create a camera view of the area shown in Figure 19.1.

FIGURE 19.1 Creating the camera view

6. Find the view in the Project Browser. It will probably be View 3 under 3D Views.

7. Once you find the view, rename it to **Rendering view corridor**.

8. Open the Rendering View Corridor view.

9. In the View Control bar, set Detail Level to Fine.

10. Change Model Graphics Style to Shading with Edges.

11. For the Shadows, select Graphic Display Options, as shown in Figure 19.2.

FIGURE 19.2 Selecting Graphic Display Options

You can also find the Graphics Display Options by clicking the small black arrow in the right corner of the Graphics panel.

12. In the Graphic Display Options dialog, click Cast Shadows and Use Sun Position for Shade Display.

13. For Edges (Silhouette Style), select Thin Lines.

14. Turn on the Gradient background.

15. Click the [...] button in the Sun Position field. This will bring up the Sun and Shadows Settings dialog.

16. Choose your geographic location for the settings Date, Time, and Place. (I am choosing Syracuse, NY, and my birthday [05/10] is the default.) You can change these settings if you would like (see Figure 19.3).

FIGURE 19.3 The Sun and Shadows Settings dialog

17. Click OK.

18. Click OK again to get back to the model.

19. Click the Show Render Dialog button on the View Control bar, as shown in Figure 19.4.

FIGURE 19.4 The Show Render Dialog button

In the Rendering dialog, you will see quite a few choices. Each choice will vary depending on the scene you are trying to capture. The following procedure will move through the Rendering dialog from the top to the bottom.

At the top of the Rendering dialog, you will see a button that says Render. This is actually the last button you are going to click. This starts the rendering process in motion. For the rest, follow these steps:

N O T E   The Region toggle (the toggle to the right of the Render button) allows you to pick a window to be rendered. Since the scene in this example is somewhat small, we won't need to click this button. If we were rendering a much larger scene, you would want to render a region. That way, it wouldn't take hours upon hours to complete the rendering and the resulting rendered scene would be a smaller size.

1. For Output Settings, set Resolution to Printer and to 300 dpi.

2. For the Lighting category, set Scheme to Sunlight Only.

3. Set Sun to Sunlight from Top Right.

4. For the Background category, set Style to Sky : Few clouds (see Figure 19.5).

5. Click the Rendering button. Once the scene is rendered, it should appear similar to Figure 19.6.

T I P   Before you click the Render button, find something else to do for about two to three hours because at this resolution, that is about the amount of time it takes for Revit to render this scene.

I recommend that you have Revit installed on another machine at your place of business. You do not want to watch the rendering process as it is very similar to gazing into a campfire. Plus, if your model is being rendered on another machine, you can actually get some work done.

Rendering

Render   Region

Quality
    Setting: High

Output Settings
    Resolution: Screen
                 Printer   300 DPI

    Width: 7 11/16" (2305 pixels)
    Height: 5 1/8" (1537 pixels)
    Uncompressed image size: 13.5 MB

Lighting
    Scheme: Exterior: Sun only
    Sun: Sunlight from Top Right

        Artificial Lights...

Background
    Style: Sky: Few Clouds

            Clear   Hazy
    Haze:

Image
        Adjust Exposure...

    Save to Project...   Export...

Display
        Show the rendering

FIGURE 19.5 The Rendering dialog

FIGURE 19.6 The 300 dpi rendering

Now that you have waited half your day for this rendering to complete, here it is. If you are like me, you are now carefully moving your mouse around wondering how long it is going to be before something happens and you lose your rendering.

The next procedure will look at how to save the rendering to the model, and also how to export the rendering to an image.

1. In the Rendering dialog, click the Save to Project button, as shown in Figure 19.7.

FIGURE 19.7 Saving the rendering to the project

2. Call the new rendering view **Exterior Rendering at corridor**.

3. Click the Export button.

4. Save the file somewhere where you will be able to retrieve it. You can choose whatever file format you prefer.

5. At the bottom of the Rendering dialog in the Display section, click Show the Model. The rendering is now reverted back to the "cartoonish" model.

6. Click the Show Rendering button. The rendering shows back up.

 W A R N I N G   The ability to jump back and forth from the model to the rendering is a nice feature, but it is short-lived. Once you close this view, the rendering is no longer available. Do not close this view until you are finished saving the view to the model and exporting it (if you wish to do so).

With our first rendering under our belts, it is time to create another exterior rendering. This time, however, we need to start adding some lighting and produce this rendering at night. There is nothing like a good before-and-after rendering to sell a project.

The objective of the next procedure is to add some exterior and interior lighting to create a nighttime rendering scene.

Rendering may or may not come easy to you. You have to remember that some of it may take trial and error. I know we are not made of money, but setting up a separate machine just for rendering is not a bad idea.

1. In the Project Browser, go to the Level 1 ceiling plan (that's *ceiling plan* in case you missed it).

2. In the Home tab on the Ribbon bar, click the Component button.

3. On the Component panel, click the Load Family button.

4. Go to the Lighting Fixtures folder.

5. Within the Lighting Fixtures directory, go to the Exterior folder.

6. Select the family called Wall Pack Light - Exterior.rfa and click Open.

7. Place the lights at the locations shown in Figure 19.8.

FIGURE 19.8 Placing the exterior lights

8. In the Project Browser, open the Level 1 floor plan.

9. On the Home tab of the Ribbon bar, click the Component button.

10. In the Place Component tab, choose the Sconce Light - Uplight 60w - 120v family, as shown in Figure 19.9.

Now that some lights are in place, it is time to look at how we can efficiently group the different types of lighting fixtures to create a nice lighting scene.

FIGURE 19.9 Placing the sconce

Creating Lighting Groups

All too often, scenes are rendered with no real consideration for the actual lighting that has been added to the model. Because we are leaning heavily on Revit to produce accurate scenarios that we are presenting to our clients, it makes sense that we spend some time thinking through our lighting before we create a rendering.

The objective of the next procedure is to create two lighting groups and to render the same view using a nighttime setting.

1. Select one of the sconces you just added to the model, as shown in Figure 19.10.

2. On the Options bar, click the Light Group menu, and select Edit / New from the list.

3. In the Artificial Lights - Level 1 dialog, click the New button in the Group Options category, as shown in Figure 19.11.

4. Call the new group **Interior Lighting Northeast**.

5. Scroll down to the bottom of the list and locate the lights Sconce Light - Uplight : 60W - 120V. Select all of them, as shown in Figure 19.12.

6. Click the Move to Group button under Fixture Options.

FIGURE 19.10   Adding a lighting group

FIGURE 19.11   Creating a new group

7. Choose the Interior Lighting Northeast group in the Light Groups dialog and click OK.

8. Click OK to close the dialog.

9. In the Project Browser, go to the Level 1 ceiling plan.

10. Select one of the exterior lights.

11. On the Options bar, click the Light groups menu, and select Edit / New.

12. Create a new group called **Exterior corridor.**

FIGURE 19.12 Moving the selected lights to the new group

13. Locate the exterior wall pack lights and add them to the group.

14. Click OK.

15. Go back to the Level 1 floor plan.

16. Add the same lights to the interior of the corridor, as shown in Figure 19.13.

17. Create a new lighting group called **Corridor Interior**, and add the corridor lights to the group. You now have three lighting groups.

18. In the Project Browser, go to the Rendering View Corridor view.

19. On the View Control bar, click the Shadows button, then select Graphic Display Options.

20. For Sun Position, click the [...] button.

21. Click the Duplicate button, as shown in Figure 19.13.

22. Call the new scene **Syracuse at dusk** (you can replace "Syracuse" with your location).

23. Set the time for 7:30 PM (see Figure 19.13).

24. Click OK twice.

25. Click the Rendering button on the View Control bar.

FIGURE 19.13 Changing the scene to dusk

26. Set the Setting value to High.

27. Make sure Lighting Scheme is set to Exterior: Sun and Artificial.

28. Click the Artificial Lights button to make sure all of your groups are present.

29. Click the Render button. Your scene should look like Figure 19.14.

FIGURE 19.14 The rendering at night

If you are actually in Syracuse during the winter, it would probably be a good idea to get inside! While we are in there, we can bring the experience that we just gained inside with us to create an interior rendering scene.

Interior Rendering

An interior rendering is going to be created almost exactly the same as an exterior rendering. If you think about it, we will definitely be using artificial lighting. We will also be using sunlight too, just to make sure we are not excluding any natural light that needs to be taken into account.

The objective of the next procedure is to create an interior lighting scene using a premade 3D perspective of a hallway.

1. In the Project Browser, find the 3D view called West Wing Corridor Perspective.

2. On the View Control bar, click the Show Render Dialog button.

3. Set the Quality setting to High.

4. Set Resolution to Printer and to 300dpi.

5. Set Lighting Scheme to Interior : Sun and Artificial.

6. Set Sun to Sunlight from Top Right.

7. Make sure Background Style is set to Color.

8. Click the Render button. Your hallway should resemble Figure 19.15.

FIGURE 19.15 The interior corridor

This is getting almost too easy! I suppose we could keep rendering all week, but in the interest of saving some trees, I encourage you to render some more. If you run into any trouble during your foray into additional rendering, give me a shout at ericaugi@gmail.com and ask your question. The winding stairs heading up to the balcony in the east wing would make a nice scene to hang on your cubicle or office wall!

If you feel as though you have enough experience with rendering, let's jump to the next section and tackle creating a nice walkthrough for a presentation.

Creating Walkthroughs

For some reason, you can show a client a beautiful rendering of a space or building you are planning on designing for them and still meet with a blasé, half-hearted reaction. Now, if you show them the same space, only this time as you are walking through it… well then! They perk right up.

Although this part of the chapter is not crucial to your expertise in Revit, it is certainly worth a glance. Sometimes it is the special tools that you can pull out of your belt that can win a job or impress your friends on a Saturday night. A walkthrough is a series of points you pick in a sequence in a plan view. It's sort of like connecting the dots, but these dots will advance a frame as if you were walking to the points that have been picked.

The objective of the next procedure is to create a walkthrough of the building and to export the walkthrough to an AVI file.

1. Go to the Level 1 floor plan.

2. On the View tab of the Ribbon bar, go to 3D ➤ Walkthrough, as shown in Figure 19.16.

FIGURE 19.16 Find the Walkthrough command.

3. Zoom in on the west entry.

4. Start picking points, as shown in Figure 19.17.

FIGURE 19.17 Picking the points in the sequence

5. Keep picking points down the hallway, into the corridor, and into the east wing, as shown in Figure 19.18.

Note that you can adjust the camera height on the Options bar. This is especially useful for walking up and down stairs.

FIGURE 19.18 Sketching the walkthrough path

6. On the Walkthrough tab of the Ribbon bar, click Finish Walkthrough.

7. On the Modify Cameras tab of the Ribbon bar, click the Edit Walkthrough button.

8. In the Project Browser, find the Walkthroughs category. Once you find that, open the Walkthrough 1 view.

9. On the Options bar, change the first frame to 1, as shown in Figure 19.19.

10. In the View Control bar, click Shading with Edges.

11. Select the crop region.

12. On the Modify Cameras tab, select the Edit Walkthrough button (again).

13. On the Modify Cameras tab, click the Play button, as shown in Figure 19.19.

FIGURE 19.19 Click the Play button to start the walkthrough.

14. Once the walkthrough is done, you can click the button that contains the value of 300 (this is the number of frames) on the Options bar, as shown in Figure 19.20.

15. In the Walkthrough Frames dialog, change the Frames per Second value to 20.

16. Run the Walkthrough again. This time it is sped up.

FIGURE 19.20 Changing the frames

The walkthrough is complete. One thing you certainly are going to be asked is if you can "give" the walkthrough to someone for a presentation. Luckily the answer is yes. The best thing about this is the fact that the person presenting does not have to be Revit literate, or even own the application.

Exporting an Animation

Exporting an animation is a great, but slightly hidden, feature. The Export function is not located on the Ribbon — you will find it in the Revit Home menu, as shown in Figure 19.21. By exporting a walkthrough, you are creating an animated vector image (AVI) that will translate the native Revit walkthrough. It is quick and almost completely painless!

To create an AVI of the walkthrough, proceed with the following activity.

1. Click the Revit Home button.

2. Go to Export ➢ Images and Animations ➢ Walkthrough, as shown in Figure 19.21.

3. Select the defaults in the next dialog.

4. Find a location for the file and click Save.

5. Click OK in the Compression dialog. (You will have to sit and wait for Revit to go through the walkthrough as it creates the AVI.)

FIGURE 19.21 Choosing to export the walkthrough

6. Find the AVI and run it to make sure it works.

 NOTE   Just in case you are wondering, yes, this AVI is over a gig. If it is necessary, you can attempt to compress the file as it is being exported, but the quality will probably degrade. Besides, memory is cheap these days.

With the walkthrough complete, there is one more animation that we need to look at. It's not as "cool" as the walkthrough but is just as interesting. This animation is called a solar study.

Creating a Solar Study

A solar study, to put simply, is a shaded 3D view that provides a time-elapsed visual image of how the building will cast shadows over the course of either a day or multiple days.

The objective of this section is to create a single-day solar study by specifying the geographical location of your building.

1. Go to the default 3D view.

2. On the View tab, click Duplicate View ➤ Duplicate with Detailing.

3. Rename the new 3D view to **One Day Solar Study.**

4. On the View Control toolbar, click the Shadows button, and then click Graphic Display Options.

5. In the Graphic Display Options dialog, turn on Cast Shadows.

6. Turn on Use Sun Position for Shaded Display.

7. Click the […] button in the Sun Position category.

8. In the Sun and Shadows Settings dialog, click the Single Day tab, as shown in Figure 19.22.

9. Click the Duplicate button.

10. Call the new configuration **Single day Syracuse, NY.**

11. Make sure Place is set to Syracuse, NY (or wherever you find yourself these days).

12. Change Date to 05/10/2009.

13. Set Time Interval to One Hour (see Figure 19.22).

FIGURE 19.22 Setting up the solar study

14. Click OK twice.

15. On the View Control bar, click the Shadows button, then select Preview Solar Study, as shown in Figure 19.23.

FIGURE 19.23 Previewing the solar study

16. On the Options bar, click the Play button, as shown in Figure 19.24.

FIGURE 19.24 Clicking Play to start the solar study

 NOTE   Unfortunately, you need to have a high-performance machine to perform this study. If you do not, this one-day solar study could almost actually take one day to complete. It will be in real time.

Creating animations such as solar studies and walkthroughs are a couple of the unique features of Revit that aid you in capturing work. Keep these features in mind next time you are working up a proposal and a presentation.

Are You Experienced?

Now You Can...

☑ **create an exterior rendering by specifying a day lighting scene based on your geographic location**

☑ **create an exterior rendering scene at dusk using lighting**

☑ **create an interior rendering using a mixture of day lighting and artificial lighting**

☑ **create a walkthrough and export it to an AVI**

☑ **create a solar study that allows you to visualize the shadowing effect spanning the course of a day**

Importing and Coordinating Revit Models

▶ Importing Revit Structure

▶ Activating Copy Monitor

▶ Running an interference detection

▶ Importing and exporting AutoCAD

t is amazing that we are up to Chapter 20, and I'm sure many readers are still unclear on how BIM is fitting in here. Yes, most of the previous chapters showed you how BIM is beneficial in that once you change an item in one place, it changes in another, yada, yada, yada. But you were probably sold on the whole "coordinating with your consultants" thing back when you were considering purchasing Revit. Well, here we are. It's time to tackle that mystical ideology that has put our industry in a loose headlock.

The first section of this chapter will focus on the actual event of importing a Revit Structure model. As you start the process, you will see that this procedure is not unfamiliar if you have any CAD background whatsoever. If you do not have a CAD background, I think you will find these procedures to be intuitive enough to get through importing Revit models with no experience whatsoever.

Importing and Linking a Revit Structure Model

As you proceed into design development, you must get your structural engineer on board. This consultant may be an external or an in-house resource. Either way, this individual will have a different model that you need to coordinate with.

This section will focus on the procedures involved with importing a Revit Structure model. We will also cover the concept of creating a live monitoring system with the structure as well as interference detection.

To get started, open the model you have been working on. If you missed the previous chapter, go to the book's web page at **www.sybex.com/go/revit2010ner**. From there you can browse to Chapter 20 and find the file called NER-37.rvt. You will also need to locate the model called NER-37_STRUCTURAL.rvt. Save this file in a location where you can retrieve it.

The objective of the following procedure is to import and link a Revit structure model.

1. In the Project Browser, go to the Level 1 floor plan.

2. Delete every structural grid and column. (Keep the canopy framing intact. Do not delete the beams and columns in these two areas.)

 N O T E   Why are you deleting these structural members you worked so hard to add? Because the structural consultant laid out their grid based on yours. You are going to copy their grid back in, and monitor any movement that may occur throughout the life of the project. As far as the columns, we are simply going to use the structural engineer's columns for our elevations, plans, and sections from this point on.

3. On the Link panel of the Insert tab, click the Link Revit button, as shown in Figure 20.1.

FIGURE 20.1 The Link Revit button on the Link panel of the Insert tab

4. Browse to the NER-37_STRUCTURAL.rvt file, but do not click Open just yet.

5. Select the file.

6. At the bottom of the dialog, you will get a choice of positioning. Select Auto - Origin to Origin, as shown in Figure 20.2.

7. Click Open. Your structural model is now linked.

FIGURE 20.2 The linked structural model

8. Open the 3D view West Entry from Corridor.

You can now see the wood framing the structural engineer added to support the cantilevered slab, as shown in Figure 20.3.

Already we are seeing the benefits of a collaborative model, and we have done nothing more than insert one model into another. This is not new technology, and we are certainly not doing anything profound here. The real benefit comes from how we can now keep track of what the structural model is doing underneath our model. We can actually copy items from the structural model, and then monitor any changes made from the linked model. This is the definition of BIM.

FIGURE 20.3 The supporting framing under the cantilevered slab at the east link

Copy Monitor

You can almost sum BIM up in one command: Copy Monitor. I hate to break down the most import acronym in our industry since "CAD" into such simple terms, but building information modeling is the process of monitoring and tracking change, and that process starts right here!

The objective of the following procedure is to copy the structural grids and apply a monitoring system that will alert you when the grids have moved. Although this book will focus solely on copying and monitoring the grids, your takeaway will be the experience required to recognize the procedure and the importance of this function.

To create a copying and monitoring system, follow this procedure:

1. Go to the Level 1 floor plan.

2. On the Coordination panel of the Collaborate tab, click the Copy/ Monitor button. On the fly-out, click Select Link, as shown in Figure 20.4.

3. Hover your pointer over one of the grids. You will see an outline of the Revit Structure model that you have linked in. Once you see the outline, pick the grid (see Figure 20.5).

FIGURE 20.4 The Copy/Monitor button on the Coordination panel of the Collaborate tab

FIGURE 20.5 Selecting the link to Copy/Monitor

4. On the Copy/Monitor tab, click the Copy button, as shown in Figure 20.6.

FIGURE 20.6 Clicking the Copy button

5. On the Options bar, click the Multiple button.

6. While pressing the Ctrl key, select all of the grids in the linked model.

7. When you are finished, click Finish on the Options bar, as shown in Figure 20.7.

8. You will get a warning saying that "The following types already exist but are different." Just click OK.

9. Close out of any warnings stating that new items have been renamed. This is inconsequential information.

It is often overlooked, but you *must* click Finish on the Options bar or the copying and monitoring process will not take effect.

FIGURE 20.7 The Finish button on the Options bar

You should have little blue eyeballs all over the model. This is an indication that you have successfully copied and now are monitoring the structural grids (see Figure 20.8).

FIGURE 20.8 The eyeballs indicate that your consultant is being watched!

Now that the grids are being monitored, it is time to take a look at what we can copy and monitor from our consultant's models by configuring the Copy/Monitor settings.

Adjusting the Copy/Monitor Settings

By copying the grids into the architectural model, we are actually proceeding with the most common, and by far the safest, function of this command. If you do choose to copy and monitor items such as foundations and columns, you can automatically replace the items being copied with an alternate component. For example, you could use Copy/Monitor on a foundation wall that is 12" thick but automatically replace it with a foundation wall that is 10" thick. I am using this example to emphasize something you would not want to do. Be careful while replacing components you are getting from the structural model.

The objective of the next procedure is to look at the Copy/Monitor settings.

1. On the Copy/Monitor tab, click the Options button on the Tools panel, as shown in Figure 20.9.

FIGURE 20.9 The Settings button on the Tools panel of the Copy/Monitor tab

2. Notice that Revit will replace any column indiscriminately with a 24"-square concrete column. Click into the first column category and replace the entry with **Copy original Type** (see Figure 20.10).

3. Change the rest of the columns to **Copy original Type** and click OK.

4. On the Copy/Monitor panel of the Copy/Monitor tab, click Finish, as shown in Figure 20.11.

5. Save the model.

Now that we have a relationship with the structural model, it is time to put this relationship to the test and generate a coordination alert. I suppose you could say that the honeymoon is over!

FIGURE 20.10 Changing to Copy original Type

FIGURE 20.11 Click Finish.

Coordination Alert

Suddenly we have been thrust into a completely different way of working. We have a structural model inserted into our architectural model that will bark at us every time something changes. There's nothing wrong with that. Sure, occasionally there will be some annoyances, but these occasional annoyances are a small concession for being truly tied in with the structure.

When something changes in the structural model that is involved with an active monitor, you will be alerted. This alert will occur when you either open your model, or when you reload the linked Revit file.

To review the coordination alert, follow this procedure:

1. Save and close your model.

2. Open the NER-37_STRUCTURAL.rvt model.

3. In the NER-37_STRUCTURAL.rvt model, move grid A to the right so it is in alignment with the beam, as shown in Figure 20.12.

FIGURE 20.12 Moving grid A

4. Save the model and close.

5. Open the architectural model. When it opens, you will get the warning shown in Figure 20.13.

6. Click OK to continue opening the model.

7. Go to Level 1.

8. Select the link (you may have to mouse over one of the grids and press the Tab key).

FIGURE 20.13 The Coordination alert

9. On the Monitor panel of the Modify RVT Links tab, click the Coordination Review button, as shown in Figure 20.14.

FIGURE 20.14 The Coordination Review button on the Monitor panel of the Modify RVT Links tab

10. In the Coordination Review dialog, expand the category for the Grids (under the New/Unresolved category), as shown in Figure 20.15.

11. Expand the Grid Moved category.

T I P   The category that says Grid Moved is the actual alteration that occurred in the structural model. Finally! Somebody is telling us what they changed without fear of us getting mad at them.

12. To the right of the Grid Moved category, you will see an Action row. Click into the cell that says Postpone and look at the list. You will see three categories:

> **Reject**   This will postpone the change. Each time you run a coordination review, this instance will be listed as rejected. You will still have a chance to modify the instance at a later date.

> **Accept Difference**   This basically skips the error. You will still be able to change it at a later date.

Rename   This will take action. If the difference is the name (which it is in this case), Revit will rename the grid. If the grid moves, Revit will move the grid for you. (Basically any modification that needs to be made can be automatically made right here.)

13. Select Modify Grid A.

FIGURE 20.15   Telling Revit to automatically move the grid

 N O T E   You can also add a comment pertaining to the change. Typically it is a note to yourself, but in some situations, you will need it when you are involved in friendly discussions about who started the chain of events.

14. Click the Create Report button at the bottom of the dialog.

15. Save the HTML file to a location where you can find it.

16. Click OK in the Coordination Review dialog. (Notice that grid A moved.)

17. Open Windows Explorer, find the HTML report and open it. This gives you an uneditable report on the coordination effort that just occurred.

18. Close the report.

19. Save the model.

20. To check and see if there are any more issues, click the Review button on the Coordination panel of the Collaboration tab, as shown in Figure 20.16.

FIGURE 20.16 The Review button on the Coordination panel of the Collaboration tab

21. Select the linked structural model. The report should be empty.

A coordination report is an excellent way to track changes, but we are alerted of these changes only if we have the elements copied and monitored. So, how are we supposed to know if other elements are colliding with one another? This question is answered by using the Interference Detection function built into Revit.

Interference Detection

What came first? The chicken or the egg? That's a tough call. Another tough call is if the beam comes before the duct or wall. Ask a structural engineer, and he will answer in the affirmative that the beam does in fact come before the wall, door, and any other architectural appointment. On the opposite hand, the architect will request to move or eliminate a structural component altogether. But, the fact is, if the architect and the structural engineer are having this argument, that means they know there is an interference, and their disagreement about the chicken and the egg is actually a good thing.

The interference detection within Revit is used in the effort of keeping the contractor from asking the question. If the contractor is asking the question, we have a problem, don't we? This means a collision occurred that nobody caught. Don't worry — you can still have the chicken argument, only it is now called litigation.

To use interference detection, you do not have to do anything more than open a single dialog. In this dialog, you can select specific elements that you are worried about colliding. Of course, in true Revit form, you can create a report and even zoom in on the issue.

The objective of the following activity is to find some clashes between the architectural model and the structural model.

1. On the Interference panel of the Collaboration tab, click the Run Check button, as shown in Figure 20.17.

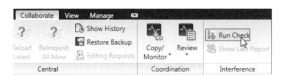

FIGURE 20.17 The Run Check button on the Interference panel of the Collaboration tab

2. In the panel to the left, select Current Project as the Categories From setting.

3. Select Doors and Stairs from the list, as shown in Figure 20.18.

4. In the panel to the right, select the NER-37_STRUCTURAL.rvt file.

5. Select Structural Framing and Structural Columns (see Figure 20.18).

FIGURE 20.18 Selecting the components to find in the interference report

6. Click OK.

7. The next dialog will show where we have a collision (it looks like all of our stairs are safe). Click on Doors : Double-Flush 72" × 84".

8. At the bottom of the dialog, click the Show button (see Figure 20.19).

FIGURE 20.19 The offending items are discovered!

9. Revit will zoom right in on the issue. Click the Export button.

10. Save the report in the same directory as the coordination report.

11. Click Close.

WHAT DO YOU MEAN, CLOSE! WE DIDN'T FIX ANYTHING

Yes, that's right — we only identified the issue. Revit does not breach into another model to fix your consultant's work. It does, however, give you a specific, detailed report for your meeting. Remember, Revit doesn't negate the need for open discussion during a project. Nor will it ever.

Boy! That is some good stuff. Lucky for you, your consultants are all up and running on Revit! Oh, they aren't? Now what kind of world are we living in here?

It's true. Your consultants aren't all going to be on Revit. If you're lucky, one in ten uses Revit in the capacity where they are ready to share a model with you. This is okay — don't panic. We are still in a great position. We can easily import AutoCAD (or MicroStation), and we can export our model just as easily.

Importing and Exporting CAD Formats

The first process we will delve into is the process of importing an AutoCAD structural floor plan. Although we have imported CAD in this book numerous times, we have yet to do so in the context of a coordinated floor plan. The mindset is a little different. And why is that? It is because we now care about where this AutoCAD drawing lands in relationship to our model, and we care also about maintaining that relationship.

For the CAD file used in the following procedure, go to the book's web page at **www.sybex.com/go/revit2010ner**. From there you can browse to Chapter 20 and find the file called NER-37.rvt. You will also need to locate the model called NER-37_STRUCTURAL.dwg. Save this file in a location where you can retrieve it.

The objective of the following procedure is to import an AutoCAD 2D floor plan, and "pin" down its coordinates.

1. Go to the Level 1 floor plan.

2. On the Create panel on the View tab, click Duplicate ➤ Duplicate with Detailing, as shown in Figure 20.20.

FIGURE 20.20 Duplicating the view

3. Rename the new view **Level 1 CAD Coordination**.

4. Open the new view.

5. Type **VG** (for Visibility Graphics).

6. Click the Revit Links tab.

Sometimes, Revit will produce a warning that you are pasting a view that references itself. This is an erroneous warning. Click Delete Items and Revit will let you proceed.

7. Uncheck the NER-37_STRUCTURAL.rvt model.

8. Click OK.

9. On the Link panel of the Insert tab, click the Link CAD button, as shown in Figure 20.21.

FIGURE 20.21   The Link CAD button on the Link panel of the Insert tab

10. At the bottom of the dialog, click the Current View Only check box.

11. Set Colors to Black and White.

12. Set Layers to All.

13. Set Import Units to Auto Detect.

14. Set Positioning to Auto: Origin-to-Origin.

15. Click Open.

16. On the View Control bar, click the Wireframe button so you can see the AutoCAD structure, as shown in Figure 20.22.

FIGURE 20.22   Clicking the Wireframe button on the View Control bar

The next step is to make sure that the coordinates in our Revit model stay true in the DWG file. With one simple procedure, we can publish the coordinates of the Revit model to the DWG file to ensure accuracy while importing.

1. On the Project Location panel of the Manage tab, click Coordinates ➤ Publish Coordinates, as shown in Figure 20.23.

2. Select the AutoCAD link by left-clicking on it in the view.

3. In the Manage Place and Locations dialog, click the Duplicate button.

FIGURE 20.23 Publishing the coordinates

4. Call the new location **Revit Position**.

5. Click Make Current.

6. Click OK.

7. Select the AutoCAD link.

8. On the Home tab, click the Element Properties button.

9. Verify that the shared location is now Revit Position.

10. Save the Revit model.

11. Once you save the Revit model, you will be prompted to save the new coordinates in the DWG. Click the Save button, as shown in Figure 20.24.

FIGURE 20.24 Saving the coordinates to the AutoCAD file

So, that's importing. Suppose we need to send our model to our clients and consultants who don't have Revit? This can be taken care of quickly and deliberately.

Exporting a Model to CAD

For some of you, this may be a nice-to-know subject. For most of you, this is a need-to-know subject. Taking the plunge into Revit means that you may be taking that plunge alone. Just because you are using Revit, that does not mean that you don't need to have the ability to give someone CAD drawings based on your models.

This section of this chapter will focus on the process of exporting your Revit model to both 2D and 3D CAD.

Exporting a 2D Model

Most of the time, this is going to be your deliverable to your clients. Also, if your consultants aren't on Revit, that also usually means that they are not using 3D CAD either. This is the "lowest common denominator." Not that it is bad — it just means we need to export our model in a way that they can just pick it up and run with it.

The objective of the next procedure is to export our model to a 2D AutoCAD drawing file.

1. In the Project Browser, open the Level 1 floor plan.

2. Click the Revit Home button, and select Export ➢ CAD Formats ➢ DWG, as shown in Figure 20.25.

3. On the View/Sheet Set panel, select In Session View/Sheet Set from the Export drop-down.

4. For the Show in List option, select All Sheets and Views in the Model.

5. Scroll down to the bottom of the list and make sure your Level 1 floor plan is checked on (see Figure 20.26). You may check on any others as you please.

6. Click the DWG Properties tab.

7. At the bottom, click Export Rooms and Areas as Polylines.

8. Click the Export button.

FIGURE 20.25 Exporting the model to CAD

FIGURE 20.26 Choosing what to export

9. Browse to the directory of your choosing.

Now that we can export to a flat 2D file, it is time to take our model and export it as a full 3D entity. The process is similar to exporting as 2D.

Exporting the Model to 3D CAD

It is such a shame to "dumb down" our 3D model to flat 2D CAD. It feels as though we are taking a step backward each time we do it. When you find yourself in the situation where your consultants are using CAD but are using the 3D modeling, you can give them the gift of 3D.

The objective of the next procedure is to export a model to 3D CAD.

1. Go to the Default 3D view.

2. Select Export ➤ CAD Formats ➤ DWG.

3. Set the Export option to Current View/Sheet Only.

4. Click the Export button.

5. Find a place to put the 3D model.

6. Save the model.

The most important step in exporting to a 3D CAD format is the fact that you need to be in a 3D view in order to do so.

As you can see, it's not a difficult process. In Chapter 23, "BIM Management," we will explore setting up the export in such a way that the layers are correct if your client is not standardized on the AIA format.

Are You Experienced?

Now You Can...

☑ **import a Revit Structure model**

☑ **copy and monitor the Revit model**

☑ **run interference checking on a linked Revit model**

☑ **export a Revit model to CAD formats (2D and 3D)**

CHAPTER 21

Phasing and Design Options

▶ Managing project phasing settings

▶ Creating an existing plan

▶ Creating a demo plan

▶ Creating phase-specific views

▶ Create design options

O f all the projects I have been involved with over the years, I can only remember a handful that didn't involve some kind of existing condition. It would be nice if we could find a giant, flat field to construct our buildings, but those projects are few and far between.

The term *phasing* in Revit is often taken quite literally, and can often become confused as *construction sequencing*. When we talk about phasing in the context of how Revit views it, we are talking about *adding new construction to an existing building*, and *the demolition of the existing structure*. Although you can use Revit to track all aspects of construction, the base use and the purpose of phasing is for existing conditions.

The first section of this chapter will focus on the setup of your actual phasing scheme. By default, Revit Architecture provides two phases: Existing and New Construction. As it stands, everything we have placed into our model for the last 20 chapters has been exclusively on the New Construction phase. We will now alter that.

Managing Project Phasing

I have seen this scenario played out more times than I would like. People get Revit, build a model, and then start clicking the Demolish button found on the Phasing panel on the Modify tab, as shown in Figure 21.1. Yes, it forces hidden lines, but what you are doing is demolishing walls that were constructed in the same phase as they are being removed. You can't just do that!

With some practice, and by following the procedures in this chapter, you will be able to swing that hammer around all you want. But for now, to get started go to the book's web page at www.sybex.com/go/revit2010ner. From there you can browse to Chapter 21 and find the file called NER-Phasing.rvt. (If you prefer, you can follow along with your own model as well.)

The objective of the following procedure is to create a "demo" phase and insert that phase between the Existing and the New Construction phase.

1. Open the file called NER-Phasing.rvt you downloaded.

2. On the Modify tab, click the small arrow on the Phasing panel (just underneath the hammer), as shown in Figure 21.1.

3. In the Phasing dialog, click on the number 1. This is the control for the Existing phase row.

4. To the right of the dialog is the Insert section. Click the After button.

FIGURE 21.1 Click the arrow on the Phasing panel.

I THOUGHT I SAW THAT BUTTON SOMEWHERE ELSE!

Although Revit Architecture 2010 has reduced the amount of button redundancy on multiple tabs, you will also see a Phases button in the Manage Project panel of the Manage tab, as shown here:

5. Rename the phase that is now in the middle to **Demolition**, as shown in Figure 21.2.

6. Click OK.

7. On the View tab, click Duplicate View ➢ Duplicate View, as shown in Figure 21.3.

8. Right-click the new view and rename it to **Level 1 Existing**.

9. Open the Level 1 Existing plan.

For now, that is all we need to do to start setting up the plans. We will create a demo plan as well, but not until we start getting some items moved over to the existing phase.

FIGURE 21.2 Adding the Demolition phase

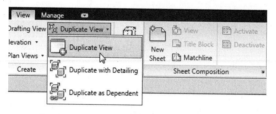

FIGURE 21.3 Duplicating the view

Creating an Existing Phasing Plan

Just because you just called it "existing," that does not, by any means, qualify this plan as an existing plan. We have a good amount of work left to do before we can consider this existing.

The first thing we need to do is to physically select each item and "move" what we want over to an existing phase. Once we have finished with that task, we need to assign the Existing phase to this plan.

The objective of the following procedure is to physically move components to the existing phase.

1. Pick a window around the entire east wing as well as the link, as shown in Figure 21.4.

2. On the Multi-Select tab, click the Filter button, as shown in Figure 12.4.

FIGURE 21.4 Filtering your selection

3. In the Filter dialog, click the Check None button, then check Walls.

4. Click OK.

5. On the Multi-Select tab, click the Element Properties button.

6. In the Instance Parameters dialog, scroll down to the bottom where you see Phasing. For Phase Created, select Existing (see Figure 21.5).

7. Click OK.

8. Pick the same window around the entire east wing.

9. Click the Filter button.

10. Select only Windows and click OK.

11. In the Element Properties dialog, change Phase Created to Existing.

Zoom in on the plan. Notice the items that have been moved to existing are gray and have lost their detail level, as shown in Figure 21.6. Also notice that some of the items are still on a heavy line weight. These items need to be selected and then moved to the existing phase.

FIGURE 21.5 Setting the Phase Created setting to Existing

FIGURE 21.6 The existing walls

Some of the items you are trying to select are still part of an array group. Since you can't actually move an array group to a phase, you can cursor over one of the arrayed items, then press your Tab key until the individual item is selected. Once it is selected, right-click and choose Select All Instances.

Keep selecting items and moving them to the existing phase created. Continue until you have every item in the east wing and the link. This includes the floors and foundations too. The only thing you want to keep is the winding stairs that connect the link to the west wing. You can select items in the 3D view as well.

Okay, it's time to create the actual existing plan. The only thing that separates an actual existing plan from a new construction plan is a single property.

The objective of the next exercise is to change the plan to an existing plan.

1. On the View tab, click the View Properties button, as shown in Figure 21.7.

2. Scroll down the list to the Phasing category.

3. Change the view phase to Existing. (Again, see Figure 21.7).

4. Click OK.

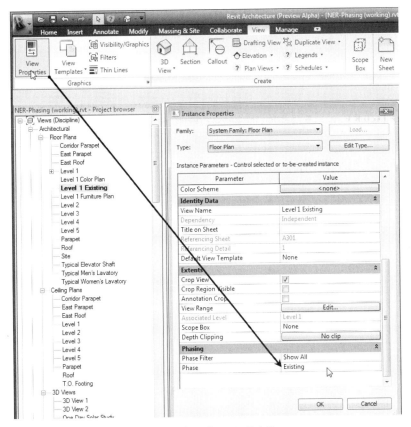

FIGURE 21.7 Changing the view phase to Existing

NOTE   If you are not catching what is going on here, here's the deal. We just added the building components to the existing phase. Now, to see the existing items only, we are changing the actual view's phase to Existing.

5. In the west end of the link, zoom in on the end. You will see a wall missing. Select one of the exterior walls, and select Create Similar from the Modify Walls tab, as shown in Figure 21.8.

6. Draw a wall across the front of the opening, as shown in Figure 21.8.

FIGURE 21.8 Drawing a new wall in the existing plan. This wall will later be demolished.

7. In the Project Browser, right-click on the {3D} view, and select Duplicate View ➤ Duplicate.

8. Rename the new 3D view to **Existing**.

9. Select the wall you just added and attach the top to the roof.

10. With the wall still selected, click the Element Properties button on the Modify Wall tab.

11. Make sure Phase Created is set to Existing.

12. Change Phase Demolished to Demolition.

13. Click OK.

14. Go to the existing 3D view. It should look like Figure 21.9.

FIGURE 21.9 The 3D existing view

Now we're getting it. The next step is to add a small addition to the north side of the east wing. We will then demo a portion of the wall.

1. In the Project Browser, go to the Level 1 floor plan.

2. Turn on the Crop region and drag the north region up about 20 or 30 feet. Do the same for the dependent crop region. It should look similar to Figure 21.10.

3. On the Home tab, click the Wall button.

4. Select Exterior - Brick and CMU on MTL. Stud.

5. On the Options bar, change the height to East Roof, and set Location Line to Wall Centerline.

6. Pick the start point, as shown in Figure 21.10.

7. Draw the wall 40' to the north.

8. Draw another vertical wall centered on the partition to the right, as shown in Figure 21.10.

9. Draw one more wall across the front.

FIGURE 21.10 Draw a small box addition.

Great! The addition is added. We could put a roof on and add some floors, but let's jump right to the good stuff. We need to start knocking out some major demolition areas. The first items we will look at are those windows, and then the area that leads into the main building.

Demolishing Components

Now that our phasing is properly set, we can really do some renovations. Since we need to cut a huge gaping hole in the north face of the building, it seems we need to demo some interior partitions back as well. Also, there are some windows that need to be demolished and in-filled. Let's start there.

The objective of the next exercise is to demolish the north exterior windows and create an automatic in-fill.

1. Go to the north elevation.

2. Zoom in on the east wing.

3. On the Modify tab, click the Demolish button (with the hammer icon) on the Phasing panel, as shown in Figure 21.11.

4. Pick the two windows to the right and the left of the addition (four demolished windows total).

5. Select the four windows.

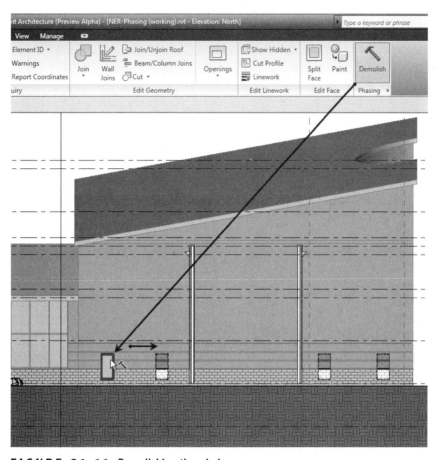

FIGURE 21.11 Demolishing the windows

 W A R N I N G   Hang on there, Thor! Do you know what phase you are in? You just demolished those windows in the new construction phase! We need to change that.

6. Click the Element Properties button on the Modify Window tab.

7. Change Phase Demolished to Demolition.

8. Click OK.

 N O T E   For all you LEED professionals, remember that you can schedule anything in Revit. You can also schedule only windows that are being demolished. With an accurate monitor of material being demolished, you can suddenly have a running tally of reusable building materials.

Because the phase of the north elevation is set to New Construction, when you demolish an item in a previous phase (the demolition phase occurs before the new construction phase), that item should not appear in the current phase. Instead of leaving a gaping hole, Revit added in-fill to the window opening.

The next demolition item will not be as easy. The next exercise will involve cutting a large hole out of the north wall at the perimeter of the addition. The height will be constrained to Level 4.

1. Make sure you are in the north elevation.

2. Select the north wall of the east wing.

3. On the Modify Walls tab, click the Edit Profile button.

4. On the Draw panel, click the Pick Lines button.

5. Pick the inside faces of the two new walls, as shown in Figure 21.12.

6. Pick the Level 4 level (again, refer to Figure 21.12).

7. Split the bottom line between the two walls. This forms the continuous loop.

FIGURE 21.12 Cutting the hole

8. On the Modify Walls tab, select Edit Profile and click Finish Wall.

9. Go to the Level 1 floor plan. Notice that the wall joins are inaccurate.

10. Select the horizontal wall. You will see arrow grips, as shown in Figure 21.13. You will also see a small "T"-shaped grip. This is an important grip.

11. Pick the "T"-shaped grip first. This will physically disallow the walls to be joined.

12. Pick the arrow grip, and drag the wall until it is aligned with the new addition wall, as shown in Figure 21.13.

13. Do the same for the other side.

FIGURE 21.13 Cleaning the join between new and existing

 NOTE Wall cleanups such as the cleanup illustrated in Figure 21.13 will be common during the phasing sequence. Don't think that Revit will automatically clean it how you would like it to. I can assure you, it will not.

14. Go to the Level 1 Existing plan.

15. Zoom in on the same intersections we just adjusted.

16. Select the middle wall, and grip-edit the walls back to the abutment, as shown in Figure 21.14.

17. Type ZA.

18. Select one of the structural grids, right-click, and select Hide in View ➢ By Category.

FIGURE 21.14 Cleaning the join in the existing plan

    19. Repeat the procedure for the reference planes.

    20. Save the model.

Now that we have an existing plan and a new construction plan, it is time to create a demo plan. Since all of the elements have been placed in the correct phases, and the phases are in place, this is the fun part!

Creating a Demo Plan

This is the type of coordination that is keeping Revit around. The fact that you can track a project from existing to demolition to completion without a single overlapping line is astounding. Granted, this sometimes does not come as easily as you may like, and you can find yourself "picking around" at wall joins to get them to display correctly. But overall, this is a marked advantage over 2D or even 3D CAD drafting.

Creating a demo plan is no more difficult than creating an existing plan. The process involves making a duplicate of Level 1, and then changing the phase to Demolition.

    1. Open the Level 1 floor plan.

    2. On the View tab, click Duplicate View ➤ Duplicate View, as shown in Figure 21.15.

FIGURE 21.15 Duplicating the Level 1 floor plan

3. Rename the new view to **Level 1 Demolition**.

4. Open the Level 1 Demolition plan.

5. On the View tab, click the View Properties button.

6. Set Phase to Demolition (see Figure 21.16).

7. Click OK.

8. Turn off the structural grids and the reference planes.

As you are building your model with view upon view, always be diligent in naming these views you are introducing to the model. It is just good practice.

 TIP   Now that you have a demo plan in place, I recommend that you do all of your demolishing here. You can just hammer away at the walls you wish to demolish without being bothered by the new construction, and you can see your work clearly and free of obstruction.

9. On the Modify tab, click the Demolish button, as shown in Figure 21.17.

10. Demolish the wall and the door shown in Figure 21.17. (Again, since we are in the demo plan, this process has never been easier.)

With the three plans assembled, it is time to make one more plan view. Although we have essentially run out of phases, we can create a new plan that will simply show the model in its completed form by using what is called a phase filter.

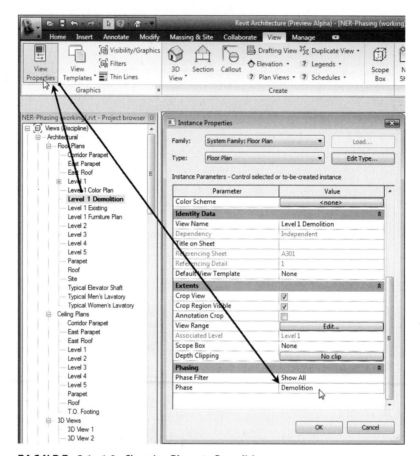

FIGURE 21.16 Changing Phase to Demolition

FIGURE 21.17 Demolishing the wall and door

Examining Phase Filters

Phase filters are created to allow the user to specify what phases they want to see in a view. For example, if your view's phase is set to New Construction, you will see the existing as well as the new information, but you won't see the demolition. In Revit, you can set up a filter to show the demolition in a new construction plan if so desired. Also, by using phase filters, you can even change how items are displayed in a specific state.

The objective of the following procedure is to create a new plan showing the model in its completed state.

   1. Duplicate the Level 1 plan (without detailing).

   2. Rename the new view to **Level 1 completed**.

   3. Go to the view's properties.

   4. Change Phase Filter to Show Complete, as shown in Figure 21.18.

   5. Click OK and investigate the plan. It looks as if we never moved anything to existing.

   6. On the Manage tab, click the Phases button, as shown in Figure 21.19.

FIGURE 21.18 The Show Complete phase filter

7. In the Phasing dialog, click the Phase Filters tab. Notice this tab contains the filtering you are using in this project. You can add or modify these filters at any time (see Figure 21.19).

FIGURE 21.19 Phase filters

8. In the Phasing dialog, click the Graphic Overrides tab. Here you can see that you can change the line types and the shading for each phase status (see Figure 21.20). Click OK.

FIGURE 21.20 Graphic Overrides tab

Typically in a set of drawings, you are not going to have a "show complete" view, but it can be extremely helpful with internal coordination throughout the life of the project. You can quickly see where there are major deficiencies while viewing a model as completed.

One problem with all this phasing is the fact that, on some projects, your Project Browser is going to become confusing and crowded quickly. Let's look at dividing the browser up into phases.

Phase filters are great, but don't get out of hand with these. You can easily create more confusion than good.

1. In the Project Browser, right-click on the Views (Discipline) heading, as shown in Figure 21.21, and click Properties.

FIGURE 21.21 Opening the browser's properties

2. Click the Edit button in the Folders row.

3. You will see that the browser is already organized by Discipline. Focus on the Then By section, and change the Then By category to Phase (as shown in Figure 21.22).

4. Click OK twice to get back to the model.

Well, I think you can see that browser organization can help you organize a project. Be careful, though. Adding random, multiple categorizations too could get out of hand and wind up more confusing than if you had just left the project browser alone.

FIGURE 21.22 Changing Then By to Phase

WHAT THE "???" IN THE PROJECT BROWSER MEANS

What the heck is that? As you can see in the following graphic, there are three question marks in our Project Browser. This will happen when you start organizing the browser by a specific property that some views do not contain. The views categorized in the ??? heading are drafting views, and they do not have a phase property.

Another functionality of Revit that we need to venture into is similar to phasing, but has an entirely different meaning when it comes to tracking aspects of a project. This function is called Design Options.

Design Options

Better known in the Design world as Bid Alternates, Revit is equipped with the functionality to allow you to actually model different Options in one model. The great thing about how Revit handles this functionality is the fact that any alternate design will never be (or at least will seldom be) a completely new structure. There will be items that are in more than one option. Revit allows you to keep "like" items intact while creating new or different items that belong to different Options. This creates a situation where you only need to model the common items once, so you can focus on the alternates.

That being said, there is a lot to be added to this functionality. Many of the examples in this section of the chapter will deal more with flaws in Revit than with actual Design option procedures.

To get started, go to the book's website at **www.sybex.com/go/revit2010ner**. From there you can browse to Chapter 21, and find the file called NER-38.rvt. From there you can follow along with the procedure.

1. On the Manage tab, click the Design Options button as shown in Figure 21.23.

2. In the Design Options dialog, click the New button under Option Set.

NOTE   You can have as many Option Sets as you choose. There will be cases where you have other, unrelated Options in other places in your model.

FIGURE 21.23 The Design Option button.

3. Select Option Set 1.

4. In the Option Set category, click the Rename button.

5. Call the Option set: East Entry.

6. Select Option 1 (Primary).

7. In the Option category, click Rename.

8. Rename it to: With Entrance.

9. In the Option category, click the New button.

10. Call the new option: Without Entry. (See Figure 21.24.)

FIGURE 21.24 Adding Options

11. Click Close.

12. In the Project Browser, go to the Level 1 floor plan.

13. Select the curtain wall to the left of the entry as shown in Figure 21.25.

14. Click the Cut button as shown in Figure 21.25.

FIGURE 21.25 Cut the curtain wall out of the host wall.

15. Delete the door family in the right side of the wall.

TIP If you have a lot of in-place families, you are going to have an extremely difficult time with Design Options. When you know you might have Design Options, create all of your families outside of the model.

16. Select the walls as shown in Figure 21.26, and click the Add to Set button in the Design Options panel on the Manage Tab. (You will have to click the Manage tab.)

FIGURE 21.26 Adding the walls to the Option Set

17. Only check With Entrance, and click OK.

18. Select the floor.

19. Click the Add to Set button.

20. Add the floor to both Options. (Keep both items checked.)

21. Go to a 3D view.

22. Select the curtain walls and the roof. (Use your filter and only check Curtain Systems and Roof.)

23. Click Add to Set.

24. Add the curtain walls to the "With Entrance" option only, and click OK.

25. Select the curved roof.

26. Add the curved roof to the With Entrance option, and click OK.

Phew! Let's take a breather! The next thing we need to do is put that curtain wall back into the model. To do this, we need to make the option we want this wall to be in current. It is almost like making a layer current in AutoCAD.

To start placing objects in a specific option, follow along with the procedure below:

1. On the Design Options panel of the Manage tab, click the (None) menu, and select: With Entrance (Primary) as shown in Figure 21.27. (This means that you are making this option current.)

FIGURE 21.27 Making the Option current

2. On the Modify tab, click Paste Aligned ➢ Same Place. Your curtain wall is back in action.

3. Go to the first floor plan.

4. On the Design Options panel, select the "Without Entry" option as shown in Figure 21.28.

5. Select the floor, and click the Edit Boundary icon on the Modify Floors tab.

6. Eliminate the jog in the floor leaving only a straight line.

7. Click Finish Floor, and click No for the next two questions.

8. On the Home tab, click the Wall button.

9. In the Change Element Type dialog, select the Exterior - Brick and CMU on MTL. Stud (No Parapet) wall type.

10. Draw a wall across the front of the building as shown in Figure 21.28.

FIGURE 21.28 Draw a new wall across the front of the building

IS THAT WALL NOT WORKING OUT?

At the ends of the walls, you may run into a join situation. If this is the case, be sure to set wall joins to Mitered.

11. Go to a 3D view. Attach the wall to the roof.

Notice that the foundation and the pad are causing trouble. You can add these items to the current option as well. To do so, follow along with the preceding exercise.

12. Click the Active only button at the bottom of the screen as shown in Figure 21.29.

13. Select the site, and click Hide in View ➢ Category.

14. Select the 5 foundation walls under the entry and the long wall, and add them to the set.

15. Go to the Top of Footing Structural Plan.

16. Change the Option to Without Entry.

17. Draw a new foundation wall and add a footing to it.

FIGURE 21.29 Active only button

18. Go to a 3D view.

19. Change the current Option to None.

Now that the Options are set, we can toggle the views to reflect the option we desire. To do so, we will create a duplicate view, and have two different option sets for a 3D view.

1. In the Project Browser, right click on the {3D} view, and duplicate it.

2. Call the new view East Entry -With Entry.

3. Duplicate the view again, and rename the second view to East Entry - Without Entry.

4. Open the East Entry - Without Entry view.

5. Type VG.

6. On the Design Options tab, select the Without Entry choice from the Design Option menu as shown in Figure 21.30.

7. Open the East Entry-With Entry view, and change the option to With Entry.

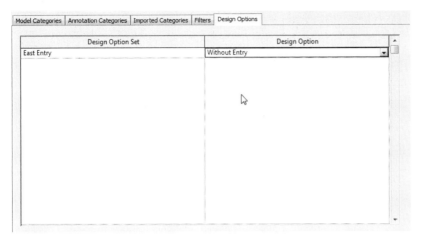

FIGURE 21.30 choosing the correct Option.

Your Options are set. Do not expect to have a graceful experience with this the first time you venture into Design Options. However, once you get it down, you will start to see the advantages of using this feature.

ACCEPTING THE PRIMARY OPTION

You will notice that when you are working in Design Options, you can only edit items belonging to the current option. If your Options set is set to (none), then you are actually in the "Main Model" option. Once you are finished with the Options and an Alternative has been accepted, you can make the accepted option the primary option and click Accept Primary. This deletes all other Options leaving just the one option. (Make *sure* you make a back up before you do this.)

Are You Experienced?

Now You Can...

- ☑ configure project phasing settings by adding new phases

- ☑ change and add phase filters, and create phasing graphical overrides

- ☑ create existing and demo plans

- ☑ organize the Project Browser to reflect your phasing

- ☑ create Design Options

CHAPTER 22

Project
Collaboration

▶ Defining and enabling worksets

▶ Defining and creating a central model

▶ Defining and creating a local model

▶ Editing requests and relinquishing objects

▶ Demand loading

I t is quite ironic that the second-to-last chapter of this book contains information that many of you will need to get your first Revit project off the ground. That is, how do we work on a project when multiple people need to be in the model? Revit is only one model, right?

You may be surprised, but the answer, and the procedure, is not as difficult as some make it out to be. I have seen many explanations on the subject of project collaboration that have been wide reaching and convoluted, thus causing an air of uneasiness. It's not as horrible as it sounds, and this chapter will explain project collaboration in the simplest terms possible.

First we'll establish exactly what we are trying to accomplish and how to go about doing it. The backbone of project collaboration is within the functionality of what is called worksharing.

Enabling and Utilizing Worksharing

The concept of worksharing in Revit, broken down into its simplest form, is this:

1. Open the model.

2. Issue a Save As command.

Now you have two models. The model you just saved is linked to the original model. Any change made in your model is saved back to the original model.

Your coworker can now open the original model and choose Save As. Now there are three models. Any change you make is saved to the original model and to your coworker model. Any change your coworker makes is saved to the original model and to your model.

The "original" model is to be considered the "central" model. The file you save is called a "local copy." So to reiterate: you open the Central model, then choose Save As. The file you now have is the local copy (see Figure 22.1). Another good way to view this setup is as a basic computer network. You have a file server, along with several desktop computers that are networked to it.

OK, so that's the concept of worksharing. It's now time to drill down and see how to activate this "network" of linked files. As mentioned before, there is a function called worksets. The worksets are the backbone of this entire concept.

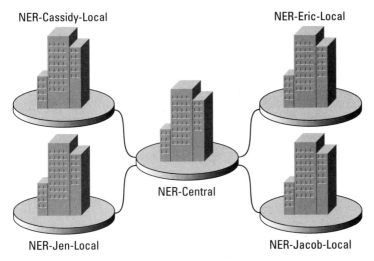

NER-Cassidy-Local

NER-Eric-Local

NER-Central

NER-Jen-Local

NER-Jacob-Local

FIGURE 22.1 The basic file-sharing configuration

Enabling Worksets

This function in Revit influences your model and the way you go about working more than anything you can do. Worksets is a "mode" you literally have to enter into. Once you have enabled worksets, there is no going back. Worksets are to the Undo button as Kryptonite is to Superman.

Essentially, worksets are a way to divide your model. You can almost look at this like phasing. Every element in your model, once you activate worksharing, will have a workset associated with it. As you will see in a moment, levels and grids will be on their own workset while everything else in the model will automatically be assigned Workset 1. This "assignment" is in the form of a parameter that you can see in the Element Properties dialog, and you can change that parameter.

Why would you want to change it? Good question. Here's an example: Say you are modifying an interior partition and your coworker (who is working on their local model) tries to edit that same wall. Your coworker will be denied access to the wall. But there is nothing stopping them from working on another wall in the same area, one that you intended on making the same modifications to. This could get messy fast. To avoid this situation, you can add all of your interior partitions to a workset called "Interior Partitions" and actually "lock" everybody else out of any item that has been placed on this workset.

Now that's the way to work!

Obviously this process is not without its rules, quirks, and parts that need further explanation, so to get started, go to the book's web page at **www.sybex.com/go/revit2010ner**. From there you can browse to Chapter 22 and find the file called NER-38.rvt.

To enable worksets and start the worksharing process, follow these steps:

1. Open the NER-38.rvt file.

2. On the Collaborate tab, click the Worksets button on the Worksets panel, as shown in Figure 22.2.

3. You will get a Worksharing dialog basically welcoming you to the point of no return. Accept the defaults for Shared Levels and Grids and for Workset 1, as shown in Figure 22.3, and click OK.

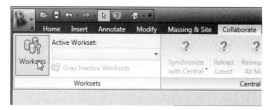

FIGURE 22.2 Once you pass this point, there is no turning back.

FIGURE 22.3 The Worksharing dialog

N O T E   Turning on your worksets is a onetime activation process. You do not have to do this every time you want to work on the project.

4. The next dialog you will arrive at is the Worksets dialog, as shown in Figure 22.4. As you can see, your two worksets are present in a spreadsheet format. It says they are both Editable and that you own them. Congratulations. There is plenty to explain here:

▶ Active Workset indicates the workset where any new item will be either drawn on or inserted on (sort of like the current "layer" in AutoCAD). There is also a Gray Inactive Workset Graphics choice. When checked on, this will shade the items not on Workset1.

▶ The Show field at the bottom of the Worksets dialog will allow you to add specific families, project standards, and views to the workset list (see Figure 22.4).

Click OK to get back to the model.

FIGURE 22.4 The Worksets dialog

 N O T E   You can turn on additional items in the Show category. Unless there is an extremely compelling reason to do so, don't — especially if this is the first project your team is taking on in Revit. Try to keep this as simple and painless as possible. Just because you can assume ultimate control over your users, that does not mean you have to.

Now that you have the worksets activated and the model is saved, it is time to create the central model. This will always be the next step in the process.

Creating a Central Model

Creating the central model is generally going to be a onetime deal. It is to be done immediately following the enabling of your worksets. Also, the individual who is creating the central model needs to be your best Revit user.

Okay, best Revit user, follow this procedure to learn how to create the central model.

1. Click the Revit Home button and choose Save As ➤ Project, as shown in Figure 22.5.

FIGURE 22.5 Save the project using Save As.

2. In the Save As dialog, click the Options button in the lower-right corner.

3. In the File Save Options dialog, change the number of backups to 1 (see Figure 22.6).

N O T E   Notice that the Worksharing area is not active. This is because you are saving the file for the first time after activating worksharing. You have no choice but to make this the central model.

4. Click OK.

5. Call the file NER-CENTRAL.rvt.

6. Click Save.

7. On the Collaborate tab, click Synchronize with Central ➤ Synchronize Now, as shown in Figure 22.7. This saves any changes made.

8. On the Worksets panel in the Collaborate tab, click the Worksets button.

Notice that on the Quick Access toolbar the Synchronize button is now available. Since this is the central model, the actual save icon is inactive.

FIGURE 22.6 Modify the settings before you save the central file.

FIGURE 22.7 Clicking the Synchronize Now button

9. Change both worksets by choosing No for Editable (see Figure 22.8).

10. Click OK. (Don't worry — I will explain what all this means in a moment.)

11. Click the Synchronize with Central button.

The reason we made these worksets not editable is because when you are working in the central file, you always want to leave it with no editable worksets. That way, users do not have access to these worksets in their local models.

FIGURE 22.8 Releasing the worksets by clicking No for Editable

The next task we need to tackle is how to make a new workset and move some components onto the new workset.

The objective of the following procedure is to create a Site workset and to move the topography and the site components to this workset.

1. Click the Worksets button on the Collaborate tab.

2. In the Worksets dialog, click the New button, as shown in Figure 22.9.

3. In the New Workset dialog, call this workset Site.

4. Set Editable for theWorkset1 workset to Yes.

5. Click OK.

6. Go to the default 3D view.

7. Select the toposurface.

8. On the Modify Topography tab, click the Element Properties button.

9. In the Identity Data category, find the Worksets row and change the workset to Site.

10. Click OK.

11. Select the rest of the site components, including the split surfaces, the tree, and the shrubs.

12. Put these items on the Site workset.

13. Change their worksets to Site. Click OK.

FIGURE 22.9 Creating a new workset

14. On the Collaborate tab, click the Synchronize with Central button.

15. On the Collaborate tab, click the Worksets button.

16. Make all worksets not editable, as shown in Figure 22.10.

If you are finding that the workset parameter in the Element Properties dialog is inactive, make sure you set the Workset1 workset to Active.

FIGURE 22.10 Making all worksets not editable

17. Click the Synchronize with Central button.

N O T E   The reason we are making sure all of the worksets are not editable is that, in the central model, everything needs to be turned off. Look at the central model as merely a "hub" that serves as a connector to pass data through as your team collaborates on the project.

It is now time to create your local model. Luckily, all of the difficult work has been done. Setting up the central file is the hardest part of the worksharing process, and is usually done by the BIM manager or at least the BIM lead person on the project. The act of creating a local file is as simple as issuing a Save As.

Creating a Local File

With the central file in place, you are ready for the rest of your team to "have at it." Although I keep mentioning how easy most of this stuff is, there are some dangers to look out for. The first danger is to never open the central file and stay in it. When you are in the process of creating a local file, you open the central file, do a Save As, and work in your new file.

N O T E   Some firms also like to have their users physically copy the central file in Windows Explorer and rename it. I err on the side of caution, and have my users open the central file and choose Save As. You may be saying to yourself "Self, why wouldn't I just take the advice of the book's author?" All I can say is, it only takes one time to have a user open the central model and start working. This generates errors, and will cause the other users to be unable to make any edits.

This section of the chapter will guide you through the process of creating a local file by opening the central model and saving the local copy as your own.

1. Make sure you are still in the central model.

2. On Revit Home button, go to Save As ➤ Project.

3. Find the folder where your central model is, and create a new folder.

4. Call the new folder **Local User**.

5. In the Save As dialog, click the Options button.

6. In the Options dialog, change the number of backups to 1, and click OK.

7. Save the model in this folder, naming it **NER-LOCAL-ERIC.rvt** (obviously you enter your name here).

Congratulations! You are the proud owner of a new Revit file that knows your name and everything! Yes, it knows your name.

You see, when you create the local file, it is yours to keep. As a matter of fact, if someone else opens your file from their computer, they will not be able to make any modifications. Not only does your local file keep a live link back to the central file, it actually knows who it belongs to. Revit does this for a good reason. This file now represents you within the team.

Working in the Revit Shared Environment

With the local model saved, you are free to work away. As you'll recall, the central model was created with three worksets: Shared Levels and Grids, Workset1, and Site. You, as a local user, can just start working away! As you start making edits to the model, however, Revit is making a note that you are actually borrowing a workset. Revit is also making a note that you physically own the item you are editing.

Borrowing? OK, let's stop right there, and take a look at what this all means. In Revit worksharing, you can either be the borrower of a workset or an owner of a workset. If you are a borrower, the rest of the design team can make modifications to elements in the workset but not to the specific element you are working on.

The objective of the next exercise is to make a modification to the site and to investigate what happens in the Worksharing dialog.

1. Go to the default 3D view.

2. Delete one of the shrubs. (Remember, we put the shrubs on the Site workset.)

3. On the Collaborate tab, click the Worksets button.

4. In the Worksets dialog, notice that you are now borrowing the Site workset, as shown in Figure 22.11.

Since there is no good way to have you go through an exercise, you can take your hand off the mouse and read for a few paragraphs. If you are at work and have another willing participant, have them create their own local file, and ask them to start making edits to the model.

FIGURE 22.11   Borrowing a workset

GET IN SYNC

Now that the local model is created, you can see what others are doing, as well as publish what you are doing for the other users. Just click the Synchronize button on the Quick Access bar, and you and your users are in sync.

Notice that the Site workset still says "No" for editable. This means that if Cassidy comes along and starts working on the shrubs right next to the one you just deleted, she still can. You don't own the workset — you are just borrowing it. Now, if you simply changed the shrub to a tree (or made any modifications whatsoever to the shrub), Cassidy cannot make any edits to the new tree. When she tries to edit the tree, she will get the error shown in Figure 22.12.

Revit Architecture (Preview Alpha)
Error - cannot be ignored
Can't edit the element until 'Eric' resaves the element to central and relinquishes it and you Reload Latest.

<u>S</u>how   More <u>I</u>nfo   Expand >>

<u>P</u>lace Request   <u>O</u>K   <u>C</u>ancel

FIGURE 22.12 Eric is modifying the element.

ERIC A.K.A. CASSIDY

If Eric decides to not relinquish an item to Cassidy, then decides to close his model and leave to go on vacation (ignoring repeated warnings), then we have a situation, don't we? His office door is locked, and we don't know his password. What you can do in these trying times is click the Settings button at the bottom of the Revit Home menu. Select the General tab, and change the username to the offender's name. You can now open his local file and relinquish the worksets. (See the following graphic.)

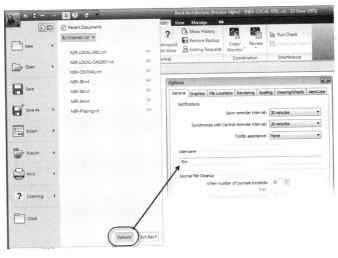

You may notice from Figure 22.12, that there is a button that allows Cassidy to place a request. When she clicks this button, a request to relinquish is sent to you. Also, she can check to see if any team members have placed a request to her (see Figure 22.13).

FIGURE 22.13 Requesting a relinquish

On the other side of the fence, there is no notification to you that anyone is asking you to cough up some site! You can check, though, by clicking Editing Requests on the Collaborate tab. From there, you will be able to expand a list of requests, as shown in Figure 22.14.

FIGURE 22.14 Checking to see who is begging

Now, once you see that Cassidy is begging you to release an item, you get to do the right thing and grant her the request. You do this by simply clicking the Relinquish All Mine button on the Collaborate tab, as shown in Figure 22.15.

FIGURE 22.15 Relinquish All Mine

See? We *can* all get along! Until you pull the next move. Suppose you didn't want anybody else on the team to modify anything in the entire Site workset. There are times when this will occur. To figure out how to do this, follow along:

1. On the Collaborate tab, click the Worksets button.

2. In the Site workset, select Yes in the Editable field, as shown in Figure 22.16. Although Cassidy is a borrower, you can still take over the workset.

3. Click OK.

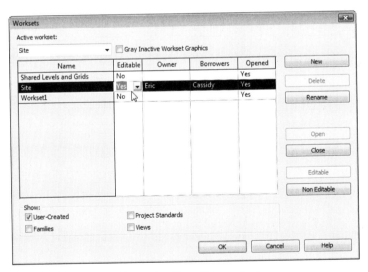

FIGURE 22.16 Occupying the entire workset

N O T E   If Cassidy was in the middle of an active edit on any items in the workset, you would not have been able to take over. You would then have to place an editing request to her. See? You should have given her the shrub when she asked for it earlier!

And so the workday goes. An environment of sharing and getting along. Speaking of environment, suppose you could not care less about the site. There is a good chance you don't even want to see it. Well, you are in luck. Because you have worksets enabled, you can make it so Revit doesn't even load the site into your local model!

Loading or Not Loading a Workset

I'm making a big deal out of a simple task only because this simple task can really speed up your performance, and nothing can bog a Revit model down more than a huge site complete with landscaping and maybe an image.

Simply switching the Opened status to No in a workset will force Revit to not load it into your model. If you make an edit that has an influence on the site, don't worry. Revit will take care of that in the central model.

To turn off the site, follow this procedure:

1. Click the Worksets button on the Collaborate tab.

2. In the Site workset, change the Opened status to No, as shown in Figure 22.17.

3. Click OK. Notice something missing?

FIGURE 22.17 Changing the Opened status to No

Having the ability to turn off large portions of a model can be a tremendous advantage as you move forward in Revit. You do need to exercise caution, however. You could easily deceive yourself into thinking that some portions of the model have not been created yet.

Are You Experienced?

Now You Can...

- ☑ activate worksharing in a Revit project

- ☑ create a central file

- ☑ create a local file

- ☑ manipulate worksets

CHAPTER 23

BIM Management

▶ Setting up the template

▶ Managing settings

▶ Setting up (and understanding) shared parameters

W ell, here we are: the last chapter. The ironic thing here is the fact that the last chapter contains much of the information you are going to need to proceed with any of this BIM stuff. All too many times I have seen firms do poorly with Revit Architecture due to one fact: they weren't prepared. "We did not find that Revit worked for us," someone tells me. I ask them what they used for a template to get started with their first project. "The default one" is always the answer.

If you think you are going to start a real project with deadlines and budget with no prior setup, you are going to fail. So don't. If you take nothing away from this chapter other than this small bit of advice, it has been successful. Granted, you don't have to get it all, but you need as smooth of a transition as possible. Also, once you start down the Revit path, don't look back, and don't say, "We can always just push it out to AutoCAD." I have found that if you think you have something to fall back on, well, you will fall.

You don't have to spend weeks upon weeks preparing for the "Coming of Revit." You can knock this stuff out if you do it in an orderly fashion, and the first order of business is the creation of your company's templates.

Setting Up the Template

If you do nothing more than simply save the default template and give it your company name, you are off to a good start. People who are jumping to a new way of working are going to be looking for any comfort they can find. No, this is not like giving someone a sugar pill for a migraine, because we are going to populate the template with custom content.

The objective of the following procedure is to save a default template and to "map" Revit to this template.

1. Open Revit.

2. In the Projects menu, click New, as shown in Figure 23.1.

3. Click the Revit Home button, and select Save As ➤ Template, as shown in Figure 23.2.

4. Save this file to your network. The file in our examples will be called NER-TEMPLATE.rte. You can call yours whatever you see fit.

FIGURE 23.1 Clicking New Project on the Recent Projects menu

FIGURE 23.2 Save as a Revit template.

 N O T E When I say save this file to your network, give this simple instruction some thought. We are going to be mapping our network deployment to this directory. Also, don't get into the habit of having errant templates scattered around your network that you are "practicing" on. You will get confused. (This author still needs to practice what he preaches regarding this matter.)

The file is now saved as NER-TEMPLATE.rte. The .rte extension indicates that you have indeed created a template and that you are now working in it.

The next order of business it to tell Revit that every time you wish to start a new project, it is this template that Revit chooses.

In your settings, if you go to the File Locations tab, you can map your Revit to always use this template as your default.

1. Click the Revit Home button. At the very bottom of the menu, you will see an Options button, as shown in Figure 23.3. Click it.

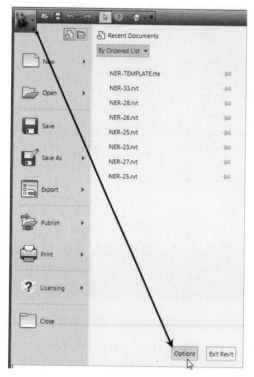

FIGURE 23.3 Finding the Options button

2. In the Options dialog, click the File Locations tab, as shown in Figure 23.4.

3. For the default template file, click the Browse button, and locate your newly saved template.

4. Once you have browsed to the .rte template, click OK.

So, it's official. You have a separate template for your company to get started with. Now the fun begins!

The first item we will look at in terms of setting up this template to your company's standards is the nagging line weight issue you have most certainly been uncomfortable with throughout this book. This is taken care of by managing your Revit settings.

FIGURE 23.4 Finding the new template

Managing Settings

Given that Revit is such a robust, deep application, you would think that there would be an endless stream of convoluted settings (like AutoCAD Architecture). Although there are quite a few settings in Revit, you will find that they are straightforward. In fact, the mapping of the default template is almost the only mapping that will be needed as you set up and work in Revit.

The objective of this section is to locate the settings for your line weights and then apply them to your object styles.

1. In Revit, select the Manage tab on the Ribbon.

2. On the Project Settings panel, click the Settings button, and then select Object Styles, as shown in Figure 23.5.

3. With the Object Styles dialog open, notice that there are categories. Click on the "+" next to the Casework category, and you'll see the subcategories.

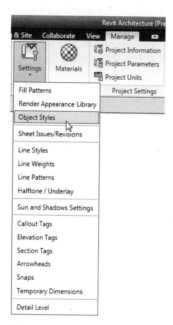

FIGURE 23.5 Selecting Object Styles

To the right of the category field is the Line Weight column. There is a projection and a cut. "Projection" refers to if the item is being viewed in plan, elevation, or a 3D view. "Cut" refers to if the item being viewed in section. (Boy, this beats layers, huh?) Notice that you can change the line color, the pattern, and the rendering material each item will use (see Figure 23.6).

FIGURE 23.6 The Object Styles dialog

Well, that was easy. I wish I could tell you specifically what number to assign each item, but that is up to you!

What do all those 1's and 2's mean? You're used to seeing something like "035mm" for a line weight, but now we are looking at plain numbers!

Don't worry — Revit has it figured out. You see, these numbers refer to a chart where you will see these familiar line weights. Also, these are line weights that comply with AIA standards.

To find the line weights associated with the object styles, follow these steps:

1. On the Project Settings panel of the Manage tab, click Settings ➢ Line Weights, as shown in Figure 23.7.

FIGURE 23.7 Click Settings ➢ Line Weights.

In the Line Weights dialog (see Figure 23.8), notice that not only are numbers 1 through 17 assigned a pen thickness, but the thickness will actually degrade as the line weights get scaled down!

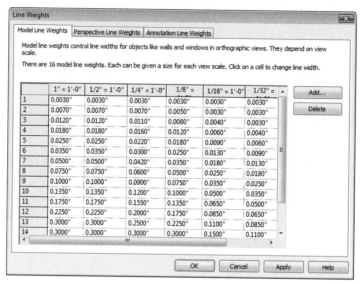

Line Weights

| Model Line Weights | Perspective Line Weights | Annotation Line Weights |

Model line weights control line widths for objects like walls and windows in orthographic views. They depend on view scale.

There are 16 model line weights. Each can be given a size for each view scale. Click on a cell to change line width.

	1" = 1'-0"	1/2" = 1'-0"	1/4" = 1'-0"	1/8" =	1/16" = 1'-0"	1/32" =
1	0.0030"	0.0030"	0.0030"	0.0030"	0.0030"	0.0030"
2	0.0070"	0.0070"	0.0070"	0.0050"	0.0030"	0.0030"
3	0.0120"	0.0120"	0.0110"	0.0080"	0.0040"	0.0030"
4	0.0180"	0.0180"	0.0160"	0.0120"	0.0060"	0.0040"
5	0.0250"	0.0250"	0.0220"	0.0180"	0.0090"	0.0060"
6	0.0350"	0.0350"	0.0300"	0.0250"	0.0130"	0.0090"
7	0.0500"	0.0500"	0.0420"	0.0350"	0.0180"	0.0130"
8	0.0750"	0.0750"	0.0600"	0.0500"	0.0250"	0.0180"
9	0.1000"	0.1000"	0.0900"	0.0750"	0.0350"	0.0250"
10	0.1350"	0.1350"	0.1200"	0.1000"	0.0500"	0.0350"
11	0.1750"	0.1750"	0.1550"	0.1350"	0.0650"	0.0500"
12	0.2250"	0.2250"	0.2000"	0.1750"	0.0850"	0.0650"
13	0.3000"	0.3000"	0.2500"	0.2250"	0.1100"	0.0850"
14	0.3000"	0.3000"	0.3000"	0.3000"	0.1500"	0.1100"

Add...

Delete

| OK | Cancel | Apply | Help |

FIGURE 23.8 The Line Weights dialog

N O T E   You may be inclined to start "tampering" with these line weights, but hold off doing that. You are probably seeing the industry finally shifting to some form of unified line weight system. This is the NCS (National CAD Standards). These line weights are set to these standards. Change the object styles all you want, but I recommend that you keep these pen assignments just the way they are.

2. Click the Perspective Line Weights tab on the Line Weights dialog. Notice that you can alter your line weights of an object in a perspective view, independent of a standard plan, elevation, or isometric view.

3. Click the Annotation Line Weights tab. Again, notice that you can set your line weights for your annotation. This tab will come in handy as you start to set up your templates. Remember it is available.

4. Click Close to leave this dialog.

I wish I could tell you that you don't have tons of work ahead of you in terms of trying to match your AutoCAD line weights, but many of you will be inundated with the effort of adjusting line weights for quite a while. You will have to make at least some tweaks before you can submit a set of drawings with your name on them.

That being said, suppose your submittal includes sending "CAD files." Hang on here, we use Revit! You can do that?

Import/Export Settings

Of course, you can do that! The beauty of it is, you can import and export to a predefined set of layers. This works wonders for firms who find themselves surrounded by "CAD people."

The objective of the next section is to learn how to deal with this issue, so follow along with this procedure:

1. Open the last model you have been working on. At this stage of the game, it does not matter which one.

2. On the Insert tab, click on the down arrow in the lower-right corner of the Import panel, as shown in Figure 23.9.

FIGURE 23.9 Click the down arrow on the Import tab

3. In the Import CAD Settings dialog, notice that all of the line weights are set to 1. This does not make for a very spectacular drawing. At the upper-right corner of the dialog is a Load button, as shown in Figure 23.10. Click it.

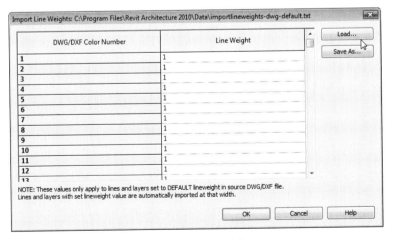

FIGURE 23.10 Importing some line weights

4. You will automatically be taken to the directory where Revit is mapped to find your line weights files. They are simple text (.txt) files. Find the file called importlineweights-dwg-AIA.txt and click Open. Notice that your line weights have been adjusted, as shown in Figure 23.11.

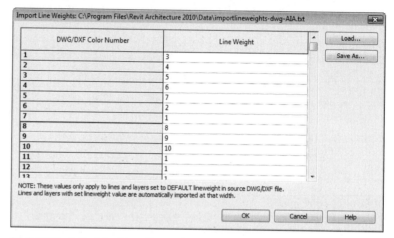

FIGURE 23.11 The adjusted line weights

5. Notice also that you have a Save As button. Change a few line weights around and click the Save As button.

6. Save the file in the same directory as NER Line Weights.txt.

As mentioned before, you will probably have a good amount of work to do configuring these line weights. If you have been sticking to the AIA or NCS layering conventions, you will not have an issue. If not, then you have some translating to do!

Great! We have importing down. Suppose we want to export a Revit model to CAD. It's a little different, but the concept is the same. You need to physically "map" the Revit objects to AutoCAD or MicroStation layers or levels.

The objective of the next exercise is to examine export settings when sending a model to CAD.

1. On the Revit Home button, select Export ➤ Options ➤ Export Layers DWG/DXF.

WAIT! I DON'T HAVE THAT CHOICE

When you are looking for an item in the Revit Home menu, notice that at the bottom of the menu is an arrow in a wide blue strip. If you hover your pointer over this blue strip, you will see the menu scroll up so you can see more choices, as shown here:

In the next dialog you will notice that all of your Revit objects are represented and are given a unique layer name. That layer name is also assigned an AutoCAD pen number. This assigns the layer a color. Both of these items can be changed in this dialog (see Figure 23.12).

2. In the Export Layers dialog, click the Standard button.

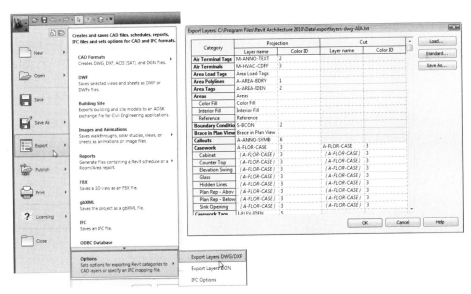

FIGURE 23.12 The Export Layers dialog

3. The Undefined Layering Standard dialog opens, as shown in Figure 23.13. Here you will get a choice of four standards. By default, the American Institute of Architects Standard (AIA) will be current, but you can change to one of the other three. Choose a standard or click Cancel.

FIGURE 23.13 The four choices for standards

4. If you want to change your layering scheme, go right ahead. Because the AIA standard is saved to an external .txt file, you will not have to worry about "messing up" that file. If you do make your changes, however, click the Save As button and save your .txt file somewhere that makes sense to you.

5. Click OK to get back to the model.

Now we are cooking here! We now know how to make the adjustments to our line weights, and how to make sure those adjustments are valid when we export the model and when we import CAD. It's time to move on to other graphical features that need to be controlled within the Revit template. These are the annotation features.

Controlling Annotations

To begin with, Revit does not accept .shx fonts. The only font that Revit accepts is a true type font (.ttf). If it is not in your Windows fonts directory, forget it. Given that, don't worry if your AutoCAD fonts are set to an SHX. Revit will convert them to Arial when you import them. If Arial is unacceptable, you are going to have to figure out what font is acceptable. I recommend Arial, but most of the SHX fonts such as architxt.shx are available in a .ttf format. You can either find them online or email me at the address in the back of the book.

The annotation we will address first is the everyday text that you will be using in your models and the accompanying leaders.

Formatting Annotations and Leaders

Just like any drafting application, Revit needs to have the text set up. Yes, you can just use it out of the box, but I assume you have standards that look better than the boxed "sample" styles that are provided.

The objective of the next procedure is to set up our default text and leaders.

1. To get started, make sure you are in the NER-TEMPLATE.rte file or the template you created.

2. On the Text panel of the Annotate tab, click the down arrow in the lower-right corner of the panel, as shown in Figure 23.14.

FIGURE 23.14 Click the down arrow in the Text panel.

3. In the Type Properties dialog, switch the Type: to $^3/_{32}$" Arial.

4. Click the Rename button.

5. Call the new text NER-$^3/_{32}$" (of course you can call it whatever you want).

6. In the type parameters, change the leader arrowhead to Arrow Filled 15 Degree.

7. Change Width Factor to .800000 (see Figure 23.15).

8. Click OK.

9. On the Home tab, click the Text button.

10. In the Change Element Type menu, make sure the NER-$^3/_{32}$" text is current.

11. Add one leadered piece of text into your model. (It's always a good idea just to check it to make sure it came out as expected.)

FIGURE 23.15 Changing the text

CLEANLINESS STARTS HERE!

We now have an extra text style kicking around. We should purge our model immediately to avoid a messy template!

1. On the Manage tab, click the Purge Unused button, as shown here:

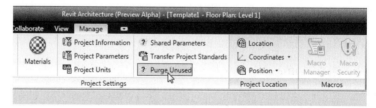

2. In the Purge Unused dialog, the first thing you must do is click the Check None button. If you just click OK, you will have purged your entire model with no warning.

3. Scroll down to the bottom of the list, find the Text category, and expand it.

4. Check the 1/4" - Arial text style.

5. Click OK. The text style is now deleted.

With the text and leaders out of the way, it is time to venture into text's close cousin: the dimension!

Formatting Dimensions

We can format dimensions in the same manner. You will, however, find this process unwieldy based on the fact that each type of dimension needs to be formatted. You cannot do just one and expect it to propagate to the other styles.

The objective of the next procedure is to format your dimension styles.

1. On the Annotate tab, click the bottom of the Dimension panel (click where it says Dimension). This will expose your dimension settings, as shown in Figure 23.16.

FIGURE 23:16 Accessing the Dimension settings

2. Click the Linear Dimension Types button.

3. In the Type Properties dialog, click Rename.

4. Rename the value to NER-$3/32$", and click OK.

5. Scroll down to the Text group, and change the Width Factor value to .8.

6. Click the button to the right of the Units Format category.

7. Uncheck Use Project Settings.

8. Change the rounding to the nearest $1/8$".

9. Check Suppress 0 Feet (see Figure 23.17).

10. Click OK twice.

FIGURE 23.17 Customizing your dimensions

Unfortunately you need to repeat this with the rest of the dimension types. I recommend you do so.

Okay, moving along with annotations, we get to the area where we need to control our levels as well as our structural grid bubbles. Since we made slight adjustments to our text and dimensions, it is time to make the same alterations to our datum items as well. Doing so, however, is not as straightforward.

Formatting Grids, Elevations Markers, and View Titles

If you don't feel like navigating through buried folders in Windows Explorer, you can click the Imperial Library button in the menu to the left of the Open dialog. This will take you directly to your default library.

If you have had any experience with Revit, I'm sure you quickly realize that there is no button to change the appearance of grids and elevations. It's not impossible to make specific alterations to these items, but it must be accomplished by editing the annotation family that is loaded into your project.

The objective of the following procedure is to alter a structural grid bubble and to modify a level indicator.

1. In Revit, click the Open button on the Quick Access toolbar.

2. Go to your Imperial Library folder.

3. Open the Annotations folder.

4. Select the file Grid Head - Circle.rfa and click Open.

5. Select the large 0. This is a tag.

6. On the Modify Label tab, click the Element Properties button.

7. Click Edit Type.

8. Check Bold.

9. Change the Width value to .8.

10. Click OK twice.

11. Save the file. Notice that Revit wants you to save a separate file. If you are the BIM manager, and nobody is going to yell at you, save it right over the existing file. If not, save it somewhere else.

12. Click the Load into Project button.

13. You will get a warning that this family already exists, as shown in Figure 23.18. Click Overwrite the Existing Version.

FIGURE 23.18 Overwriting the existing version

Sweet! You just replaced the grid bubble. See the trick? Some elements can be edited within the model, while some you have to go ferret the family out of its hiding place. Let's keep rolling and do a level head!

1. On the Quick Access toolbar, click the Open button.

2. Browse to the Imperial Library and then the Annotations folder.

3. Select the file Level Head - Circle and click Open.

4. Select the text Name.

5. On the Modify Label tab, click the Element Properties button.

6. Click the Edit Type button.

7. Click Bold.

8. Change the Width Factor value to .800000.

9. Click OK twice.

10. Save the file.

11. Click Load into Project, as shown in Figure 23.19.

FIGURE 23.19 Click Load into Project.

12. Select Overwrite the Existing Version.

13. Go to an elevation view just to make sure it worked.

YEAH, BUT WHERE DID THIS FAMILY GO?

You loaded it into your project and it just magically worked, right? No. There is no magic here. In the elevation view, if you select the level, click the Element Properties button, and then click Edit Type, you will see that the symbol this specific family is using is the one we just modified, as shown here. Also, this means that you can load any level head into the model and apply that to the family.

Okay, now this is just getting to be downright fun. Let's go ahead and modify a view title, shall we?

1. On the Quick Access toolbar, click the Open button.

2. Browse back to the `Annotations` directory.

3. Select the file `View Title.rfa` and click Open.

4. Select the View Name tag, and click the Element Properties button.

5. Click the Type Properties button.

6. Check the Bold option, and change Width Factor to .8000000.

7. Click OK twice.

8. Select the ⅛" = 1'–0" tag.

9. Click the Element Properties button.

10. Click Type Properties.

11. Click Duplicate.

12. Call the new tag ³/₃₂".

13. Change the text size to ³/₃₂".

14. Click OK twice.

15. Save the view title family.

16. Load it into your project.

17. Overwrite the existing version.

18. Stand up and clap loudly because you are actually creating a nice template! (Optional.)

This is looking great. Now for the harder stuff. When it comes to additional information that Revit does not provide, you are going to need an outside influence. Or, at least you are going to need to physically create a text file loaded with some of your "oddball" parameters that you can share between projects, families, and possibly other disciplines.

Creating and Understanding Shared Parameters

This is a convoluted subject, so I am going to try to explain it in terms that I can understand — because this had to be explained to me over and over until I finally got it.

Suppose you are doing a project for a school. All of your drawings need to have an SED (State Education Department) number. (I'm in New York, so if it is called something different in your state, province, or country, please forgive me.) This SED number belongs in with your project parameters so when you are filling out the job information, this SED number can be included. The issue is we need to add this parameter to the project you are working on *and* this same exact parameter needs to be added to the title block family. When you inset the title block into the project, this SED number will populate the title block.

Still foggy? Okay, let's just do it, and see what shakes out! The objective of the following exercise is to create a shared parameter .txt file and add it to a title block and your project.

1. In the Manage tab, click the Project Parameters button, as shown in Figure 23.20.

FIGURE 23.20 Clicking the Project Parameters button

2. In the Project Parameters dialog, click the Add button.

3. In the Parameter Properties dialog, click the Shared Parameter button.

4. In the Categories field, check Project Information.

5. In the middle of the dialog, click the Select button (see Figure 23.21).

6. You will get a dialog stating that you have not specified a shared parameter. Click Yes to choose one.

7. In the next dialog, there is still an issue because you don't actually have a shared parameter file. Click the Create button.

FIGURE 23.21 Filling out the information for the shared parameter

8. Save the file as **NER-Shared Parameters**. (Of course you can name it anything you choose.)

9. In the Groups field, click the New button, as shown in Figure 23.22.

10. Call the new parameter group **Project Information** and click OK.

11. In the Parameters field, click New.

12. Name it **SED Number**.

13. Click OK.

14. Keep clicking OK until you are back to the model.

15. On the Manage tab, click the Project Information button, as shown in Figure 23.22. Notice that SED Number has been added to the list.

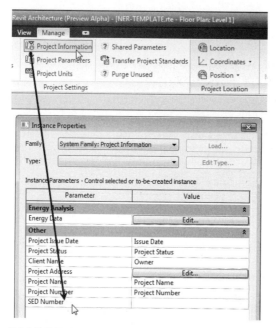

FIGURE 23.22   Violà! The new shared parameter!

If you type your long SED number, where does this number wind up? This is where the shared part comes into play. Suppose we need this SED number displayed in our title block? It's just a matter of adding this same parameter to the title block family.

Still don't believe me? Okay, let's add the same exact shared parameter to a title block, and then load it into the model.

1. On the View tab, click the New Sheet button, as shown in Figure 23.23.

FIGURE 23.23   Creating a new sheet

2. Click OK in the next dialog.

3. Select the title block, and click the Edit Family button in the Modify Title Blocks tab, as shown in Figure 23.24.

FIGURE 23.24 Editing the title block family

4. Click Yes to open the title block.

5. Zoom into the lower-right corner, and select the Date label, as shown in Figure 23.25.

6. Click the Create Similar button on the Create panel, as shown in Figure 23.25.

7. Pick a point, as shown in Figure 23.25.

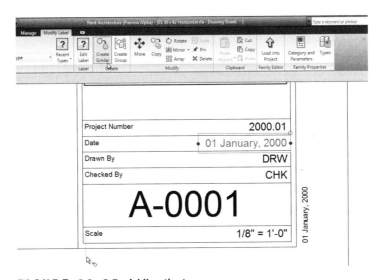

FIGURE 23.25 Adding the tag

8. Once you pick the point, you will see an Edit Label dialog. Click the New button, as shown in Figure 23.26.

9. In the Parameter Properties dialog, click Select. (I think you know where we are going here.)

10. Select the SED number (it is the only one), and click OK.

11. Click OK again.

12. Click the Add button, as shown in Figure 23.26.

FIGURE 23.26 Adding the parameter to the label

13. Click OK.

14. Load the title block into the model.

15. Click Overwrite the Existing Version.

16. Nothing changed? Well, let's see about that! Click the Project Information button on the Manage tab.

17. Give it an SED number such as 123.456.789.

18. Click OK. The title block now contains this information.

Now, that's how you create and utilize shared parameters. Although this trick is useful for project parameters, it is useful for object parameters as well. This is just another way we can control the flow of information!

Are You Experienced?

Now You Can...

- ☑ begin to set up a companywide template
- ☑ set up text styles and dimension styles
- ☑ edit the families of various symbols used in your models
- ☑ create and utilize shared parameters

INDEX

Note to reader: **Bolded** page numbers refer to definitions and main discussions of a topic. *Italicized* page numbers refer to illustrations.